The Economics of
Ancient Greece

THE ECONOMICS OF ANCIENT GREECE

Τῇ Ἑλλάδι πενίη μὲν αἰεί
κοτε σύντροφος ἐστί

BY

H. MICHELL, M.A.

PROFESSOR OF POLITICAL ECONOMY IN MCMASTER UNIVERSITY,
HAMILTON, ONTARIO

CAMBRIDGE
AT THE UNIVERSITY PRESS
1940

CAMBRIDGE
UNIVERSITY PRESS

32 Avenue of the Americas, New York NY 10013-2473, USA

Cambridge University Press is part of the University of Cambridge.

It furthers the University's mission by disseminating knowledge in the pursuit of education, learning and research at the highest international levels of excellence.

www.cambridge.org
Information on this title: www.cambridge.org/9781107419117

© Cambridge University Press 1940

First published 1940
First paperback edition 2014

A catalogue record for this publication is available from the British Library

ISBN 978-1-107-41911-7 Paperback

COLLEGIO · REGINAE · OXONIENSI
NUTRICI · ALMAE
D. D.
ALUMNUS · PIUS

CONTENTS

CONTENTS

PREFACE

SINCE the day when Boeckh published his *Political Economy of the Athenians*, now a hundred and twenty years ago, the study of Greek economic life has advanced considerably, more particularly in the epigraphical field, and much attention is now being given thereto. I have endeavoured in the following chapters to give, in short compass, the results of modern research, and the conclusions of scholars working in this fascinating field. Many of the problems are of almost baffling complexity and have given rise to much controversy. I have not attempted to set out in detail the views, often sharply divergent, of various scholars on this or that question, but have been content to refer those who desire to go deeper to the sources where they can find a great mass of material, much of it of importance. Our knowledge on many points is lamentably imperfect, and all we can do is to make intelligent guesses. I have thought it best to end the survey at the conquests of Alexander. The developments of the Hellenistic Age were so great and far-reaching that they demand a far more extended treatment than could conveniently be included in a book of this size.

During the several years that I have been engaged in this work, I have had occasion to correspond with many scholars who have, without exception, responded most courteously to my inquiries and given me much help. I cannot name them all here, but I am grateful for their generous assistance. I cannot, however, fail to mention the constant help I received from my colleague in this university, Dr E. T. Salmon. Dr F. M. Heichelheim read the manuscript, and his meticulous scholarship and profound knowledge of the subject have been invaluable to me. The acute criticisms of Dr J. H. Clapham and Dr Max Cary have saved me from many serious mistakes in fact and method of treatment.

But for such errors as have crept in, and I cannot hope that many will not be found, these scholars are assuredly not accountable.

H. MICHELL

McMaster University,
Hamilton, Ont.

ABBREVIATIONS

P.W.   Pauly-Wissowa-Kroll, *Realencyklopädie der Klassischen Altertumswissenschaft.*

D.S.   Daremberg-Saglio, *Dictionnaire des Antiquités Grecques et Romaines.*

J.H.S.   *Journal of Hellenic Studies.*

C.A.H.   *Cambridge Ancient History.*

Rhein. Mus.   *Rheinisches Museum für Philologie.*

Klio.   Klio, *Beiträge zur alten Geschichte.*

I.G.   *Inscriptiones Graecae.*

*I.G.*²   *Inscriptiones Graecae*, Editio Minor.

C.I.G.   *Corpus Inscriptionum Graecarum.*

Ditt. *Syll.*   Dittenberger, *Sylloge Inscriptionum Graecarum.*

Michel.   *Recueil d'Inscriptions Grecques.*

All dates are B.C. unless specifically marked A.D.

The spelling of proper names follows the recommendation of the Council of the Hellenic Society for use in the *Journal of Hellenic Studies*, where all Greek proper names are transliterated into the Latin alphabet, according to the practice of educated Romans of the Augustan Age.

CHAPTER I

THE BACKGROUND OF GREEK ECONOMICS

THE GREEKS

ALFRED MARSHALL once said that it was as difficult, or impossible, to interpret the past as to anticipate the future, and the truth of that statement becomes abundantly evident to the modern economist who essays the difficult task of evaluating the economic life of the ancient Greeks. To the modern mind their history is full of events that amaze and perturb the reader; their actions and policies are such as to baffle our theories and defeat our sympathies. In art and philosophy, poetry and the drama we may draw very near to them, for such are timeless and the spirit of man is eternal. But politics and statecraft, social systems and economic expedients, are of the age of which they are a product, and we of another age cannot enter fully into the spirit that prompted them. We may chronicle their happening, and explain with reasonable certainty the circumstances that led to their adoption; but that is as far as we can go; between us and them time has reared an impassable barrier. Our vision is obscured by the preoccupations of our own age. We see the long vistas of antiquity fore-shortened, and we do not comprehend, or but dimly grasp, the passage of centuries. The economic conditions of the ancient world were radically different from those of to-day and must be judged, if they ever can be judged, by totally different standards.

But the difficulties that confront us need not deter us from trying our best to form a picture, faulty though it may be, of the economic system of that ancient people to whom we owe so much. We shall find ourselves only too often in uncertainty; and at best our conclusions, especially in the earlier periods, and hardly less so even in the later, in default of actual written records, and sometimes in spite of them, can only be intelligent guesses, which are constantly modified, corrected, and restated as modern discoveries bring new evidences to bear on the problems concerned. It is like trying to fit together a mosaic that has been broken up and even some of the pieces lost. Here and there can be found pieces that evidently go together, while other fragments are too small to allow of more than tentative and, very often no doubt, wrong reconstructions. A chance reference, a few words in one of the ancient authors, an inscription, only too often broken and half defaced, a papyrus found in desert sands, such are the materials with which we must work; never perfectly sure, but always trying new combinations, new arrangements, hoping that our guesses are right; a fascinating, tantalising and often a wearisome task. There is a romance, an adventurousness, in the patient toil of the archaeologist as he digs in the mounds that once were great cities. At any moment his spade may unearth a treasure that will throw a flood of light on questions that now baffle the learned world. And so we need not utterly despair, as we watch year by year the records of remote times being pieced together.

THE GEOGRAPHIC FACTOR[1]

True though it may be that much in the character of the Greeks is difficult to understand and disconcerting to realise, yet there are factors to be taken into account which may well prove illuminating in our study. Of these the principal is, what we may call, the geographic or environmental, which must in every age and place profoundly modify the circumstances of existence of the people living within its influence.

We are accustomed to speak of two great factors which shape the destiny of races, heredity and environment, and of these the Greeks were very well aware. Strabo, criticising the theories of Poseidonius, remarks: "As regards the various arts and faculties and institutions of mankind, most of them, when all men have made a beginning, flourish in any latitude whatsoever, and in certain instances even in spite of the latitude. So that some local characteristics of a people come by nature, others by training and habit. For instance, it was not by nature that the Athenians were fond of letters, whereas the Lacedaemonians and also the Thebans, who are still closer to the Athenians,

[1] E. C. Semple, *Influence of Geographic Environment, passim*; Holland Rose, *The Mediterranean in the Ancient World*; Busolt, *Griechische Staatskunde*, I, 102 ff.

were not so; but rather by habit. So also the Babylonians and the Egyptians are philosophers, not by nature but by training and habit."[1] In this judgment we may agree with Strabo, although he leaves serious questions still unanswered. It was not by "nature" that the Athenians were different from the Spartans; to that we may assent. But from whence came that "habit" that shaped their destiny? The point is an interesting one. The Athenian was a cosmopolitan; to his harbour came all the ships of the world, and his wits were sharpened by daily contact with the people of all nations. Upon him had been thrust the government of an empire, and his navy policed the seas. Whatever else the Athenians did, they "thought imperially"; which was a very different "habit" from that of the Spartans, who were singularly averse from thinking of anything that lay beyond the narrow confines of their own small land. The Spartan had shut himself in and applied himself with extraordinary precautions and elaborate safeguards to one single thing—his domination as a privileged caste in his own land. It was inevitable that a different habit of mind should have shaped itself in the consciousness of the Spartan. It is illuminating in this connection to realise that early Laconian art was equal to any produced in other parts of Greece. But the Spartan had turned away from such distractions; his political necessities had made him into a specialist in one thing only, domination through military fitness. To that all his efforts were turned; his very existence depended upon it.

It has been remarked, and there is a great deal of truth in it although it must not be pushed too far, that the Greek could not extend the sphere of his cultural influence beyond the limit of cultivation of the olive, a delicate plant and one demanding a climate peculiar to itself.[2] Alexander, a Macedonian who came from a region outside the olive belt, pushed his victories to the extreme limit of the cultivation of the vine, a far sturdier plant. It might be argued with considerable plausibility, if not with entire conviction, that the shrivelling of his empire was due to the absence of those climatic conditions which favoured the genius of the Greek husbandman. Certainly the Greek was

[1] ii, 3, 7 (c. 103) (Loeb trans.).
[2] Newbigin, *Mediterranean Lands*, p. 24.

not a success in Egypt, in which neither olive nor vine attains successful cultivation.

In Greece itself the smallness of the holdings and the intensity of agriculture allowed of a dense population where large-scale production was impossible. The Greek could not have used the modern agricultural machinery; his fields were too small, so he tilled his lands with the ox-drawn plough, or more often with hoe and mattock and lived in villages.[1] He was typically a town-dweller, as the Chinese are to-day; the isolated farm in the middle of a hundred acres or more was unknown to him.

The problem of subsistence was an ever-pressing one which allowed of no slackening in effort. An interruption of the day-to-day toil was serious; war and the destruction of vineyards and olive groves was an almost irremediable disaster, as the Athenians found after the Peloponnesian war. So priceless were the gifts of nature and so anxiously must the gods be propitiated that around their agriculture was thrown the sanctity of religion. The olive was sacred, a gift from Heaven, and to cut down a tree was sacrilege. The rites of Demeter the Corn Goddess as practised in the Eleusinian mysteries are significant. Water was poured on the earth, for water is a precious thing and fit offering to give a goddess; without water the earth will not yield its fruits. A sacred drama in honour of the deity was performed in a hall brilliantly lit by torches to represent the sunshine necessary for ripening the crops.[2] To trifle with these mysteries was a very serious thing, as Alcibiades found to his cost.

As the standard of living rose with increased wealth the problem of feeding the populace became more acute as wheat was demanded in place of the more easily grown barley. In this Attica was at a great disadvantage; like the modern Great Britain she could not possibly feed her own people and foreign wheat had to be imported which must be paid for somehow, either by silver from the mines of Laurium or by exports. Boeotia was a far richer country, but without access to the sea, and the Athenians thought the Boeotians dull and stupid. Such a community could satisfy all its own material needs. The

---

[1] Newbigin, *Mediterranean Lands*, p. 55.
[2] References to cult of Demeter very numerous. Cf. Frazer in *Golden Bough*, "Spirits of the Corn and the Wild", cap. 2.

Boeotians did not even want Athenian pottery, and living within a severely restricted area could not help but be backward as compared with Attica, where poor lands and ready access to the sea provided an unending stimulus, for hunger is a wonderful sharpener of wits. The Saronic gulf is calm and sheltered, and on the north-east the isthmus of Megara contains Mount Geraneia, which served as a natural rampart for Athens.

Easy access to the sea made communication by land unnecessary, especially when land routes are difficult through the complex relief and indented coast-line of the mainland. The Greeks were not great road builders, because they did not find any pressing need for them. Similarity of climate and natural products made inland commerce within Greece unnecessary; they had little to exchange. Athens bought vegetables and eels from Boeotia, but had little to give in exchange except money.[1] But overseas were to be found wheat in limitless quantities and timber, a vital necessity for a land denuded of its forests, and these could be paid for with oil, wine, figs and pottery, which the barbarians of Macedonia and South Russia were eager to buy. To keep the trade routes open, to police the Aegean and keep the pirates in order became a vital necessity if Athens was not to starve, so the Athenians were forced onto the sea. If the typical Athenian was none too fond of hard labour he could hardly have been any fonder of the back-breaking labour of tugging at an oar. But if he shirked his duty on shipboard he knew his city would go hungry; so he served as a rower in the war galleys as cheerfully as the trying circumstances allowed and made the best of a bad job.

It is to the influence of the sea that we must attribute most of the prevailing forms of Greek culture and economic evolution. Living in lands none too fertile and often rocky and barren, where the increase of population beyond the limits of subsistence drove them of necessity to seek new homes, the early Greeks built their frail ships and launched out into the deep. We must not forget that the Greeks were never a seafaring nation like their great rivals the Phoenicians, nor like the modern British and other peoples on the Atlantic sea-board.

---

[1] Newbigin, *Mediterranean Lands*, pp. 132, 137–8. Boeotia wants nothing from Attica (Aristoph. *Acharn.* 899).

They dreaded and hated the sea, than which "there is nought else worse to confound a man howsoever hardy he may be".[1] They never really forgot that they were sprung from inland dwellers of the grassy steppes, and their seafaring was forced upon them not by choice but of necessity. As Mr Holland Rose appositely says, not in all Greek literature, nor in Latin for the matter of that, do we ever find any lyrical outburst in praise of the sea, which was no "lover and mother of men" to them.[2] Such epithets as are applied to it are invariably harsh. The "wine-dark" of Homer pictures a forbidding tide under a lowering sky. Poseidon was always an angry god, who resented the presumption of man to invade his domain. So the Greeks gritted their teeth and took to the sea, not because they liked it but because they had to; it was their pathway about the world. Go on it they must, and there they found a wonderful source of foodstuffs in the fish, especially the tunny, which abounded in its waters. It has been suggested, with a good deal of reason, that it was following the tunny shoals that led the earlier Greek mariners up the Hellespont to the fishes' starting-point in the Black Sea and westwards to the coasts of Italy in their long summer migration.[3] The absence of currents and the generally calm weather which prevailed from April to October made navigation possible for the little square-rigged ships and clumsy gear of the pioneer Greek sailors. The Aegean is thickly dotted with islands, 483 of them, which allowed even the tiny craft of the early Greeks to put to sea without too great risk of disaster, when, on a storm approaching, a quick dash for land would carry them to safety. And lastly, the wind system of the Eastern Mediterranean was favourable to navigation in the summer months. The Etesian winds, the prevailing northerlies, carried them from Greece to Crete and Egypt; from whence by way of Syria, Cyprus and under the lee of Asia Minor they crept to the shelter of the Sporades.[4]

From the shores of Thrace to the southernmost point of the Peloponnesus all the valleys of Greece open out on the East or Asiatic side. Greece was at the threshold of the Orient, and the

[1] *Od.* viii, 138.
[2] With the possible exception of Aesch. *Prom.* 90.
[3] Holland Rose, *The Mediterranean in the Ancient World*, p. 8.
[4] *Ibid.* p. 11.

destiny of the Greek led him eastwards; there he won his greatest triumphs and there he met his final overthrow. From the first heroic struggle with the Persian, to the last convulsion of the Mithradatic wars, Greek and Asiatic found their destinies intermingled, and to this very day that fate has shaped his destiny.[1]

Greece was, and still is, a little and a poor country; her agricultural resources were scanty and the configuration of the land prevented easy communication. Her little states were shut in by mountains, separated from one another by obstacles that induced a proud seclusion and a fierce and, only too often, an aggressive and truculent patriotism. In the plains between the mountains numbers multiplied, and there was always the problem of population increase pressing upon the bare means of subsistence. It was not to be wondered at, therefore, that there arose a vexing and oftentimes desperate land question, such as all countries encounter where a land-hungry people finds itself thwarted by a vicious or antiquated system of capitalist proprietorship, and where the problem can only be solved by violence or emigration, if it ever be completely solved. It was indeed this littleness that, in large degree, stimulated that early and precocious maturity which was so soon to wither and die. Life in a little Greek city was very vivid; it could also be very petty, and we cannot doubt tiresome and boring. The young men of spirit become restless, and, as Thucydides says at the beginning of the Peloponnesian war, are simply "spoiling for a fight".[2] From the narrow confines of their homeland the surplus population is forced out to find a livelihood elsewhere. "A small cup soon overflows", and finally the limitations of too small a home area step in to arrest national development, which in the end fades and decays.[3]

Do we not find in this never-ending land problem which, in the last analysis, was one of actual subsistence, the explanation of the extraordinary spirit of seclusion and aloofness that was so characteristic of the Greek? Why did the Spartan withdraw himself from the rest of Greece and refuse citizenship to any

---

[1] Semple, *Influence of Geographic Environment*, pp. 3, 259.
[2] ii, 8.
[3] Semple, *Influence of Geographic Environment*, p. 416.

that did not belong to the privileged class of "superiors"? Why do we find in the writings of the philosophers that never-ending insistence on exclusiveness, that deliberate attempt to shut out the foreigner and to limit the size of the state? The ostensible reason is the fear of corruption from outside sources, more particularly contamination from the Persians, and we must not disregard that motive. But deep down, unperceived by its authors, there must have been the age-long fear of over-population pressing upon the means of subsistence. The Spartan sought to exclude the foreigner because Laconia had little enough to support even the Spartan population, dwindling though its numbers were. Plato and Aristotle sought to limit the numbers of the citizens in their ideal states because they knew from actual observation the troubles that over-population engendered. They had anticipated by two thousand years the theories of Malthus.[1]

The Greeks utterly failed to build up a political structure commensurate with their cultural achievements. This tragic failure, to which in the last analysis must be attributed their final downfall, may be traced principally to their inability to throw off those vicious animosities that had become so ingrained in them that a united Greece was an impossibility. And when the horizon so suddenly and amazingly widened, and Alexander gave the world to the Greek to play with, the old rivalries, the unappeasable jealousies of Greek towards Greek, continued on a vaster and more tragic scale. The confusion of the Hellenistic era which succeeded the conquests of Alexander was beyond description. Three great royal houses, that of Macedonia, the Seleucids of Asia and the Ptolemies of Egypt fought themselves to a standstill, and when they were not fighting each other they were tearing themselves to pieces in internecine strife within their own borders.[2] Rome was practically forced to step in and impose peace upon the successors of Alexander. But even after it had done so, the last and worst "flare up" followed in the terrible wars of Mithradates of

---

[1] A modern parallel may be found in the troubles that beset the Pitcairn islanders when newcomers invaded their little domain.

[2] Mr Tarn, in his *Hellenistic Civilisation*, is forced to the conclusion that in that age men were "a little mad". World empire is a heady draught for any people; even the Romans yielded to its intoxication.

Pontus against the Romans, and Hellenism went down in irretrievable ruin.

That last appalling catastrophe induces some sad reflections. That Athens should have thrown in her lot with Mithradates and defied the Romans was a piece of folly that is, at least to later observers, almost inconceivable. It is, of course, only too easy to be wise after the event, and it may even be agreed that Mithradates had at least even chances of beating the Romans. But in any event it was madness for Athens to risk everything by abandoning a neutrality that was her only chance of existence. It is related that the destruction of Corinth by Mummius was the outcome of an exasperation that at last broke down the patience of the Romans, whose treatment of Old Greece up to that time had not, on the whole, been ungenerous. If the Greeks would not behave themselves, if they were blind to their best interests and incapable of accepting the inevitable, they must be taught a lesson, and a bitter and sharp one it was. It is significant that Roman despised Greek; the "hungry Greekling" of Juvenal is not a pretty picture. We who study the writings of their philosophers, who find in the teachings of Aristotle and Plato the highest expression of political thought, must turn away in weariness and disgust from what we can only call the "political wrongheadedness" of the very people whose teachers they were.

THE ECONOMIC LIFE OF GREECE

But it is not with such sad reflections that we are concerned here. What of the Greek in his economic life, in the workshop, the market place, the counting house and in international commerce? Such is to be the theme of our inquiry, and although much of it will be interesting, even fascinating, yet we must realise that we are not treading the mountain tops nor concerning ourselves with the glories of Greek art or philosophy, but rather with the humdrum things of daily life, petty, mean affairs of shopkeepers, artificers and peddlers. We may even ask ourselves whether, after all, it is worth while to bother ourselves with such things. If we may thrill to the immortal protests of Demosthenes against the Macedonian who was to rob his city of her liberty, why should we bother ourselves with the speeches that he made in the law courts, or have been attributed to him, over some sordid case of cheating and sharp practice among the merchants of his time? Many will think the point well taken; but if we are to understand the Greeks we must know them in all the various aspects of their lives; in their great moments and in their pettiness, in their masterpieces and in their daily life of making a living. And so it is with the Greek as tradesman and worker and merchant, not as poet or artist or philosopher that we are concerned.

While the Greek was an excellent technician, so far as his limited means allowed him, a clever business man (a little too clever sometimes as the cases in the law courts show) and an extremely competent trader, yet we are confronted with what appears at first as a strange and anomalous contradiction that, apparently, the Greek despised work as beneath the dignity of a free man, and left to his slaves the labours that he was unwilling to perform himself. But we must be careful not to jump to a conclusion that is not really consonant with the facts. As a matter of actual fact, were manual labour, and indeed all gainful occupations, despised and shunned? Were the Greeks "workshy" idlers, who lived on the industry of their slaves and allowed foreigners, "Metics", to amass wealth, without an effort to compete with them, content to mulct them with heavy taxes, and themselves live "on the dole"? It would be all too easy to answer all these in the affirmative, and dismiss the whole subject with a few well-known passages from the historians and philosophers. But the problem is not quite so easy and demands further scrutiny.

In the first place, it must be noted that any prejudice against manual labour among the Greeks was of comparatively late origin. Certainly, in the Homeric age, to labour with one's hands was no disgrace; witness the prowess of Odysseus, who was a mighty worker, built his own house and even his own bedstead.[1] Nor was there any prejudice against manual labour in the time of Solon, who decreed that a father must see that his son be taught a craft.[2] Undoubtedly in the time of the

---

[1] But they did not like agricultural labour, which was beneath the dignity of a high-spirited warrior. Cf. *Od*. xiii, 31–4, xiv, 222–3.

[2] Plut. *Solon*, 22.

tyrants, and right up to the Persian wars, it was no disgrace to "learn the works of Athena and Hephaestus of the many arts and with his hands to earn his living".[1]

To what, then, must be attributed the undoubted prejudice against manual labour in the latter part of the fifth and throughout the fourth century? It is quite evident that it arose after the Persian wars, when the "Marathon men" were the heroes, and the life of the soldier was magnified as the only fit one for freemen. The plunder gained from the wars, and after the founding of the Delian League, the revenues from the allies, set up new standards of values and conduct.[2] Herodotus remarked upon this as something quite new and wondered whether they had learned it from the Egyptians and barbarians. "All the Greeks have adopted the same notion, and especially the Lacedaemonians; but the Corinthians hold handicraftsmen in least disesteem."[3]

It would be easy to quote passages from Aristotle and Plato showing their attitude towards gainful occupations.[4] They did not so much despise "honest toil" as consider it incompatible with the life of the lawgiver and ruler; in which perhaps they were not very far wrong. They simply would not allow that a man, whose whole energies were devoted to making a living, could possibly at the same time fulfil his duties as a citizen in the law courts, the Assembly and the army. They also deeply distrusted the acquisitive instinct; the ruler must be entirely separated from the commercial and labouring classes, or else he would be corrupted by them.

But the theories of the philosophers and the jeers of the comic playwrights like Aristophanes, who never misses any opportunity to gibe at Cleon for making his living at the vulgar trade of a tanner, which, be it said, was in particular disrepute because of the unpleasant odours therefrom, do not by any means indicate that the Athenian citizen actually despised and shunned all gainful occupations. The laws by no means encouraged idleness; we hear of accusations brought against individuals for

---

[1] *Anth. Lyr.* (Diehl), Solon, 1, 49–50.
[2] Cf. W. Drumann, *Arbeiter u. Communisten in Griechenland u. Rom*, p. 46.
[3] Herod. ii, 166–7.
[4] E.g. Arist. *Pol.* 1278 A; Plato, *Laws*, viii, 846 ff. But cf. *Critias*, 110 C, and *Apol.* 22 C; Neurath, *Staat und Gesellschaft*, p. 594.

having no visible means of support. In the first half of the third century we hear of a prosecution of the philosopher Cleanthes on such a charge. But when he showed that he worked at night drawing water for gardens, the Areopagus was so delighted with his industry that it voted him ten minas in order to continue his studies.[1] We have already mentioned the law of Solon that a parent who failed to have his son taught a trade could not demand support from him in his old age. Pericles in his funeral oration boasts of the fact that the Athenians combine the pursuit of culture with useful occupations. "Wealth we employ for use rather than for show, and place the real disgrace of poverty not in owning to the fact but in declining to struggle against it. Our public men have, besides politics, their private affairs to attend to, and our ordinary citizens, though occupied with the pursuits of industry, are still fair judges of public matters."[2] We know from the speech of Demosthenes against Eubulides that for anyone to sneer at a citizen for making his livelihood in the market laid him open to a prosecution for evil-speaking.[3] What is troubling poor Euxitheus, the plaintiff in this case, is not so much the fact that his parents were poor and had to earn their living, although he apologises abjectly for that fact, but rather that aspersions had been cast on his mother's virtue; a very serious charge when he is claiming Athenian citizenship.[4] Undoubtedly there was a good deal of snobbery in Athens, as everywhere, and the well-to-do looked down on the workers. Demosthenes does not appear in a very pleasing light when he sneers at the humble origin of Aeschines, who had to work for his living when a boy; so different from his own upbringing as the son of a wealthy parent; and then, with artless naïveté, hopes he will not be accused of bad taste in alluding to these vulgar matters![5]

Although both Plato and Aristotle considered that the worker could not be a lawgiver, yet we find that artisans were not only numerous but in the majority of the Assembly. Xenophon tells us that it was composed in Athens of fullers, shoemakers,

----

[1] Diog. Laert. vii, 168. Also the story of Menedemus and Asclepiades who ground at a mill all night and were handsomely rewarded for their industry (Athen. iv, 168 A). Cf. Plut. *Apoph. Lac.* 221 C.

[2] Thuc. ii, 40.   [3] Cf. also *in Mid.* 32.
[4] Dem. *in Eubul.* 30.   [5] *De Corona*, 255.

carpenters, blacksmiths, farmers, merchants and shopkeepers.[1] Plato says that in democracies the most influential and numerous class in the Assembly is that of the artisans.[2] Although in earlier times office was restricted to owners of land, certainly by the end of the fifth century manufacturers or merchants were eligible even for the highest. Eucrates, a dealer in oakum, was elected general in 432;[3] Lysicles, who dealt in sheep, in 428,[4] and Cleon, a tanner, in 425. Demosthenes was the son of a manufacturer of armour; Socrates of a mason; Aeschines was an actor before he made his reputation as an orator, and possibly he sold perfumes, although there is doubt on the point.[5]

There is in Greek a word *banausia* which denotes vulgarity, and a workman was called *banausos*, a low, vulgar fellow.[6] Possibly, but by no means certainly, the word is derived from the verb *bauno*, which means to work in a constricted space before a fire.[7] If so, it might not unreasonably be argued that in a hot country such would be distasteful to people who much preferred to work in the open air. But even at that they greatly disliked digging and heavy manual labour in agriculture,[8] for which they may be pardoned in a warm climate; the stony soil is hard on the muscles of those who must perforce wrest their livelihood from it. There is an amusing passage in one of the plays of Aristophanes[9] in which the God of Riches argues against an even distribution of wealth, on the ground that it would destroy the slave trade and drive citizens to work, a result most fervently to be deplored. From whatever side we look at it, the conclusion is inescapable that the Greeks greatly disliked manual labour, and looked down on those who were unfortunate enough to have to betake themselves thereto. The ideal of the gentleman of leisure was somewhat over-developed

---

[1] *Memor.* iii, 7, 6.
[2] *Repub.* viii, 565 A.   [3] Aristoph. *Equites*, 130.
[4] That is to say if we identify the Lysicles of Thuc. iii, 19, with that in Aristoph. *Equites*, 131.
[5] Athen. xiii, 611 F.
[6] Numerous references, e.g. Plato, *Rep.* 495; *Laws*, 741 E. Cf. Busolt's remarks on this, *Griech. Staatsk.* I, 182, n. 5.
[7] Cf. Liddell and Scott (new ed.) and E. Boisacq, *Dictionnaire Étymologique de la Langue Grecque*, s.v. Zimmern, in his role of *advocatus dei*, argues eloquently for this view.
[8] E.g. Aristoph. *Aves*, 1431–2; cf. Luke xvi. 3.
[9] *Plutus*, 510–25.

in the ancient world; just as it is in any society to-day where the accumulation of acquired or inherited wealth is sufficient to allow of it to flourish.

On further reflection it will be seen that the degradation of labour is characteristic of an economy founded upon the system of slavery. The slave worked, that was what he was for; therefore if a freeman also worked, he brought himself down to the level of the slave and suffered the competition of cheap labour. The Greek was not unique in this attitude; it was found universally in the ancient world. Looked at in this light the aversion from manual toil is at least understandable if not, according to our modern ideas, entirely commendable. The phrase "nobility of toil" is a very modern one, and would have been meaningless to the ancients. With our multitudinous wants and means of supplying them through large-scale production, the vast majority of mankind to-day works by hand or brain, and finds no social stigma attached thereto; except, perhaps, where a military or aristocratic caste is still able, however precariously, to maintain an attitude of superiority.

It is interesting to note that St Paul is anxious to justify himself, a tentmaker, in the eyes of those who would look down their noses at his honest toil, and acknowledges that he is subject to social ostracism thereby. "We labour, working with our hands, being reviled;"[1] he "suffers reproach" as a manual labourer.[2] He is afraid, and not without justification, that the Christian converts, who were generally drawn from the artisan classes, should, in their enthusiasm for the new revelation, throw up their occupations and become an embarrassment to the infant religion through idleness and over-much preoccupation with the things of eternity. Such an admonition as "servants (i.e. slaves) be obedient to them that are your masters" was very necessary if the Christian religion was to escape, and it did not wholly escape, the reproach of being subversive of the social system of the day.

It is not fair to accuse the Greek citizen of being "work-shy"; he was not so much lazy as occupied with things that he considered better than mere working to acquire money. There was in him something of the artist who was careless of riches. Not

1 Cor. iv. 12.   [2] 1 Tim. iv. 10.

that he did not understand perfectly the use of wealth; but wealth was to him a means to an end, not an end in itself; so he looked down on those mean souls who worked without imagination or the divine fire of inspiration. When he did work he liked to work in the open air. To rear a magnificent edifice, a deathless work of art, was a supreme satisfaction. But, unfortunately, building Parthenons did not claim all his attention; the workaday necessity for earning a living imposed its burdens upon him. Not everybody had private means, or a farm in the country, or was an artist, or poet, or philosopher. And so the great majority of the Greeks both in classical and Hellenistic times worked just as hard as anybody else in any time or country. The honest labouring-man, a free citizen and not ashamed of it, with good reason we may readily agree, is a familiar figure in the Greek comedies.

There is one factor in the economy of the Athenian state which must always be reckoned with, the wholesale payment of citizens. Ostensibly for services rendered on the juries and in the Assembly, such payments were in reality of the nature of relief, the "dole". It may be argued, not without some justification, that if the state demanded the presence of its citizens in the courts, and juries of five hundred drew largely on a small population, in the Assembly and in the various public offices, they not unreasonably had to be paid for their services. Athens, when head of the Delian League, was the capital city of a great confederacy, and to the Athenian courts came all the cases which the intensely litigious Greeks so freely indulged in.[1] But while it is not impossible to excuse payment of citizens on these grounds, it is far more difficult to do so when we find that they also drew their pay, three obols a day, for attending the dramatic presentations in the theatre and the religious festivals. Again it may be argued that such were civic celebrations, an act of obligation on the citizens to attend, and if they were to leave their occupations to do so, they must be compensated. Such a plea can only be entertained hardly; the argument in justification becomes a trifle strained, and we are forced to look upon the practice as a dole to the Athenian citizen, in other words as relief. Aristophanes in *The Wasps* ridicules the whole system.[2]

[1] Cf. Xen. *Mem.* iii, 5, 16.   [2] Cf. also *Equites*, 797, 1350.

The old men come trudging along the country roads before dawn with their lanterns, eager to be in time for the opening of the courts, where they can earn their three obols comfortably by sitting all day, and no doubt napping when the case is dull. "How shall we get our breakfast, if the courts don't open soon?" cries the son of one of them. And so a very large proportion, how large it is impossible to compute, lived partly or wholly on payments from the state.

That the clearer thinkers of the time were uncomfortably aware of the dangers of such a system of wholesale payment of citizens is very evident. Plato, particularly in the *Gorgias*, has grave doubts as to the statesmanship of Pericles who introduced the system, and acknowledges that it has laid the Athenians open to the accusation of being "lazy, cowardly, loquacious and avaricious".[1] Aristotle characterises as the worst form of democracy that in which the citizens are numerous and can only be made to assemble when they are paid. "Where there are revenues the demagogues should not be allowed after their manner to distribute the surplus; the poor are always receiving and always wanting more and more, for such help is like water poured into a leaky cask. Yet the true friend of the people should see that they be not too poor, for extreme poverty lowers the character of the democracy; measures also should be taken which will give them lasting prosperity; and as this is equally the interest of all classes, the proceeds of the public revenues should be accumulated and distributed among them, if possible, in such quantities as may enable them to purchase a little farm, or at any rate make a beginning in trade and husbandry."[2]

And yet, looking at the whole matter from a practical point of view, it is difficult, even with our modern notions, to condemn the Athenians for spending the money they had in a way that gave themselves the greatest satisfaction. We must always remember that it was rooted in the Greek mind that the wealth of the state ought to be divided among its citizens. Athens was rich; she enjoyed substantial revenues from the mines of Laurium, and, while head of the Delian League, the tribute of the allies. As their ambassadors to Sparta say with engaging frankness, they proposed to spend the money on themselves.

[1] *Gorgias*, 515 E.   [2] *Pol.* 1320 A.

"It has always been the rule that the weaker should be constrained by the stronger."[1]

If we may define with Chesterton the state of being poor as that of "not having very much money", perhaps the best definition that has ever been given, the Greeks were poor and did not care very much whether they were or not; a state of mind assuredly beyond all praise. So, why work? The question is a pertinent one and, looked at in that light, not so very easy to answer. Perhaps we to-day work too hard and are not much the better for our unceasing toil. We may be more comfortable, live easier and enjoy all the blessings of modern plumbing. But it is open to doubt if we are, in actual fact, really very much happier. The Athenian must have had a magnificent time and enjoyed himself immensely, chattering with his friends, serving as a juryman in an interesting case in the courts, sitting in the Assembly, watching or taking part in athletic contests, participating in the great and beautiful religious festivals, or sitting in the theatre thrilling at the grandeur of a tragedy or splitting his sides at some rare, and rather broad, joke in a comedy. It was a gorgeous life, and as long as slaves and Metics would do the dirty work the Athenian enjoyed it to the full. It takes a very stern asceticism to blame him for it.

But although a plausible case can be made out for the Greek, yet there were grave sources of decay at work which, in the end, worked their inevitable destruction. In the last analysis we must come to the conclusion, which seems inescapable, that the whole political and economic system was essentially and irremediably unsound and wrought its own destruction. Bemused with that land-hunger, which the scanty soil of Greece was unable to appease, the citizen despised the manual labour of industry, and yet was forced to the town, where he met the competition of Metic and slave. An easy way out of his difficulties, a fatally easy one we may say, was found in his being able to "cash-in" on his citizenship, and eke out a more or less unsatisfactory and comfortless existence "on the dole".[2] Irritated by his sense of economic failure, and arrogant from his feeling of political superiority, he was the natural prey of the demagogue, who found in his restless dissatisfaction the tool to be used with

---

[1] Thuc. i, 26. [2] Hasebroek, *Trade and Politics*, p. 33 ff.

fatal facility in political faction. The principle of democratic government, reduced to a logical absurdity, allowed him no rest, little opportunity to go about his own affairs without the unceasing distractions of politics. If he was poor himself, the citizen saw no particular reason why others should be rich, and his democratic form of government gave him plenty of opportunities to make that admirable sentiment effective.

By such taxes as the capital levy and the Liturgies or compulsory "Benevolences", the rich could be easily mulcted and their wealth spent in various ways pleasing to the multitude. As we see in our chapter on Public Finance, this perpetual antagonism between rich and poor was fatal in the end, and the whole Athenian state, after the tribute from the Delian League could no longer be collected, drifted into bankruptcy. It was highly diverting for the citizen to witness fine spectacles, and amusing to sit in the theatre or the law courts and be paid for the sitting. But it ruined him in the end. If he could have been put into a more stable and satisfactory condition, it is more than probable that the Athenian state, and indeed all Greece, would have avoided or at least weathered some, if not all, of the disasters that overtook it. Certainly many of the mistakes that were committed might have been avoided had strong leadership been present. Apart from politics, only in war could the citizen find a career consonant with his dignity. The pay was good, and the chances of plunder, the capture of an enemy who could be sold as a slave, were always present. War distributed money, and made additional burdens on the well-to-do both possible and justifiable. War was, therefore, a blessing and not to be avoided, if the chances of success seemed good.[1] Not that some of the shrewder minds did not see perfectly clearly that the senseless bellicosity of the Greeks was fatal to material prosperity. The fifth chapter in the little pamphlet entitled "On the Revenues of Athens", attributed to Xenophon, is a sensible and eminently reasonable plea for a pacific policy which should avoid the disasters of war, and the orator Isocrates in his speech on Peace[2] has a fine passage that, if acted upon, would have saved Athens

---

[1] Cf. Xen. *Mem.* iii, 6, 7.

[2] *de Pace*, 20. Aristotle's argument in his *Politics* (1256 B) that war against a "servile" race is natural and just is an ingenious one. But cf. *ibid.* 1324 B, 1333 B, 1334 A. Aristotle entirely missed the economic argument against war.

from many tribulations. But fight and quarrel the Greeks would and did, and destroyed themselves in their folly.

POPULATION[1]

Of all the baffling problems for which no definite solution may be offered, perhaps the most obscure is that of the population of Ancient Greece, or of the ancient world in general for the matter of that. It seems practically impossible to arrive at any satisfactory conclusion merely by accepting the figures given in ancient writers, since these figures are so palpably absurd in many instances that no reliance can be placed upon them. Why this should be it is very difficult indeed to say. It is entirely possible, in fact practically certain, that in many cases the notation used has been wrongly transcribed through the corruption of manuscripts, or the carelessness of early copyists. In some cases the original author was clearly wrong in his estimates and made a bad mistake. In other cases we must seek an explanation in the attitude of practically all ancient peoples in grossly over-estimating numbers. Why this should have been so is hard to say, except on the ground that very large numbers baffled their powers of imagination. Anything beyond a few thousand seemed to them "an awful lot", and they were just as apt to say five hundred thousand as fifty thousand. And yet such an explanation is hard to accept when we remember the amazingly accurate calculations of the Alexandrian astronomer of the circumference of the earth. Perhaps another and easier explanation may be that the ancient scribes betrayed an almost childish vanity in magnifying numbers; for instance, the vastness of the Persian armies that a handful of Greeks defeated or the mighty men of valour of the children of Israel.

One of the most notorious of all exaggerations, which has been the subject of endless controversy in the past, and will be

---

[1] Beloch, *Bevölkerung der Griechisch-Römischen Welt*; A. W. Gomme, *Population of Athens in Fifth and Fourth Centuries B.C.*; R. L. Sargent, *Size of Slave Population at Athens*; Cavaignac, *Population et Capital*, caps. vi–viii; Gernet, *L'Approvisionnement d'Athènes en Blé*, cap. i; Andreades, *Hist. Greek Publ. Finance*, pp. 285 ff.; Jardé, *Céréales*, cap. 2; Schwahn, art. "Theten" in *P.W.*; Westermann, art. "Sklaverei" in *P.W.* Suppl. vi, pp. 905 ff.; Boeckh, i, 7; G. E. Fawcus, "The Athenian army in 431", *J.H.S.* xxix (1909), p. 23.

no doubt in the future, is that of Athenaeus who, quoting from Ctesicles, states that in the census taken by Demetrius of Phalerum (317–307) there were 21,000 citizens, 10,000 Metics and 400,000 slaves in Athens. The same author, purporting to quote from Timaeus and Aristotle, gravely informs us that there were at one time 470,000 slaves on the island of Aegina and 460,000 in Corinth.[1] These figures have been rejected ever since the time of Hume who, in his "Populousness of Ancient Nations", began the long controversy on the subject.[2] The island of Aegina has an area of approximately 35 sq. miles, of which the greater part is mountainous and rocky.[3] At the present time its population is about 8000. By no stretch of the imagination is it conceivable that this small and mountainous island could possibly contain so enormous a number, even granting that the port did have a fairly large population, and the same is true of Corinth. All attempts, therefore, at justifying the numbers given by Athenaeus for Attica must break down on the palpable exaggerations of the other two estimates; if one figure is wrong, we must assume that the other is equally fallacious.[4] Beloch[5] made the suggestion that 40,000 were meant, not 400,000; but this rests on no certain ground and is as impossible of substantiation as the figures of Athenaeus. We are thus driven back to the conclusion that they are unexplainable and must be rejected.

Attempts at attacking the puzzle from another side are equally unsatisfactory. In a famous passage[6] Demosthenes states that in the year 338 there were imported from Pontus 400,000 medimni of grain, that is, wheat, and that this quantity was equal to all the wheat imported from other countries, such figures, he says, being verifiable from the books of the port

---

[1] Athen. vi, 272 B, C, D.

[2] Miss Sargent, *Size of Slave Population at Athens*, pp. 14 ff. summarises and comments upon Hume's conclusions.

[3] Strabo, viii, 6, 16 (c. 375).

[4] Mr N. G. L. Hammond in a paper on "The Slave Population of Attica circa 350 B.C.", *Cambridge University Reporter*, March 12th, 1935, argues that the figures for Attica must be correct because of the figures for Aegina and Corinth. But if the latter are wrong they invalidate the former and the argument is in a circle.

[5] *Bevölkerung*, pp. 54f. Cf. also *Griech. Gesch.* iii, 2 (2nd ed.), pp. 414f.

[6] *In Lept.* 31.

authorities at the Piraeus.[1] If we accept these figures, then, obviously the total import of grain was 800,000 med., or 1,200,000 bushels. There is evidence to show that in 329 the Attic crop amounted to 340,350 med. of barley and 28,500 of wheat or 368,850 med. in all, or about 553,000 bushels, and this was apparently, although not certainly, a poor crop. If we were to reckon a normal crop of not more than 600,000 med. or 900,000 bushels, barley and wheat, we should arrive at a total consumption in Attica in a "normal" year of something in the neighbourhood of 2,100,000 bushels of grain. What amount was fed to livestock we have no idea, a factor which once more clouds the issue severely. Dr Beloch assumes an average per capita consumption of 6 med. of wheat and barley, and this is a reasonable figure to accept.[2] We, therefore, arrive at a population for Attica in the latter part of the fourth century of about 233,000, which compares with Beloch's 215,000 and Mr Gomme's 270,000, which he regards as a maximum.[3]

These figures must be accepted, if at all, with the utmost possible caution and regarded as no better than a guess. If we were to surmise that the population of Attica never exceeded 300,000, nor dropped, except probably in the second century, below 200,000, we should, in all likelihood, be not very far from the truth. Complete accuracy is quite impossible, and at that we have to leave it.

As to the population of all Greece our guess is even more impossibly short of an approach towards a reasonable approximation. Beloch estimated it at 2,228,000, a figure which Mr Grundy considers too low.[4] According to the census of 1907 the population of "Old Greece" amounted to 2,631,000.[5] It is not likely that Greece of the fourth century B.C. contained more people than in the twentieth A.D. If we were to con-

---

[1] But for another interpretation of this passage cf. Kocevalov, *Die Einfuhr von Getreide nach Athen*, in *Rhein. Mus.* xxxi (1932), p. 321. Mr Kocevalov holds that the passage points to double that amount coming from "Pontus".

[2] Sir George Knibbs reckoned 5·7 bushels of wheat at the present time; with barley 9 bushels would be quite reasonable. Cf. *Mathematical Theory of Population*, p. 455.

[3] *Bevölkerung*, p. 33; Gomme, *Population*, p. 32f.

[4] *Thucydides and History of his Age*, p. 213f.

[5] Probably the best figures to take; subsequent additions of territory and influx of refugees make later figures too confused to be useful.

jecture, therefore, a population of about two-and-a-half millions probably we should not be very far wrong.

But whatever our guesses may be at actual figures, there is little doubt that we can assume broad general movements of population. From the Persian to the Peloponnesian war there was clearly an increase, due to increasing wealth and, we may suppose, better living conditions. Any diminution of numbers owing to casualties in warfare or emigration was doubtless offset by new arrivals of Metics and slaves; perhaps we should not be far wrong if we surmised that it was the increase in slaves that accounted for the greater part of population growth at this period. The decrease in numbers during the Peloponnesian war was due not only to heavy casualties but also to the great plague that ravaged Athens; Beloch believes that a quarter of the population died.[1] Thucydides in his vivid description of the epidemic says,[2] "such a pestilence and loss of life as this was nowhere remembered to have happened", and further "nothing reduced the power of the Athenians more than this. For not less than four thousand four hundred heavy armed in the ranks died of it, and three hundred of the equestrian order, with a number of the multitude that was never ascertained."[3] It is to be conjectured that the poorer classes suffered more than the richer, and we cannot doubt that the loss of life in the overcrowded tenements of Athens and the Piraeus was very severe. With regard to war casualties it is unsafe to speak with any certainty, but they were undoubtedly heavy. Added to which there must have been a marked diminution in the slave population. We know that "more than 20,000" ran away when the Spartans occupied Decelea.[4] This is obviously a round number and we need not regard it as absolutely authentic; but we may be sure that there was a heavy loss on that account. We may also conjecture that the diminution in wealth during this distressful epoch must have curtailed the ability of many to keep slaves or rather to purchase new ones when their former ones had died or deserted. Added to which the foreign population of Metics, mostly merchants, must have diminished to some

---

[1] *Griech. Gesch.* II, 1, pp. 308 ff. (2nd. ed. 1914).
[2] ii, 47.   [3] iii, 87.
[4] Thuc. vii, 27.

extent owing to the dislocation of trade; although possibly so long as the Athenians controlled the seas they may have considered the Piraeus the safest place for them. With the return of peace there was another rise in population due very largely to an influx of foreigners and the renewed purchase of slaves, who were cheap, and also to more peaceful times and the employment of mercenary soldiers in campaigns rather than a levy of citizens. The marked drop in the number of citizens from 338 to 313 is to be explained by emigration to the new countries conquered by Alexander, and colonisation of Thrace in part by Athenians by Antipater.[1] Undoubtedly there was a severe drop in population, as noted by Polybius, in the third century, which can be attributed to the disorders of the time, general distress and emigration.

While we are treating of the vexed subject of population it may be opportune to speak of another troublesome problem, that of infanticide. This is another of those dark shadows across the life of the ancient world of which it is very difficult if not impossible to speak with certainty. That it existed is, of course, well known and widely attested; to what extent it was practised cannot be determined. Malthus assumed, more or less on general grounds and without any definite evidence to go on, that infanticide was a very definite and powerful check to the increase of population in Greece.[2] Modern writers are more cautious; Mr Gomme gives excellent arguments in favour of the view that, in actual fact, it was rare. "Certainly we have no reason to suppose that the movement of population was sensibly affected by the practice."[3] This is very likely true, and in any case, as we know for certain in Sparta, it may be conjectured that it largely appertained to weakly or deformed infants.[4] Aristotle disliked the practice but, under certain circumstances, advocated abortion. Infanticide, where a people or tribe is living on the verge of starvation, on what the economist calls "subsistence level", is a necessity; one more mouth to feed is too much for their severely restricted resources. We may, therefore, conclude with some degree of certainty that in

---

[1] Plut. *Phocion*, 28; Diod. Sic. xviii, 18, 4.
[2] *Essays*, Book i, cap. 13.   [3] *Population*, pp. 75 f.
[4] Cf. Arist. *Pol.* 1335 B.

the more prosperous periods of Greek history it was rare or non-existent. Mr Tarn, speaking of the third century, a time of the gravest economic and political distress, says that infanticide "on a considerable scale" was not in doubt.[1] The evidence of the New Comedy is not necessarily convincing; the theme of the son or daughter that has been exposed or kidnapped, to turn up later to the embarrassment or joy of its parents, is a very old one and belongs to all ages.

But if we may suppose that infanticide among citizens was exceptional, what are we to say about the slaves? We know that it was always considered bad business to breed slaves, it being more satisfactory and cheaper to buy imported adults. What then are we to think about the slave birth-rate and the morals of those unfortunates? Evidently that is a subject of which the less said the better.[2]

Another dark corner into which, for the sake of our peace of mind, we had better not pry too closely is the effect upon the birth-rate of a certain aspect of Greek morals which is highly disconcerting to modern susceptibilities. Aristotle seems quite sure that homosexuality had kept down the natural increase in numbers in Crete, and even states that the practice was introduced and encouraged for that particular purpose,[3] an assertion that is highly open to doubt. It is hard to suppose that such practices had any real effect upon the birth-rate, and the whole subject may be dismissed with a verdict of *non probatum*.

GREEK ECONOMIC THOUGHT[4]

It will be well to examine briefly the economic thought of the Greek philosophers. While it cannot be said that anything approaching a systematic theory of Political Economy was ever formulated in ancient times, such is the accomplishment of the

[1] *Hellenistic Civilisation*, pp. 82, 85.
[2] For further references cf. A. Cameron, "The exposure of children and Greek ethics", *Class. Rev.* xlvi (1932), p. 105; H. Bolkestein, *Class. Philol.* xvii (1922), p. 222; L. Van Hook, *Trans. Am. Philol. Ass.* li (1920), p. 104.
[3] *Pol.* 1272 A.
[4] M. L. W. Laistner, *Greek Economics*; L. H. Haney, *History of Economic Thought*, cap. iv; J. K. Ingram, *History of Political Economy*, cap. i; J. Kinkel, *Die sozialökonomischen Grundlagen der Staats und Wirtschaftslehre von Aristoteles* (1911); T. Bisinger, "Der Agrarstaat in Platons Gesetzen", *Klio*, Beiheft xiii (1925).

moderns, yet there are scattered in fair abundance through the writings of Plato, Aristotle, and Xenophon sufficient indications to show that even the philosophers were well aware of economic problems, and had given thought and consideration thereto. If Plato is to discuss his ideal Republic, he must also discuss its economic underpinning, and Aristotle, both in his Politics, Laws and Ethics, envisages many problems that are essentially, in the strictest sense, more economic than political.

It is notable to observe that Plato based his Republic upon what is, in fact, an economic interpretation of history. "A city comes into being because individually we are not self-sufficing but have a variety of wants. Then, as men have many wants and many persons are needed to supply them, one takes a helper for one purpose and another for another; and when these partners and helpers are gathered together in one habitation the body of inhabitants is termed a state. Then men give or receive in exchange because they think it is to their advantage. Our mutual needs will, it appears, lead to the formation of the state."[1] Aristotle, on the other hand, while acknowledging that the household is formed for the provision of everyday wants, yet bases his theory upon the dictum that man is by nature a "political being", and that, unable to exist in solitude, the state is necessary to make life possible for him;[2] a view which on consideration will be seen to be essentially the same as Plato's in its final analysis.

The idea of division of labour is explicit in their writings and is based quite simply upon such human wants as food, clothing and shelter, which will be produced most efficiently if each individual confines himself to what he can do best. The necessity of finding an easy means of exchanging products will lead to a class of merchants and shopkeepers, the use of money, and finally to a class of hired labourers. So far the concept of division of labour has proceeded on lines familiar and simple to the modern mind; but from then on it is given a twist, which presents the theory of the state, not from the standpoint of individual well-being, but from that of the welfare of the state. In the subordination of the individual to the state is to be found the keynote of all Greek philosophic theory in the political and

[1] *Rep.* 369 B.   [2] *Pol.* 1252 B, 1253 A.

social sphere. If the end of man is to do the will of the Gods, he will find it in being the good citizen, and thus alone he will attain felicity. If the form of government is right, then the citizens will find in it their opportunity for self-expression; wherefore the theory of the state is of paramount importance, transcending all other considerations. The Greek thinker started, therefore, from the top, the state, and so worked downwards to the individual; while modern political philosophers of the liberal school, rightly or wrongly, start from the individual and work up to the state. The difference of approach between ancient and modern thinker is profound and ineradicable; it is still to appear which is the better. Perhaps no final judgment can ever be come to on such a problem.[1]

It is when we study Plato's so-called theory of communism that we find the greatest misapprehension on the part of many who have read his Republic and Laws. In the first place, it must be clearly understood that his "communistic" system did not apply to all classes in the state but only to the highest, the rulers and philosophers. It was not an economic doctrine in any way; it had not anything whatever to do with solving the evils of poverty through a distribution of wealth or a regimentation of the productive efforts of society. The rulers, the philosophers of the ideal state, were to devote themselves to their task of government with a single-hearted devotion that allowed of no selfish individualism. If they are to do this successfully, then private property, and, as a logical corollary, the most individualistic of all the institutions of society—marriage and the family—must disappear. All things for these transcendental rulers must be in common; for the baser orders, the workers, such was too high for attainment. It is to be noted that if the family among the rulers is to disappear the woman is, *ipso facto*, to be emancipated from the traditional seclusion of her sex among the Greeks. It must be acknowledged, however, that such freedom or emancipation as Plato designs for women of the highest class confounds the imagination in its practical working out. But no doubt when one is letting one's fancy go, and under no obligation whatever to restrict it within the con-

---

[1] The doctrine of the Totalitarian State is a return to the Greek concept, from which nineteenth-century Liberalism had broken away.

fines of possibility, one need not bother with such limitations. But, on the other hand, Aristotle will have none of it, maintaining that property must be in private hands, but pleading for an unselfishness that will find delight in sharing with others. "It is clearly better that property should be private, but the use of it common; and the special business of the legislator is to create in men this benevolent disposition.... There is the greatest pleasure in doing a kindness or service to friends or guests or companions which can only be rendered when a man has private property."[1] Plato's distrust of the acquisitive instinct and the profit motive was the basis of his scheme of government for the ideal state. To him the possession of wealth and the pursuit of gain must be an insuperable barrier to the exercise of political power. To those whose economic interests might be subserved by the possession of such power, the temptation to use it for their own ends is too great for the state to run any risk of such abuse. Nor were the working classes to be any the more trusted; selfishness either of rich or poor, if given the chance of being exercised in the affairs of state, could only lead to the corruption of politics for the sake of class interests. The only way to avoid such corruption must be by placing all government in the hands of a *corps d'élite*, from whom all temptation to abuse of power for economic ends should be eliminated. From them the acquisitive instinct and the motive of profit must be totally banished. Only by giving this class unlimited dictatorial powers could the welfare of humanity be attained. Such was, indeed, the aim of Lycurgus, to whom were attributed the singular rules of life of the Spartan aristocracy, with their iron money and system of rigid asceticism, coupled with unlimited power over those who did not belong to the dominant class.

We are reminded of the Samurai of Japan, and reflect that such an aristocratic system must inevitably degenerate into a conservatism that, in the end, can only break down under its own weight and be unable to withstand the impact of other forms of civilisation upon it. The instinct of exclusivism that locked both Sparta and Japan against intrusion of other nations was one of self-preservation of a class that could not adapt itself

[1] *Pol.* 1263 A.

to other modes of life. It is also significant to reflect that the Japanese were able to reconstitute their whole economic and political system, which the Spartans were unable to do. Further than that it is unwise to push the analogy.

But for those who do not constitute the ruling class, Plato sees clearly that social solidarity can only be achieved by eliminating both the plutocrat and the beggar.[1] But how that was to be attained was a problem that he was honest enough to admit was excessively difficult. He was acute enough to perceive very clearly that neither colonisation nor confiscation was better than a merely temporary expedient, which could not permanently solve the problem of inequality of wealth.[2] The only real and lasting cure must be through a complete moral change by means of education and long and patient training. This, he acknowledges, will be hard, so he proposes to get rid of all the older people, whose minds are not amenable to new ideas, and concentrate upon the training of the children.[3]

It is clear that Plato did not really believe that his ideal state as outlined in the Republic was actually possible, and so we find in the Laws certain modifications which he considers would make his system practicable. In the Laws we find a kind of trained democracy with a rigid system of land-holding. The number of citizens is to be limited to 5040.[4] Every citizen is to have an allotment of land which shall be inalienable, and in case of a childless possessor may be secured by adoption. This parcel of land is to be the limit of poverty, the minimum possession beyond which the poor cannot sink.[5] It is apparent here that Plato understands very clearly the fundamental weakness of the Spartan system which broke down exactly upon that point, the alienation of land that left the citizen penniless. On the other hand, excessive wealth was to be curbed by a kind of super income tax which would amount to confiscation beyond a certain maximum.[6] Each lot was to be in two parts, one near the city, the other on the frontier, by which means he hoped to

---

[1] *Rep.* 421; *Laws*, 936 B–C.   [2] *Rep.* 565 A–B; *Laws*, 735 D–6 C.
[3] *Rep.* 540 E–1 A.
[4] *Laws*, 737 E. The number 5040 is chosen because, for a number of moderate size, it has the greatest possible number of divisors (59), including all the digits from 1 to 10.
[5] *Laws*, 744 E.   [6] *Laws*, 745 A.

prevent any concentration of the best and most favourably situated land.[1] As no importation of foodstuffs was to be allowed, everyone will have to cultivate the soil.[2] Only the most absolutely necessary things that cannot be produced within the borders are to be imported. There is to be an international currency for buying abroad, and a domestic one for local needs.[3] The evils of commercialism will thus, he hopes, be avoided.

It may be remarked that such speculations on the ideal state would by no means strike those who listened to Socrates as extraordinary or unpractical. All through Greek history expeditions of Greek colonists were sent out to found new commonwealths in distant lands, and the idea of adopting, at least as an experiment, some such system as the philosopher dreamed of, was not at all an impossible one to entertain. The idea, to use a much later appellation, of a "Utopia" was always an attractive one to the Greek; the whole Spartan system was an attempt at such. Much later, in Hellenistic times, we find it cropping up again in the Sun State of Iambulus, of which Diodorus Siculus gives us a remarkable account,[4] and in the Fortunate Isle of Panchaea which Euemerus discovered in the Atlantic Ocean.[5]

It is in the treatment of money that the ideas of Aristotle have, at least for modern minds, their greatest interest and their most powerful influence.[6] Money is necessary; society cannot function without a medium of exchange or a measure of value.[7] A distinction is very properly drawn between money and wealth, as the story of King Midas, whose touch turned everything to gold, very clearly shows. But, while necessary, money is not "natural", such as are the kindly fruits of the earth. Money does not breed; it is a dead thing which is useful as a medium of exchange but for nothing else. Wherefore "usury is most reasonably detested, as it is increasing our fortune by money itself and not employing it for the purpose it was originally

---

[1] 745 C.   [2] 842 C.
[3] 742 B. An interesting example of early control of the foreign exchanges.
[4] Diod. ii, 55 ff. Cf. art. "Iambulus" by Kroll in *P.W.*
[5] Diod. v, 42 ff. Cf. art. "Euemerus" by Jacoby in *P.W.*; E. Rohde, *Der griechische Roman*, Index, s.v. Euemerus; E. Salin, *Platon und die griechische Utopie*, pp. 220 f.
[6] *Pol.* 1257 A.   [7] *Ethics*, v, 8.

intended, namely exchange ".[1] It is generally explained that the
condemnation of the charging of interest on loans which was
widespread among the ancients—the Old Testament is full of
it[2]—may be attributed to the fact that ancient economy had not
advanced to that point where loans were made for productive
purposes; they had not evolved a commercial banking system
that was in partnership with production. Loans were usually
made to relieve distress; and not without justification the idea
of benefiting by the misfortunes of others was condemned.
There is, doubtless, a certain amount of truth in this view; but
it is difficult to suppose that Aristotle was not perfectly well
aware of the importance of banking and money-lending in the
world of his day, when loans for highly productive purposes
which benefited both borrower and lender were of vital importance for both industry and commerce. If Aristotle were
merely protesting against the high interest rates his stand might
be applauded. Otherwise it is difficult for the modern mind to
accept such a theory as would condemn the charging of interest
under any circumstances. The argument that money is a dead
thing and does not breed must be rejected absolutely. It would
be just as reasonable to assert that, because a spade or a plough
is "dead" and can only be made productive in the hands of the
workman, therefore no charge should be made for it. It is to
be noted that even so good an Aristotelian as St Thomas
Aquinas has grave difficulty with this doctrine, and is forced to
some damaging admissions before he is done with it.

It may plausibly be argued that the Greek philosophers, and
indeed the Christian Church, when condemning the payment
of interest on ethical grounds were, from a strictly economic
point of view, arguing on sounder premises than perhaps they
were aware of. At a time when capital was scarce and its

---

[1] *Pol.* 1258 B. Cf. also Plato's *Laws*, v, 742 C; xi, 921 C. Plato forbade
even the repayment of capital borrowed in his desire to exclude private
possession of wealth from the rulers of his ideal state. But cf. Boeckh, i, 22,
on this point. Cf. E. Salin, "Kapitalbegriff u. Kapitallehre von der Antike
zu den Physiokraten", *Vierteljahrschr. f. Sozial u. Wirtsch. Gesch.* xxiii, 4
(1930), p. 401. Aristotle distinguished between active and inactive wealth
and between visible and invisible capital; to loan out the latter was contrary
to nature. Woodhouse, *Solon the Liberator*, p. 122.

[2] Many references, e.g. Exod. xxii. 25. But exacting usury from Gentiles
was not forbidden (Deut. xxiii. 20).

"liquidity" very restricted, the need for it was greatest, and high interest rates prevented its free circulation. One of the greatest needs of the ancient and medieval world was a plentiful supply of capital which could be utilised at reasonable rates of interest. Unfortunately the disorders of the age made the risks encountered by capital so great that, to protect themselves, lenders were forced to charge very high, no doubt in many cases exorbitant, rates. These same disorders drove capital to shelter, to be locked up in safety deposits, the temples for choice as being the safest places, and so become "thesaurised" and made of no avail in the commerce and finance which so sorely needed it. But even if capital had been readily available in large quantities for commercial or industrial enterprises, yet the primitive character of the technical processes and the small scale of production made the demand for it a very restricted one. To-day, when machine production has almost entirely displaced hand processes, the demand for capital is very great. Even a small factory requires large amounts of money to equip it with up-to-date machinery. The Greek entrepreneur had no such heavy outlay to face in setting up a business. He did not need to go to a bank to help him start; probably he financed it out of his own pocket or with the help of partners. The whole complicated technique of credit had not been evolved. The manufacturer did not receive large orders whose execution he must finance through his bank. No such alliance between banker and manufacturer, such as is characteristic of modern conditions, had been established.

Another point that must be remembered is that such modern methods of gathering great amounts of capital as the joint stock company with limited liability were entirely unknown. Partnerships there were, but their command of money was strictly limited.[1] It is pertinent to recall that the vast aggregations of capital which are familiar to us to-day are of very recent growth, made possible by the subscriptions of innumerable small investors who are able to buy a few shares in some company. The small investor was unknown to the ancient world: there was nothing for him to invest in.

[1] E.g. in shipping loans, banking, mining and tax-farming, but they were temporary associations and not on the joint-stock principle; cf. "Business partnerships in Ancient Greece", *Class. Rev.* lii (1938), p. 30.

We should, therefore, be correct if we were to say that while lack of capital was one of the greatest hindrances to economic development, yet that lack of capital, as distinguished from wealth in the economic sense, was occasioned in large measure by lack of enterprises in which it could be profitably employed and the absence of any financial technique for its accumulation and disposition.[1] Adam Smith, in a celebrated passage, when reflecting upon the fall in interest rates which had puzzled other writers, put his finger unerringly upon the cause—greater security and the competition of lenders. If the ancient philosophers and the Christian Church had argued along those lines they would have been on surer ground. As it is, it is difficult to acquit Aristotle of a wilful exercise in logomachy, a playing with words, when he says that money cannot breed. It is interesting to reflect that the Greek word *Tokos* means both child-bearing and interest on loans.[2]

The treatment of the problem of poverty and wealth both by Aristotle and Plato is sound but limited in the view of the modern economist. Riches lead to deterioration of character in those who possess them, while poverty is a deterrent to the best work.[3] Plato finds it hard to believe that a man can be rich, happy and good at the same time. Aristotle had no particular dislike for riches, except in so far as they gave too much power to the wealthy, which he fears even more than power given to the poor.[4] Poverty is the parent of revolution and crime, and in his anxiety to preserve the constitution and the forms of law, Aristotle is willing to come to terms with the poor. It is absolutely necessary that the property of the rich should be spared; but if heavy taxation is necessary, then at least some of it should be devoted to the services of religion. Better far that the pay of the citizens be cut down by limiting the number of meetings of the Assembly and the law courts. Let part of the revenue, if need be, be devoted to the purchase of small farms or the provision of some sort of occupation for the destitute.[5] Any surplus, he says, left in the treasury should be divided among the

---

[1] Salvioli, *Le Capitalisme dans le monde antique*, brings this aspect out very clearly.
[2] *Pol.* 1258 B; cf. Plato, *Rep.* 555 E; *Laws*, 742 C.
[3] *Rep.* iv, 421 D.   [4] *Pol.* 1297 A.
[5] *Ibid.* 1320 A.

people, a surprising proposal when it is remembered that such primitive ideas of a "share-out" had been rejected as long before as the days of Themistocles. But such at best is a *pis-aller*, and he is by no means happy about it. He is not moved by compassion for the needy, but troubled at the dangers which confront the constitution from the divergent interests of rich and poor.

It must not be overlooked, and it comes as a shock to the modern reader, that the whole of Plato's system is founded on slavery, with an undefined and vaguely outlined system of serfdom.[1] In the chapter on Labour the whole question of slavery in Greece is treated at some length and it is unnecessary to speak of it here. We cannot acquit Plato of inconsistency when he condemns the kidnapping of free individuals for the slave trade,[2] but allows the purchase of slaves, who he knew perfectly well must have been kidnapped; such is one of the inconsistencies into which he must have fallen inevitably, if he is to build his state on a foundation of slavery.

It is true that Aristotle is uneasy about slavery. While he can argue confidently that some are born with the servile disposition, and are by nature fit for nothing better than discipline and direction by their superiors, he begins to falter when he considers the case of those who have been enslaved by the fortunes of war and who may actually be superior to their masters. To that he gives no satisfactory solution and leaves the problem unsolved.[3]

In general it may be asserted that whatever economic theory is to be found among Greek writers was immature. Modern political economy is far in advance of any to be found among the ancients; for one reason at least in that the data at the disposal of the modern economist, the field of observation and the corpus of knowledge, are all immensely greater than for the ancient observer. But however true that may be, it is difficult to acquit the philosopher of a conscious unwillingness to condescend to such vulgar and mundane matters as stood in the way of the development of economic theory. Problems enough in the economic field were to be found; the whole subject of public finance was sufficiently pressing to call for the best brains to

---

[1] *Laws*, 806 E.   [2] *Ibid.* 823 E.   [3] *Pol.* 1254 A ff.

devote themselves to it. But any idea that the state had a right to expect such service was alien to the philosopher. With endless, and it must be said fruitless, speculations as to the ideal state, the philosopher could with propriety occupy his mind; but neither propriety nor dignity would allow him to devote his very considerable powers to the problem of how the state was to preserve its solvency and escape from the hopeless bankruptcy into which it inevitably drifted. Political speculation was so all-absorbing that economic problems were thrust aside and disregarded.[1]

So great a gulf is fixed between our modern thought and that of the ancients that it is utterly impossible to bridge it. To read into the writings of the Greek philosophers a conception of economic theory which is recognisable to-day is a vain endeavour. Their thought was entirely dominated by ethical ideas; there was an absolute separation of the ideas of right and wrong in human conduct from that of economic advantage and disadvantage. It might, at first sight, be thought that in this the Greek philosopher was superior to the modern economist who is, apparently, too prone to overlook the ethical in favour of the practical, and to preach a materialism in which spiritual values have no place. Reflection will reveal that such would be far from the reality. The Greek philosopher's outlook was too constricted for him to appreciate the fact, which the modern economist has grasped, that economic advantage or disadvantage is, in the last analysis, conditioned by ethical values. "Honesty is the best policy" is a trite old saying, but profoundly true; we cannot gain the whole world if we are willing to lose our own soul.

And so the fact remains that while we may learn from the philosophers the great truths and noble ideals of the relation of the human soul to God, they have nothing to tell us regarding those perplexing problems that so occupy our minds to-day. And that for the simple reason that economic considerations did not primarily occupy their attention, and only incidentally are mentioned to be hastily brushed aside when they obtrude themselves upon their main consideration.

[1] This aspect of Greek thought is well brought out in Cornford's *Thucydides Mythistoricus*, p. 32.

To what may this inattention to economic questions be ascribed? Perhaps to a certain degree of intellectual superiority or spiritual arrogance, of which it is difficult to acquit the philosophers. But we cannot leave it at that; especially when we reflect that the Romans were even more neglectful of economic inquiry. The preoccupation of our own age with the problems of Political Economy is of very modern growth; it is indeed a consequence of what we call the Industrial Revolution of the latter part of the eighteenth century. We are rich and have a lot of money; so we think a great deal about our money and our possessions, for where our treasure is there will our heart be also. But the Greek was poor and had not very much money; so he did not think about it a lot, but made the best of what he had, and a very good best it was too. We may reasonably doubt whether he would have been helped a great deal if Aristotle had been the Adam Smith of his day. But in any case he did pretty well with what he had, and we do not seem to be doing any too well with what we have, vastly greater though it may be; so our criticisms of the Greek in his economic life may only too easily be ungenerous, and lacking in an appreciation of an age upon which we are presumptuous enough to sit in judgment.

The Greeks were a very wonderful, and in many ways, at least to our modern eyes, a very strange and baffling people. Again and again, as we read of their doings, we are pulled up short to wonder if we have read aright, and are not being deceived by some deliberate falsehood, some lying accusation brought by a vindictive historian who has chosen to besmirch the fame of a brave and generous race. We read the lofty utterances of their philosophers with reverence; we are thrilled and awed with the majesty of their poets; we gaze at the most perfect art to which man has ever attained, and then, when we read of the dealings of Greek with Greek, we become all too sadly aware that there was a very dark side to "The Glory that was Greece". It ill befits us to sit in judgment; there is too much in our dealings with our fellow-men of which to be ashamed for any delusions of superiority on our part. But the old tag "to know all is to forgive all" is never wholly true, and the history of the Greeks is stained with too much savagery, perfidy and treachery to shut our eyes to; that is, if we are honest, and not

too dazzled with our intellectual, we may also say our senti-
mental, preoccupations with their achievements.[1]

And again, there is another side to Greek life which we would
willingly ignore, and yet obtrudes itself upon our sensibilities.
Plato in the *Phaedrus* has Socrates liken man to a charioteer
who drives a pair of horses, one white and the other black. The
white horse personifies the nobler aspirations, the black the
baser passions. They are an ill-matched pair and the driver
must strive to keep the ill-favoured horse from running away
and bringing both driver and chariot to destruction. It is
but too apparent that the black horse had much to do in that
degradation of morals which was the canker at the heart of all
Greek life. It is not necessary to dilate upon a painful subject;
all that we can do is to put such distressing things aside and
strive to forget them. God would not have destroyed the cities
of the plain if even ten righteous men had been found there,
and there were many more than ten in ancient Greece. Like
the brave Socrates, who would not take the chance of escape
from death offered to him by his friend Crito, we must stop
our ears to all but those sounds of flutes in the air, such as the
Corybants listened to, and let the words of her noblest sons
echo in our ears and listen to nothing else.

Why did the Greeks fail? Or perhaps we should be nearer
the truth if we asked, Did the Greeks fail? Can we really use
such a term as failure of a people whose achievements in art,
literature and philosophy are still a source of respectful admiration to the whole world? We might just as well say that the
Greek architects failed because their buildings are now in ruins.
The Greeks never failed; they were gloriously and eternally
successful.

But for all that, there came upon them political and economic
ruin. Perhaps, after all, Spengler is right when he says that the
Greek, having had his day, passed away according to the
universal and eternal law of the rise and fall of civilisations in
all ages. But that is a facile explanation that leaves the outward
phenomena untouched. Dr Andreades holds, and there is much
to be said for his view, that the Greek system of public finance

[1] Dr Gilbert Murray has some wise and eminently fair remarks on this
subject in Wells's *Outline of History*, I, xxiii, 3.

was so radically unsound that his political institutions were bound inevitably to decay and breed that "stasis", that sickness of the state, which corrupted all public life. Or we may say that the incurable bellicosity of the Greeks tore them to pieces, and be equally right. In the last analysis no people, however gifted, can rise superior to its political and economic institutions, since they are the expression of its practical everyday genius; and, after all, man does live by bread and in the sweat of his face he eats it. We cannot avoid the conclusion that Greek statesmanship was inefficient, which is another way of saying that Greek democracy was unequal to the task of ruling and destroyed itself in its own weakness.

CHAPTER II

AGRICULTURE[1]

"I SHOULD be surprised for my own part", says Socrates to Critobulus, "if any man of liberal feelings has met with any possession more pleasing than a farm, or discovered any pursuit more attractive, or more conducive to the means of life, than agriculture."[2] Socrates, himself no farmer, then goes on to demonstrate how agriculture may be successfully pursued simply in the light of reason, and how the philosopher, if he puts his mind to it, could make a first-class farmer, proving his argument by recounting a conversation he had had with Ischomachus, a country gentleman, whom he had lately met when on a visit to the city. Certainly, according to Ischomachus, farming was a most delightful occupation and by no means difficult to master; you left it all to your bailiffs. True it was necessary to be about early, riding round your estate to see that your servants were busy at their tasks. But as soon as the morning inspection was over, the rest of the day was your own and could be employed by a visit to the city, to mingle with other gentlemen of leisure, and talk to Socrates, and so home to observe the admirable direction of one's household by the wife you have so carefully trained for her duties.

Such was the ideal life, and in all fairness to the Athenians we must agree that such has been the ideal in all ages and countries, and still is to-day. Whether or not Ischomachus made it pay is quite another thing altogether. The gentleman farmer

[1] General references: Jardé, *Les Céréales dans l'Antiquité Grecque*; Gernet, *L'Approvisionnement d'Athènes en Blé*; Guiraud, *La Propriété Foncière en Grèce jusqu'à la Conquête Romaine*; Glotz, *Ancient Greece at Work*, cap. viii; Grundy, *Thucydides and the History of his Age*, caps. 3, 4; E. C. Semple, "Ancient Mediterranean Agriculture", *Agricultural History*, April, July, 1928; Sauciuc-Saveanu, *Cultura Cerealelor Athénielor*; Cavaignac, *Population et Capital dans le Monde Mediterranéen Antique*. Arts. in *P.W.*: "Ackerbau, Landwirthschaft, Bauernstand", Suppl. iv; "Domanen", Suppl. iv; "Sitos", Suppl. vi. K. C. Bailey, *The Elder Pliny's Chapters on Chemical Subjects*. Heichelheim, *Wirtschaftsgeschichte des Altertums*, p. 386 ff.

[2] Xen. *Oecon.* v, 11.

seldom looks upon his occupation in the cold light of a business proposition. Luckily for Ischomachus he has inherited a fortune from a shrewd father who, after the destruction of the Peloponnesian war, made a business of buying up ruined properties, reconditioning them, and selling them at a handsome profit as going concerns.

Not that we must be unfair to him; he evidently does know his business, and as he goes on his rounds his eye is quick to note the progress made by his labourers and direct his bailiffs in the proper methods. Something of the business sense of his father still clings to him; he is by no means the idle son of the rich father. We may, however, shrewdly doubt if he will add to his patrimony, and still more so if his sons will preserve the family fortune.[1] That may not be wholly his, or their, fault. The founder of the fortune was lucky, and clever enough, to grasp an opportunity that allowed him to profit handsomely by the ruination of the former landed proprietors. Such a chance comes but seldom, and we can easily conjure up a mental vision of the family, little by little relinquishing their hold upon the land and slipping back to the status of the petty bourgeoisie from which they rose. It may not be a matter of "three generations from shirt sleeves to shirt sleeves", for landed proprietorship endows a family with a more solid foundation than the fortune won in commerce or speculation. The descent is more gradual and may even be indefinitely postponed if the structure is buttressed with rich marriage alliances.

The picture given of the science of agriculture is charming in its simplicity. Nothing is easier for a man of intelligence than to manage an estate. Socrates is delighted to find out how much he knows about farming already. "I am thinking, Ischomachus," he says, "how admirably you have adapted your whole train of argument to support your proposition; for you laid it down as a fact that the art of agriculture was the most easy to learn of all arts, and I am now convinced, from everything you have said, that such is indisputably the case." Of course we may be sure that Socrates does not really think it is as simple as Ischomachus tries to make out. It is easy enough to instruct the sower how

---

[1] He left 20 talents to his two sons, although at one time he had 70. Lysias, xix, 46. Athen. xii, 537 c suggests the whole fortune was lost.

to spread the seed evenly; but a lot of knowledge is necessary as to what seed to sow. Figs and vines may be planted in the light of reason, and Socrates would probably be intelligent enough not to make fatal mistakes in that operation. But the tending and pruning of the trees demanded long experience and great skill, which Socrates assuredly would not have possessed. And so on through the whole category of farming operations.

But in any case Greek agriculture was a poor business except in a few favoured districts. Barely 22 per cent of the land is to-day cultivable, and we may surmise that the proportion was not very substantially more in ancient times. Mountainous and barren except for the valleys, the land yielded a livelihood hardly and the struggle for existence was unremitting. Under such conditions population must always be severely restricted; which explains the colonising activities which carried off the surplus. We may even go so far as to say that the incessant warfare of the petty states was a means of keeping down numbers; although it is only fair to remember that the battles were never very deadly, at least on land. We might go farther and explain, if not excuse, the sinister practice of infanticide on the same grounds, although not too much must be made of that.

The Land Question

The problem of land ownership was an acute one in all the states of Greece, and was settled, or not settled, in various distressing and violent ways. The old aristocratic system of ownership, so vividly depicted in Homer, had lingered on into the historical age, and with the increase of population, the pressure of a "land-hungry" people, just as in Ireland in the nineteenth century, upon the land had become acute, a pressure which successive waves of emigration had only temporarily alleviated, and by no means permanently cured. In Hesiod we find unmistakable evidence of a vicious state of affairs in Boeotia in the eighth century, where the poor were ground down by the rich, and an even worse situation some time later in Megara where, according to Theognis, an agrarian revolution which rivalled the French Jacquerie in outrage, had swept the landed classes from their estates.

Attica was at least fortunate in a more peaceful solution of the problem, that is to say, as far as the evidence goes. In 594 Solon, the lawgiver, was called to the office of Archon to find a way out of a situation which boded ill for the peace of the state. The best land was in the possession of nobles, *Eupatrids*, the "sons of noble fathers", an hereditary aristocracy, or perhaps more accurately, a landed gentry, farmers on a large scale, or as large as the circumstances of the land and time permitted. On the plains they cultivated barley, and perhaps a little wheat, vines, figs and olives, as the early coins of Attica with their likeness of an oil jar testify. On parts unsuitable for cultivation they raised sheep, goats and some cattle. They were great horsemen, "knights", as the rich always are, and a few well-armed knights could always ride down a rabble of peasants.[1] The little man, the countryman, was in a bad way. Aristotle tells us that the lower classes were in a state of hopeless indebtedness. "Not only was the constitution at this time oligarchical in its every respect, but the poorer classes, men, women and children, were the serfs of the rich. They were known as *Pelatae* and also as *Hectemori*, because they cultivated the lands of the rich at the rent thus indicated."[2] The whole

---

[1] The mail-clad knight was invincible until gunpowder conquered him. Cf. Arist. *Pol.* 1289 B; Polyaenus, v, 47.

[2] *Ath. Pol.* ii, 2. *Pelatae*, "dependents". No really satisfactory translation of this word is possible. Perhaps the Latin *cliens* comes as near as any. But also perhaps *obaerarius* (Varro, *Res Rust.* i, 17, 2) and *obaeratus* (*ibid.* vii, 105). Cf. Pliny, *Nat. Hist.* xxxiv, 1, which seems to refer to some sort of undefined serfdom, may be a Latin counterpart. Cf. Tenney Frank, *Economic Survey*, i, 14. Whatever the *Pelatae* were they lingered on in Naxos, if not in Attica, as we see in Plato's *Euthyphro*, where a *pelates* had been killed by his master. Woodhouse, *Solon the Liberator*, p. 52.

Hectemori, "sixth-partners". This term has been variously explained as labourers who received one-sixth of the produce as wages; or tenants who paid five-sixths of the produce as rent; or tenants who paid one-sixth as rent and retained the rest. All these contain difficulties; the first because they were evidently not merely labourers but tenants; the second because it appears difficult for them to subsist on only one-sixth of the produce of a small farm; the third because a rent of one-sixth seems small. In Cato (*de Agri Cult.* 136), various shares are discussed, varying from one-fifth to one-ninth, according to the goodness of the soil, which would seem to make the second explanation possible. It must be acknowledged, however, that these shares were given, not to tenants working all the year round, but to "politores", or "finishers", who were hired for one particular job only, and were presumably itinerant harvesters. But cf. Adcock in *C.A.H.* iv, 35, and art. "Hektemorioi" by Swoboda in *P.W.* Woodhouse, *Solon*, p. 45 f.

country was in the hands of a few rich men, and if the tenants failed to pay their rent, they were liable to be cast into slavery and their children with them. Loans were secured upon the debtor's person, a custom which prevailed until the time of Solon, who was the deliverer of the oppressed through his *Seisachtheia*, or "casting-off of burdens", by his cancellation of mortgages[1] and prohibition of enslavement for debt. There are several obscurities here which are difficult, if not impossible to resolve. There is no evidence that Solon went any further in cancelling all debts, nor any that did not involve servitude of the debtor. Nor was there any attempt at breaking up the estates of the nobles, although it is fairly obvious that many of them must have lost land which they had acquired, or perhaps were likely to acquire, through foreclosure.[2]

The reforms of Solon did not by any means solve the land problem. The rich landowners retained their powers of government, while the poor were merely protected against their more flagrant abuses. But, as has been found in every age, an aristocracy whose privileges rest in the possession of land alone, cannot indefinitely withstand the growing power of commercialism and the greater diffusion of wealth. As Athens became more and more a centre of trade and manufacture there arose a bourgeois element, not only lacking in sympathy and reverence for the older landed gentry, but even bitterly opposed thereto. *Mutatis mutandis*, the parallel between the sixth century B.C. in Attica and the fifteenth A.D. in England is curiously suggestive. In both cases a dying feudalism, if we may apply that term to ancient Attica, was given its death-blow by the town, which was ever the foe of the owners of the great estates. A "feudal" aristocracy is an anachronism in an age of advancing wealth and culture and, sooner or later as circumstances dictate, must be supplanted by a more democratic, or perhaps more accurately, a more bourgeois form of economy. But a bourgeoisie can only effectively function through a leader, and such was found in Attica in the "tyrant" Peisistratus who seized

[1] Woodhouse, *Solon the Liberator*, discusses the point at considerable length, p. 169f.

[2] Solon was accused, characteristically, of playing into the hands of land speculators (*Ath. Pol.* vi). Cf. also Busolt, *Griech. Staatsk.* iii, 17ff.; art. "Solon" by Aly in *P.W.*

the power in 540, and in furtherance of his own designs forcibly dispossessed such of the *Eupatrids* as had not made terms with him of their estates, and divided them among the agricultural population. By these means he abolished the *Hectemori*, creating in their place a body of small owners and peasant proprietors, whose only financial burden was the payment of the land tax assessed on the value of the annual produce of their farms.[1]

If we accept M. Glotz's calculation with regard to the size of the farms in Solon's division of classes,[2] we have in the largest 75–125 acres under grain, or 20–25 in vineyards, or 50–75 mixed. In the second or knight's class, there were 45–75 acres under grain, or 12–15 in vines, or 30–45 mixed. In the third, or Zeugites class, there were 30–50 acres under grain, or 7–10 in vines, or 25 mixed. The Thetes, or lowest class, had 22 acres under grain, 6 in vines and 15 mixed. These were very small holdings, and the subsequent legislation of Peisistratus increased the tendency to minute subdivision. According to one reckoning at the end of the fourth century the average farm in Attica could not have contained more than ten acres of land capable of cultivation.[3] A working farmer (*autourgos*) could probably live fairly well on such a holding, especially if it were well planted with olives, figs or vines. If it were under grain, wheat or barley, his position was more hazardous, as he had to meet foreign competition in cheap grain. It must be added, however, on the other hand, that the grain farmer had less to fear from invasion than the olive or fruit farmer, to whom the destruction of his grove brought irreparable disaster. Such a holding was certainly about the smallest that could possibly support a family. A farm of 70 acres, such as the wealthy Alcibiades possessed, was considered a large estate,[4] as was also one in Euboea, where the farms were probably larger than in Attica, of 43 acres.[5] Not only was the insatiable land-hunger

---

[1] One-tenth according to Arist. *Ath. Pol.* xvi, 4; one-twentieth according to Thuc. vi, 54. Which is correct is impossible to say, except that one-tenth would have been a fairly heavy tax for Attica at that time and one-twentieth would seem the more likely of the two.

[2] *Ancient Greece at Work*, p. 247.

[3] Busolt, *Griech. Staatsk.* i, 180; cf. also Guiraud, *Propriété Foncière*, pp. 388ff.

[4] Plato, *Alc.* i, 123 C. For other examples cf. Jardé, *Céréales*, p. 121.

[5] Dem. *in Lept.* 115; cf. Plut. *Aristid.* 27.

responsible for the smallness of the holdings, but the legal system of division of land among the children at the death of the owner also contributed thereto, as it does in France to-day. Many devices were used to counteract this, families agreeing to the eldest son farming the whole inheritance and paying rent to the others. Fathers, instead of giving a part of their land as dowry for a daughter, gave a mortgage bond.[1] That this tendency to minute subdivision led, at least after the Peloponnesian war, to capitalistic exploitation was inevitable. Since through its very process holdings became too small to support their owners, it became necessary to unite them into larger ones that at least were economically adequate for efficient production.

Tenant farming never spread far in Greece, which escaped at least the problem of absentee-landlordism. Except for the state and the temples which leased their lands, individuals did not commonly rent their properties, preferring to manage them themselves, sometimes putting in stewards at a wage, or making trusted slaves their bailiffs. Such leases as were made were for ten, twenty or even forty years, sometimes with a clause providing for the planting of olives on waste ground.[2]

Our knowledge with regard to the rents paid by tenants on farms is unfortunately so scanty as to be of little use in determining any scale of average payments. We have a fair number of references to the renting of agricultural land, but from the information contained therein practically no safe conclusions can be drawn. Only in one instance can a rough calculation be made, that of the rent paid by one Hyperides for a farm at Eleusis, from which it would appear that it was reckoned on a basis of about 8 per cent of the annual value of production.[3] It must, however, be remarked that we are here on not too safe ground. It is one thing to say that the rate was reckoned as equivalent to 8 per cent of the annual value and another that such was the actual rent paid. The tenant paid what he could. If we can suppose that from 8 to 10 per cent was the usual rent

---

[1] Cf. Busolt-Swoboda, *Griech. Staatsk.* i, 142, ii, 1578; art. "Bauernstand" by Kornemann in *P.W.* Suppl. iv.

[2] *I.G.* ii^2, 2492 (=*Syll.*^{3} 966); 2493–7; 2498 (=*Syll.*^{3} 965); *I.G.* ii, 1055, lease of Deme Aexoneis; art. "Misthosis" by Schultheis in *P.W.*

[3] Plut. *Vit. X. Orat.* 849 D; Jardé, *Céréales*, p. 96, n. 2, p. 116, n. 2; Heichelheim, *Wirtschaftsgeschichte des Altertums*, p. 315.

exacted, we perceive that the return on capital invested in land was very notably below that invested in commercial ventures.[1] Obviously the risk was far greater in the latter than the former and the rate correspondingly higher. It is, however, somewhat remarkable that the return from investment in agricultural land was so low in view of the "land-hunger" that always was prevalent in Greece.

The Geology of Greece[2]

In order to understand the problems that confronted the Greek farmer it is necessary to set them against their geological framework. In the idiom of the geologist, Greece, and indeed most if not all the Mediterranean area, presents a typically *karst* formation, i.e. that of a succession of limestone mountain belts from which the rain water runs down to the valleys and gorges below. Limestone is soluble in water, and the percolation of the moisture along the joints in the rocks and through subterranean drainage washes down both the soluble and insoluble residues to where they collect in what are known to the geologists as *poljens* or *dolines*, pockets or small plains covered with *terra rossa*, soil composed of the insoluble matter present in limestone. In these *poljens* the water-table is high, i.e. water is near the surface, and so such water-loving plants as maize find suitable conditions for their growth and in modern agriculture form a highly important crop. Unfortunately for the ancient world maize was unknown; had it been known conditions would have been very different and the task of providing foodstuffs considerably simplified. The formation of these infertile red clays, from which all alkalies have been leached and the humus carried away, depends upon the rainfall. Where that is heavy the soil is poor in the lower valleys; where it is light the evil of leaching and loss of humus is much less or non-existent. Lime furnishes supplies of calcium carbonate which are valuable in counteracting the natural tendency to the formation of acid which leads to deflocculation, i.e. the destruction of the flocculent or

---

[1] According to Jardé's calculations Phaenippus got about $9\frac{1}{2}$ per cent on the capital represented in his farm—*Céréales*, pp. 151–6; cf. Heichelheim, *Wirtschaftsgeschichte des Altertums*, p. 389.

[2] Semple, *Ancient Mediterranean Agriculture, passim*.

flaky character of the soil which tends to preserve indefinitely its fertility.

The key to Greek agriculture, therefore, lies in the rain system. Like all the Mediterranean area, Greece is a region of winter rains and summer droughts. The annual precipitation is moderate, but varies markedly from one district to another. Generally speaking, it declines from north to south, from the highlands to the lowlands, and from west to east of the mountains, peninsulas and islands. Thus on the west, it ranges from 60 in. on the Alpine slopes near Trieste to 50 in. at Corfu, 27 at Patros, 21 in Crete and 11 in Cyrenaica on the coast of North Africa. In Cephallenia, on the west coast, the annual precipitation is 40 in., in Attica, in the rain-shadow of the Pindus mountains, it is 16, to rise once more to 26 at Smyrna on the west coast of Asia Minor. It will, therefore, be readily seen that the Greek farmer of antiquity, exactly as his descendant of to-day, had to contend with two problems, that of excessive rainfall in some districts which washed away the humus and formed an infertile red clay deposit, and an aridity that preserved the valuable soil constituents but demanded irrigation. Where that was impossible or difficult, a dry-farming technique with constant manuring and resort to summer fallow was necessary, a wasteful but unavoidable utilisation of the limited amount of land available for cultivation in the valleys and small coastal plains.

That the ancient farmer was able to adapt himself to these conditions and evolve a scientific form of agriculture, argues well for his intelligence and still more for his diligence. The most careful discrimination between those soils that were dry and those retentive of moisture, frequent manuring and selection of seed, incessant working of the soil by the plough, both in fallow and crop-land, were the tasks imposed upon him in his struggle against aridity. Not that nature did not compensate him in many ways. The mild winters with their rains allowed of a long growing season and for work to be carried on at all seasons, except in the torrid heat of summer, when he sat under his own fig tree and watched the fruit of vine, fig and olive ripen to maturity. In spite of difficulties he evolved a system of agriculture that was, and still is, superior to that of other regions where a single crop as, for instance, wheat on the North

American continent, compels the farmer to be absolutely dependent upon its success or failure. A threefold system of agriculture guarded against total failure of one or more of its constituents. Winter grains maturing in the spring and early summer; planted olives, grapes and figs ripening in the autumn and so independent of artificial watering, and thirdly, widely distributed summer crops of vegetables and fodder raised by irrigation, kept him busy but gave him a certain livelihood. It was essentially a capitalistic form of agriculture that demanded money to buy seed and manure and the incessant toil of irrigation. It was also small-scale agriculture, as will be seen later. But it was sure and stable—provided some disaster such as war did not upset the year-long toil of the fields.

In such "garden spots" of Greece population concentrated. Life was toilsome but not too difficult and numbers increased quickly. Intensive tillage supplied the necessaries of life; water-borne commerce provided such luxuries as were available. With the increase of population came an intensification of farming technique. The mountain sides were terraced to extend the area available for cultivation and retaining walls were necessary to prevent erosion. Manuring was absolutely necessary to retain fertility, and where manure was not available in sufficient quantities, summer fallow was unavoidable; all combined to constitute a "precocious form of intensive tillage".[1]

GRAIN-RAISING AREAS

A survey of Ancient Greece shows that by far the most fertile part was Thessaly, whose rich plains were capable of feeding all the rest of Greece,[2] in spite of occasional famines caused, probably, more by the ravages of war than failures of the crops through natural causes.[3] Grain from Thessaly was exported through Pagasae.[4] In Central Greece Phocis was not a favoured farming country owing, as Theophrastus tells us, to the coldness

---

[1] Semple, *Ancient Mediterranean Agriculture*, p. 62.
[2] Xen. *Hell.* vi, 1, 11. Wheat from Thessaly, Theoph. *C.P.* iii, 20, 8. *H.P.* vii, 7, 4, 10, 4; Athen. iii, 127 D.
[3] E.g. *I.G.* ix, 2, 517, lin. 9, 30 (= *Syll.*³ 543). Philip and Flamininus fought for the harvest of Skotoussa (Polyb. xviii, 20).
[4] Xen. *Hell.* v, 4, 56, vi, 1, 11.

of the soil which compelled early sowing to avoid autumn frosts.[1] Locris, a mountainous land, only grew grain, that is barley, on the plains bordering the Gulf of Corinth and the valley of the River Euripus. Aetolia, semi-barbarous, was little cultivated, except in certain parts of the coast-lands, and in the plains about Lake Trichonis.[2] Acarnania raised cattle, horses and other livestock,[3] and if we are to judge from the representations of wheat and barley and a plough upon the coins of several cities of Acarnania, it would appear to have had a flourishing agriculture.[4] Right across Central Greece stretches a chain of valleys, from the high valley of the River Cephisus to the arm of the sea which separates Euboea from the mainland. Irrigated by mountain streams bringing down alluvial soil, these valleys are very fertile, although inclined to be marshy, and there were found pastures suitable for the raising of cattle. Lake Copais was famous for its eels and wild fowl,[5] delicacies much appreciated in the Athenian markets. Boeotia was famous for the richness of its farming lands,[6] which produced, we are told, such wonderful grain that "the athletes of Boeotia consumed scarcely three pints while when they came to Athens they easily managed five".[7]

Attica, more than half covered with mountains, did not raise enough grain to feed its population, but specialised in olives, vines and figs. Xenophon thought so little of Attica as a farming country that he considered its wealth to lie under the ground in its silver mines rather than on it.[8] The Peloponnesus, a jumble of mountains, has, however, many rich valleys. The plain of Sicyon was well tilled; Elis was rich in flocks,[9] but also raised a sufficiency of barley. Phlius in Argolis owes its name, apparently, to the fertility of its soil.[10] Arcadia was excepted from the statement of Thucydides that the Peloponnesus was fertile.[11] The

---

[1] Theoph. *H.P.* viii, 1, 7, viii, 2, 2; Dem. *de Falsa Leg.* 123.
[2] Polyb. v, 8, 4.   [3] Xen. *Hell.* iv, 6, 4–6.
[4] E.g. Argos, Amphilochicum, Anactorium, Leucas.
[5] Aristoph. *Acharn.* 874–80, *Pax*, 1003–5.
[6] Thuc. i, 2; Strabo, ix, 2, 1 (*c.* 400).
[7] Theoph. *H.P.* viii, 4–5.
[8] Xen. *Revenues*, i, 5.   [9] Xen. *Hell.* iii, 2, 26.
[10] Probably fanciful, like so many ancient etymological derivations (Steph. Byz. s.v.).
[11] Thuc. i, 2.

plain of Elis was famous both for arable and pastoral agriculture.[1] Theophrastus tells us that a two-months' wheat had been brought to Achaea from Sicily, but adds that although as a food it was light and sweet, it was neither prolific nor fertile.[2] Evidently Mantinea grew enough wheat not only to feed itself but send supplies to its allies, which caused its destruction by the Lacedaemonians.[3] "Argos of the Wheatfields" was celebrated for its fertility in the time of Homer,[4] and a rich prize for raiders in search of booty.[5] Laconia, about Pylos, in Homer's time was "a wide plain, wherein is much clover and feed for horses and wheat and spelt and widely growing barley",[6] but Theophrastus classes its wheat among the lighter and less prolific sorts.[7] It is difficult to decide whether the Peloponnesus as a whole was able to feed itself without importing wheat; undoubtedly it was necessary at times to bring it from Sicily, but perhaps we may look upon this as a war-time measure.[8] In any case the necessity for such help from other countries cannot have been so pressing as in the case of Attica. But the problems of the grain trade are discussed more fully elsewhere.

The islands of the Aegean are for the most part rocky and infertile, exposed to constant winds, and fit only for the cultivation of olives and vines laboriously propagated in terraces on the hillsides. Only on some of the larger islands is cultivation of grain possible. Euboea was one of the granaries of Attica;[9] in it was cultivated the "two-months" wheat introduced from Sicily of which mention has already been made. The seizure of Decelea by the Spartans in the closing stages of the Peloponnesian war, whereby the route from Oropus was cut, was a disaster of the first magnitude to the Athenians. The large island of Lemnos produced wheat that was highly esteemed in the market of the Piraeus for the heaviness of its grains.[10]

---

[1] Xen. *Hell.* iii, 2, 26; Paus. v, 4, 1.
[2] Theoph. *H.P.* viii, 4, 4.   [3] Xen. *Hell.* v, 2, 2.
[4] *Il.* xv, 372.
[5] Thuc. vi, 7; Plut. *Cleom.* 26; Livy, xxxiv, 26, 8.
[6] *Od.* iv, 602–4. Not rye, as Butcher and Lang translate Zeia.
[7] Theoph. *H.P.* viii, 4, 5.
[8] Thuc. iii, 86. Cf. Gernet, *L'Approvisionnement d'Athènes*, pp. 310–12.
[9] Aristoph. *Vespae*, 715; Theoph. *H.P.* viii, 8, 5; 11, 7. The seizure of Decelea is treated more fully in the chapter on the grain trade.
[10] Theoph. *C.P.* iv, 9, 6. Dem. *in Phil.* i, 32.

Theophrastus calls the soil of Melos "wonderfully productive...
good for wheat and olives and fairly good for vines....They
tell us of an even more wonderful thing in Melos; there they
reap thirty or forty days after sowing; wherefore it is a saying
of the islanders 'one should continue sowing till one sees a
swathe'."[1]

GRAIN PRODUCTION

With regard to the volume of crops raised we are in great uncertainty and only the most elusive references are available.
According to an inscription at Eleusis,[2] the Attic crop in 329
reached a total of 363,400 med. of barley and 39,112 of wheat.
From the same source we learn that the island of Salamis produced 24,525 med. of barley; Imbros 70,200 med. in all, of
which 44,200 were wheat; Scyros 38,400 med. of which 9600
were wheat; Lemnos 305,275 med. of which 56,750 were wheat.[3]
Possibly, but not certainly, this was a year of severe shortage
and we may take the figure as a minimum.[4] Without an adequate
supply of animal manure and no chemical fertilisers,[5] and with
an unscientific system of crop rotation, the production of foodstuffs, as indeed in all ancient and medieval agriculture, was
low.[6] As a consequence competition with foreign grain was
next to impossible for Attic farmers, who took to "truck-

[1] *H.P.* viii, 2, 8.

[2] *I.G.* ii², 1672; cf. Schwahn, *Rhein. Mus.* (1933), p. 254, n. 3.

[3] Cf. Tarn, *C.A.H.* ii, 448; Jardé, *Céréales*, pp. 36 f., 95 f.; Gomme, *Population*, p. 28; art. "Sitos" in *P.W.* supt. ii, p. 846.

[4] The problem as to whether the years of famine, during which Cleomenes engineered his famous "corner", were occasioned by crop shortage or dis-location of the grain trade is discussed elsewhere. Cf. p. 275.

[5] Cf. Woodhouse, *Solon*, p. 163.

[6] Kinkel (*Sozialök. Grundl. d. Staats u. Wirthschaftsleben von Aristoteles*, p. 76) concludes, on very uncertain grounds, that the ratio of production to seed sown was 7 : 1, as compared with from 20 to 30 : 1 in Egypt and Pontus. Schwahn (*Rhein. Mus.* (1933), p. 254) reckons that Attic agriculture was barely one-third as fruitful as modern. An acre sowed with barley would produce 11 bushels, while a fair crop to-day will average at least 36 or more. Jardé (*Céréales*, cap. iii) while not arriving at any definite conclusion is certain the return was very small as compared with modern farming (cf. *Rev. Et. Anc.* xi (1910), pp. 373–6). It may be remarked, however, that Schwahn is speaking of the best tillage land of England or Germany, but not of Mediterranean lands in general where 12 bushels per acre is an average yield. Cicero (II *Verr.* iii, 116) speaks of 20–24 bushels of wheat to the acre in Sicily. Columella (iii, 3–4), writing not very long after, says that 8 bushels was an average crop in Italy.

farming", or market gardening, where, however, they met the competition of Boeotia which seems to have largely supplied the Athenian market with vegetables, game and eels.[1] In the end, therefore, cultivation of the fig, olive and vine became practically the only paying form of agriculture in Attica.

With regard to the various forms of grain raised, barley was, as we have already seen, by far the commonest, about ten to twelve times more barley being raised than wheat. This was to be expected in the case of a country of poor soil and undeveloped agricultural science. M. Jardé is probably correct when he says that rye was unknown, although the whole point is obscure. We are not even sure whether Pliny's *Secale* was rye;[2] it may have been black spelt, and we are on even more doubtful ground in identifying *Briza* with rye.[3] Rye is essentially a North European plant, and the amount grown in Greece to-day is inconsiderable. Oats were regarded as noxious weeds, or rather the wild plant was. It is very uncertain whether cultivated oats were known; the word *Bromos* provides some puzzles which seem insoluble.[4] Millet was well known and apparently widely cultivated.[5] Our difficulties in identifying the various kinds of wheat in cultivation are very great owing to the unfortunate practice of ancient writers in using the word *Sitos* as a generic term to denote almost any food grain.[6] It may be remarked that the use of the English word "corn" is also fruitful of uncertainties to-day. In earlier times three kinds of "wheat" were distinguishable, *Zeia*, *Olyra* and *Tiphe*,[7] which may tenta-

[1] Many references: e.g. Aristoph. *Acharn.* 729, 860, 874; *Pax*, 1003. Cf. also E. Meyer, *Gesch. d. Alt.* iii, 546.

[2] xviii, 40 (141). The rye of the Bible is certainly spelt. Exod. ix. 32; Isaiah xxviii. 25; Ezek. iv. 9.

[3] Athen. x, 447 C. Galen, *de Alim. Fac.* i, 13. Cf. Sauciuc-Saveanu, *Cultura*, p. 38. Art. "Getreide" by Orth in *P.W.*

[4] Theoph. *C.P.* iv, 4, 5, iv, 5, 2, iv, 6, 3; *H.P.* viii, 9, 2. Cf. Vergil, *Georg.* i, 77; Col. ii, 10, 32; Pliny, *H.N.* xviii, 149. A harmful weed in Vergil, but Columella regards them as a useful forage crop.

[5] Many references: e.g. Theoph. *H.P.* viii, *passim*. Kaeppel, *Off the Beaten Track in the Classics*, p. 125, commenting on the account given by Strabo (iv, 5, 5, c. 201) of Pytheas finding the inhabitants of Thule living on millet, remarks that he must have meant oats, which were unknown to him, and that Thule was beyond the northern limit of cultivation of millet. The point is well taken but we cannot be certain that oats were unknown to him.

[6] Art. "Sitos" by Heichelheim in *P.W.* Suppl. vi.

[7] Theoph. *H.P.* viii, 1, 3. Jardé discusses the varieties at length in his first chapter.

tively be identified as spelt, emmer and einkorn, or one-grained wheat, i.e. *triticum sativum*, *dicoccum* and *monococcum*.[1] Except for the first which certainly was, and for the matter of that, still is cultivated to a certain extent, such "hulled" varieties gave way to the bread wheat, or *sitos*, such as we know to-day.[2] Except for the elementary necessity of only planting the best seeds and the introduction of foreign wheats, the Greeks displayed, so far as we know, no knowledge of the art of improving the strains by cross-fertilisation. A passage in Theophrastus[3] speaks of the alleged degeneration of wheat and barley into darnel,[4] a misapprehension which persists to the present day. It is fair to Theophrastus, however, to say that he is very doubtful on the point.

An interesting passage[5] speaks of the practice of turning animals into the sprouting crops to prevent the plants running wildly to leaf, and says that this was done in the wheat fields of Thessaly and particularly in Babylon, where it was done twice in the growing season. Such is well known in modern times as "sheeping off", i.e. the practice of grazing forward or "winter proud" young wheat to prevent too rank growth.[6] Theophrastus continues by saying that in Babylon if the ground is ill-cultivated it produces only fiftyfold, but if carefully a hundredfold. Such figures are grossly exaggerated; the best modern conditions being unable to reproduce them.[7]

The Study of Soils

The Greek farmer was keenly alive to the necessity of studying his soil. Contrasted kinds should be mixed, heavy with light, red with white. "For the mixture not only remedies defects, but adds strength. To mix another soil with what is exhausted and unsuited to grains will make it bear again as if renewed."[8] Seed

---

[1] Cf. Sauciuc-Saveanu, *Cultura*, p. 43.
[2] Cf. art. "Ackerbau" by Olck in *P.W.*
[3] *H.P.* viii, 7, 1; cf. ii, 4, 1; *C.P.* iv, 4, 5, v, 3, 6, v, 15, 5.
[4] Sometimes known as "chess" in North America. The "tares" of the Bible (Matt. xiii. 25).
[5] *H.P.* viii, 7, 4.
[6] Cf. Jardé, *Céréales*, p. 21, n. 6; J. Sinclair, *Code of Agriculture* (5th ed. London 1832), p. 347.
[7] It is curious to compare this statement with the parable of the sower.
[8] Theoph. *C.P.* iii, 20, 3.

should be sowed thickly or scantily according to the nature of
the soil; a fat soil will take more seed than a thin.[1] Deep working
was necessary and was well understood in Homeric times.[2] The
peasants in Thessaly had a kind of spade, called *Mischos*, which
enabled them to turn over the top soil and get to the fruitful
undersoil.[3] On the island of Aegina, which is covered with a
thin surface stratum of freshwater limestone over fertile marl,
the inhabitants burrowed down to the marl to mix it with the
soil above. This habit of burrowing earned for the Aeginetans
the nickname of Ants or Myrmidons, at least according to
Strabo's account,[4] and the same practice was followed in
Megara.[5]

THE USE OF FERTILISERS

The necessity of using fertiliser was well understood where the
areas under cultivation were severely restricted, and the danger of
over-cropping an ever-present one. The first mention of the use
of manure has been, possibly fancifully, identified with the
cleaning of the Augean stables by Hercules. However that may
be, there are several allusions to manure heaps in Homer.[6]
The collection of manure was of the utmost importance,[7] and
Theophrastus rates the various sorts in their order of strength
and utility.[8] He very strongly recommends the compost heap
of straw, leaves and weeds bedded under farm animals and well
trodden down to add to the bulk and conserve the moisture.[9]
In Palestine salt was added—a sound practice.[10] There is reason
to suppose that city sewage was used for fertilising the surround-
ing land. The main cloaca in Athens ran across the city and
through the Dipylon to a reservoir outside, from which brick-
lined canals carried the contents to the plain of the Cephisus.
One canal seems to show a device for regulating the flow and
suggests that the sewage was sold to farmers for spreading on

---

[1] Theoph. *H.P.* viii, 6, 2; Xen. *Oecon.* xvii, 8–11.
[2] *Od.* ix, 136; cf. Col. ii, 2, 3.   [3] Theoph. *C.P.* iii, 20, 8.
[4] Strabo, viii, 16, 6 (c. 375).
[5] Theoph. *C.P.* iii, 20, 4; cf. Col. ii, 16; Pliny, *H.N.* xvii, 4, 6–8.
[6] E.g. *Od.* xvii, 297, xxiv, 225.
[7] Xen. *Oecon.* xx, 10; cf. Woodhouse, *Solon*, p. 163.
[8] *H.P.* ii, 7, 4, vii, 5, 1; *C.P.* iii, 9, 2.
[9] *Ibid.*; cf. Isaiah xxv. 10; Xen. *Oecon.* xviii, 2.
[10] Luke xiv. 35.

their fields.[1] This is, however, conjectural. Nitre was used[2] and salt was recommended for palm trees,[3] but neither of these provided humus for the soil. Xenophon speaks of ploughing under green wheat,[4] and Theophrastus says that farmers in Thessaly and Macedonia ploughed under beans.[5] Legumes with the exception of chickpeas gave the soil new strength, but the best of all were lupines.[6] It is curious to note that Theophrastus does not mention pigeon guano, although we know that it was an object of revenue to the temple of Delos.[7] Both Varro and Columella give figures for the amount of manure which should be used per acre; but Greek writers say nothing of this, the only reference being in the Amorgos lease, where the figures do not convey very much.[8] A curious, but not very important point, is whether or not pasturing sheep on green fallow was practised in the pre-hellenistic period. Several leases seem to forbid the practice.[9] Certainly it was known in the time of Theocritus,[10] and there seems no particular reason why the custom should not have been general in quite early times.[11]

Fallow was constantly worked to keep down weeds and make the soil moister and lighter.[12] Hesiod `called fallow land a guardian against death and ruin.[13] In early times the fallow was ploughed thrice.[14] Theophrastus recommends a fourth ploughing in winter for light, dry soils,[15] as was done in Elis.[16] In Palestine also a fourth, or midwinter working, was necessary; the sluggard who will not do so by reason of the cold shall beg in harvest and have nothing.[17] Ploughing was the essence of good farming.[18] Lacking any device of the nature of a

---

[1] Art. "Cloaca" in *P.W.*; Ziller, *Athen. Mitt.* ii (1877), p. 17, and Dörpfeld, *ibid.* xiii (1888), p. 211. Possibly the Dung Gate of Jerusalem served the same purpose (Nehem. iii. 13; xii. 31).
[2] Theoph. *C.P.* iii, 7, 8; cf. Luke xiv. 35.
[3] *C.P.* ii, 5, 3, iii, 7, 1–4.
[4] *Oecon.* xvii, 10.   [5] *H.P.* viii, 9, 1.
[6] *C.P.* iv, 7, 3, iv, 8, 1–3; *H.P.* viii, 11, 8.
[7] *I.G.* xi, 2, 161 A, 43, 162 A, 39, 287 A, 20; cf. Cato, *de Agri Cult.* 36.
[8] *I.G.* xii, 7, 62 = *Syll.*³ 963.
[9] *I.G.* xii, 7, 62, xiv, 645.   [10] *Idyll.* xxxv, 99.
[11] Cf. Brendel, *Die Schafzucht*, p. 102.
[12] *C.P.* iii, 10, 1; Xen. *Oecon.* xvi, 11–15.
[13] *W.D.* 464; Pindar, *Od. Nem.* vi, 10–12.
[14] Hes. *Theog.* 971; cf. *Il.* xviii, 542; *Od.* v, 127, xiii, 32.
[15] *C.P.* iii, 20, 2, 6–7.   [16] Theocr. *Idyll.* xxv.
[17] Prov. xx. 4.   [18] *C.P.* iii, 10, 6.

harrow, the clods had to be broken up with a hoe,[1] or a heavy mallet or "beetle".

SOWING

Generally winter wheat was grown in Greece. "Sow in the Autumn", says Hesiod, "when the yearly cry of the crane from the cloud is the sign of the approaching rains of winter. Then all hands must plough and sow early and late, on wet days and on dry, that the harvest may come with the white blossoms of spring."[2] Great care had to be taken in planting wheat which required immediate showers for germination, and therefore was sown after barley at successive intervals during the autumn to insure at least some yield.[3] Never sow on a dry soil.[4] Crops mature quickly in the heat of summer and must be gathered "when the snail seeks the shade of the leaf to escape the heat of the sun".[5]

Spring wheat, or three months' wheat, was less common, but was grown in Thrace, Southern Euboea and Boeotia and yielded a hard heavy grain. On the Scythian plains of South Russia both winter and spring wheats were raised, but the soft winter wheat was inferior to the hard spring variety.[6] The famous heavy Boeotian variety was spring-sown, as it is to-day, on the shores of Lake Copais when the winter flood waters had receded, the rich lacustrine soil and high water table giving it a superior quality.[7] Millet or "panic grass", i.e. Italian millet, was sown where summer showers or irrigation afforded adequate moisture.[8]

Legumes were usually planted in the autumn, but peas and lentils, as not being able to stand winter cold, were sown in spring.[9] Sesame, with millet and "panic", were a summer crop, and did well with irrigation.[10] Great care must be taken in the selection of seed.[11] A good plant will not grow from bad

---

[1] Cf. Hosea x. 11; Isaiah xxviii. 24.

[2] *W.D.* 248; cf. Verg. *Georg.* i, 213.

[3] Xen. *Oecon.* xvii, 4–6; Theoph. *H.P.* viii, 1; *C.P.* iv, 4, 7. "The former and the latter rain", i.e. autumn and spring (cf. Amos iv. 7).

[4] Xen. *Oecon.* xvii, 2.   [5] Hes. *W.D.* 260.

[6] Theoph. *H.P.* viii, 4, 5–6.

[7] *C.P.* iv, 9, 5. Lake Copais has been drained.

[8] *H.P.* viii, 3, 3; *C.P.* ii, 7.   [9] *H.P.* vi, 5, viii, 1, 3.

[10] *H.P.* viii, 7, 3.   [11] Cf. Lev. xix. 19; Deut. xxii. 9.

seed;[1] seeds must be gathered from plants in their prime;[2] seedlings must be transplanted.[3] Wheat exhausts the land more than any other crop, and next to it barley, wherefore the former requires good soil, while barley will bear even on somewhat crumbling soils.[4] Cereals are prone to rust,[5] more particularly barley, of which the variety known as "Achillean" is highly susceptible to that disease. Lands exposed to the wind and elevated are not so liable to rust as low-lying lands.[6] High winds are destructive when the grain is in flower, or immediately after the flower has fallen.[7] Seed that has been kept for a year is best for germination; that kept for more than three years is infertile. At Petra in Cappadocia it is said that seed remains fertile for forty years, and may be used for food for as long as seventy years.

The principle of irrigation was well understood and practised from an early date, as two passages in Homer testify.[8] Plato gives an eloquent description of its benefits, along with drainage and flood control.[9] It must, however, be said that probably Greek irrigation was on a very small scale, the watering of gardens and orchards.

The whole question of the Greek plough is far from simple. It seems to have had an iron share (although this is not certain), but no coulter or spreader; thus it was not particularly effective and allowed many of the weeds to survive.[10]

Reaping was done with the sickle. If the straw was short it was cut close to the ground, if long about halfway up.[11] What straw was left was either burned or ploughed under. Threshing was done by horses, mules or oxen treading out the grain on a circular floor paved with cobble stones.[12] The grain was spread out a little at a time and evenly before the animals as they circulated. It may be remarked here parenthetically that there is

---

[1] Arist. *de Plant.* 1, 6, ii, 6.
[2] Theoph. *H.P.* vii, 3, 3, 4.   [3] *H.P.* vii, 4, 3, 5, 3.
[4] *H.P.* viii, 9, 1.   [5] Cf. Pliny, *H.N.* xviii, 44 (154).
[6] Cf. *C.P.* iii, 22, 2.   [7] *C.P.* iv, 13, 4; Pliny, *H.N.* xviii, 44 (151).
[8] *Il.* xxi, 257; *Od.* vii, 129. The first is often referred to as the only passage describing irrigation but that on the garden of Alcinous is unmistakable.
[9] *Laws*, vi, 761, viii, 844 A.
[10] Theoph. *C.P.* iii, 20, 8. Homeric plough, *Od.* xiii, 31; Hes. *W.D.* 427. Cf. Jardé, *Céréales*, p. 19 f.; also P. Leser, "Entstehung u. Verbreitung des Pfluges", *Anthropos Bibl.* iii (1931), p. 211; A. S. F. Gow, "The ancient plough", *J.H.S.* xxxiv (1914), p. 249. Iron share, *Il.* xxiii, 834-5.
[11] Xen. *Oecon.* xviii, 1.   [12] *Ibid.* xviii, 3 f.

no extant reference to either Greeks or Romans using the flail. St Jerome uses the word *flagellum*, but evidently this refers to a stick used in beating out small grains such as millet.[1] The heavy hinged flail was a medieval discovery. A well-known picture on a vase from Hagia Triada in Crete depicting harvesters returning from work with wands over their shoulders is no evidence of the use of the flail; such wands were almost certainly used for knocking down olives from the trees. After tossing and winnowing done with the cradle, *liknon*, which, if the story in Homer is to be followed, was shaped like an oar,[2] the grain and chaff were heaped in a broad basket and then thrown against the wind which blew away the chaff.[3] In Palestine, if not in Greece, the refuse was given to the poor who extracted whatever they could out of it. One accusation against the rich was that they sold and did not give the refuse away.[4]

The question of how far Greek farmers practised a regular system of crop rotation has been a matter of doubt, at least one authority denying it altogether.[5] A passage in the *Oeconomicus* of Xenophon does not shed very much light on the problem, since it obviously refers merely to ploughing under of weeds, and gives no indication of any settled rotation.[6] A newly found inscription[7] dating from the years 339–338, seems, however, to indicate clearly a three-year rotation. Undoubtedly in Italy in the time of Pliny, a regular three-year rotation of millet, turnip or radish, barley or wheat was well established.[8] The whole problem with regard to Greece must be left in some uncertainty.

The essential feature of Mediterranean agriculture is what may be called the "gardener cultivator", who can use the constantly renewed moisture of the upper layers of soil in winter for short-lived herbaceous plants that require little heat, and the deeper lying sub-soil water in summer for deep rooting shrubby plants which require much heat.[9] It is, therefore, characteristic of this form of agricultural economy that Theo-

---

[1] *Comment. in Iesaiam Proph.* 380, referring to Isaiah xxviii. 27.
[2] *Od.* xi, 128.
[3] Xen. *Oecon.* xviii, 6; cf. Varro, i, 50–2.
[4] Amos viii. 6.   [5] Jardé, *Céréales*, p. 86.
[6] *Oecon.* xvi, 10.   [7] *I.G.* ii², 2493.
[8] *H.N.* xviii, 23 (191); cf. *ibid.* xviii, 11 (111).
[9] Newbigin, *Mediterranean Lands*, p. 58.

phrastus should give a long list of various vegetables such as asparagus, beans, beets, cabbage, celery, chickpeas, cucumbers, gourds, leeks, lettuce, lentils, onions, radishes and turnips. He also mentions many of the well-known fruits such as apples, almonds, dates, figs, pears, plums, pomegranates and quinces. Of relishes and herbs he speaks of garlic, horseradish, mint, parsley, rue, sage, savory and shallot.[1] Market gardening, especially in Boeotia which extensively supplied the Athenian demand, was an important business to which a great many references may be found.

FLAX

Flax, which exhausted the ground and required a rich, moist soil, was not much grown, since both climate and soil in Greece were generally too dry.[2] It had always been raised in Egypt, and in Palestine, where its cultivation was limited by law to once in seven years.[3] Such places in Greece as were favourable to flax were the plain of Elis, but Pausanias says that, although the Greek variety was as fine as that of Judea, it was not of so yellow a colour.[4] It was also grown in the rich alluvial plain of the River Phasis in Colchis where, according to Herodotus, it had been introduced by the Egyptians.[5] Greek authors evidently look upon flax as a fairly late importation and there are certainly no references in Homer to its cultivation. But we are left with the problem as to where the yarn came from whose weaving we hear of on several occasions. It is hard to suppose that the Phoenicians imported flax yarn when they could more advantageously have brought the finished cloth. We are, therefore, constrained to suppose that its cultivation was far older and more widespread than would appear. Flax fibres were woven into linen and the seeds used as food.[6] Hemp was apparently not known in Greece until late, although Herodotus mentions it as being cultivated by the Scythians.[7] Hiero II of

---

[1] Athenaeus supplies many more in his third book; cf. Arist. *Probl.* xx, 923 A, for problems in growing vegetables.
[2] Theoph. *C.P.* iv, 5, 4; cf. Col. ii, 10, 17.
[3] Joshua ii. 6; Hosea ii. 9.
[4] Paus. v, 5, 2, vi, 26, 6, vii, 21, 14.
[5] Her. ii, 105; Strabo, xi, 2, 17 (c. 498).
[6] Thuc. iv, 26, 8.   [7] Her. iv, 74.

Syracuse used it for making ships' cables, and seems to have bought it from the region of the River Rhone and Iberia.[1] Ropes of white flax were used by the Phoenicians and of papyrus by the Egyptians in making the bridges across the Hellespont for Xerxes.[2]

ANIMAL HUSBANDRY[3]

The nomad tribes, the "Dorians", who came from the grassy steppes with their herds of cattle and horses found very different conditions in Greece, and stock raising had perforce to give place to tillage. Pasturage on the lowlands was impossible in summer when the herbage shrivelled under the torrid sun. Shallow-rooted herbage would only grow on the swampy coastal plains and deltaic flats of the rivers and higher up where mountain-locked lake basins and a high water-table afforded wet meadows or marsh pastures. The quality of these mountain pastures declined from north to south and from west to east. On the rainy western flanks of the mountains they were numerous and fertile, but in the rain shadow of the eastern sides they were poor and scattered, while summer drought increased in intensity south of the fortieth parallel. On the mountain sides a thorny vegetation, with clumps of deciduous trees growing in pockets where humus and moisture collect, creeps up to 3000 feet. These lower slopes give pasturage fit only for sheep, goats or swine, except in spring and in the warm rainy autumn. But there are no grazing grounds for cattle or horses, which cannot subsist on the meagre fare suitable for sheep and goats, and require the succulent herbage of rain-fed pastures. As is done to-day, so in ancient Greece the herds were kept in the valleys and plains during the winter, and with the approach of summer were driven to the uplands, where it was cool and green pastures could be found in the upper valleys fed by the snows. The shepherd of Sophocles "loved the upland pastures", and when he lived near Cithaeron "for full three half-years", from spring to autumn, he fraternised

[1] Athen, v, 206 F. Cf. Judges xvi. 9; Isaiah i. 31, where the word translated "tow" means rather lint or the discards of flax.

[2] Her. vii, 34.

[3] E. C. Semple, "Influence of geographic conditions upon ancient Mediterranean stock-raising", *Ann. Ass. Amer. Geog.* xii (1922), p. 3.

with other shepherds, to return to the lowlands as winter approached.[1] It is easy to realise how serious a problem was the obtaining of manure when the animals were shifted every six months. Farm animals were kept down to the actual needs of the farm and were stall-fed throughout the year

Cattle

In animal husbandry the Greeks had considerable success, although they never attained to such results as modern scientific breeding has achieved. Aristotle in his *Natural History* shows a sound knowledge of the elementary rules of breeding from the best stock. We find two predominant strains of cattle, the long- and short-horned.[2] Of the former the most notable examples are found in the Minoan and Mycenaean remains, where they are depicted in the exciting scenes of bull-fighting; possibly they were only kept for that sport. Both long- and short-horns apparently came from Egypt,[3] the short-horns possibly coming into that country with the Hyksos, whence the breed spread all over the Mediterranean as far west as Sicily, Sardinia and Corsica. In Homer, as befitting a record of a people which had lately turned from a nomadic to a settled form of economy, references to cattle are very numerous. As remarked elsewhere, the earliest form of "money" was apparently the ox, and the nobles are great cattle breeders who count their riches in their herds. As population increased in the restricted areas of Greece the keeping of large herds became impossible, and in historical times, so far as we can tell, cattle became more or less the sacred animals of the temples, bred for sacrifice.[4]

The most famous country for cattle was Epirus, which had the finest pastures.[5] Aristotle's account of the Epirote cattle is prodigious;[6] the cows were so big that the milker had to stand

---

[1] *Oed. Rex*, 1103, 1127f.; cf. Woodhouse, *Solon*, p. 54.

[2] K. Zeissig, *Die Rinderzucht im alten Griechenland*.

[3] Importation of long-horns from Africa, Polyb. iv, 38, 4; from Mygdonia north of Chalcidice in Macedonia, Her. vii, 126.

[4] There was certainly a great scarcity of draught oxen in Attica. In 330–329 Eudemos of Plataea had to send his own teams to Athens as he could not get enough animals on the spot. *I.G.* ii², 351.

[5] Arrian, ii. Cf. Hes. *Cat. of Women*, 97: "There is a land Ellopia with much glebe and rich meadows and rich in flocks and shambling kine. There dwell men who have many sheep and many oxen."

[6] Arist. *H.A.* iii, 16, 7.

up; if he sat he could not reach up to the udder. Such cows gave, he said, 1½ amphorae of milk a day, i.e. about 8½ gallons. It is to be remarked that the world's champion milker, one of the Holstein-Friesian breed, to-day has given as much as an average of 10 gallons a day over a period of one year. We may discount the enormous size of the animals, but we can see that even if the yield of milk was as Aristotle affirms, which we may doubt, the milk-producing qualities of the modern animals are in excess of those of antiquity. So famous was the breed of Epirote cattle that prize bulls were imported into Italy to improve the Italian strains.[1] Thessaly as providing fine pastures also was famous for its cattle.[2] In the centre of Greece Acarnania and Phocaea raised cattle, the plains of the former affording good pasturage.[3] Aetolia apparently was only good for goats, but Boeotia and Euboea[4] were cattle raisers, as the names compounded with *bous* suggest. The coins of Eretria show longhorns, those of Euboea short-horns, and Aelian informs us that in the latter the colour of the animals was silver grey.[5] Little cattle raising was practised in Attica owing to lack of pasture, and all animals were imported from Euboea, Boeotia, the Peloponnese, the coasts of Asia Minor and from even as far east as the Black Sea. The breed in the Peloponnese was generally a small active mountain animal and could have been of little value. The pastures of Arcadia were good according to Ovid,[6] as were those of Elis[7] and Messenia.[8] In Laconia we only know of sheep and goats, although a passage in Pausanias[9] must be mentioned in which he says that the Spartan Euaephnus rented his pastures to herdsmen, receiving in return part of the animals. North of Laconia lay Argos, the "thirsty land", to which the south winds blowing over the Arcadian and Laconian mountains brought insufficient moisture for pasture land but enough for wheat and barley raising. But the alluvial plain of the Argolis raised, at least in Mycenaean times if not later,

---

[1] Varro, ii, 5, 10.
[2] Strabo, ix, 5 (c. 429), *passim*.   [3] Xen. *Hell.* iv, 6, 4.
[4] Cattle in Euboea. Dio Chrys. vii, 11.
[5] *de Nat. An.* xii, 36. For types of Eretrian coins, cf. Barclay Head, *Hist. Numm.* 2, s.v. Eretria.
[6] *Fast.* ii, 273.   [7] Hom. *Od.* iv, 634.
[8] Strabo, viii, 5, 6 (c. 366).   [9] iv, 4, 5.

both long- and short-horns as the excavations of Schliemann testify.

The service of the temples required only the most perfect animals for sacrifice,[1] and the duty of selecting suitable victims in Attica was delegated to twelve *Hieropoei*, one from each tribe, who also superintended the distribution of the meat. Very high prices were given for the best animals;[2] we know that at the festival of Apollo at Delos 109 bullocks cost 8419 drs. A donation of such animals was a kingly gift; Seleucus I sent twelve bullocks to the shrine of Apollo Didymaios.[3] In conclusion it may be added that draught oxen were stalled and fed on dry fodder.

It is curious to note that butter made of cow's milk played no part in the Greek dietary, for the two reasons that, owing to the scarcity of animals, cow's milk was hard to come by, and that butter is difficult to keep fresh in a warm country; its place is taken by the ever-useful olive oil. It may be remarked that the word *Bouturon* found in the Periplus of the Red Sea clearly refers to the clarified butter called Ghi so extensively used to-day in India. Generally when used at all it was as a salve or ointment.[4] It is also pertinent to remember that in the Old Testament the word translated "butter" indicates rather curdled milk, and the passage in Proverbs rendered "churning" and "butter" in the English version means rather the pressing of curds to make cheese.[5] It is tantalising to be told by Varro[6] that Greek writers on agriculture had much to say on the making of cheese, for none of their treatises have survived. Cheese in Greece was made mostly from the milk of sheep and goats, which was considered superior to that of cows for the purpose.

[1] Beef was seldom eaten as being too expensive, except when the meat was distributed after the sacrifices. Athenaeus (ix, 377 A) speaks of roasting an ox at a wedding feast in a rich household; cf. also vii, 282 B. The Man of Petty Pride in the *Characters* of Theophrastus (xxi, 7) when he has sacrificed an ox nails the scalp above his door so that everyone may see.

[2] But Varro says that buyers for sacrificial purposes did not demand a guarantee of soundness (ii, 5, 11).

[3] Dittenberger, *Orient. Graec. Inscr. Sel.* no. 215, line 62; Michel, *Recueil*, 577 A.

[4] Cf. Athen. x, 447 D; also vi, 225 D, iv, 131 B; Varro, ii, xi.

[5] Prov. xxx. 33.

[6] *Res Rust.* ii, 1, 28. Athenaeus (xiv, 658 A–C) gives a list of various sorts of cheese. For further on cheese-making cf. Galen, i, 15, 58.

We have a picture of the Cyclops milking his ewes and goats; half the milk he curdled to make cheese and put aside in wicker baskets and half he kept for drinking at supper.[1] To curdle the milk rennet was used,[2] or earlier the juice of the wild fig.[3]

Horses[4]

Always a luxury of the rich their possession betokened a land-owning class of "knights", e.g. the Hippobotae of Euboea and the Hippeis of Attica. We hear that the noble Alcmaeonid family were great horse breeders and raised blood stock to win races at Olympia.[5] It is important to note that cavalry were always a negligible force in Greek armies owing to the mountainous nature of the land, and it is also interesting to realise that those armies that possessed sufficient cavalry always tried to manœuvre their opponents onto a plain where it could be used. For instance the Persians chose to fight at Plataea,[6] and the broad plain of Boeotia[7] was the scene of such decisive battles as Chaeronea and Coronea, where cavalry was effectively used. Regions where fine horses could be raised were confined to those of good pastures characterised by marsh meadows with heavy winter rainfall and summer showers to prevent scorching of the grasses in the heat. Other regions were found where lacustrine basins surrounded by high mountains ensured permanently moist soils. Such were Thrace, Thessaly, Messenia, Arcadia, Elis, Argos and Epirus.

By far the most famous of all horse-raising countries was Thessaly, where the lacustrine plains are alternately flooded and drained by the River Peneus. These rich pastures had provided horses for cavalry since the days of Peisistratus.[8] In the *Electra* of Sophocles, Orestes competes in the Pythian games with a team of Thessalian horses. It is interesting to observe

---

[1] *Od.* ix, 244; cf. Theocr. xi, 34; xxv, 101. It is curious to note that there are few references in Greek, or indeed in any ancient literature, to the drinking of milk, except by infants. Plutarch, *de Tuenda San. Praec.* 131 D, regards it as an unhealthy article of food. Cf. Pindar, *ap.* Athen. xi, 476, 477 A; also remarkable description given by Herodotus (iv, 2) of the Scythian method of milking mares.

[2] Arist. *H.A.* iii, 20 (xvi, 6); *G.A.* i, 20 (729 A); Varro, ii, xi, 4–5.

[3] *Il.* v, 902.

[4] Hörnschemeyer, *Die Pferdezucht im klassischen Altertum.*

[5] Her. vi, 125. [6] Her. vi, 102.

[7] Her. ix, 13. [8] Her. v, 63; Thuc. i, 107, ii, 22.

the places from which the contestants came. There was one Achaean team, one from Sparta, two from Libya, one from Magnesia, another Aenian, by which is meant Thessaly. Orestes was fifth in the race, the ninth was an Athenian, the tenth a Boeotian.[1] Bucephalus, the famous charger of Alexander, came from a stud farm at Pharsalus on the banks of the River Apidanus in Thessaly.[2] Aristotle attributes the strong oligarchy in Thessaly to the command of cavalry by the knights who could subdue the rabble.[3] Homer speaks of the horses of "deep-soiled" Phthia in Thessaly.[4] It is to be noted, however, that while Xerxes considered Thessalian horses the best in Greece they were, in his opinion, inferior to the breeds of his own land, in which he was undoubtedly correct.[5]

The only region in the southern part of Greece outside of the Peloponnesus that was capable of horse raising on even a moderate scale was Boeotia with its moist lacustrine plain, "grassy Haliartus" in the reed-grown basin of lake Copais.[6] Boeotia was "a land of goodly steeds".[7] From Thucydides we learn[8] that Boeotia, Phocis, and Locris provided cavalry to the Spartans. Locris must have depended on the pastures of the rich coastal plain of Opous bordering on the sound of Euboea. Attica was no place for either horses or cattle, and only when Athens acquired the lower Asopus plain from Boeotia and the rich island of Euboea[9] could horses be raised. The Peloponnesus gave little scope for cavalry movements, and whatever pastures there were were of small extent. Argos, which stood on a small silted plain at the head of the Argolic gulf, certainly raised horses.[10] Homeric Sparta, which included Laconia and Messenia, was early famous for its meadows. But when population began to increase in the plain of the Eurotas river, which is only 40 sq. miles in extent, the keeping of live stock became more restricted and the war to seize the broad Messenian plain became a necessity. The alluvial Messenian plain, on the windward side of the Taygetus range, had sufficient rainfall of 39 in. a year to ensure good pastures. We hear of "grassy Hire", "divine

[1] Soph. *Elect.* 703.
[2] Arrian, *Anab.* v, 19, 5.
[3] *Pol.* 1289 B.
[4] *Il.* i, 154.
[5] Her. vii, 196.
[6] *Il.* ii, 503; Strabo, ix, 2, 18 (c. 407).
[7] Soph. *Oed. Col.* 668.
[8] ii, 9.
[9] Her. v, 77.
[10] *Il.* iii, 74.

Pherae" and "Antheia deep in meads", on the deltaic flats along the Messenian gulf.[1] These were famous for their cattle and sheep.[2] We hear later in the third century that this region sent a shipload of horses to Egypt.[3] The broad tertiary plain of Elis watered by the Alpheus and Peneus and with lagoons in the coastal belt had the best lowland pastures in the Peloponnesus.[4] Here were the cattle of King Augeas and, in a raid on Elis, Nestor of Pylos carried off 50 herds of kine, 50 flocks of sheep, 50 flocks of goats and 150 mares with their foals,[5] when mounted Epeians pursued the marauder.[6] In 218 Philip V of Macedon secured great booty of cattle from this district,[7] and to this day it is well stocked with animals.

The plateau of Arcadia, dotted with small lakes drained by "swallow holes" (*katavothra*) but flooded after winter rains and the thawing snow from the mountains in spring, provided excellent pastures. The lake plain of Orchomenus is marshy,[8] and on the plain of the Pheneus Odysseus pastured his mares.[9] Arcadia was famous for its horses.[10] The islands gave little or no pastures suitable for horse or cattle raising, but the hillsides where the trees afforded mast raised pigs, sheep and goats. The description that Telemachus gives of Ithaca is typical. "In Ithaca there are no wide courses, nor meadow land at all. It is a pasture land of goats and more pleasant in my sight than one that pastureth horses; for of the islands that lie upon the sea none are fit for the driving of horses, or rich in meadow land, and least of all is Ithaca."[11] An Ithacan chieftain kept a stud farm of twelve mares in Elis and bred mules there.[12] From outside of Greece fine horses were brought from Sicily to compete at the great festivals.[13]

Probably the horse was brought to Greece by the nomad invaders who came from the horse-breeding steppes.[14] In Homer

---

[1] Strabo, viii, 4, 1 (c. 359).   [2] Strabo, viii, 5, 6 (c. 366).
[3] Polyb. v, 37.   [4] Theocr. *Id.* xxv.
[5] *Il.* xi, 671.   [6] *Il.* xi, 707.
[7] Polyb. iv, 75.   [8] Paus. viii, 14, 1–4.
[9] Paus. viii, 14, 5–6.   [10] Varro, ii, 1, 14, iv, 12, vi, 2, viii, 3.
[11] *Od.* iv, 604; cf. xiii, 241.   [12] *Od.* iv, 634.
[13] Pind. *Pyth.* 1, 2, 3, 6; *Olym.* 1, 2, 3; *Nem.* 9.
[14] The point is very uncertain. Possibly it came from Asia Minor. There is a well-known picture from a Minoan-Cretan vase of a horse being conveyed in a ship, which may suggest it was imported from Hittite sources. The problem is impossible of solution.

mention of horses is frequent. Ancient sculptures, especially those of the Parthenon frieze, show that the Greek horse was small, not much bigger than the modern pony; doubtless it showed considerable speed; but since it was not used as a draught animal it was not bred for size or strength. The use of cavalry before Alexander was small. In Homer the heroes were driven to the battlefield in their chariots and fought on foot. The style of fighting of Greek armies, the heavy phalanx, gave little chance for effective cavalry work except for scouting and following up a retreat. The fact that the saddle was unknown, and consequently also stirrups, must have made a charge almost impossible. With a more flexible battle array Alexander made considerable use of cavalry with great effect. Greek horses were unshod, as were the Roman which, however, had leather foot coverings; the iron shoe was a late introduction, probably not earlier than the second century B.C. For this reason Greek horsemen were very careful of their animals and were unwilling to use them over stony ground. Xenophon, in his short treatise On Horsemanship, gives elaborate and very sound instructions on the good points of the horse and its management. We know that very great pains and considerable sums were expended on the breeding and training of teams for the races at the great games, especially at Olympia.[1]

Sheep

Of the breeding of sheep we know a good deal, since sheep occupied a much more important position in Greek agriculture than any other of the domesticated animals.[2] The ancestry of the sheep is of immense antiquity, and our present-day breeds are the outcome of crossing between various races of the animal inhabiting different parts of the world. Undoubtedly the sheep as known to the Greeks was an importation from Asia and North Africa and the types known in classical times the result of many cross-breedings.

Generally speaking the various strains incorporated were the

[1] Prices of horses—12 minas, Aristoph. *Nubes*, 21. A horse pawned for the same sum, Lysias, *de Maled.* 307. Three minas a very low price, Isaeus, *de Dicaeog. Her.* 116. Cf. Boeckh, i, p. 92.

[2] Otto Brendel, *Die Schafzucht im alten Griechenland*. Max Hilzheimer, "Sheep", *Antiquity*, x (1936), pp. 195, 358, 359.

fat-tailed and fat-rumped sheep of Asia Minor, the great wild sheep, the Argali, the small mountain sheep, the Mouflon of Cyprus, originally we must suppose from Armenia, and the Merino of North Africa. From these four were evolved the various types which are recognisable in coins and works of art from Mycenaean to late classical times. From seals and gold objects found at Mycenae, it is evident that the sheep of those times represented two main breeds, the big Argali and the smaller "maned" sheep of Africa with big backward-curving horns. Neither of these are wool sheep, their bodies being covered with hair, dark brown or mottled. Later, certainly before Homeric times, the long-tailed, long-woolled sheep of Arabia and Syria were imported. These animals were valued for their milk, to which innumerable references are found in Homer, while their long tails and fat rumps gave fat and flesh for eating. The fleeces were yellow, and it is perfectly possible that we have here at least one explanation of the quest of the Argonauts for the golden fleece in an attempt to bring back those wonderful sheep to Greece. This yellow colour of the wool was bred out by crossing, and in Homer we have many references to white-fleeced animals. Such crossing evidently was between the long coarse-woolled variety with the short fine-woolled mountain type, either the mouflon or merino, which resulted in an animal producing a high-grade fleece. Certainly by the time of Herodotus the typical fat-tailed sheep had been very considerably modified and indeed changed altogether by cross-breeding, for he describes with astonishment the fat-tailed sheep of Arabia as something well worth recording.[1]

Turning now to the various parts of Greece particularly favourable for sheep breeding, it may be said, as in the case of cattle and horses, that they flourished wherever pastures were good, although generally the sheep and goat can find a living where the larger animals cannot. Greece in general is favourable to sheep, and to-day in comparison with other countries of the same size it is a notable sheep-raising country. Thessaly was famous for its sheep as for other animals from early times. Iton "the mother of sheep" is mentioned by Homer,[2] and Strabo

---

[1] Her. iii, 113. Cf. Aelian's description of fat-tailed sheep of India, *V.H.* iv, 32.　　　　　[2] *Il.* ii, 696.

says that in Thessaly the people wore long woollen cloaks because
of the cold climate.[1] Epirus was famous for its sheep, which
were much prized in Italy, Varro mentioning the so-called
"Pyrrhic" breed which gave a wonderful wool.[2] Boeotia of old
was a notable sheep country, as it is to-day.[3] Many coins of
Phocis show rams' heads. Attica was the greatest centre of
sheep breeding in continental Greece, the climate being particularly adapted thereto, although Athenaeus says that Attic flocks
were pastured in Euboea.[4] Three main varieties of Attic sheep
are clearly distinguishable, first a long-woolled, high-standing
animal, as seen from a figure on the Parthenon frieze; secondly
a smaller mountain sheep, evolved from an argali-mouflon cross,
and third another breed evidently derived from a mouflon-
merino cross. Many references are to be found to the excellence
of the Attic breeds.[5] The finer animals were covered with skins
to improve the softness of the fleece, a custom that still survives.[6]
So famous and valuable were these animals that Ptolemy exhibited
twenty of them in his wonderful festival procession.[7] From
Attica they spread widely, notably to Miletus and the islands.

Lying so close to Attica, Megara was also well adapted to
sheep raising, and we have one facetious remark of Diogenes
Laertius who says he would not like to be a child in Megara as
the inhabitants dress their children in rags but put blankets on
their sheep.[8] Arcadia, famous for its pastoral pursuits, was
early mentioned with Orchomenus "of the many sheep".[9]
Coins of Arcadia show a cross between the old long-woolled
fat-tailed sheep with the Cyprian mouflon, to produce a very
fine type of big sheep. In the Peloponnese, Messenia was most
suitable for sheep. We have an interesting story in Homer of
how the Messenians had stolen 300 sheep from Ithaca along
with their shepherds, which seems to suggest the first introduction of the animal there, since they had to take the shepherds
to look after animals they knew nothing about themselves.[10]

---

[1] xi, 14, 12 (c. 530).   [2] ii, 2, 1 ff.
[3] Hes. *Theog.* 23.   [4] Athen. i, 27 F.
[5] Varro, ii, 2, 18; Athen. xii, 540 D, v, 219 A: "What other wool is softer
than the Attic?"
[6] Varro, ii, 2, 18; Pliny, *H.N.* viii, 73.
[7] Athen. v, 201 C.   [8] vi, 41.
[9] *Il.* ii, 605.   [10] *Od.* xxi, 18.

In the islands we find in seals from Crete a small, sturdy, mountain type, evidently an argali-merino cross. Samos was well adapted to sheep raising.[1] Athenaeus says that the tyrant Polycrates at the end of the sixth century brought them from Attica to cross with the Milesian breed.[2] In Sicily there was a cross between the Attic mouflon-merino with the argali-merino, the result being an excellent wool-bearing animal which gave rise to a large wool trade with Rome; Athenaeus speaks of Sicilian wool.[3] Over the whole of the Ionian Greek colonies the sheep were everywhere; those of Miletus were specially famous, Milesian wool fabrics being particularly valuable.[4] It will be seen that the evolution of the animal in Greece was definitely from one that would yield milk and mutton to a wool sheep. This is quite understandable with an increase of population that demanded wool for clothing more insistently than the comparative luxuries of milk and meat. Among the Egyptians and Israelites, in early times at least, the fat-tailed and fat-rumped animal was highly prized as a fat producer; lard from pigs was scarce owing to the tabu of the animal on the ground of its uncleanness.

We find many references containing careful instructions with regard to feeding. Great stress is laid on the importance of giving the animals salt.[5] Aristotle recommends clover, trefoil and lucerne, branches of the wild olive and vetches and lentils.[6] Much stress is laid on water, which for winter feeding should come from the south and for summer pastures from the north, i.e. warm and cold. Pastures should look "towards the evening", i.e. the west, so that they should not get the hot noon-day sun. Herds were turned out to grass in the spring and autumn; in summer, when the pastures were parched, they were fed on leaves. The care taken of the animals was notable. They were kept at night in folds of very substantial stone construction as a protection against wolves and robbers.[7] A good picture of such

---

[1] Strabo, xiv, 1, 15 (c. 637); Theocr. xv, 125.
[2] xii, 540 D.   [3] v, 209 A.
[4] Athen. xii, 519 B, 540 D, 553 B. Cf. Aristoph. *Lys.* 729; Aelian, *Nat. an.* xvii, 34.
[5] Arist. *H.A.* viii, 10 (12); Pliny, *H.N.* xxxi, 41.
[6] Pliny, *ibid.*
[7] Many references in Homer to sheepfolds; e.g. *Il.* ii, 470; xix, 377.

a fold is seen in a relief of the second century from Alexandria showing a very solid stone structure proof against heat in summer and cold in winter. The folds were placed in sheltered spots facing east or south for warmth. On the pastures the sheep were penned with hurdles which could easily be moved.[1] The value of the manure was well understood, and we may conclude that the practice of stall-feeding was largely in order to collect it; we are told that the main duty of the stall servant was to clean them.[2] Sheep were so valuable for their wool that they were seldom sacrificed. Lambs were a very special offering to the gods and a great luxury to eat.[3]

Shearing took place twice yearly;[4] the first beginning on the twelfth day of the spring moon. Animals were never shorn during the moon's waning and only in sunny, warm weather.[5] After shearing any cuts were dressed with tar and the whole body anointed with pigs' fat, and four days after a bath in salt water as a preventive against mange was given.

Generally it may be said that the Greeks showed a remarkable grasp of the essentials of scientific breeding and care of sheep, and their practice has not been changed to any great extent to the present time.

Swine

The keeping of pigs[6] is as old as man's settled life on earth, when he had emerged from the purely "collectional" stage, abandoned a nomadic existence, and found in agriculture and the domestication of animals the supports of a fixed occupation of a chosen territory. *Sus mediterraneus*, probably if not certainly, a cross between *sus vittatus*, the wild pig of Asia Minor, and *sus scrofa*, the wild boar of Europe, is like all his race no wanderer like the sheep, goat or ox, and is therefore un-suitable for the unstable economy of the nomad; he is typically an animal of a sedentary and unmoving existence. He is also, for all the fierceness of his wild species, an animal peculiarly

---

[1] Theocr. xxv, 99.   [2] *Od.* xvii, 223.
[3] Theocr. v, 140; Quint. Smyrn. v, 493; *Il.* xxiv, 620; cf. *J.H.S.* ix, 325. Many references in the Bible.
[4] Theocr. xxviii, 12; cf. Aristoph. *Aves*, 712-13.
[5] Varro, ii, 11, 5; Col. xi, 2.
[6] K. Winkelstern, *Die Schweinezucht im klassischen Altertum.*

adapted to domestication. The beech, oak and chestnut forests of the Balkan area and much of Greece have been since time immemorial, and still are, areas well adapted for his nurture.

The references in Homer to the craft of the swineherd and its importance in the economy of the day are numerous. Eumaeus, the bailiff of Odysseus, had a large herd carefully tended and guarded. The pen he had built himself. "With stones dragged thither had he builded it, and coped it with a fence of white thorn, and he had split an oak to the dark core and without he had driven stakes the whole length thereof on either side, set thick and close; and within the courtyard he made twelve styes hard by one another to be beds for the swine and in each stye fifty grovelling swine were penned, brood swine, but the boars slept without...and their tale was three hundred and three score. And by them slept four dogs, as fierce as wild beasts, which the swineherd had bred."[1] By day the herd was driven out to feed in the woods and back to the styes at night. Aristotle in his *Historia Animalium* has much to say on breeding,[2] and diseases of pigs,[3] with careful directions on the care of sows with young and the management of the litter. The animals should be fed on acorns and nuts, but he recommends also a mixed diet, with barley, beans, millet and other sorts of grain, in order to give the meat a better flavour; to feed them on acorns alone makes it taste insipid. The acorns are stored in the barn for the winter, and dried figs give a delicate flavour. He gives the rather curious information that at the beginning of the fattening period the Thracian swineherds allow the animals to drink, but from the second to the seventh day give them no water.[4] Pigs can be fattened in sixty days, during which time they must be confined to the styes and not allowed to wander: the weight of the meat was reckoned as one-sixth of the live weight. Evidently in Homeric times the art of intensive fattening was not understood or practised. A fat hog five years old was fit for a feast,[5] and those of Circe were nine years old.[6] Eumaeus gave the suitors the older animals to eat but to the poor beggar he gave a sucking pig, such being fit

---

[1] *Od.* xiv, 11ff.   [2] *H.A.* v, 14 (12), (546 A).
[3] viii, 21.   [4] viii, 8 (6).
[5] *Od.* xiv, 419.   [6] *Od.* x 390.

food for herdsmen and poor people.[1] We have no mention of smoked ham or bacon, but numerous references to salted or pickled pork.[2] It is interesting to note that, among the Greeks and Arabs, swine were regarded as animals highly prized for sacrifice to the gods; there was no tabu as among the Egyptians and Israelites. Aristophanes abounds in references to pig keeping and the animal was regarded quite as one of the family.[3]

Asses and Mules

The ass and mule[4] had been known and prized in Greece from very early days. The ass, although as always the butt of many jokes for its stupidity, was held in honour for its noble qualities.[5] We hear of the wild asses of Phrygia, Lycaonia and Africa.[6] The asses of Arcadia were especially esteemed.[7] The animal was used, as to-day, for transport purposes and was valued for the loads he could carry on his back.[8] But it could not have been a very strong animal, since the asses that took their daily loads of firewood to Athens from the estate of Phaenippus carried a maximum of 70 lb. on their backs.[9] Whether from taste or necessity, in a land where meat was a luxury, the flesh of the ass was eaten, as indeed it is to-day.[10]

There are many references in Homer to mules which were thought superior to oxen for ploughing.[11] We are told that the Mysians were the first to breed mules,[12] and we hear of those of Cappadocia as famous,[13] as were those of Arcadia;[14] and Homer says they were bred in Elis,[15] but Pausanias contradicts this, saying that mules were not raised there on account of a curse, but gives no further explanation of this.[16] That mules were

[1] *Od.* xiv, 80; cf. Athen. ix, 375 B.
[2] Col. xii, 53. It is highly probable the Greeks smoked the meat.
[3] E.g. *Plutus*, 820, 1106; *Pax*, 24, 927; *Vesp.* 36; *Lysist.* 684.
[4] Arts. "Asinus" and "Mulus" in *D.S.*
[5] E.g. Arist. *de Gen. An.* ii, 8.
[6] Strabo, xii, 6, 1 (c. 568).
[7] Varro, ii, 1, 14; Strabo, viii, 8, 1 (c. 388).
[8] E.g. Arist. *Lys.* 290; Xen. *Cyrop.* vii, 5, 11. No record of prices paid for asses.   [9] Dem. *in Phaen.* 7.
[10] Aristoph. *Vesp.* 195; cf. Lucian, *Luc.* 31; Her. i, 133.
[11] *Il.* x, 352. Cf. *Od.* viii, 124, an obscure passage. Price of a pair of mules 5½ to 8 minas, Isaeus, *de Philoct. Hered.* 33.
[12] Anacr., Frag. 36.   [13] Arist. *de Mir. Ausc.* 69, 835 B.
[14] Herds of horses and mules in Peloponnesus—Varro, ii, 7, 1.
[15] *Od.* iv, 635.   [16] Paus. v, 5, 2, 9, 2.

sterile was often the occasion of comment, and Aristotle describes the animal carefully.[1] For some reason not clear, the mule was considered a mountain animal;[2] but there seems to have been a disposition to confuse the mule with the wild ass, or at least it would appear so in Homer.[3]

Goats

The goat was everywhere, and his depredations among the young saplings on the hillsides must have done much to hasten the deforestation which was so serious in Greece. He could live and thrive where cattle could not find enough for subsistence, on the terebinth or turpentine tree[4] or heath.[5] References in the Bible to goat keeping are very numerous. In Homeric times goats' flesh seems to have been a delicacy, otherwise the suitors of Penelope would not have accepted the meat of the fattest animals.[6] The horns from which the bow of Pandarus was made sixteen hand-breadths wide, must have been a prodigious animal if it were a wild goat; but probably it was an ibex.[7] As already noted, goats' milk was used for cheesemaking. Goats from Scyros and Naxos were famous and were imported into other countries to improve local breeds.[8]

Beekeeping

Beekeeping was general at a time when sugar was not used and only known as an Asiatic rarity.[9] It was so common in Attica that regulations were necessary as to the distance between the hives on the hillsides.[10] Attic honey was famous, especially that from Hymettus.[11] It may be remarked that the scrub of the Greek uplands contains many aromatic plants, notably thyme,

[1] Arist. *de Gen. An.* ii, 8; *H.A.* vi, 24, 36 (29). Cf. the story of the mule giving birth to a foal in Her. iii, 153; Varro, ii, 1, 27; Columella, vi, 37, 3; Livy, xxvi, 23, xxxvii, 3. Numerous modern instances.
[2] Aristoph. *Ranae*, 290. The point is quite obscure.
[3] *Il.* ii, 852.
[4] *Anth. Pal.* vi, 336. Cf. Eupolis, *ap.* Macrob. vii, 5, 9.
[5] Theocr. i, 13; *Anth. Pal.* vi, 99, 334.
[6] *Od.* xiv, 106. But later it seems to have been fit only for slaves.
[7] *Il.* iv, 104.
[8] Athen. xii, 540 D. Polycrates, tyrant of Samos.
[9] Strabo, xv, 1, 20 (c. 694).
[10] Plut. *Solon*, 23. Cf. Plato, *Laws*, viii, 843 E, attracting another's swarm.
[11] Paus. i, 32, 1.

which gives the honey a distinctive flavour. Strabo affords us the information that honey from the Laurium district was famous because it was taken from the hives without smoking the bees.[1] Why this should have been so, and why so unpromising a district as that of the mining area of Laurium should have been favourable for bees, we do not know.[2] The bitter taste of honey from Pontus was disliked in Greece and Italy.

Poultry[3]

Scattered references to the keeping of poultry are numerous. In the Homeric age the barnyard cock and hen seem to have been unknown in Greece, and the first extant reference is apparently that in Theognis, who wrote sometime in the sixth century.[4] The so-called Homeric Battle of the Frogs and Mice, in which the cock is mentioned, is of much later date.[5] Evidently this breed of bird was either brought to Greece by the Persians, or came supposedly from Persia, that is from Asia; this agrees with its known origin which is undoubtedly Asiatic. Several authors refer to them as Persian birds.[6] The cock was sacred to Athena, we are told by Pausanias,[7] somewhat curiously in view of its late introduction to Greece, and to Hermes by Plutarch.[8] His plumage was greatly admired as outshining all the gold of Croesus.[9] Representations of cocks are found upon the coins of Himera, Dardanus, Carystus and Phaestus.

Aristotle has many references to domestic fowls,[10] and particularly remarks on the characteristic care of the hen for her eggs and chickens. The way in which a hen guards her young under her wings has always interested observers.[11] Aristotle deals with the structure and development of the egg,[12] and Dioscorides

---

[1] Strabo, ix, 1, 23 (c. 400).

[2] Dio Chrys. ix, 6. Arist. *H.A.* ix, 40 (27), (627 B) has observations on bee-keeping.

[3] Cf. Vickery, *Food in Early Greece*, p. 66, for references to early poultry keeping.

[4] 862.   [5] *Batr.* 192.

[6] E.g. Aristoph. *Aves*, 277, 483, 707; Cratinus, *ap.* Athen. ix, 374 D, and others.   [7] vi, 26, 3.

[8] *Conv.* 666.   [9] Diog. Laert. i, 51.

[10] Many references in Book vi of the *Hist. An.*

[11] *H.A.* ix, 7 (613 B 14). Cf. Matth. xxiii. 37.

[12] *H.A.* vi, 3 (561 A).

says that hens' eggs were used medicinally.[1] Artificial incuba-
tion of eggs was well understood.[2] Both Varro and Columella
treat the breeding and care of poultry in detail, as also, at a
much later date, Cassianus Bassus in the *Geoponica*.[3] The art
of "caponising", or fattening birds for the market was widely
practised;[4] the Delians were especially successful therein and
Pliny says they were first to do so,[5] but such attributions are,
as usual, very doubtful. Several varieties and breeds were
recognised, of which Tanagrians from Boeotia were particularly
well known. Pausanias says of them that there were two breeds,
"of which the cocks were called 'Fighters' and 'Blackbirds'.
The size of these Blackbirds is the same as the Lydian birds,
but in colour they are like crows, while wattles and comb are
very like the anemone. They have small white markings at the
end of the beak and at the end of the tail."[6] We hear of fowls
from Chalcidice, which were good fighters but poor layers,[7]
and from Africa that were called *Meleagrides* by the Greeks,
"large, speckled, with rounded backs",[8] which seem to suggest
a kind of Plymouth Rock. Varro also remarks that the name
Melic as applied to poultry was a misnomer; they should be
called *Medic*.[9] A miniature Bantam or "Adriatic" breed was
well known and mentioned by various authors.[10] Aristotle
speaks of fowls from Illyria that lay two or three times a day as
a wonderful thing, which no doubt it was.[11] Egyptian hens were
famous for their patience in sitting.[12] Cock-fighting was a craze,
and references thereto very numerous.[13] Aelian says that the
annual great cock-fighting festival at Athens was started by

[1] Diosc. ii, 50. But Plutarch, *de Tuenda San. Praec.* 131 D, regards them
as an undesirable article of diet. Athenaeus speaks of dishes made of eggs
xii, 516 E, F, xiv, 640 D, 641 F, 642 E.
[2] Arist. *H.A.* vi, 2 (559 B 1); Diod. Sic. 1, 74.
[3] *Geop.* xiv, 7–17.
[4] Arist. *H.A.* ix, 50 (631 B); cf. Poseid. *ap.* Athen. xii, 549 F.
[5] *H.A.* x (21), 24.
[6] Paus. ix, 22, 4.   [7] Varro, iii, 9, 6.
[8] *Ibid.* iii, 9, 18.   [9] *Ibid.*
[10] Arist. *H.A.* vi, 1 (558 B); *Gen. An.* iii, 1 (749 B). Chrysipp. *ap.* Athen.
vii, 285 E. Pliny, *H.N.* x (56), 77; Col. viii, 2, 13.
[11] *de Mir.* 842 B 27; cf. *H.A.* 558 B 20 (vi, 1).
[12] *Geop.* xiv, 7, 30.
[13] E.g. Aesch. *Eum.* 866; Plato, *Laws*, vii, 789; Theocr. xxiii, 73, and many
others. The popularity of quail fighting was even greater; cf. Athen. xi,
464 (numerous references).

Themistocles to commemorate the victories of the Persian war.[1]
References to the crowing cock that heralds the dawn are innumerable.[2]

Geese were very early bred and cared for, as several references
in Homer testify, although it must be remarked that all are in
the *Odyssey* and none in the *Iliad*.[3] Aristotle speaks of the goose
in several places.[4] Fattening geese to obtain foie gras was
practised.[5] Geese and other birds were brought from Boeotia
to the Athenian market.[6] They were raised in Macedonia and
Thessaly,[7] and Athenaeus speaks of goose eggs as a delicacy.[8]

It is curious to note that there is no clear reference to the
keeping of domestic ducks, although Varro speaks of a place
where such birds were reared.[9] There are numerous references
to them; one in Aristophanes where "duckling" is used as a
term of endearment, which would suggest they were domesticated.[10] Pigeon fancying was fashionable and pheasants were
regarded as a great luxury. Whether they were preserved we do
not know.[11]

Olives

Of all trees the olive was, and still is, the most valuable and most
carefully tended in the Mediterranean area. It is practically
certain that the olive came from Asia Minor—references in the
Bible to it are very numerous—and was a comparatively late
importation into Greece and still later into Italy, where it was
taken in all probability by Greek colonists. References in
Homer to the olive are few and evidently the oil was highly

[1] *V.H.* ii, 2, 8.

[2] E.g. Soph. *Elect.* 17; Plato, *Symp.* 223 C; and many others.

[3] xv, 161, 174; xix, 536f.

[4] ii, 1 (499 A), ii, 17 (509 A), vi, 2 (560 B 10), vi, 8 (564 A 10).

[5] Athen. ix, 384; *Anth. Pal.* ix, 377.

[6] Aristoph. *Acharn.* 878; *Pax*, 1004. Art. "Gans" by Olck in *P.W.*

[7] Plato, *Gorg.* 471 C; *Pol.* 264 C.

[8] Athen. ii, 58 A; cf. also xii, 540 B.

[9] *Res Rust.* iii, 11, 1. The references in Theophrastus (Signs of Weather,
18, 28) to the behaviour of ducks are not very clear, but they seem to indicate
both tame and wild.

[10] *Plutus*, 1011, cf. *Aves*, 566; Arist. *H.A.* 593 B 16, 509 A 4.

[11] Pigeons: Theoph. *Char.* xxi, 15; Plato, *Theaet.* 197. Many references
to pigeons in *H.A.* of Aristotle. He seems to have been interested in them and
watched their habits carefully. Pheasants: Athen. ix, 387.

prized.[1] That Solon introduced the olive into Attica is mani-
festly absurd, but it is not unlikely that he first made laws as to
the regulation of its culture, forbidding any trees to be planted
nearer than nine feet from a neighbour's boundary owing to
the great spread of the roots.[2] Olives thrive in a dry, calcareous
soil, such as that of Attica, and Athenian oil was famous everywhere, especially in Egypt which is unsuited to the tree and
whose oil was poor in spite of the best efforts of the Ptolemies to
improve it.[3] Since the roots do not go deep into the soil but
spread out, continual irrigation is essential[4] and much pruning
is necessary.[5]

The young trees were raised in nursery beds for five years
and then transplanted, and under the best conditions the trees
would bear seven to ten years after planting.[6] Once the trees
were well established their care demanded little labour and gave
a high return to the cultivator.[7] It may be observed that, since
the olive harvest falls in mid-winter, labour is available in an
otherwise slack season. So valuable were the olive trees not
only to their owner but to the state, that there was a law pro-
hibiting any proprietor from rooting up more than two trees
in any year for public festivals or for his own use in case of
death, the fine being 100 drs. for each tree destroyed and a
reward of a like sum to the informer.[8]

FIGS

Figs were propagated by cuttings or grafting; if from seed the
species degenerated.[9] Slips will do best when planted in a

---

[1] E.g. *Od.* ii, 339.

[2] Plut. *Solon*, 23; Theoph. *H.P.* ii, 5, 6; cf. Plato, *Laws*, viii B, 43 E.

[3] Theoph. *H.P.* iv, 2, 8. Oil not inferior but lacks a pleasing smell and
has not enough salt in it. Cf. Strabo, xvii, 1, 35 (c. 809).

[4] *H.P.* i, 6, 4, ii, 7, 3.   [5] *H.P.* ii, 7, 2.

[6] Cf. the prohibition in Lev. xix. 23 ff. against eating the fruit before five
years after planting.

[7] Jardé, *Céréales*, p. 186, reckons that an olive grove would yield three
times the value of a similar area under wheat. Cf. Col. iii, 3, v, 8.

[8] Dem. *in Macart.* 71; cf. Lysias, vii, *passim*. The point is by no means
clear, but olive trees played a large part in Attic religious ritual. Cf. art.
"Baumkultus" in *P.W.*; L. Weniger, "Altgriechischer Baumkultus", *Das
Erbe der Alten*, ii, pp. 40f. Cf. also Jews forbidden to destroy olive trees in
war-time, or to use the wood in besieging a city (Deut. xx. 19).

[9] Theoph. *H.P.* ii, 1, 2; ii, 2, 4; ii, 5, 3.

squill bulb.[1] The trees should be planted far apart and in low ground.[2] If watered the tree grows vigorously, but the fruit is inferior, except that growing in Laconia which does better for water.[3] Dust is dug in round trees where it is deficient.[4] Root pruning is beneficial if the tree is running to leaf; ashes are sprinkled about it and gashes made in the stems, when it will bear better.[5] It was in fig culture that the Ancients made their most interesting scientific study to prevent the dropping of the immature fruit. A remedy was found in the process known as caprification by mixing wild with cultivated trees, so that the cultivated figs, which bore only female flowers, should be cross-fertilised by the small gall wasp, Blastophaga, which fed on the wild trees, bearing male flowers.[6] The process is still followed wherever the fig is cultivated. Theophrastus says that the fig will bear debarking for some time, which hardly agrees with the complaint of the prophet Joel where the final desolation of the land is compared with the stripping of the bark from the fig trees.[7]

The large sugar content of dried figs made a highly sustaining army ration.[8] Unlike the olive the fig is short-lived.[9]

VITICULTURE[10]

As being so important a branch of agriculture, great attention was paid to scientific viticulture. The first care is the choice of suitable soil.[11] Generally low ground is the most favoured, for the vine is a water-loving tree.[12] But each variety requires its appropriate soil, for there are as many varieties of vines as there

[1] Theoph. *H.P.* ii, 5, 5, vii, 13, 4; *C.P.* v, 6, 10; Pliny, *H.N.* xvii, 87. Possibly this may have had a magical significance. Cf. Frazer, *Golden Bough*, "The Scapegoat", p. 255; cf. also Athen. iii, 77 E.

[2] *H.P.* ii, 5, 6.   [3] *H.P.* ii, 7, 1; *C.P.* iii, 6, 6.

[4] *H.P.* ii, 7, 5; *C.P.* iii, 16, 3.   [5] *H.P.* ii, 7, 6; Pliny, xvii, 253.

[6] *H.P.* ii, 8, 1; *C.P.* ii, 9, 5, iii, 18, 1; falling of figs from the tree, Isaiah xxxiv. 4; Rev. vi. 13. Cf. also Athen. xiv, 651 C.

[7] *H.P.* iv, 15, 2; Joel i. 7.

[8] Polyb. xii, 10; cf. 1 Sam. xxv. 18. References in the Bible to dried figs numerous.

[9] Theoph. *H.P.* iv, 13, 2. Attic figs, Athen. xiv, 652 B.

[10] Art. "Vin" by Jardé in *D.S.* The equipment necessary for a vineyard of about 65 acres in the estimation of Cato is interesting (*de Agri Cult.* xi).

[11] Xen. *Oecon.* xx, 3.

[12] Theoph. *H.P.* ii, 7, 1.

are lands.[1] Vines are not propagated by grafting[2] but by slips or by "layering",[3] i.e. by covering a branch still growing on the tree with earth. Vines climbing a tree are always raised in this way.[4] If they are propagated from seed they will degenerate.[5] The slips are set separately in rows;[6] sometimes they are put in upside down; but Theophrastus holds that this makes no difference in their growth.[7] Ischomachus instructs Socrates in the art of planting. The slip must be put into well-dug earth, with a layer of soft soil underneath. It must not be placed upright, but laid a little obliquely so that it may lie like a "gamma" turned up, in order that there may be more buds under the soil; since, from the buds, shoots spring above the earth, so that when many shoots take root in the earth, the plant will spring up quickly and with great vigour. The earth round the young plants must be trodden down hard, so that it may not turn into mud in wet weather and rot them, nor be dried up in hot weather and the roots become heated from the dryness or porousness of the earth.[8] When the plants are well established and the roots gone down far into the earth, cultivation round the trees is necessary as will be seen later. The intervals between the rows may be widened if it is desired to cultivate other trees between them.[9] Fruit trees are most suitable for this purpose.[10] But such trees must be those that do not have very spreading roots, like apples or pomegranates.[11]

Some species of vines creep on the ground.[12] Grapes from these varieties are large but are liable to be eaten by mice and foxes. When planted on moist ground they must be raised on poles, a practice which proved so disappointing to the fox in Aesop's fable. Those that grow upright without support must be pruned so that there is an equal growth of branches all round to keep the trees steady and not one-sided.[13] Most vines need

[1] Theoph. *H.P.* ii, 5, 7.
[2] Theoph. *H.P.* ii, 5, 3. But cf. Varro, i, 41, 3; Cato, xli.
[3] Pliny, *H.N.* xviii, 22, 23, 26; Col. iii, 9, iv, 29; Cato, xxxii, lii, cxxiii.
[4] Col. *de Arb.* 7.   [5] Theoph. *H.P.* ii, 2, 4.
[6] *Ibid.* ii, 5, 3, iv, 4, 8.   [7] *Ibid.* ii, 6, 12.
[8] Xen. *Oecon.* xix, 8–11. Cf. method advocated by Theoph. *H.P.* ii, 5, 5; *C.P.* iii, 12, 1; Cato, *de Agri Cult.* 33.
[9] Aristoph. *Pax*, 566 f.
[10] Aristoph. *Acharn.* 995 f.   [11] Theoph. *C.P.* iii, 10, 6–7.
[12] *Geop.* iii, 1, 5; Varro, i, 8.   [13] Col. iv, 17, v, 4.

props of one sort or another.[1] Allowing vines to grow up trees was sometimes practised, but it was not approved of by the best authorities.[2] The vine, unlike the olive, demands incessant care, and the earth between the rows must be constantly turned over. It is, therefore, necessary to dig round the trees either twice or three times a year.[3] Great care must be taken in digging, otherwise injury may be done to the roots, which will make them less able to bear variations of heat and cold by being weakened, some authorities attributing sun-scorch and rot to the same cause.[4] As the summer advanced the leaves were thinned out and those remaining shrivelled in the heat, thus reducing the surface of evaporation.[5] By the end of August, when the summer's heat had reached a maximum and evaporation was greatest, the soil round the trees was pulverised and tossed in the air to settle on the clusters of grapes as a protection against the sun.[6] This checked evaporation from the leaves and soil round the trees by preventing capillary attraction of underground water.[7] The same thing, it may be mentioned, was done at Megara during the September heat to protect cucumbers and pumpkins, whose fruits were made sweeter by the conservation of the natural moisture.[8]

Incessant hoe and spade work was necessary in the vineyard for dry farming.[9] Nothing should be planted between the vines, as a clean culture was highly necessary to increase absorption of moisture.[10] But Columella did not object to a short-lived green crop, that could be ploughed under for manure.[11] With regard to manuring there is much disagreement, as some hold that it affects the flavour of the grapes, but Theophrastus recommends a moderate use.[12] Pruning is highly necessary[13] and

---

[1] *Il.* xviii, 563; Hes. *Scut. Herc.* 298; Aristoph. *Acharn.* 986; Theocr. iii, 70; Varro, i, 8.

[2] Theoph. *C.P.* i, 10, 4, iii, 10, 8; Polyb. xxxiv, 11, 1; Aristoph. *Vespae*, 326 *et schol.*; Xen. *Oecon.* xix, 18; Dem. *in Nicost.* 15.

[3] *C.P.* iii, 12, 2; 16, 1. The Amorgos lease, *I.G.* xii, 7, 62, i, 9–10, requires twice a year.   [4] *H.P.* iv, 14, 7.   [5] Xen. *Oecon.* xix, 19.

[6] *H.P.* ii, 7, 5; *C.P.* iii, 16, 3. Cf. Col. iv, 28, 1, xi, 2, 60.

[7] Semple, *Ancient Mediterranean Agriculture*, p. 96.

[8] *H.P.* ii, 7, 5.   [9] Hes. *W.D.* 250; *Od.* xxiv, 224; Isaiah v. 6.

[10] Cf. Deut. xxii. 9.   [11] Col. xi, 2, 60.

[12] *C.P.* iii, 9, 5; cf. Col. xi, 2. In the Amorgos lease the fertilising of the land is required of the tenant, but no distinction is drawn between arable land and vineyards.

[13] Theoph. *C.P.* iii, 13, v, 5, vii, 7; cf. Cato, *de Agri Cult.* 32.

should be done twice a year.[1] Surface roots must be pruned when the tree runs to leaf. "Young vines are very liable to be worm-eaten and suffer from over luxurious growth and sun-scorch especially when the tree has suffered from bad cultivation, or when it has been pruned upwards." The last seems to be a technical term for pruning in such a way that the growth of the new wood is encouraged at the expense of the fruit. The sense is obscure but "pruned upwards" suggests from below, i.e. with the blade of the knife pointing upwards.[2] The heads of the buds must be nipped off[3] and the dropping of the buds may be controlled by cutting round the bark once a year.[4]

The vine casts its fruit if it be snowed or rained on at the time when the flowers fall or the tree is over-luxuriant, and such grapes as remain are small.[5] The vine is a prey to many dangers; in Miletus they are attacked by caterpillars which eat both flowers and leaves when there is a south wind and sunny weather.[6] Hot winds scorch the clusters.[7] The vine is popularly supposed to be the longest-lived of all trees, but Theophrastus denies this is so in nature, the reason being that its life is pro-longed artificially.[8] If the trees are tapped for their juice, it is best done a little before the budding begins.[9]

The vintage, as ever, is a time of rejoicing, and the scene on the shield of Ajax is a very pleasing one, "where the youths and maidens, blithe at heart, carried the honey-sweet fruit in plaited baskets. And in the midst a boy played delightfully on the ringing lyre, and sang sweetly in his clear voice the song of Linus; and stamping all together they bounded with their feet and went along with dancing and with shouting."[10] The process of wine-making is described at length in the chapter on Industry.

How far the planting of olive trees and vines encroached upon the arable land in Attica, thus curtailing the growth of cereals, is

[1] Theoph. *C.P.* ii, 14, 4.
[2] Theoph. *H.P.* iv, 14, 6; Hort's note, *Enquiry*, i, 394.
[3] Theoph. *C.P.* iii, 14, 8.
[4] *Ibid.* i, 5, 5; 17, 10; v, 4, 9; Pliny, *H.N.* xvii, 39, 1.
[5] Theoph. *H.P.* iv, 14, 6–7.
[6] *Ibid.* iv, 14, 9. The "Palmer worm" of Joel i. 4, ii. 25; Amos iv. 9.
[7] Theoph. *H.P.* iv, 14, 10.
[8] *Ibid.* iv, 13, 4.
[9] *Ibid.* ix, 1, 6.
[10] *Il.* xviii, 561 f.

a difficult question and probably no definite answer can be given. Mr Grundy[1] is of the opinion that much of the land formerly devoted to cereal cultivation before the import of foreign grain became general was diverted to vineyards and in a lesser degree to olive groves. This would appear to be a reasonable assumption; but it must be regarded merely as one for which no conclusive proof can be given. M. Jardé[2] is inclined to believe that the encroachment upon arable lands must have been small, vines and olive being planted upon lands which had been cleared of forests and scrub.[3] In any case the raising of cereals was always the most important part of Greek agriculture except in Attica, which at an early date found it impossible to feed the large population in Athens and the Piraeus. But again we must be careful not to take conditions in Attica as typical of the whole of Greece.

DEFORESTATION

Another difficult problem is that of deforestation.[4] That Greece had lost all or most of its forests by the end of the fifth century is undoubtedly true; a fact which Plato deplores.[5] But we must be careful in our use of the word "forest", if we mean by that term areas containing large trees fit for the construction of houses and particularly for shipbuilding. Greece was early stripped bare: we know with certainty that practically all lumber used in construction was imported. But there is no evidence to show that Greece was denuded of all woods. The trade of the charcoal burner was always an important one in an age that did not use coal. Nor is there any evidence that deforestation had

---

[1] *Thucydides and the History of his Age*, p. 73.

[2] *Céréales*, pp. 101–5.

[3] Cf. Theoph. *C.P.* ii, 4, 2: "Use your rich soils for grains and thin soils for trees."

[4] Jardé, *Céréales*, pp. 67, 99; Zimmern, *Greek Commonwealth*, pp. 44, 47; Hassinger, *Geographische Grundlagen der Geschichte*, pp. 27, 143 ff., 165 ff.; K. G. Sklawunos, "Über die Holzversorgung Griechenlands im Altertum", *Forstwissenschaft Centralblatt*, lii (1930), p. 868.

[5] *Crit.* 3 c. Cf. Bursian, *Geographie von Griechenland*, i, 252 ff. For similar deforestation in Crete cf. Myres, *Who were the Greeks?*, p. 6. Perhaps *Od.* xviii, 357, refers to a very early effort at reforestation. For destruction of forests in Cyprus, Strabo, xiv, 6, 5 (c. 684). Cf. also Theoph. *H.P.* v, 3, 7, disappearance of thyine trees in Attica.

in any marked degree affected the lands formerly under timber through soil erosion, or the climate through a change in the rainfall. It is also to be remarked that at least in Attica a large part of the area cleared of woods was replanted with olive groves. But it is certain that the question of deforestation was a matter of grave concern, and we find in leases of land careful restrictions as to the felling of timber, or where cut stipulations for replanting.[1] The whole subject is a difficult one, of which it is impossible to speak with certainty.

ADEQUACY OF GREEK FARMING

How far the agricultural resources of Greece were sufficient, except in times of crop failure, to feed its population must remain in considerable doubt. Mr Grundy[2] makes the struggle for supplies of overseas wheat the key to all Grecian diplomacy. Outside of Thessaly, he asserts,[3] the Greek states bought a large part of their daily bread; they did not produce it at home. "So long as the stream of foreign corn could flow in uninterruptedly, the economic situation showed a balance on the right side. But the margin of balance was very small. The slightest disturbance of foreign trade caused it to incline the other way. The purchasing power of the majority of the Greek states was just sufficient to provide their inhabitants with food from year to year." M. Jardé, on the other hand, is inclined to regard this as an overstatement. "As a matter of fact there is often a tendency to exaggerate the problem of food supply and policy necessitated by the exigencies of subsistence. We always think of Athens, which, at an early date, was over-populous for her agricultural resources and was forced to seek the same ways and means of alleviation which face Great Britain and Japan to-day. Undoubtedly the case of Athens was not an isolated one. Corinth and Aegina were also populous cities, whose territories were unable to support them and for whom the importation of cereals had necessitated such development of industry as was adequate to provide commodities in exchange. But along with

[1] *I.G.* xii, 5, 568, xiv, 645; *I.G.* ii², 1241.
[2] *Thucydides and the History of his Age*, especially part iii, caps. 3–5.
[3] *Ibid.* p. 91.

such over-populous cities, there were others where the gap between production and consumption was less wide because the population was smaller or increased more slowly.... In such countries production on an average was sufficient for consumption and the question of subsistence, which sometimes arose but never in such a tragic way as in Athens, did not have the repercussions upon public policy which it so frequently had in that of the Athenians."[1]

The divergence between these two views is less of fact than of emphasis. Undoubtedly the whole problem of subsistence was always a major one for all the Greeks; sometimes more pressing than others. When population increased, as it did notably during the fifth century, the pressure upon means of subsistence became greater and could only be relieved by war, pestilence or emigration. In addition to which, as we have occasion to observe elsewhere, the Greek system of land tenure had possibilities of grave imperfections which could only be corrected, if they ever were, by violent disturbances ruinous alike to debtors and creditors, landlords and tenants.

In conclusion we may affirm that grain farming over much of Greece, and more especially in Attica, was a poor business. Especially was this the case when we remember that less than 10 per cent was wheat, the rest barley and that the public taste greatly preferred wheat: we are told that at the public distribution of grain the recipients despised barley and clamoured for wheat. In any case the poor Athenian grain farmer had a hard struggle to compete with imported wheat, and when the price was very low he was hopelessly beaten.[2] Olive, vine and fig culture paid handsomely. But on anything like a large commercial scale this required more capital than the little man could afford, and so it was left to the rich who could employ hired labour and slaves.

The parallel between English farming and Athenian is curiously close. With large industrial populations dependent upon imported foodstuffs, agriculture must languish. To such countries the maintenance of the trade routes is of vital importance, necessitating large fleets and a constantly watchful foreign policy to seek and maintain markets for manufactured

[1] *Céréales*, pp. 198–9.   [2] Xen. *Revenues*, iv, 6.

products. It would be unfair to accuse the Greeks of lack of enterprise or dullness with regard to their agricultural methods to account for any apparent backwardness. Everything combined to make the worst possible conditions for the Greek farmer. Too poorly endowed with cultivable lands; too dry to afford pasture to raise cattle for manure, Greece had all the disadvantages of intensive cultivation without any of the advantages.[1]

AGRICULTURE AFTER THE PELOPONNESIAN WAR

It was in agriculture that the worst destruction of the wars was seen. Year after year the fields of the combatants on both sides had been harried and the crops destroyed. To burn standing grain was at worst only a temporary loss to the owners which could be repaired in no long time: to cut down the olive plantations of the enemy was an almost irreplaceable loss. Such was the fate of Attica, and nothing shows the bitterness of the struggle more than this action.[2] Not only were the plantations destroyed but their enemies had burned down all farm buildings and driven off such livestock as remained.[3] The loss of life in the war had been heavy; many had died in the great plague of 430, and slave labour was scarce owing to desertions to the enemy. There is reason to suppose that the soil of Attica never wholly regained its former fertility, and it has also been suggested that owing to neglect of the land and proper drainage, malaria, hitherto unknown in Greece, began to sap the vitality of the people.[4]

The task of restoring the farms of Attica from the destruction of war, replanting of olive groves and vineyards was a slow and very expensive one, which gave ample scope to the moneylender to drive extortionate bargains with poor borrowers. As

---

[1] Jardé, *Céréales*, p. 89.   [2] Cf. Deut. xx. 19.
[3] Thuc. vii, 27.
[4] Jones, *Malaria: A Neglected Factor in the History of Greece and Rome*. Dr Jones gives evidence to suggest that up to 400 in Greece and 200 in Italy malaria was almost unknown. It may be remarked that the intensive methods of the best period of Greek agriculture would of themselves prevent malaria. It is reasonable to suppose that Dr Jones has put the date at least one century too early for Greece.

in the time of Solon the land became overburdened with debts, as the number of steles or mortgage stones of the fourth century testify. The small farmer began to be forced off the land; he had no capital to repair the losses he had sustained nor even to carry on. Evidently a lot of land went right out of cultivation altogether owing to its owners having been evicted for debt. A paying business was done by capitalists buying such impoverished lands up and reconditioning them for resale. The father of Ischomachus, the model farmer (and husband), had made a good thing out of such transactions.[1] More and more agriculture became capitalistic in form. It is significant that we hear in the later fourth century from a speech attributed to Demosthenes of the largest estate on record, that of Phaenippus, which we are told had a circumference of 40 stades, which must have been about 750 acres and produced 1000 medimni of barley (about 2500 bushels) and 800 metretes of wine. Isaeus[2] mentions a farm worth $2\frac{1}{2}$ talents, which brought in an income of 12 minae per annum, i.e. 8 per cent, not a very large return. No wonder capitalists preferred to invest their money in ship loans.

With the wars of the successors of Alexander and all the dislocations and troubles that followed, the small farmer was ruined, deserted his little holding or was forced off it, and enlisted in one of the mercenary armies. If he survived he could get land from Ptolemy or Seleucus, who were only too glad to have Greek settlers in their dominions. While there never were in Greece the great farms, the "latifundia" of Italy, because the configuration of the land did not permit of such, except perhaps to a small extent in Boeotia and Thessaly, yet large landowners possessed a number of holdings scattered about which they operated by means of bailiffs and slave gangs. The violent agrarian troubles seen in Laconia connected with Agis and Cleomenes were symptomatic of that very deep-rooted antagonism between the landless man and the rich capitalist which became worse in the Hellenistic era. The small farmer had gone, and the so-called "reforms" of the Spartan revolutionaries were attempts to get the people back on the land,

---

[1] Xen. *Oecon.* xx, 22. Cf. Heitland, *Agricola*, p. 36.
[2] xi, 42.

a hopeless and impossible thing at so late a time. Roman capitalism, when it began to exploit the world, had no place for the small farmer, and it is to be noted that often the capitalist class in Greece was pro-Roman. Greek agriculture under Rome went from bad to worse, and it is probably correct to say that the free population declined absolutely.[1]

The grinding burden of taxation, the exactions of the Roman Publicani had done their work at last and Greece was exhausted. The land had been overcropped and soil exhaustion and deforestation advanced rapidly. Dio Chrysostom[2] presents a lamentable picture of the state of affairs in Euboea. Two-thirds of the territory belonging to Chalcis were completely deserted owing, he says, to carelessness and lack of men to cultivate the land. Large proprietors were only too glad to pay if anyone could be found willing to work. The land outside the gates looked like a wilderness rather than a prosperous suburb, as in former times. Strabo tells us of Eurycles of Sparta who owned the entire island of Cythera.[3] The old evil, to which no solution had ever been found, of subdivision of land to the point where the individual holdings were too small for economic efficiency, had at last solved itself very drastically and the reverse process set in; the possessions of landowners became ever larger. Emigrants sold their lands, or even abandoned them; families died out and their little possessions were absorbed into the great estates. We hear of estates of 5000 acres; we are told that 100 proprietors possessed 200,000 acres in Laconia. Boeotia, once the most fertile country of Greece, became a land of large estates held by hard-drinking country squires, who cared more for hunting and carousals than for the welfare of their miserable tenants.[4] In Attica the rural parts steadily dwindled in population. In Thessaly the cities tried a back-to-the-land policy by buying up estates and planting urban dwellers on small holdings, but without success. The brilliance of the Hellenistic era covered a deep-seated and ineradicable canker of agrarian decay. The Turk has often enough been accused of misrule and the ruination of the lands he conquered, and much of the backwardness of Eastern European agriculture may no doubt be attributed to

---

[1] Heitland, *Agricola*, p. 129.
[2] *Orat.* vii, *passim.*
[3] viii, 5, 1 (c. 365).
[4] Polyb. xx, 4.

his oppression. One thing, however, can be placed to his credit, the introduction of the raisin which for centuries has been the backbone of whatever prosperity modern Greece enjoys.

THE SLAVE IN AGRICULTURE[1]

In another chapter it is remarked that probably, if not certainly, the number of slaves employed in agriculture was comparatively small. Slave labour, except on big estates engaged in large-scale production, does not pay on the land. How many slaves were working in agriculture in Attica it is quite impossible to say. Cato estimated that a farm of 150 acres, devoted principally to olives, required thirteen people. Sixty-two and one-half acres mostly in vineyards required sixteen workers, or an average of one worker to 7·3 acres.[2] What was the cultivable area of Attica? If we put it at about 140,000 acres, we should have a total of agricultural workers of something under 20,000. But Cato was reckoning on units of 150 acres, which certainly was too big for Attica in the fifth and fourth centuries. We should probably be safe, therefore, in halving that number and saying that less than 10,000 slaves were working on the land. Even the very large farm of Phaenippus had only seven slaves working on it. It is hard to suppose that on little holdings of 10 or 15 acres more than one slave was kept, more probably none at all. It must have been one of the more prosperous farmers who possessed a field slave and an indoor domestic servant, as Aristophanes depicts in a rather pleasing scene of rustic jollity.[3] At harvest time gangs of hired workers went from farm to farm to help out, but whether they were slave or free is hard to tell.[4]

---

[1] Sargent, *Size of Slave Population in Attica*; Heitland, *Agricola*.
[2] *De Agri Cult.* x, 11. Varro, *Res Rust.* i, 18, agrees with these figures.
[3] *Pax*, 1140.
[4] *Vespae*, 712. Cf. Heitland, *Agricola*, p. 47. In a record of seventy-nine male slaves who had been set free, only twelve were agricultural workers; out of fifty-six women there were none (*I.G.* ii², 1553 ff.).

CHAPTER III

MINING AND MINERALS[1]

I T is typical of the difficulty so often found in obtaining exact knowledge of the economic conditions of Ancient Greece, that with the exception of the mines of Laurium, of which we know a good deal, evidence with regard to mining is very scanty. This is particularly noticeable in the case of iron, so important a metal that it could be not unreasonably expected to have yielded many references in ancient authors. The very reverse is, however, the case, and we must be content with a few scattered and unsatisfactory sources of evidence, and such inferences as we may reasonably draw therefrom. Not only is this the case, but the Greeks laboured with such perseverance in their mining operations as to have completely worked out the deposits, and the course of time has obliterated all trace of them in many instances, so that positive identification is sometimes impossible.

GOLD[2]

It is most noticeable in Homer to observe the apparent richness of the kings in gold, and the wonderful hoards discovered by Schliemann in Mycenae go far to substantiate this. We must, of course, discount very heavily the fairy tales that represent the vast wealth of the heroes; but nevertheless it cannot be doubted that there was a great deal of the metal in Greece in the time of Homer; the references are too frequent and exact to permit any other conclusion. If we conclude that the Mycenaeans were rich in gold, we are left with the problem of its origin. Mr O. Davies in a paper entitled "Bronze Age Mining round

---

[1] Gen. references: Orth, art. "Bergbau" in *P.W.* Suppl. iv, 108ff.; art. "Metalla" in *D.S.*; arts. "Bergbau", "Edelmetall", "Metall" by Ebert in *Reallex. der Vorgeschichte*; H. Bluemner, *Technologie und Terminologie der Griechen und Römern*; E. Schönbauer, "Beiträge zur Geschichte des Bergbaurechtes," *Münch. Beiträge zur Papyrusforschung und Antiken Rechtsgeschichte*, xii (1929), pp. 13ff.; K. C. Bailey, *The Elder Pliny's Chapters on Chemical Subjects*.

[2] Art. "Gold" in *P.W.* iii, 1555ff.

the Aegean ",[1] gives reasons to conclude that probably some came from Macedonia or Thasos. Siphnos did not produce any as early as that, but Egypt was working gold mines at a very early age, and probably some went from there to Greece in trade, or captured by pirates. Mr Davies is of the opinion that local sources were early worked out and their origin lost. Undoubtedly some came from the Danube valley and Transylvania, a conclusion which is supported by the evidence of chemical analysis. We are left, therefore, in a good deal of uncertainty as to the sources of gold in the Mycenaean Age, except that most of it reached Greece through the depredations of the pirates.

But if at an early date gold was plentiful in Greece, it certainly was not in historical times. The frequent references to the awe with which the riches of Croesus and Midas were regarded, show that the hoards of Mycenaean times no longer existed, but were buried or dissipated. So scarce was gold that Herodotus tells us that when the Lacedaemonians wished to make a statue of Apollo in gold, they had none and had to procure it from Croesus.[2] Hiero of Syracuse could find none to make a statue of Victory and a tripod for Delphi, and at last found some at Corinth, which he purchased from one Archiletes who had gathered it in small quantities. So valuable was it that Hiero paid him with a whole shipload of wheat and many other gifts.[3] Athenaeus speaks of the scarcity of gold right up to the time of Philip of Macedon.[4] Evidently what gold came to Greece was in small quantities until Philip began to exploit the Macedonian mines.

With regard to the sources of gold supply in the post-Mycenaean era the evidence is scanty.[5] Strabo says: "The wealth of Tantalus and the Pelopidae arose from the mines round Phrygia and Sipylus; that of Cadmus from those round Thrace and Mount Pangaeus; that of Priam from gold mines at Astyra near Abydos [of which to-day there are still small remains, here the amount of earth thrown out is considerable and the excavations are signs of mining in olden times]; that

---

[1] *Nature*, December 31st, 1932.   [2] Her. i, 69.
[3] Athen. vi, 232 B.   [4] Athen. vi, 230 F.
[5] But cf. Bluemner, *Technologie*, iv, 20f., who thinks that considerable quantities came from Thrace.

of Midas from those round Mount Bermius; that of Gyges and Alyattes and Croesus from those in Lydia, and from the region between Atarneus and Pergamum, where is a small deserted town, whose lands have been exhausted of ore."[1] Turning to more certain evidence, the most famous sources were the islands of Thasos and Siphnos. Of Thasos, Herodotus says: "The inhabitants of the island were so rich that they were able to fortify their city to resist the onslaught of the Persians [in 491] and the siege of Histiaeus. Their revenues arose both from the continent and from their own mines. From the gold mines of Scapte-Hyle came in all eighty talents every year, and from those in Thasos less indeed than that amount yet so much that as they were exempt from taxes on the produce of the soil, there came in to the Thasians in all from the continent and the mines a revenue of two hundred talents yearly, and when production was at its height, three hundred talents. I myself have seen these mines, and by far the most wonderful of them are those which the Phoenicians discovered, who with Thasus colonised the island and gave it his name. These Phoenician mines are in that part of the island between a place called Aenyra and Coenyra, opposite Samothrace, where a large mountain has been thrown upside down in the search."[2] With regard to Siphnos Herodotus says: "They were the richest of all the islanders, having in their island both gold and silver mines, so that from the tenth of the money accruing from thence a treasure is laid up in Delphi equal to the richest, and they used every year to divide the riches that came from the mines."[3] It is always unwise to give too much credence to statements of amounts or numbers in ancient times, and these with regard to the gold from both islands are undoubtedly exaggerations, except in so far as they refer to the production over a few years. These deposits were, in fact, not mines but pockets of gold which were quickly exhausted. The failure of the Siphnian supply was attributed by the ancients to the resentment of Apollo at their failure to give a tithe to Delphi.[4] The riches of Siphnos attracted the cupidity of the

---

[1] Strabo, xiv, 5, 28 (c. 680).
[2] Her. vi, 46–7.　　　　　　　　　[3] Her. iii, 57.
[4] Paus. x, 11, 2; J. T. Bent, "On the mines of Siphnos", *J.H.S.* vi (1885), p. 231 ff.

Samians who were, as Herodotus dryly remarks, "in want of money", and in 524, in consequence of a piratical expedition, extorted a ransom of 100 talents. This led to reprisals from Aegina, which suggests either that from the island it drew much of its wealth, or that the Aeginetans punished the Samians as pirates in their endeavour to maintain the safety of the seas. We have no direct evidence that Siphnos was in the possession of Aegina, and Herodotus puts the punishment of the Samians down to an old grudge.[1]

The most famous of all gold-mining regions was that of the River Strymon in Thracian Paeonia along with the silver mines of Mount Pangaeus, which was, according to Herodotus, "a great and high mountain abounding in mines of gold and silver belonging to the Pierians, Odomanti and especially the Satrae".[2] As a matter of fact the mines were not in the mountain, but in the alluvial deposits in the foothills washed down from the mountain above. On the southern spur there can still be seen old workings called Asemotrupai, or "silver holes", in modern Greek.[3] Near by were the mines in Krenides, the centre of the mining district, later named Philippi when under Macedonian rule. Strabo mentions it as follows: "There are numerous gold mines near to Krenides, where the city of Philippi now stands, near Mount Pangaeus. Pangaeus itself, and the country on the east of the Strymon and on the west as far as Paeonia, contains gold and silver mines. Particles of gold, it is said, are found in Paeonia in ploughing the land."[4] Eastwards was the hill of Asyla from which Philip obtained, at least according to Diodorus, a thousand talents of gold a year.[5] The first reference to silver from Pangaeus is when Peisistratus, on his second exile in 556, according to Aristotle "went to the parts about Pangaeus, where he coined money; and having hired soldiers he went back to Eretria, and in the eleventh year made his first attempt to recover his position by force".[6]

In a passage from Agatharchides quoted by Diodorus,[7] we have the best description of the process of gold mining and smelting in the Nubian workings carried on under the monopoly

[1] Her. iii, 59.　　　　　　　　　　[2] Her. vii, 112.
[3] Casson, *Macedonia*, p. 63.　　　[4] Strabo, vii, Fragment, 34.
[5] Diod. xvi, 8, 6.　　　　　　　　　[6] Arist. *Ath. Pol.* xv, 2.
[7] iii, 12.

of the Ptolemies. The mines are situated "in the extremities of Egypt on the frontiers of Arabia and Ethiopia". There is found a country where "the earth is of a black colour full of streaks and veins of a remarkable whiteness which surpasses the most brilliant natural products"..."the hardest of the earth that contains the gold is exposed to a fierce fire so that it cracks and then they apply hand labour to it; when the rock is soft it is worked by iron tools in the hands of the labourers. The foreman, who distinguishes one sort of rock from another, instructs the workers and assigns them their tasks. The strongest pound the shining rock with iron hammers, driving galleries, though not in a straight line but in the direction taken naturally by the glistening stone. These workers on account of the windings of these galleries live in darkness and carry lamps attached to their foreheads. According to the peculiarities of the veins they have to get into all sorts of positions and throw on the floor the fragments they hew out. Young children crawl through the galleries and bring up to the surface the broken stones. Those workers who are over thirty years of age take an assigned portion of these stones and crush them in stone mortars with iron pestles to the size of a pea. Women and old men then take these and put them into mills, of which there are a number in a row, and grind them to the consistency of flour. Finally other workers rub the reduced white rock, pouring on water on a wide board slightly inclined. Thereby the earthy part is dissolved and runs down the slope of the board and the gold sticking to the wood remains because of its weight, and doing this often, first they rub it slightly with their hands and then with fine sponges gently pressing the powdered earth, lifting it by these means until the gold-dust is pure. Lastly other workers take over by measure and weight what is left and put it into earthenware pots, mixing with the gold a proportionate lump of lead and grains of salt with a little tin and barley bran. Having fitted a cover to the pot and smeared it round the edges very carefully with clay, they bake it in an oven five days and as many nights without ceasing, and when it is cold they find nothing left in the pots of the other things, but the gold is pure although a little reduced in quantity."

Such a description is perfectly recognisable to the modern

metallurgist. The white stone is obviously quartz containing native gold. The veins were exploited by means of a series of adit-levels. The rock was loosened by the fire-setting method, a fire being placed against the face of the rock, which on cooling cracked so as easily to be broken with picks. After pulverising in hand querns the gold was separated from the "gangue" or earth by the aid of water on the washing tables. The smelting was done in cupels, the covers of which were "luted" to stop all cracks. Lead was added as a scorifier, salt as a flux, barley bran as a reducing agent. The only explanation of the addition of tin was that it was needed as an alloy for hardening. After a long exposure to heat the lead and salt had been absorbed in the clay cupel, the gold and tin remained.

It is unnecessary here to speak of the really appalling conditions under which the miserable labourers worked. "There is no one who seeing these luckless people would not pity them in their misery; for there is no forgiveness or relaxation at all for the sick or the lame, the aged or for the weakness of the women, but all with blows are kept at their labour until they die worn out by their servitude. Thus the poor wretches dread the future more than the present because of the horrors of their state and look to death as preferable to life."[1]

Silver[2]

In many mines gold and silver were found together in the form of natural amalgam, electrum, which the metallurgical skill of the earlier miners was unable to separate. We have no record of when this was first accomplished, perhaps in the time of Croesus. Pure silver was found apparently in only two places in Greece proper and one in Macedonia. Of the silver mines of Damastium in Epirus, now Monastir, we know very little, the only reference being in Strabo, who says they lay between the Ceraunian promontory, north of Corcyra, and the territories of Epidamnus and Apollonia; of how early they were first worked

---

[1] Diod. *loc. cit.*

[2] Ardaillon, *Les mines de Laurion dans l'antiquité*; M. Cary, *Sources of Silver for the Greek World* in *Mélanges Gustave Glotz*, Paris, 1932; art. "Silber" by Bluemner in *P.W.*; Momigliano, A., *Sull' Amministrazione del Miniere del Laurio.* Athenaeum x (1932), p. 247.

we have no information.[1] In Macedonia were the silver mines of Dysorum, from which Herodotus says "in later times a talent of silver came in daily to Alexander".[2]

By far the most famous and valuable of all silver mines worked by the Greeks were those of Laurium in Attica, from which the Athenians derived great wealth. Of these our knowledge is fairly extensive owing to careful exploration of the site, which has been left substantially in the condition it was when the workings were finally abandoned. M. Ardaillon, in his invaluable treatise, has told us practically everything that can be ascertained of these mines, and in our consideration of the subject we will follow him closely.

We have no information as to the first discovery of silver in the locality; we can but conjecture that the sharp eyes of the Phoenicians as they sailed by Sunium saw the red of the silver-bearing limestone and marked it down as a likely place for profitable working. "That they were worked in very ancient times is well known to all; for assuredly no one tries to specify at what time they began to be worked," says Xenophon.[3] In any case such exploitation must have been very crude, a mere scratching of the ground, and it was probably not until the time of Peisistratus that anything like systematic exploitation took place. It is also clear that Peisistratus owed much of his success as a ruler, at least after his return from exile for the second time in 546, to his command of the mines, and it has been suggested by Mr Ure that he re-entered Athens victoriously as the leader of the miners.[4] A tyrant in command of large resources, and revenues "partly collected at home and partly drawn from the river Strymon",[5] was sure of an enthusiastic support from the more needy of the citizens; "home" here clearly indicating the silver workings of Laurium. In any case the "owls" coined first by Peisistratus evidently were made from silver from Laurium. It is possible that he brought experienced miners from Thrace, since there is a Maroneia in

---

[1] Strabo, vii, 7, 8 (c. 326); cf. Beaumont, *J.H.S.* lvi (1936), p. 181; O. Davies, *Roman Mines in Europe*, p. 239, who is doubtful of the early working of the Damastium mines.

[2] Her. v, 17.　　　　　　　　　　[3] *Revenues*, iv, 2.

[4] P. N. Ure, *Origin of Tyranny*, p. 38.

[5] Her. i, 64.

Thrace as well as Attica; but this is pure conjecture. We know little of the history of the mines after Peisistratus, but must suppose that exploitation went on continuously. It was not, apparently, until the beginning of the fifth century that really valuable ore masses were encountered.[1] Indeed it is possible to fix the date within the decade 490–80, since it is quite certain that the Athenians possessed no considerable treasure at the first invasion of the Persians, and in 480 we have the action of Themistocles in restraining them from dividing the silver coming from the mines between them, but instead spending it on building a fleet. Aristotle recounts the incident thus. "The third year after this when Nicomedes was archon (484–3) the mines at Maroneia were discovered, and their working gave the state a revenue of a hundred talents. While sundry persons advised the people to divide the money among themselves, Themistocles dissuaded them; he did not make clear what use he proposed to make of the money, but he asked them to lend one talent apiece to one hundred of the richest citizens. If later the use made of the money was approved, it could be debited to the state, and if not, they could recall the money and dispose of it as they thought fit. He obtained the money on these conditions, each of the hundred citizens building one ship, and with these ships they fought the barbarian at Salamis."[2] For the next seventy years the mines were vigorously worked, and from them as well as from the tributes of the allies, Athens obtained the wealth that enabled her to rule as an empire the Delian League. In 413 came the seizure of Decelea by the Spartans on the advice of Alcibiades. "You will be masters of the greater part of the wealth of the country. By the same stroke the Athenians will be deprived of the product of their silver mines and all that they yield."[3] The effect upon Athens was disastrous, twenty thousand slaves ran away, among them apparently the whole number of those at work in the mines; at least we may be sure that these over-worked unfortunates would

[1] Mr Cary makes the interesting suggestion that Callias, named Lakko-ploutos, the richest man of his day, made his fortune by opening up new veins of ore; *Class. Rev.* May 1936, p. 55. But much uncertainty as to Callias; cf. Athen. xii, 536 F; Plut. *Arist.* 5.

[2] Arist. *Ath. Pol.* xxii, 7. Cf. also Thuc. i, 14; Plutarch, *Themistocles*, 4.

[3] Thuc. vi, 91, 6.

be the first to snatch at the chance of flying from their unhappy toil. Athens was cut off from her richest source of revenue, and it is significant that in 407 the Athenians were forced to melt down the golden treasures of the temples and issue the first gold coins in the history of the city, and in 406 a copper issue appeared, much to the discontent of the populace.

For the next half century we hear almost nothing of the mines, but it is quite certain that work was not entirely abandoned;[1] in fact we have evidence that work went on during the first half of the fourth century. Xenophon, in his pamphlet "On Revenues", in which he advocates state action to exploit the mines, writing in 354 says that many fortunes have been and still are being made by private individuals as lessees of mining claims. Evidently Xenophon's scheme was not acted upon and private exploitation under state leases continued.[2] Certainly during the second half of the fourth century activity was maintained, as we hear of various cases coming up in the courts dealing with affairs at Laurium. Teisis, an informer, denounces Philippus and Nausicles for concealing the large income they got from their concessions.[3] Lysander, another informer, prosecutes Epicrates who with others had taken 300 talents in three years from the same source.[4] Diphilus at some date between 345–325 was condemned to death for having removed the pillars or stopes in the mines, and his fortune amounting to 160 talents was confiscated.[5] Under Lycurgus, the best finance minister the Athenians ever had, the public receipts from the mines were said to have amounted to 200 talents a year for twelve years after 338. These enormous sums seem to point to intensive

[1] As Bury suggests: "The mines of Laurium were not to be reopened again till three-quarters of a century had passed" (*History of Greece*, p. 485). Socrates asks Glaucon why the mines were producing less than formerly, not why they were closed down (Xen. *Mem.* iii, 6, 12).

[2] Schwahn, "Die Xenophontischen Poroi", *Rhein. Mus.* 1931, p. 253.
Schwahn is of the opinion that the proposals of Xenophon were impossible and never acted upon. In any case, under the most favourable circumstances, the benefits to accrue to Athens would only come very slowly, in his estimation not for a hundred years.

[3] Hyperides, *Pro Eux.* 36.   [4] *Ibid.* 37.

[5] Plut. *Vit. X Orat. Lyc.* 343 D. Miss Sargent suggests that investors pooled their interests in some sort of organised companies, and that the fortune of Diphilus really represented the assets of Diphilus and Co.; the silent partners in the firm would not have cared to make themselves known under the circumstances—*Size of Slave Population*, p. 92.

working, probably on a new and rich seam in the ore bodies.[1] From that time forward we hear little of Laurium; possibly the richer veins had been worked out, and in any event after Alexander the immense amount of treasure poured into the world from the Persian hoards, which raised prices and particularly the cost of working the mines, made further exploitation unprofitable. Modern examination of the ancient workings reveals that the ores had been exhausted. We do know, however, that some work was going on in the second century. Athenaeus, quoting Demetrius of Phalerum, speaks of the activity of Attic miners. "To see these men digging into the earth with so much ardour, one might suppose that they hoped to dig out Pluto himself."[2] A century later Strabo says that work was going on in resmelting the lead that had been left.[3] Such, as far as we know, was the end of the mines of Laurium in ancient times, "that fountain of running silver, a treasure of the land", as Aeschylus called it.[4] In 1864 a French company reopened the mines, and by 1870 had shipped 8670 tons of argentiferous lead from Ergasteria, and since then the deposits have been regularly worked, principally for zinc. At the present time small quantities of iron, lead, copper, sulphur and arsenic are also regularly produced.

THE LAURIUM REGION

To turn now to the region where mining was carried on, it will be observed that it lay in the southern part of Attica near the promontory of Sunium, about 25 miles south of Athens. The workings penetrate to low rocky hills that reach from Thoricus on the Aegean to Anaphlystus on the west, a distance of about 7 miles. In order to comprehend fully the problems which faced the Athenian miners, it is essential that the geology of the region be understood. The argentiferous ore occurs in a limestone of cretaceous age near its contact with schist. There are in all three of these "contacts" or layers of ore to which the miners have penetrated. On the top is a layer of limestone partly eroded, under which lies the first contact imposed upon

[1] Ardaillon, *Les mines de Laurion*, p. 158.
[2] Athen. vi, 233 E.
[3] Strabo, ix, 1, 23 (c. 399).
[4] *Persae*, 238.

mica schist. Most of this first contact had already been removed by erosion when the mines were first worked, but what remained was undoubtedly the scene of the earliest operations. Horizontal cuts or adits (the *laurai* or alleys from which the place took its name) were driven into the hillsides and the first layer removed before the miners penetrated deeper. As they drove their galleries they noticed that in the underlying schist were veins of ore, and in following these downwards they struck the second contact which lay above another stratum of limestone. Having cut through this, they reached the third and by far the richest contact. There is no means by which we can arrive at any date at which the second and third levels were reached. Perhaps the second level was found at the time of the Persian invasion and the third in the second half of the fourth century, but this is pure conjecture.

The ore was chiefly galena, the sulphide of lead, which yielded in different places from 30 to 300 oz. of silver per ton. It can easily be seen how rich a prize the best workings must have been, and how hazardous the speculation which provided the capital for exploitation; it all depended, as does mining to-day, whether the ore struck was rich or poor in silver. In all three contacts the ore was found in globular masses of irregular shape and size, at times as much as 35 ft. thick, imbedded in fissures of the schist. Along with the galena went pyrite and blende, the sulphides of iron and zinc. Over 2000 shafts were sunk to reach the second and third contacts, the deepest of them 386 ft. deep, the main shafts being from 4 to 6 ft. in diameter. From these shafts branched off galleries, many of them only 2 ft. in height and width, along which the miners crawled on their way to the ore masses upon which they worked and through which the extracted ore was hauled to the shafts for raising to the surface. The extraordinary smallness of many of these passages would almost suggest that children were used to carry out the ore, a by no means impossible thing when we remember that at the beginning of the nineteenth century in the coal mines of England such were regularly employed in this labour; this is, however, purely conjectural.[1]

[1] Cf. Ardaillon, *Les mines de Laurion*, p. 91. We know that children were so employed in the Nubian gold mines. It is extremely doubtful, however, if the more humane attitude of the Athenians towards slave labour would have tolerated such practice.

The larger ore masses were removed by digging downwards, this "underhand stoping" being aided by inclined drifts up or down as required to connect with the nearest level, but some was done upward or "overhand", followed by underfoot filling. The system of stoping was of the "pillar and stall" type.[1] Mining was carried on in "good ground" and there was little need for propping, although we do know that lumber for pit props was imported,[2] and remains of props, curiously enough of olive wood, have been found.[3] The workings were dry, but must have been hard to ventilate since the passages are small and crooked. How ventilation was managed is, however, fairly evident. The main drifts run in duplicate parallel to each other, connected by cross-cuts for the circulation of air. These drifts were helped by numerous entries which were closed or opened to control the current of air. One way by which presumably ventilation was secured was by lighting a fire at the bottom of one shaft to draw the air upwards so that cold air should fall down a parallel shaft. This primitive but effectual method is well known to miners, and may explain a very obscure passage in one of the speeches of Demosthenes which refers to "under-firing" in a mine.[4] But in any case we know that there was difficulty in ventilation and that, in consequence, the mines were unhealthy.[5] Each miner had a lamp which held enough oil to last for 10 hours, the length of his shift;[6] niches in the rock are to be seen where the lamps were placed. His tools were hammer, pick and shovel and wedges made of iron tempered by plunging in water. Each miner broke about 25 tons of ore a month, and this ore was carried to the shafts by basket carriers (*thulakophoroi*).[7] There is no actual evidence that ore was hoisted to the surface by windlasses, but as M. Ardaillon

[1] Cf. Poll. iii, 87, vii, 98; Plut. *Vit. X Orat. Lyc.* 843 D.

[2] Dem. *in Mid.* 167.

[3] Ardaillon, *Les mines de Laurion*, p. 56; cf. Vitruvius, v, 12, 6. Olive wood piles for under-water work. But the Laurium workings were dry.

[4] *In Pantaen.* 36. Boeckh suggests it refers to burning props. It is hard to suppose it means fire setting to loosen the ore, as probably this method was not used, the difficulty of getting the smoke out would be too great. Perhaps it was a deliberate attempt to smother the miners. No satisfactory explanation can be given. Cf. Ardaillon, *Les mines de Laurion*, pp. 56, 203.

[5] Plut. *Comp. Nicias et Crassus*, 1; Xen. *Mem.* iii, 6, 12.

[6] Cf. Pliny, *H.N.* xxxiii, 4, 70; 6, 97.

[7] Poll. vii, 100. Hesych. s.v.; Pliny, *H.N.* xxxiii, 4, 71.

remarks, since that was the means employed in Roman mines we may conclude it was also practised at Laurium.

When the ore reached the surface it was first crushed in mortars with an iron pestle. These mortars, of which remains have been found, were of very hard trachyte, which came undoubtedly from Melos. After being reduced in this fashion the ore was milled.[1] These mills were made of the same hard rock, and consisted of a round central stone set in the ground and tapering towards the top. Over this was fitted another hollow stone, shaped somewhat like a cup without a bottom, which revolved on the centre stone. The ore was poured in at the top, and as the outer stone revolved it was ground and filtered through between the two. The outer stone was suspended on an upright pillar of wood imbedded in the centre stone, revolving on an iron collar. By raising or lowering this collar, the interstice between the outer and inner stones could be widened or contracted in order to obtain a coarser or finer grinding. Very probably the ore was put through several times to obtain the finest results. To the outer stone were attached by sockets bars like those of a capstan by which it was made to revolve. Evidently this was done by man-power; there are no indications that horses or mules were used to turn the mill.

The ore having been milled the next process was to wash it. Since the district has no running streams, the miners were forced to rely on rainfall which was carefully gathered in large cisterns. From these the water was led by runlets to a series of inclined planes or washing tables made of masonry covered with cement and provided with "riffles" or ridges. As the water flowed over the tables the lighter and worthless material was carried away and the heavier ore was caught by these riffles. So precious was the water that when it had flowed to the end of the inclined wash-tables it was carried back to the upper reservoir for use again. We must conclude that this was done by hand with buckets as there are no signs of pumps, and although the principle of the siphon was known it was impossible to use in this connection.[2]

---

[1] Diod. iii, 13, 2.

[2] No evidence that the principle of the pump was known to the Greeks before the invention of Ctesibius of Alexandria (c. 250); cf. Vitruv. x, 4f. For the siphon cf. Aristoph. *Thesm.* 557.

The next operation was to smelt the washed ore, which was done in blast furnaces of which remains have been found. The ore was mixed with layers of wood and charcoal[1] which were set alight and blown with a leather bellows. By this process the various chemical impurities were expelled by burning, and the resultant metal residue in the form of "work-lead" trickled to the bottom to be collected in the form of pigs. In this work-lead was contained the silver which had still to be extracted. This was done by "cupellation", that is, by melting the lead in "cupels" or cup-like hearths made of clay. In this process the lead is separated from the silver by being converted into fusible lead oxide or litharge,[2] which is partly absorbed by the cupel, and of which great quantities have been found on the ground. The residue of silver was then taken to the mint where it was given a last refining in a cupel[3] which produced a silver of extreme fineness, the average of a number of coins analysed showing 978 parts fine out of 1000; an extraordinary degree when the crudeness of the method is remembered. Lastly the litharge was resmelted to obtain the lead contained therein. Pigs weighing half a talent or about 33 lb. sold, we are told, in the fourth century for 2 drs. the talent. Pythocles, the Athenian, advised the state to take all the lead from the mines at the regular market price of 2 drs. and sell it at 6 drs. We do not know if his advice was acted upon.[4] By-products were mercuric sulphide or cinnabar[5] and red oxide of lead, or minium.[6]

[1] Cf. Pliny, *H.N.* xviii, 99, xxxiii, 60, 94; Plut. *Symp.* iii, 10 (658 D); Strabo, iii, 2, 8 (c. 146). In these passages a straw fire is said to be superior to one of charcoal; cf. Bailey's note, i, 194.

[2] Cf. Athen. x, 451 D; also Pliny, *H.N.* xxxiii, 60.

[3] Arist. *Probl.* xxiv, 936 B 9; M. Stephanides, "L'essai des Substances chez les Anciens", *Archeion*, xi (1929), p. 375.

[4] Ps.-Arist. *Oecon.* 1353 A; cf. Besnier, "La commerce de plomb dans l'antiquité", *Rev. Arch.* xii (1920), p. 211, xiii, p. 36, xiv, p. 98.

[5] Theoph. *de Lap.* 58; Poll. vii, 129; Diosc. v, 109. The word *Kinnabari* as denoting mercuric sulphide is correctly used both by Theophrastus and Dioscorides. Pliny accuses the Greeks unjustly of confusing Cinnabar with dragon's blood (*Sanies draconis*), a resin from the tree *Pterocarpus draco*. Cf. Pliny, *H.N.* xxxiii, 111 f., xxxv, 50, and Bailey's notes, i, 217.

The confusion as to the use of *Kinnabari* becomes greater when we find it used by Pausanias as a red paint (viii, 39, 6, vii, 26, 11) and in another passage (ii, 2, 6) the word *Eruthra* also indicates some red pigment.

[6] Theoph. *de Lap.* 40, 51; Poll. vii, 100; more correctly *massicot*, which is produced at a temperature below the fusing point of monoxide of lead, the raw material from which minium is made.

From the soot in the flue of the furnace were gathered three compounds whose identification provides some difficulties. *Molybdena* was not, as might be imagined, the modern molybdenum but lead sulphide or galena.[1] *Cadmia*[2] was not the modern cadmium but oxide of zinc or calamine. *Spodos* is not exactly identifiable, but almost certainly was an impure form of zinc oxide.[3]

Into the long and somewhat complicated question as to what was *miltos* and its uses it is unnecessary to enter here in detail. Generally speaking it was red ochre used as a paint and for the glazing of ceramics. That *miltos* was used as a kind of generic name for various medicaments known as Sinopic earth, Lemnian earth and Lemnian Sphragis, appears from references in Pliny, Galen, Dioscorides and Theophrastus. What makes it of some importance in Greek commerce was the fact that it was subject of a treaty between Athens and the island of Ceos, which may be dated conjecturally about the middle of the fourth century. According to this treaty, which was a renewal of an earlier one, the Cean *miltos* was to be exported exclusively to Athens without any duty levied thereon and on Athenian ships.[4] It is a little puzzling to account for the importance of *miltos* that would make it subject of a special treaty. Dr Hasebroek[5] suggests that it was used in painting warships, presumably as an anti-fouling composition. This is possible, were it mixed with some poisonous compound such as red mercuric sulphide. As noted elsewhere, Miss Richter has pointed out very clearly that it did not enter very largely into the ceramic industry; it was not mixed with the clay, but used as a pigment, and it is therefore hard to suppose that it was in great demand by Greek potters. It is true that Theophrastus says that the Cean product was the best,[6] superior to that from Lemnos and Sinope. In default of further evidence as to its importance as a drug, we may accept Dr Hasebroek's conjecture

[1] Arist. *de Gen. An.* ii, 1 (735 B); Diosc. v, 85; Pliny, *H.N.* xxxiv, 173. Cf. Bailey's note, ii, 203, where an alternative, *massicot*, is favoured.

[2] Diosc. v, 84, 3; cf. Bailey's note, ii, 166.

[3] Pliny, *H.N.* xxxiv, 128; cf. Bailey's note, ii, 181.

[4] *I.G.* ii², 1128; cf. Ziebarth, *Beiträge*, p. 72; Heichelheim, art. "Monopole" in *P.W.* xvi, 156.

[5] *Trade and Politics*, p. 141.   [6] *de Lap.* viii, 52.

as to its use in shipbuilding as probably the explanation why *miltos* was valued so highly in Athens.[1]

MINING LEASES

There are a few problems with regard to the leasing of mining properties which have given rise to a considerable amount of controversy from the time of Boeckh until now. Into the various views put forward it is unnecessary to enter here, especially since it seems as if M. Ardaillon had given the best interpretation and it will therefore be convenient to follow him closely.

In the first place we know from Aristotle's *Athenaion Politeia* that there was a board of ten commissioners for Public Contracts (*Poletae*) who "lease the mines and taxes in conjunction with the Military Secretary and the Commissioners of the Theoric fund, in the presence of the Council, and grant to the persons indicated by the vote of the Council, the mines which are let out by the State, including both the 'workable' ones, which are let for three years and those which are let under special agreements for (ten?) years."[2] This passage is obscure, but on consideration it will be seen that it is capable of reasonable interpretation. The whole mining district of Laurium was public domain which was never alienated but let to lessees for a stated number of years. The leases were of two sorts, those of mines which had already been worked, i.e. upon which the preliminary exploration had been effected. These were let for three-year periods. The other sort was for ten years and comprised those which had not been opened and upon which all the preliminary work had still to be done. This explanation is at least a reasonable one and we may suppose is in all probability right. The opening up of a new mine, the sinking of shafts, the exploratory labour before the ore was struck and extraction started must have taken a considerable time, and a shorter lease than ten years would not have been sufficiently attractive to induce speculators to bid for such a privilege. For mines already opened, and the chances they offered for

---

[1] Pliny, *H.N.* xxxv, 33. Bailey, ii, 209, has collected all other references which need not be elaborated here. No red ochre is now produced in the island, but a little is mined at Siderocastro in Arcadia.

[2] *Ath. Pol.* xlvii, 2 (Kenyon's trans.).

profitable exploitation sufficiently apparent, a shorter lease was deemed best. In any case it is practically certain that no mine was held in fee simple. The whole area had been surveyed and mapped by state surveyors and in the archonship of Callimachus a list of "workable" mines had been drawn up to which reference was made when a lease was granted. We have examples of these leases in the fourth century, as for example one which refers to a mine named Hermaikon, which is marked by a pillar, bounded on the north by the wall on the property of Diotimus of Euonymon, on the south by the smelting works of the same Diotimus, on the east by the road from Thoricus to Laurium, and on the west by the road from Laurium to Thrasymus. The lessee was Onetor, son of Arcesilas of Melite, and for it he had given 150 drs.[1] This sum was a common one in the fourth century, not a very large price to pay, while others went for as little as 20 drs. The last must have been hardly more than holes in the ground where a single man worked, or at best with one or two helpers. Such little producers could not possibly have run their own grinders and washing tables. We may surmise these were operated by large concerns which ground, washed and smelted for smaller contractors.

A question to which there is no definite answer through lack of clear evidence is whether the mining rights were apart from those of occupation above ground. All that can be said in that respect is that in all probability a definite area was leased upon which the lessee could sink his shafts, set up his washers and furnaces, and we must suppose the living quarters of his workers. We must conclude that the whole region belonged to the state, and that all private occupation and agriculture had ceased with the expropriation of any landholders who may have been on the spot before mining became important in the locality.[2]

If the question of occupation is obscure, that of the system upon which rent or royalties were paid to the state is even more

---

[1] *I.G.*[2] 2, 1582, Michel, *Rec.* 1514; *I.G.*[2] 2, 1588 (1st ed. 781).

[2] M. Ardaillon discusses these points at considerable length, p. 166ff. Cf. also Meier, Schoemann, Lipsius, *Der Attische Prozess*, p. 1022; Busolt, *Griech. Staats.* ii, 1222, n. 2; Kahrstedt, *Staatsgebiet und Staatsangehörige in Alten*, p. 24; Schönbauer, *Beitr. z. Gesch. des Bergbaurechts*, p. 276; A. Momigliano, *Sull' Amministrazione del Miniere del Laurio* in *Athenaeum* x (1932).

difficult to elucidate. According to Suidas "Those who worked the mines whenever they wished to begin operations made a declaration to the overseers appointed by the state, and for the purposes of taxation were held responsible for a twenty-fourth part of the ore mined." At first sight this would seem to settle the question at once; the state demanded a royalty of slightly over four per cent. But it is not quite as simple as that, for what are we to make of a passage in the speech of Demosthenes against Pantaenetus, in which the plaintiff accuses Nicobulus of having robbed his slave when he was on the way to pay the public treasury the rent of the mine, which he had bought for a talent and a half?[1] Boeckh was the first to suggest that this sum was a premium paid for the right to work a certain property. This is entirely reasonable, and we can easily imagine that when a lease fell in, as it would at the end of three or ten years, as the case might be, it was put up for auction and sold to the highest bidder. But in this case Pantaenetus had bought the lease not from the state but from one Telemachus. We must conclude that Pantaenetus was a sub-lessee. It is easy to imagine that at the auction of leases speculators would try to buy them up in order to make a profit by transferring their lease to another who was willing to take it over. We do not know what Telemachus had given for the lease to the *Poletae*, perhaps a talent, and was making a handsome profit on the principle of a kind of "lease scalping". But however that might have been, we have from this case an unmistakable indication that the four per cent royalty was not the only return that the state received from the mines; leases were sold at auction and from these a considerable revenue must have been derived. M. Ardaillon points out with truth that the statement of Aristotle that in 484 the state received a revenue of 100 talents from the mines[2] would argue a colossal output for that year if that sum came alone from the four per cent royalty,[3] and if it means that such was the income for a single year.

---

[1] *In Pant.* 22.

[2] *Ath. Pol.* xxii, 7; cf. Her. vii, 144; Polyaen. i, 30, 5.

[3] Ardaillon discusses the problem at length, *Les mines de Laurion*, pp. 188 ff.; also in art. "Metalla" in *D.S.* Cf. also Calhoun, "Ancient Athenian mining", *Journ. Econ. and Bus. Hist.* iii, 333 f.; Schönbauer, *Beitr. z. Gesch. d. Bergbaurechts*, pp. 13 f.; Momigliano, *Amministrazione*, p. 247.

A point of considerable uncertainty which has given rise to controversy is whether or not the lessee of a mine enjoyed exemption from the eisphora and performance of liturgies. The supposition that he did so rests upon a passage in one of the speeches of Demosthenes. In the case against Phaenippus, which had to do with an exchange of property or *antidosis*, the plaintiff says that when the parties to the exchange make out an inventory of their possessions they declare on oath that they have given a true account of everything "except property in the silver mines which the laws have made exempt from duty".[1] It would certainly appear strange that the state should exempt from such important taxes the wealthy men who drew large incomes from the mines. Boeckh explains this apparent anomaly on the ground that "the mine proprietor was a tenant in fee-farm who was permitted the use of public property in consideration of the payment of a sum of money and a portion of the yearly produce as rent. But the property taxes and liturgies only fell upon freehold property while the mines being conveyed by the people under the condition that the tenants made an annual payment to the state, were for this reason considered as tax-free." Ardaillon conjectures that the capital that was invested in the mine and the revenue drawn from it were exempt from taxation because they already paid a heavy tax in the form of rent and it was considered just that they should not suffer from a form of double taxation.[2] Such is the only possible conclusion that can be arrived at upon this very obscure and puzzling point. We may suppose that when bidding for a mine lease this fact was kept well in mind and the price paid was in consequence a high one. To secure exemption from such onerous taxation as the Liturgies and Eisphora would be worth while paying a good deal for; we know that Phaenippus paid 90 minas for his.

LABOUR IN THE MINES

The common labour of the mines was performed by slaves, "malefactors and barbarians, some of them in chains, perishing

[1] *In Phaen.* 18.
[2] *Les mines de Laurion*, p. 199. Curiously enough Andreades has nothing to say upon the point.

in these close and unhealthy places".[1] Although there is no recorded instance of a freeman working as a labourer in the underground workings, yet foremen were not invariably slaves,[2] and concessionaires on a small scale, who could not afford an overseer, worked themselves.[3] We know from his tombstone of one Atotes, a Paphlagonian, who boasts of his skill as a metallurgist.[4] A first-class slave foreman was a very valuable possession; we know that Nicias paid a talent for one, an enormous price.[5] Slaves, when not actually owned by the concessionaires themselves, were available for hire in gangs at what was apparently a flat rate of an obol a day, the lessee to provide food, clothing and lodging. We hear of several who owned great numbers who were let out in this way, notably Nicias who had a thousand, Hipponicus six hundred and Philemonides three hundred.[6]

In another chapter we comment upon the treatment of their slaves by the Athenians, and it is not necessary to repeat our observations here, except to say that it is unsafe, and we may affirm unfair, to draw any comparison between the horrifying conditions in the gold mines of Nubia and those at Laurium. The Nubian mines were worked by forced labour which could easily be renewed through the effective means of the press gang. The slaves at Laurium were an investment which had cost a good deal of money; we know from the proposals of Xenophon for working the mines that they cost on an average something over 150 drs.[7] It would be entirely to the interest of their owner to feed them well and keep their health and strength at a high level. M. Ardaillon, on the analogy of the Nubian mines, supposes that some of the lighter work above ground was performed by women; this is possible but we have no evidence on the point. We have already suggested that the smallness of the underground passages would give the impression that the ore was carried out by children. We have no idea as to where or how the slaves were housed; but an allusion in the *Revenues* suggests in barracks close to the mines.[8]

---

[1] Plut. *Comp. Nicias et Crassus*, 1.
[2] Xen. *Revenues*, iv, 22.   [3] *I.G.* ii², 1582–9.
[4] Bérard, *Bull. Corr. Hell.* xii (1888), p. 246.
[5] Xen. *Mem.* ii, 5, 2.   [6] Xen. *Revenues*, iv, 14.
[7] Thiel, *Xen. Por.* p. 53.   [8] Xen. *Revenues*, iv, 49.

As to the numbers employed we have no certainty, although a good many ingenious calculations have been made on the point. Xenophon proposes a maximum purchase of twelve thousand. But as we remark in our section on population, any estimate of the number of slaves in Attica is wildly conjectural and entirely unsafe.

XENOPHON'S PROPOSALS[1]

The author of the little pamphlet, whether he be Xenophon or not—and almost certainly he was not, yet for simplicity we will call him Xenophon—advances a highly ingenious argument for the exploitation of the mines at Laurium at the public expense. With all the persuasiveness of a modern mining prospectus, he paints the picture of the advantages to be gained thereby in the brightest colours. The date can be set with almost certainty at 355–354.[2] He begins by pointing out that the mines are by no means exhausted, in fact he calls them "inexhaustible", which was far from the truth. If so many people were constantly increasing the number of the workers engaged and making large fortunes, why should not the state go into the mining business on a large scale, buy slaves and work the mines itself? He proposes first to buy 1200 slaves, and from the profits made from their work in five or six years the number could be raised to six thousand, and from that number an annual income of sixty talents would be derived from which twenty could be used for the purchase of more slaves.[3] When the number had been brought up to 10,000, the annual income would be 100 talents. That such a number could easily find profitable work can be seen from the fact that normally almost double that number were regularly employed. He also thinks that the state might undertake prospecting for new ore beds in which there might be risk of loss, since private prospectors had often been deterred from doing so on account of the speculative nature of the undertaking. Finally he proposes that the undertaking of the scheme be

[1] J. H. Thiel, *Xenophontos Poroi*; K. von der Liek, *Die Xen. Schrift von den Einkünften.*

[2] Thiel, *Xenophontos Poroi*, p. viii.

[3] I.e. at an obol per day per slave. Xenophon reckons a year at 360 days, so 6000 × 360 = 2,160,000 obols, 36,000 obols to the talent = 60 talents.

divided between the ten tribes, each to open new mines and share the profits and losses between them. He answers the objection that the sudden purchase of large numbers of slaves would tend to raise the price unduly by saying that the affair must be gone about with great circumspection and not in a hurry, so that the market should not be unduly disturbed. And, lastly, he says that a good income could be derived from those who supplied necessities to the mines and set up a market close by.

We have no record of how these proposals were received but evidently they were not acted upon by the state, presumably because of the very large initial outlay involved and the risks attendant upon carrying on the scheme. We can easily imagine that the Athenians would reply that the city was already getting a good revenue from the mines without any risk at all, and to embark on public exploitation would be a most hazardous venture.

MINING LAW

It remains to say a little on the laws governing mining. Civil cases pertaining to mining came before the Thesmothetae, judges who sat in the Commercial court.[1] We have already mentioned the sale of leases and payment of royalties to the Poletae. Any unauthorised working of mining property was an indictable offence before the Assembly. The royalties must be paid promptly at the appointed time; failure to do so involved imprisonment and payment of double the amount.[2] One particularly serious offence was that of cutting away the stopes left to support the excavations; such was punishable by death and confiscation of property.[3] All cases arising from the mines were tried by a special "Mining Court" and, like all commercial causes, belonged to the category of monthly cases, i.e. the judgment had to be delivered within one month. Other offences under the mining law were encroachment upon the ground of another lessee,[4] armed intrusion, the expulsion of the lessee from his ground, and that somewhat mysterious act of "underfiring", whatever that may be, but probably straight arson, the

---

[1] Arist. *Ath. Pol.* lix, 5.   [2] Dem. *in Pant.* 22.

[3] E.g. the case of Diphilus.

[4] E.g. Hyperides, *Pro Eux.*, where Epicrates of Pallene had gone over the limits of his concession.

malicious burning of pit-props to injure the property of another or drive him out because of the smoke.

We find in the suits argued by Demosthenes several that bear very interestingly upon affairs connected with Laurium. In that against Pantaenetus a concession had been bought by the defendant from a certain Telemachus for 90 minas, and in order to do so he had borrowed 105 minas from two friends, Euergus and Nicobulus. While Nicobulus was away Pantaenetus defaulted in his payment of interest, whereupon Euergus seized the mine and started to work it on his own account. He also seized some silver that a slave of Pantaenetus was taking to the public treasury to pay the taxes on the mine, thereby making the original lessee default in his payment and laying him open to a payment of double the amount. Pantaenetus brought suit against Euergus and obtained a verdict with damages of two talents. When Nicobulus returned he arranged with Pantaenetus for the repayment of the 105 minas to Euergus and himself, giving in return the mine and slaves and receiving a release from all demands. But this failed to satisfy Pantaenetus, who saw further chances of harrying the two partners. He started a suit against Euergus, who had not got the same release from him of all claims, and another against Nicobulus alleging that it had been a slave of Nicobulus who had seized the silver, and although he had acted under the orders of Euergus, Nicobulus was responsible for the actions of his servant. Evidently Pantaenetus, having won his original case, was playing the game against the two defendants for all it was worth.

The business of mining was a very risky one. In the case of Phaenippus the plaintiff had lost three talents through forfeiture of his claim, and tells the jury that he has merely shared the general misfortune of all those operating mining concessions. It seems, however, that entire or partial remission of the rent was possible, although we have no clear evidence on the point other than the plea in the same case, "Since you give aid and protection to all that work the mines, come also now to our assistance."[1] Possibly this may refer to a license to explore hitherto unexploited ground, payment to be contingent upon success in finding new ore bodies. There is no way of arriving

[1] Dem. *in Phaen.* 31. The date is about 330.

at the amount of silver taken from the mines, although it has been estimated that well over two million tons of argentiferous lead were treated during the time the mines were being worked.

COPPER[1]

The whole question of the provenance and working of copper is beset with difficulties which are hard and, in some cases, impossible to resolve. These arise from the fact that the Greek word *chalkos* is used indifferently for copper, bronze and very possibly brass, and it may be remarked that the same confusion is found in the Latin *aes*. Since copper, as being comparatively easy to smelt, was (with the possible exception of gold and silver) the first metal to be used by man, the word *chalkos* became identified with metal in general, and the *chalkeus* was a metal worker, a smith, whether it was in copper, iron or the precious metals.

References in Homer to copper and workers in metal are very numerous. Sometimes, as when allusion is made to weapons, the word *chalkos* undoubtedly refers to bronze; at others, when tripods and caldrons are mentioned, it equally undoubtedly means copper. This is substantiated by finds of bronze weapons and copper utensils at Mycenae and Tiryns. With regard to brass, as is mentioned in our section on zinc, there is no certainty whatever. No implements made of brass have been discovered but, on the other hand, there is no reason why brass should not have been known to the ancient world, and there was plenty of zinc in Greece.

Greece at the present time is entirely denuded of copper, and in historic times the Greek got that metal by importation from other countries. There are traces of small workings in the neighbourhood of Mycenae, evidently early exhausted, and we may suppose that some of the copper of Homeric times came from these, but even then most of it must have come from Cyprus. One curious misapprehension which still persists to-day is

[1] Art. "Metalla" in *D.S.*; arts. "Bronze", "Erzguss", "Hydrargyrum", "Kupfer", "Schwefel", in *P.W.*; G. A. Wainwright, "The occurrence of tin and copper near Byblos", *J.E.A.* xx (1934), p. 29; Bluemner, *Technologie*, pp. 38, 64, 81, 88, 91. O. Davies, "Bronze Age mining round the Aegean", *Nature*, December 31st, 1932; *ibid.* "Roman mines"; Lucas, "Notes on the early use of tin and bronze", *J.E.A.* xiv (1928).

that which attributed copper working to Chalcis in Euboea.[1] Geologists have failed to discover the slightest trace of copper in the vicinity, and we must put down the legend to the Greek etymologist's inveterate habit of misunderstanding his own language. It has been suggested with a good deal of plausibility that Chalcis comes from *Kalche*, the purple murex, and that is the more probable since Chalcis was one of the localities in which its fishery was carried on.[2] We may be fairly certain that in Homeric times, apart from the small native supplies, Greece got its copper from Cyprus. Athena, when she took the form of the Taphian Mentes, carried a cargo of iron to Temesa to exchange for copper.[3] It is much more likely to identify Temesa with that place in Cyprus rather than with Tempsa on the west coast of Southern Italy, although admittedly the latter also produced copper. References to copper from Cyprus are frequent and need not be enumerated here.[4] Other sources of supply were Elba,[5] northern Africa on the Numidian coast in Libya;[6] the Thebais[7] and the island of Meroe.[8] Certainly the Egyptians got most of their supplies from the Sinai peninsula, where there are many old copper mines. Whether any copper came west from Chaldaea, the modern Kurdistan where there is copper near Diarbekr, and from Carmania,[9] is very doubtful. Probably little came from India which, as Pliny remarks, was poor in copper and lead,[10] and Theophrastus speaks of copper from an island near the city of Chalcedon:[11] it is not improbable that the Greeks obtained supplies from that source. Copper-zinc ores were plentiful, and still are on the southern shores of the Black Sea.[12] There

---

[1] Strabo, x, 1, 9 (c. 447).
[2] Bluemner, *Technologie*, iv, p. 62, n. 2, p. 74, n. 6.
[3] *Od.* i, 182; cf. Bluemner, *Technologie*, iv, p. 60, n. 6.
[4] E.g. Theoph. *de Lap.* 25; Strabo, xiv, 6, 5 (c. 684), iii, 163; Pliny, *H.N.* vii, 195. Cf. O. Davies, "Copper mines of Cyprus", *Ann. Brit. Sch. Ath.* xxx (1932), p. 74.
[5] Arist. *de Mir. Ausc.* 93, 837 B. Aristotle says the deposits were worked out, but copper is still produced in Elba.
[6] Strabo, xvii, 3, 11 (830).　　　[7] Diod. i, 15, 5.
[8] Strabo, xvii, 2, 2 (c. 821).　　　[9] Strabo, xv, 2, 14 (726).
[10] *H.N.* xxxiv, 163. But Aristotle speaks of the beauty of Indian copper, *de Mir. Ausc.* xlix, 834 A.
[11] *de Lap.* 25; Arist. *de Mir. Ausc.* lviii, 834 B.
[12] Arist. *de Mir. Ausc.* lxii, 835 A. Cf. Ezekiel xxvii. 13, Tubal and Meshech.

was a good deal of copper in Magna Graecia, e.g. from Tempsa in Calabria.[1] And lastly through the Phoenicians the Greeks must have obtained unlimited quantities from Spain, Turdetania and Baetica, and from the mysterious Tartessus which was we must suppose in the vicinity of the rich modern mines of Rio Tinto.[2] On the islands of Siphnos and Paros large quantities of copper slag have been found. The copper mines of Western Crete, supposed to be prehistoric, were only opened in Hellenistic times and continued to be worked until the Middle Ages. On the neighbouring island of Gaudo, the ancient Clauda, there are extensive copper ore deposits. We have no information whatever with regard to the smelting of the ore nor the working of the metal.

ASPHALT

As will be remarked in the section on shipbuilding in the chapter on Industry, there is considerable doubt as to whether wood tar was used exclusively in calking or whether bitumen was also employed, and our knowledge of the use of asphalt or bitumen is very defective. Undoubtedly it was well known, and there are many references to *asphaltos* and *pissasphaltos*. It was found at Zacynthus, the modern Zante;[3] at Epidamnus, or Dyrrhachium, in the land of the Apolloniates, where at the modern Selenizza it is worked to-day.[4] Aristotle says it was common in Macedonia, Thrace and Illyria.[5] But modern surveys reveal no bitumen in Thrace. The Sicilian deposits at the modern Ragusa were well known.[6] It is almost certain that this is the source referred to by Theophrastus as Erineas near Syracuse.[7] A deposit at Gargaliani in Messenia is being worked at the present time.

ASBESTOS

A small deposit of asbestos, early worked out, was found at Karystos at the southern extremity of Euboea and in Cyprus,

[1] Strabo, vi, 1, 5 (c. 255).   [2] Strabo, iii, 2, 11 (c. 148).
[3] Her. iv, 195; Diosc. i, 93; Vitruv. viii, 3, 8.
[4] Strabo, vii (c. 316).
[5] *de Mir. Ausc.* 35, 41, 113, 116, 127. He may possibly be referring to Spinos. Cf. Theoph. *de Lap.* ii, 13.
[6] Pliny, *H.N.* xxxv, 179.   [7] *de Lap.* ii, 15.

where it is still found. Various writers describe its use as a non-inflammable material mostly for lamp-wicks. Investigation of the Cyprus deposits show that it is chrysotile, a green fibrous magnesium silicate, not asbestos proper.[1]

TIN

In the problem of the early provenance of tin we encounter almost insoluble difficulties, which never have been and possibly never will be satisfactorily cleared up. There is much uncertainty as to the derivation of the word *kassiteros*, but in all probability it came from the Sanscrit; which would presumably point to an early supply from the Far East, perhaps through Phoenician middlemen; but of this nothing whatever is known.

It is perfectly certain that tin was well known in Homeric times. Not only did they use it as an amalgam to make bronze, but also they evidently well understood the art of tin plating and apparently, but not certainly, used the pure metal for armour and other purposes.[2] But where the metal came from at that time is more than we can tell with any certainty; perhaps through Phoenicians. Mr Davies suggests that it is not impossible that small deposits were worked in Greece in Mycenaean times at Cirrha near Delphi.[3] Perhaps some came down the Adriatic from Bohemia; whether or not British tin reached Greece in Homeric times is impossible to say.[4]

In historic times it is quite certain that tin came from Britain; but what or where the Kassiterides, the Tin Isles, were, is beyond all reasonable conjecture. Into the long and interminable controversy that would seek to identify them with the Scilly Isles it is quite unnecessary to enter here. Even in ancient times the story of these wonderful isles was doubted, and Herodotus with his usual candour says he cannot identify them.[5] We may, therefore, dismiss the whole muddled controversy, and conclude

[1] Strabo, x, 1, 6 (c. 446); Pliny, *H.N.* xix, 19, xxxvi, 139; Diosc. v, 115; Paus. i, 26, 7; J. W. Evans, *Mineral Mag.* xiv, 143; Bailey, ii, 256; Steph. Byz. *s.v.* Karystos.
[2] Many references, all in *Iliad*, none in *Od.*; e.g. xi, 25, xviii, 613, xxi, 592, xxiii, 503.
[3] "Two north Greek mining towns", *J.H.S.* xlix (1929), p. 89.
[4] Cf. V. G. Childe, *Dawn of European Civilization*; Tozer, *Hist. Anc. Geog.* p. 35, and Cary's note, p. viii (2nd ed.).
[5] iii, 115.

with Mr Haverfield that the Tin Isles were "either a myth or a misunderstanding".[1]

Undoubtedly tin from Cornwall did reach the Mediterranean. Probably before its destruction Tartessus commanded this trade which was taken over by its conquerors the Carthaginians, in whose hands the sea route remained until in their turn they were supplanted by the Romans. But the sea route was not the only one, since there is every reason to suppose that much tin came down to Massalia through its enterprising Phocaean colonists, who worked up the River Rhone into the Rhine and Lake Leman and through the Seine, Loire and Garonne.

Concerning this trade with Britain Diodorus Siculus has some information for us. He says: "The nations of Britain by the headland of Belerium[2] are unusually hospitable, and thanks to their intercourse with foreign traders have grown quite gentle in their manner. They extract the tin from its bed by a cunning process. The bed is of rock but contains earthy interstices along which they cut their galleries. Having smelted the tin, they hammer it into knuckle-bones and convey it to an adjacent island named Ictis. They wait until the ebb-tide has drained the intervening channel, and then convey thither whole loads of tin on waggons."[3] This passage merely plunges us into even worse difficulties. Where was Ictis? Its identification with Vectis, the Isle of Wight, is impossible, and the Mictis of Timaeus does not seem any more plausible.[4] The only place that would seem remotely to correspond with the description is Mount St Michael off Marazion in Mount's Bay, and with that highly dubious identification we must leave the problem unsettled.[5]

We have already mentioned tin from Bohemia, and it is highly probable that some came to Greece from that source in

[1] Art. "Kassiterides" in *P.W.* Cf. R. Hennig, "Zur Frage der Zinninseln", *Rhein. Mus.* lxxxiii (1934), p. 162; Tozer, *Hist. Anc. Geog.* p. 35; Bérard, *Phéniciens et l'Odyssée*, i, 385. Possibly the Coptic "pitran" for tin may be connected with the name Britain first used in Demotic texts from Persian Egypt. Cf. W. Spiegelberg, *Demotisches Handwörterbuch, s.v.*
[2] Probably, but not certainly, Land's End.   [3] Diod. v, 22.
[4] Art. "Ictis" (Haverfield) in *P.W.* on Diod. v, 22; Pliny, *H.N.* v, 104.
[5] Cf. Cary, *J.H.S.* (1924), p. 166; T. Rice Holmes, *Ancient Britain and the Invasions of Julius Caesar*, pp. 499ff.; H. O. Hencken, *The archaeology of Cornwall and Scilly.*

historic times.[1] Strabo talks of tin from Spain; but there is no evidence of its reaching Greece, although there is nothing impossible on that score.[2] He also speaks of tin from the country of the Drangae,[3] which may be identified with modern Afghanistan or Seistan. But of these deposits nothing is known, and it is quite possible that he is confusing tin with zinc, which is found in that region. It may be remarked that the use of the word *plumbum*[4] by Latin writers, especially Pliny, leads to confusion as to whether tin or lead is indicated.[5]

Numismatic evidence, based on an analysis of Athenian bronze coins minted in the late fourth and middle third centuries, shows a marked fall in the amount of tin alloy, from 13·0 to 6·5 per cent, and a rise in the lead from 0·06 to 4·45 per cent.[6] This may simply mean a progressive impoverishment of the Athenian state which entailed using the less valuable metal, or it may indicate a rising tin price owing to a diminution of supplies from Phoenician sources. In support of the latter hypothesis it is observed that after the destruction of Carthage in 146, the tin content falls even more drastically. It is quite possible that until the Romans reopened the tin trade with Britain, there was a scarcity of the metal in the Mediterranean.

ZINC

The knowledge of Greek metallurgists of the working of zinc was imperfect. This is hardly to be wondered at, since a full comprehension of its chemical properties is of recent date, and to this day there is a certain amount of confusion in nomenclature. In its native state zinc is exceedingly rare, only a few

---

[1] R. L. Beaumont, *J.H.S.* lvi (1936), p. 190.

[2] iii, 2, 9 (c. 147). S. Fawns, *Tin Deposits of the World*, pp. 5, 145.

[3] xv, 2, 10 (c. 724).

[4] I.e. *plumbum album* and *plumbum nigrum*.

[5] Pliny, *H.N.* ix, 133, xxxiv, 156. Cf. Bailey's notes, i, 155, ii, 191, where the position of the Tin Isles is discussed once more inconclusively. For further references to tin cf. Arist. *de Color.* 794 B. Tin and copper statues in *Electrides Islands* in the Adriatic (*de Mir. Ausc.* 81, 836 A). One possible source of early tin was Aethalia or Elba, where it is being mined at the present time (*de Mir. Ausc.* 93, 837 B). *Antiquity*, xii (1938), p. 79.

[6] E. R. Caley, "Investigations on the composition of ancient bronzes", *Museum News*, New York, September 1937.

known specimens existing, and in conjunction with other metals it is difficult to smelt, demanding a higher temperature than early metallurgists were ordinarily able to generate.

In dealing with the use of zinc among the Greeks we have to work back and trace the use of the word *oreichalkos*, which we may assume to denote brass, i.e. an amalgam of copper and zinc. Its first extant mention is in one of the Homeric hymns,[1] and the word is used by Hesiod.[2] Very much later Aristotle[3] speaks of a brilliant white copper, produced by the Mossynoeci,[4] who made it not by melting tin with copper but by adding "some kind of" earth. This is probably calamine or Smithsonite (zinc carbonate, $ZnCO_3$),[5] and the copper is brass. Plato in describing Atlantis[6] says that *oreichalkos* is the most precious of all metals after gold, which might have been true in Atlantis, but probably refers here to electrum, a not inexcusable confusion owing to the resemblance of colour. Theophrastus mentions an ore which, when mixed with copper, makes it superior in beauty and colour,[7] which we may infer to be zinc. Strabo,[8] in speaking of Andeira in Asia Minor, mentions an ore "which when burned becomes iron and when heated in furnaces with a certain earth distils 'mock-silver' (*pseudargyros*), and this with the addition of copper makes the 'mixture' as it is called, by others named *oreichalkos*." *Pseudargyros* is zinc, and the method of smelting through distillation is correct, from which we may conclude that the art of metallurgy had considerably developed, although a somewhat puzzling reference in Pollux[9] would seem to suggest that the true nature of *oreichalkos* was not understood.

Into the subsequent use of zinc, both as a metal and as a medicament, it is needless to go, except that it is not without interest to note that, by what is presumably a misunderstanding, Pliny turned *oreichalkos* into *aurichalcum*, misled no doubt by its golden colour.[10] Aurichalcum is evidently "Pinchbeck" or

---

[1] vi, 9. [2] *Scut. Herc.* 122.
[3] *de Mir. Ausc.* lxii, 835 A.
[4] The derivation of the German *Messing* from this is fanciful.
[5] Or, according to American usage, zinc silicate.
[6] *Critias*, 114 E, 116 C. [7] *de Lap.* 49.
[8] xiii, 1, 56 (c. 610). Andeira, the modern village of In-önü. Cf. Leaf, *Strabo in the Troad*, pp. 205, 284, 325.
[9] vii, 100. [10] *H.N.* xxxiv, 2.

"Tombac", a form of Ormolu, which is brass with a low zinc content (10–15 per cent instead of 37 per cent as in true brass). Evidently the early metallurgists had difficulty in using zinc, which accounts for the predominance of bronze. We may, however, conclude that brass was not unknown to the Greeks.[1]

QUICKSILVER

Hydrargyros, or sometimes *argyros chytos*, liquid silver, was well known, but it is doubtful if Greek metallurgists knew of any useful purpose to which it could be put; it is practically certain it was not used in metallurgical processes. Theophrastus[2] says it was made from cinnabar by heating the latter with copper and vinegar. This is perfectly recognisable, and may be explained by saying that the cinnabar dissolved in the vinegar to give an acetate of mercury, the copper reacting with this acetate to give copper acetate and free mercury. Dioscorides[3] obtained it from cinnabar by the aid of iron, using a distillation process. The iron reacted with the mercuric sulphide to give iron sulphide and free mercury.

IRON[4]

Into the long and confused controversy on the provenance and early use of iron it is unnecessary to enter here. Probably, if not certainly, the earliest appearance of iron as a metal was in the mountainous region between the Caspian and Black Seas, inhabited by various tribes such as the Chalybes[5] and Mossynoeci, of whom we have already spoken. From thence the iron-armed, conquering Assyrians obtained their weapons, as did also the Hittites. Farther west on the slopes of Mount Ida the Dactyli made iron at an early date, which led Strabo to make the some-

---

[1] For further on zinc cf. Bluemner, *Technologie*, iv, 96, 193. It may be noted that a sort of brass made of copper with an alloy of 1·35–5·30 per cent of arsenic has been found in Egypt and Cyprus. The whole question of the use of bronze and brass by the ancients is discussed by Bailey, ii, 159. W. Gowland, *Journ. Inst. Metals*, vii (1912), pp. 35 f., concludes from various analyses of coins and other objects that brass was a Roman invention.

[2] *de Lap.* 60; Pliny, *H.N.* xxxiii, 64, 100, 123; cf. Bailey's note, i, 223.

[3] Diosc. v, 95; cf. also i, 72.

[4] Art. "Metalla" in *D.S.*; "Bergbau" and "Eisen" by Bluemner, "Stahl" by Romel in *P.W.*

[5] Xen. *Anab.* v, 5, 1; Aesch. *Prom.* 714; Arist. *de Mir. Ausc.* xlviii, 833 B.

what incautious remark that all are agreed that iron was first
worked by the Dactyli on Mount Ida,[1] but later, a trifle inconsis-
tently, he says that iron and bronze were first worked at Rhodes.

It is not improbable that the Homeric Greeks got their iron,
and that was little enough, from these same Dactyli, although
we are puzzled by that mysterious cargo of iron that Mentes
took from Taphos to Cyprus. There is no iron in Taphos, and
if we are to take the story at all seriously we must suppose it
came in trade, possibly down the Adriatic from Central Europe,
but that is wildly conjectural.[2] Sir Flinders Petrie advances
the view that iron, except as a precious curiosity, was not used
until the ninth century B.C.[3] However that may be, it is certain
that the Phoenicians did not bring any iron with them when
trading with the Greeks, or presumably we should have heard
of it among their cargoes. On the other hand, we know the
Greeks gave iron to the Phoenicians in exchange for wine, and
it is perfectly possible to suppose that this iron had been taken
from the Dactyli.[4] There were large iron-ore deposits both in
Cyprus and Crete, but there are no early objects of that metal
found, or rather only such small ones as nails; larger objects
such as swords are of the Hallstatt type, undoubtedly not the
product of Minoan workmen.

Iron in the Homeric age was very valuable; at the funeral
games of Patroclus the prize offered for "putting the shot"
was the shot itself, a great mass of rough-cast iron so valuable
that Achilles says it will last him for making iron implements
for five years.[5] There is only one reference in all Homer to an
iron weapon—the mace of Areithous,[6] but the arrow with
which Pandarus wounded Menelaus had an iron head.[7] That
the weapons of Odysseus which Telemachus hid from the

[1] x, 3, 22 (c. 473); cf. also xiv, 2, 7 (c. 654); Diod. v, 4.
[2] Ridgeway, *Early Age of Greece*, i, ix. For the Mentes story cf. *Od.* i, 184;
Bérard, *Phéniciens et l'Odyssée*, i, 160; F. B. Jevons, "Iron in Homer",
J.H.S. 1892, p. 25. Seymour, *Life in the Homeric Age*, p. 77, identifies Ithaca
with Leucas, and suggests that the home of the Taphians was on the island
of Kalamo off the coast of Acarnania, where iron ore has been found.
[3] Very doubtful: cf. Heichelheim, *Schmoller's Jahrb.* lvi (1932–3), p. 174.
Id. in *Gnomon*, vii (1931), p. 588; G. A. Wainwright, "Iron in Egypt",
J.E.A. xviii (1932), p. 3; Seymour, *Life in the Homeric Age*, p. 299.
[4] *Il.* vii, 472; cf. Bérard, *Phéniciens et l'Odyssée*, p. 329.
[5] *Il.* xxiii, 826, or perhaps meteoric iron.
[6] *Il.* vii, 141.   [7] *Il.* iv, 123.

suitors were made of iron or steel is hard to credit, and the reference to "iron that draws a man" would appear to be a late interpolation.[1] M. Glotz remarks that in the first half of the *Iliad*, 309 cases of the use of bronze are mentioned as against 16 of iron, whereas in the second half and in the whole of the *Odyssey* the corresponding figures are 109 and 32. "But we must not draw from this the mathematical deduction that at the beginning of the Homeric Age bronze was used 19 times more than iron and at the end of the period 3 or 4 times, for poetic tradition always favoured bronze. But we see in what direction and to what extent the relative position of the two metals altered."[2]

Turning now to historic times, we find Greece plentifully supplied with iron ore. The report of the modern Department of Mines at Athens shows that it is now being worked at Laurium; at St Elisse on the Maleian promontory near the ancient Epidelium; at Larymna in Locris; at Atalanti also in Locris, which may possibly be identified with Elateia, and on the islands of Seriphos, Cythnos and Crete.

In Ancient Greece there is some uncertainty as to the actual working of iron deposits. The Laurium district is very rich in iron ore, but we have no mention of its exploitation. It is hard to suppose that the Athenians were wholly indifferent to it, as a plentiful supply of iron was obviously a necessity to them; but, as Bluemner remarks, the immense quantity of iron ore found there to-day certainly suggests neglect.[3] It is very probable that this neglect was due to the faultiness of their methods of extraction, which left a good deal of iron in the slag, but could not get rid of the phosphorus. So long as they had access to magnetite or haematite deposits with a high percentage of pure iron, they would hardly want to work the inferior ores. Probably the more valuable silver occupied their attention, and it was easier to import their iron. In Laconia, as already mentioned, there was a famous mine on the Maleian promontory, which was worked by the Spartans.[4] Strabo speaks of iron deposits in

[1] *Od.* xvi, 294.   [2] *Ancient Greece at Work*, p. 45.
[3] *Technologie*, iv, 96; cf. also Ardaillon, *Les mines de Laurion*, p. 36.
[4] Mr Tarn, *Hellenistic Civilization*, p. 220, is hardly correct when he says the deposits were worked out in Hellenistic times. There are large quantities there now which are being worked to-day. We may suppose that the degeneration of the times had made for neglect. Cf. Bluemner, *Technologie*, iv, 74.

Euboea "in the Lelantine plain above the city of Chalcis which contained copper and iron together, a thing not reported as occurring elsewhere, but now both metals have given out".[1] This is probably as mythical as the supposed occurrence of copper in this district. Iron was plentiful in the islands, e.g. in Andros, Ceos, Cythnos, Melos, Siphnos, Scyros, Syra and Gyaros.[2]

If Greece obtained iron from Spain, which is very doubtful, it must have been at a late date. Strabo mentions extensive workings of the ore in Turdetania and Iberia.[3] There were also iron quarries in Macedonia. Nor have we any evidence of imports into Greece from Aethalia (Elba). Strabo says: "The iron [from Elba] cannot be brought into complete coalescence by heating in the furnaces of the island, but it is brought over immediately from the mines to the mainland."[4] Diodorus supplements this by describing how the people of Elba broke up the masses of rock, burning and smelting the pieces and dividing the resultant masses into lumps of convenient size, like large sponges, to sell to merchants for conveyance to the mainland.[5] There doubtless it was resmelted and reduced by hammering to wrought iron.[6] Aristotle speaks of iron mines in Sicily, and recounts the story of the successful "corner" in iron by a resourceful Sicilian who gained a profit of 200 per cent, but found his activities stopped by Dionysius, who did not care for anyone else competing with him.[7]

COAL[8]

Greece is by no means destitute of coal, but it is a low-quality lignite. At the present time it is mined at Coumi in Euboea in fairly large quantities, and in several other places, such as Oropus and Aliveri.[9] The only references we have to coal in the

[1] Strabo, x, 1, 9 (c. 447). But not consistent with his statement about Andeira.
[2] Ardaillon, *Les mines de Laurion*; art. "Metalla" in *D.S.*
[3] iii, 2, 8 (c. 146); iii, 4, 6 (c. 159).
[4] v, 2, 6 (c. 223).
[5] v, 13. Cf. also Arist. *de Mir. Ausc.* 837 B; Bluemner, *Technologie*, iv, 64.
[6] For further on iron working cf. p. 204.
[7] Arist. *Pol.* 1259 A.
[8] Art. "Kohle" by Lagerkrantz in *P.W.*
[9] About 150,000 metric tons according to reports of the Department of Mines at Athens.

ancient writers are first, in the fragment "On Stones" by Theophrastus, who says it was found in Liguria and Elis. "Some of the more brittle stones become as it were charcoal when put into the fire, and will continue to burn for a long time. Of this kind are those found in the neighbourhood of Binai.[1] These are found in mines and are also washed down by the streams. They will take fire on throwing charcoal on them, and continue to burn as long as anyone blows on them, but afterwards they will deaden and may later be made to burn again. They are therefore of long continuance, but their smell is troublesome and disagreeable. There is also a stone called *Spinos*, which, when cut in pieces and thrown together in a heap exposed to the sun, burns and does so the more when it is moistened or sprinkled with water."[2] The reference here is possibly to pyritic shale. A little later Theophrastus says: "In the promontory called Erineas there is a great quantity of stone like that found at Binai, which when burned emits a bituminous smell and leaves matter resembling calcined earth. These stones are called coals (*anthrakes*), and are broken for use; they are earthy, but kindle and burn like charcoal. These are found in Liguria, where also is amber, and in Elis on the way to Olympia over the mountains, and are used by blacksmiths."[3] It is noteworthy that the coal mine spoken of here as found near Olympia is worked at the present time. It is a poor bituminous sort, containing pyrite which produces unpleasant sulphur fumes. There is also a reference in Pliny to red hot stones, used by the Gauls to smelt copper, which may conceivably refer to coal.[4]

[1] Binai is unidentified, but probably in Macedonia, presumably blotted out by the Celtic invasions. Herodotus (iv, 195) says that the asphalt found at Zacynthus was better than the Pierian. If he refers to the Binai workings here the identification with Pieria in Macedonia seems fairly certain.

[2] *de Lap.* ii, 12–13; cf. Arist. *de Mir. Ausc.* 833 A, 841 A. Pliny, *H.N.* xxxvi, 141; cf. Bailey's note, ii, 258; cf. also *ibid.* xxxiii, 94, and Bailey's note, i, 209. There seems to be no explanation of this whatever, and the reference in Aristotle only makes the confusion worse. There is no stone that burns when moistened with water and there seems no reason to think that quicklime is suggested here.

[3] *de Lap.* ii, 16.

[4] *H.N.* xxxiv, 20 (96). Bailey, ii, 166, rejects the possibility of coal being indicated here.

SALT[1]

Greece has no deposits of rock salt, and domestic supply was derived wholly from evaporation from brine springs or sea water. In Attica there were such brine springs opposite Gephyra on the other side of the Cephisus, and salt works on the sea-shore.[2] A plentiful supply could always be procured from Megara; that city apparently specialising in it.[3] Pliny says that Megarian salt was of excellent quality, and that salt was also made on the coasts of Euboea and Crete. There were great quantities at the mouth of the Borysthenes or Dnieper.[4] As the inland Thracians, with the exception of the Dacians, had no salt, they were obliged to buy it from the Greeks, and on the lower Strymon this trade was in the hands of the Athenians, who received in exchange slaves. We are told that a cheap Thracian was called a "salt-slave" (*Halonetos*).[5] The Greek colonies on the shores of the Aegean and the Euxine used to dry salt from the waters of the lagoons in Mesembria, Anchialus and Aenus, and then take it inland to sell,[6] "among such men as know not the sea, neither eat meat savoured with salt".[7] The regular price seems to have been one-seventh that of the same weight of wheat, and Plutarch says that during the siege of Athens by Demetrius a medimnus of salt sold for 40 drs.[8] There is an obscure reference in Aristophanes to a decree of the people of Athens, which would suggest that measures had been taken against a monopoly of the product and an undue rise in price; but of this nothing is known.[9]

---

[1] Art. "Salz" in *P.W.* by Bluemner; "Sal" in *D.S.* by Besnier; Pliny, *H.N.* xxxi, 73.

[2] Boeckh, *Staatshaushaltung*, i, 126. Cf. art. in *P.W.* p. 2077. Export of salt, presumably from Attica, to Byzantium, Theoph. *Char.* xxi, 14.

[3] Aristoph. *Acharn.* 521, 760.

[4] Her. iv, 53; Dio Chrys. xxxvi, 437 M 25.   [5] Zenob. ii, 12.

[6] Kazarow, *C.A.H.* viii, 542.   [7] *Od.* xi, 123.

[8] *Demetrius*, xxxiii, 3.   [9] *Eccles.* 814.

CHAPTER IV

LABOUR[1]

The Citizen

WE have already in our introductory chapter discussed at sufficient length the attitude of the Greeks towards labour, and it is needless to say anything more on the subject. The citizen worked in every profession and trade; the Metic certainly had no monopoly, nor, as we shall see later, did the slave by any means displace the free labourer, at least in the more skilled trades.

It would be no difficult task to give a lengthy list of citizens, whose names we know, who were engaged in every conceivable trade and profession. To give but a few instances, among the more well-to-do we know of Anytus, Cleainetus and his son Cleon, who were prosperous tanners; Hyperbolus, who made lamps; Cyrebus, who had made a fortune as a miller and baker; Cephalus, who made earthenware;[2] Eucrates the tow and oakum merchant; Diitrephes, who made baskets; Demeas and Menon, who were large manufacturers of men's garments; Leocrates, Euphemus and Sophilus the father of Sophocles, who were ironfounders; Theodorus, father of Isocrates, a flute-maker; Cleophon, a lyre-maker; the father of Demosthenes, who made swords and bedsteads; Lycidas, father of the orator Pytheas, who was a baker; Pammenes, the goldsmith, who made a crown for Demosthenes when he was Choregus. The list might easily be extended to scores of others of whom we hear from one source or another, all of whom were substantial citizens, some of them rich, others comfortably off. Some very large fortunes were

---

[1] General references: Bluemner, *Gewerbliche Tätigkeit der Griechen u. Römern. Technologie u. Terminologie der Gewerbe u. Künste bei Griechen u. Römern*—old, but still indispensable—the first volume of *Technologie* was revised and much enlarged in 1912; Guiraud, *La Main d'Œuvre Industrielle dans l'Ancienne Grèce*, cap. iv; Francotte, *L'Industrie dans la Grèce Ancienne*, i, caps. vi, viii; art. "Industrie u. Handel" in *P.W.*; F. Heichelheim, in *Schmoller's Jahrb.* lvii (1933), pp. 308 ff.; Frohberger, *De opificum apud veteres Graecos condicione*, cap. ii.

[2] Plato, *Rep.* 421 D, speaks of many rich potters.

made by citizens, as, for instance, Nicias who owned slaves in
the mines, Epicrates and Diphilus rich mine-owners, Philippus
and Nausicles. Among the petty contractors who undertook
small building jobs, we hear of many citizens, Diitrephes,
Apollophanes, Solon, Heracleides, Phalacros, Timomachus,
Thesias, Euthydemus and Cteson, as well as many who undertook small jobs at stonemasonry and carpentering. Such names
are known to us through various chance references; obviously
they must have formed but a very small fraction of a great
multitude of citizen workers.

It remains to be seen how the Athenian citizen fared in
competition with the Metic. From such records as we have we
are led to suppose not very well. We have the accounts of the
building of the Erechtheum in 409–408[1] and we find that out
of seventy-one contractors and labourers there are only twenty
Athenian citizens; among fourteen carpenters they number five;
among forty stonecutters there are ten citizens; among fourteen
labourers and two sawyers there are none; out of eight sculptors'
roughing assistants there are three; of ten carvers of decorations
one is an Athenian; neither goldsmith nor painter is a citizen.
In shaping beams, at so much a foot, there are three citizens and
two Metics. The former do not seem to have exerted themselves
particularly, since they do 9, 47 and 68 ft. respectively, and earn
31 drs. between them. The two Metics do 84 and 180 ft. respectively and earn 66 drs. between them. Towards the end of
the next century we have the building accounts of Eleusis in
329–328,[2] from which we can easily see that the number of
citizens at work has fallen proportionately in the last 80 years.
Out of ninety-four professionals only twenty-one are citizens;
the percentage of citizens among the freemen engaged has
dropped from thirty-six in 408 to twenty-seven in 329. Among
twenty-seven contractors there are nine citizens; among forty-
one merchants, eleven citizens. At this time the only superiority
citizens have in industry is in that of pig-breeding, and the
transport of lime and brickmaking, and this was due solely to
the exclusive right of owning land. In all other branches of
trade and industry they are in a striking minority. There are no

[1] *I.G.* i², 374; cf. also 372–3.
[2] *I.G.* ii², 1672.

citizen metal workers; no carpenters and joiners; hardly a stonemason, and the Metic importers of timber from Macedonia have almost driven them out of the lumber trade.

What conclusion, therefore, are we to come to with regard to the economic status of the citizen? As we have seen, not all the free citizens could live a life of cultured idleness; many of them, we may surmise the majority, had to work and work very hard, under conditions that were the reverse of favourable. Between the competition of the energetic Metic, who had no scruples about his social position whatever, and the slave who had to work, the poorer class of citizen came off badly.[1] Liable for war service in army or fleet, an interruption to his work which he probably rather welcomed, and often called upon to do his duty in the courts, the citizen had many distractions, and for these the state must pay. If the state insisted upon its citizens taking an active part in government, it was obliged to compensate them for the time thus withdrawn from earning their living. It is hardly too much to conceive of the citizenry of Athens as forming a gigantic civil service, more especially in the time of the Delian Confederacy when all lawsuits had to come to the Athenian courts, and therefore payments for attendance in the Assembly and for jury duty were something more than poor relief occasioned by failure to compete successfully in industry with more energetic rivals. The citizen was an aristocrat who disliked manual labour; lounging in the market-place and gossiping, or occupying himself with the endless political intrigues of the state was much more to his taste, if he could afford it. Such pleasant ways of passing their days were much more to the taste of the citizens who only took to hard manual labour when they were utterly destitute,[2] and Euxitheus, who is trying to establish his Athenian citizenship, says: "Poverty compels freemen to do many mean and servile acts for which they deserve rather to be pitied than to be utterly ruined. I am told that many women of civic origin have become nurses and wooldressers and vintagers owing to the misfortunes that overtook the state; and many have since been raised from poverty to wealth."[3]

---

[1] But cf. Guiraud, *Main d'Œuvre*, p. 173, who holds that the evidence too meagre for us to draw positive conclusions therefrom.

[2] Isaeus, v, 39.   [3] Dem. *in Eubul.* 45.

Agriculture alone remained the sole preserve of the citizen, and unless he had capital to sink in his farm—and the cultivation of olives, vines and figs demanded capital—he was at a severe disadvantage in the face of importation of foreign grain, and the competition of Boeotian vegetable growers in the market at Athens.

LABOUR IN CONSTRUCTION INDUSTRY

Of labour in the construction industry we have fuller details than almost any other, because we have records of public expenditure and accounts of sums paid to workmen and contractors. Plutarch in speaking of the magnificent public buildings erected by Pericles says: "The materials were stone, bronze, ivory, gold, ebony, cypress wood; and the arts and trades that wrought and fashioned them were smiths and carpenters, moulders, founders and braziers, stone-cutters, dyers, goldsmiths, ivory-workers, painters, embroiderers, turners; those again that conveyed them to the town for use, merchants, mariners and ship-masters by sea, and by land cartwrights, cattle-breeders, waggoners, rope-makers, flax-workers, shoemakers and leather-dressers, road-makers and miners. And every trade in the same nature, as a captain in an army has his particular company of soldiers under him, had its own hired company of journeymen and labourers belonging to it, banded together as in array, to be as it were the instrument and body for the performance of the service. Thus, to sum up in a word, the occasions and services of these public works distributed plenty through every age and condition."[1]

In an account for roofing a temple in Athens we have a sawyer, a painter, and workmen who fixed carved wooden blocks on the top, which had been prepared by other workers.[2] In an inscription dealing with the building of the Erechtheum there are recorded the names of stone-cutters who fluted the columns; marble workers who carved the rosettes on the ceiling from patterns modelled in wax; painters in encaustic; gilders; sawyers; carpenters who build the roof and put up and take down the scaffolding.[3] In 279 we have the building of the

---

[1] *Pericles*, xii, 6.
[2] Guiraud, *Main d'Œuvre*, p. 58ff.; *I.G.* i², 373.
[3] *I.G.* i², 372–4.

temple of Apollo at Delos, where the mason Nicon levelled the top course of the wall to receive the roof, and the carpenter Dinocrates who laid on the wooden wall-plate to support the joists.[1] When the doors of the Propylaeum were broken by the collapse of a pillar, they were repaired by a carpenter and the pillar repaired by a mason with the aid of a crane or windlass, which was brought to the place, set up and then taken down by other workmen.[2] Inscriptions from Epidauros record the various workmen engaged in the building of temples during the fourth century B.C., such as stonemasons, roughers, finishers, joiners, carpenters, decorators, tilers, roofers, gilders, goldsmiths and sculptors.[3] Generally the workmen are confined to their own job, but sometimes we find the same man doing several. It is not clear whether these were contractors who undertook to supply labour for the different jobs or whether they were the same workmen. For instance, in the same job at Epidauros, we have Aristaeus who gave a door a coat of pitch, laid tiles on the roof and built a small shed; Sotaerus, who supplied nails, elm, lotus and box wood; Lykios, who supplied pine and worked as a stone-cutter; Euterpidas a stonemason, who also sawed the wooden joists.

At Athens we have several inscriptions detailing the payments made to various workmen.[4] In making the doors Carion is paid 23 drs. for sawing three pieces of wood from Macedonia for the door sills, and two pieces for the doors themselves. Dionysios, a Metic living in Eleusis, makes the doors for 65 drs.; 190 nails cost an obol a piece; the door posts are bought from Syros, a merchant, for 28 drs., 3 obols; two pivots on which the cedar-wood doors of the treasury turn are supplied by Pamphilos, who lives at the Piraeus; cedar for the doors is supplied by Simmias for 210 drs. Dressed planks for the doors and the platform of the treasury cost 512 drs.; five joists are bought from Phormio of the Piraeus for 130 drs.; seven joists of elm wood cost 98 drs., and so on through the whole list of accounts. Sawyers are paid 3 obols a day; bricklayers 17 drs. for laying 1000 bricks, each a foot and a half long, which have cost 36 drs.

---

[1] *I.G.* xi, 2, 161 A, 49–50. [2] *Ibid.* i, 66.
[3] *I.G.* i², 102–20.
[4] *I.G.* ii², 1672; cf. also 1665–85, *passim*.

per thousand, or with mortar 40 drs. Transport for the same number cost 25 drs. Masons received 1 dr. and an obol for each flagstone cut; transport of each stone cost 1 dr. 3 obols; laying 1 dr. Throughout all the many accounts relative to public works on a large scale, it is to be particularly noted that in most cases the payments are small and the contractors in a small way of business, who each do their part with perhaps the help of a few free workers or a few slaves, while the materials are bought in small quantities wherever they can be picked up. As M. Francotte remarks: "One would imagine that a small building were being put up in a village with only local labour to help."[1] Possibly, however, there were a few contractors in a large way, if we are to accept Plutarch's statement that Callicrates and Ictinus contracted together to build the entire Parthenon. Coroebus began the temple at Eleusis and after his death it was finished by Metagenes. Xenocles roofed the temple of Castor and Pollux and the same Callicrates built the long walls, which must have been an enormous undertaking.[2]

Throughout these accounts one finds the same names of contractors doing different jobs; a carpenter also lays tiles; a stonemason lays bricks and so on. From this arises the question as to how far the division of labour had really gone in Ancient Greece, and to that no definite answer can be given. M. Guiraud remarks that while we know that division existed, we are in almost complete ignorance as to its more minute details.[3] For instance, we know that in the workshop of the father of Demosthenes some of the slaves were occupied entirely in making beds; but we are not told whether each had his appointed task or whether each workman made the entire article. In our chapter on Industry we give examples of different tasks performed in various trades, but these do not constitute more than a very simple form of division of labour. We have no evidence to show that large-scale production was aimed at by a division of operations such as is familiar in the modern factory; actually the "factory" was really non-existent, although fairly large work-

[1] *L'Industrie*, ii, 90; cf. also Guiraud, *Main d'Œuvre*, p. 80.
[2] Plut. *Pericles*, 13; cf. also Her. v, 62, the Alcmaeonidae building the temple at Delphi.
[3] *Main d'Œuvre*, p. 64.

shops employing some scores of workers, in nearly all cases slaves, were found.

WAGES[1]

Towards the close of the fifth century the daily general wage of workmen, whether skilled or unskilled no apparent distinction was made between them, was 1 dr.;[2] while assistants got 3 obols. Agricultural labourers received 4 obols in cash and their food, which was reckoned at 2 obols. In the fourth century wages rose, and in 395–391 a foreman of a gang of bricklayers got 2 drs., and two lads received 1 or 1½. At Delphi, in the middle of the century, plasterers got from 1 to 2½ drs. At Eleusis in 329–328, labourers received 1½, sawyers 2, bricklayers, carpenters and plasterers 2½.[3]

In any calculation with regard to a "living wage", however, the problem is always hopelessly complicated by the factor of unemployment. It is always fatally easy to assume that work is continuous and to draw conclusions that are, as every statistician of labour conditions knows only too well, not only erroneous but highly deceptive. There were in Attica about sixty holidays a year;[4] naturally there was no regular weekly rest on Sunday, and so we may reckon that in ancient times the number of possible full working days was approximately the same as to-day. From such figures as we have, it is very evident that, even with legal holidays, work was far from continuous. At Eleusis[5] we have figures with regard to marble workers employed in fluting columns. Three gangs, in which citizens are employed, work over a period of 36–37 days, and never do more than 22–23 drs. worth of work per man. Three other gangs of slaves do work

---

[1] Glotz, *Mélanges*, 282 ff. Boeckh, i, 21; Francotte, *L'Industrie*, ii, vi; Guiraud, *Main d'Œuvre*, 182 ff. Schwahn, *Gehalts und Lohnzahlung in Athen, Rhein. Mus.* lxxix (1930), pp. 170 ff.; Busolt, *Griech. Staatsk.* i, p. 201.

[2] The question is very obscure for lack of sufficient evidence. It is hard to believe that the more skilled workers did not receive a higher wage. Cf. *I.G.* i², 374, where the wages of various labourers are recorded. These are probably all unskilled; we have no records of the payments to others of a higher class.

[3] *I.G.* ii², 1672.

[4] Xen. *Govt. of Athens*, iii, 2, 8, remarks that these were more than in other states of Greece; cf. also Plato, *Alcib.* ii, 12. Strabo, vi, 3, 4 (c. 280), says that in Tarentum the holidays outnumbered the working days.

[5] *I.G.* ii², 1658, 1659, 1662, 1667, 1672, 1673.

worth 27, 35 and 38 drs. during the same time. It is hard to suppose that the slaves were better workmen than the citizens; we must rather conclude that the citizens were either laid off or stopped work voluntarily, which affords a rather striking instance of the competition of slave with free labour. Gradually piece work displaced day work.[1] At Eleusis the labour of moulding bricks $1\frac{1}{2}$ feet square was paid at the rate of 36 drs. per 1000, the worker to find the clay. Laying bricks cost from 12 to 15 drs. per 1000 in 395–391; the price had risen to 17 in 329–328.

THE COST OF LIVING[2]

The notoriously difficult question of cost of living and what constitutes a "living wage" is hardly less obscure in Ancient Greece than it is to-day. But in view of the simple character of existence, the absence of luxuries and cheapness of articles of clothing, it is not impossible to arrive at a probable approximation. The Greek labourer ate little or no meat, except when he got a share from the public sacrifices; his principal articles of diet were grain, wheat or barley, fruit or vegetables, and very weak wine diluted with water. Barley was reckoned as only half as nourishing as wheat, and therefore the regular army ration of a Spartan soldier was fixed at 1 choinix (about 2 pints) of wheat, or 2 choinices of barley per diem.[3] This, it must be noted, was considered a highly liberal allowance, fit for soldiers on campaign, and half that amount was considered sufficient for his Helot servant. But doubtless the latter made up the deficiency when possible by stealing. One choinix of wheat a day would give a yearly consumption of about $7\frac{1}{2}$ med. a year.[4] At the end of the fifth century when wheat sold for 3 drs. per med., a full allowance would therefore cost a workman about $22\frac{1}{2}$ drs. If a married man earned a drachma a day and worked

---

[1] In Ciccotti's view because the workers wanted to take their own time at their jobs. *Il Tramonto della Schiavitù* (1899), p. 124.

[2] Busolt, *Griech. Staatsk.* i, p. 195 ff.

[3] Jardé, *Céréales*, discusses the point fully, pp. 128 ff. Apparently at the end of the first century A.D. the ratio had risen to 3 : 1; cf. Rev. vi. 6. Daily ration of one choinix, cf. Her. vii, 187; Diog. Laert. viii, 18; Thuc. iv, 16, vii, 87. Cf. also Busolt, *Griech. Staatsk.* i, 202. Busolt discusses the competition of slave with free labour, i, 195.

[4] Forty-eight choinices to the medimnus.

300 days, and had two children besides his wife, allowing three full rations of breadstuffs for the four, the family would spend about 68 drs. a year on that item of their budget. What then was spent on other foods? At that point we are entirely at fault, and our estimates of cost of living become merely conjectures, of which there have been many. M. Glotz reckons 180 drs. for food, 50 for clothing, 36 for rent and 14 for sundries.[1] Boeckh puts it at 396 drs. in the time of Socrates, for a year of 360 days, and at 486 in the time of Demosthenes.[2] M. Mauri puts it at a slightly higher figure, 400 and 525 drs.[3] M. Guiraud remarks that these are quite arbitrary estimates, and appeals to surer evidence in the *Wasps* of Aristophanes, written in 422. There we find a labourer married and with one child able to feed himself and family on 3 obols a day or 177 drs. a year of 354 days.[4] If we add 45 drs. for clothing, 36 for rent, as Boeckh and Mauri agree, and 14 for sundries, we arrive at 272 drs. a year which would allow a workman to live, provided that unemployment did not cut his earnings down considerably.[5] Possibly the wife may have contributed to the family income by spinning and weaving; we do not hear of charwomen, but perhaps they did exist. We cannot wonder that small families were the rule; and the instant distress and necessity for public relief whenever the cost of imported grain rose become entirely understandable. The margin between existence and starvation was a very narrow one.

In the fourth century when grain rose to 5 drs. the medimnus and frequently higher, the cost of food for a family of four must have risen to nearly 300 drs. It does not appear, however, that other expenses had risen to any extent, and a workman could support his family on 450 drs. a year, if he earned $1\frac{1}{2}$ a day. The skilled worker was probably as well off as before, but the unskilled, who still only earned one, was in a bad way. In conclusion it is interesting to note that Lysias in his speech against Diogeiton reckons 1000 drs. a year sufficient to support comfortably three orphans, an attendant and a maid, and Demos-

---

[1] *Ancient Greece at Work*, p. 286.   [2] *Staatshaushaltung*, i, p. 141 ff.
[3] *I cittadini Lavoratori dell' Attica*, p. 78.   [4] *Vesp.* 300–1.
[5] *Main d'Œuvre*, pp. 191–2. Busolt, *Griech. Staatsk.* p. 203, puts the minimum at 360 drs.

thenes reckons about the same amount in his own case when prosecuting his guardians for embezzlement of his patrimony. These cases are, of course, for the wealthy; but the ratio between the incomes of the rich and those of the labouring classes is obviously a reasonable one.[1]

WOMEN'S LABOUR[2]

Women worked in Greece, as they have in every time and place. We are even tempted to think that often they worked harder than the men, but that would hardly be true. Everybody, except the fortunate rich, worked hard; they had to, and women entered fully into the economic life of the community. Nor must we think of women as being invariably shut up in their houses; such was the lot of the well-to-do. They were everywhere, doing everything but the tasks that were impossible for them, as innumerable allusions in literature attest.

As shown in our chapter on Industry, the occupation above all others pursued by women was the making of clothing for themselves and their families. Spinning and weaving were their speciality, and in it their skill was superior to that of men.[3] Not only did they make the clothes for the family but sold their cloth. Xenophon in his *Memorabilia*[4] has a most edifying story in which Socrates advises Aristarchus, who has been ruined by the war, to set the fourteen female relations who have fled to him for protection to spinning and weaving, and so relieve the distress of the sorely tried man and bring in money to keep them all going. Aristarchus follows his advice with the happiest results. "The necessary means were accordingly provided; wool was bought, and the women took their dinners as they continued at work and supped when they had finished their tasks. They became cheerful instead of gloomy of countenance and, instead of regarding each other with dislike, met the looks

---

[1] Lysias, *in Diog.* 28; Dem. *in Aphob.* i, 36.
[2] P. Herfst, *Le travail de la femme dans la Grèce Ancienne*.
[3] Plato, *Alcib.* i, 126 E; *Lysis*, 208 E; Xen. *Mem.* iii, 9, 11; Aeschines, *in Timarch.* 97 (flax-workers); Aristoph. *Ranae*, 1346. Out of fifty-six women slaves manumitted, forty were wool-workers, three general store keepers, two sesame sellers, one vegetable seller, one honey seller, one zither-player, one nurse, and six domestics; *I.G.* ii², 1553 ff.
[4] *Mem.* ii, 7.

of one another with pleasure. They loved Aristarchus as their protector, and he loved them as being of use to him."

Fulling the cloth, as being beyond their physical strength, was probably, at least in the absence of evidence to the contrary, not an occupation followed by women, although there is no reason why they should not have helped in the less heavy tasks. As it was an unpleasant trade, perhaps they refused to assist in it; but of that we know nothing. We do know, however, for certain that they were helpers in the dyeing industry.[1] We have a reference in the New Testament to a seller of purple, Lydia of Thyatira, and to dealers in Cos and Hierapolis from other sources.[2]

How far there were dressmaking establishments, fashionable *couturières*, is difficult to say. We know that there were dressmakers (*akestriai*); but it seems more likely they were seamstresses who went to work in the houses where they were needed.[3] But no doubt the Hetairae needed the services of experts to provide them with the most fashionable creations, which they had no inclination to make for themselves. We do know that women sold ribbons,[4] and we have one reference to a woman named Elephantis who sold ready-made garments;[5] we do not know if they were of her own making.

With regard to women selling in the market some uncertainty has arisen. Theophrastus speaks of the "women's market",[6] which would seem to designate that quarter where women sellers displayed their wares. But Pollux[7] seems to suggest that it was the place where articles mostly used by women were sold. The point is obscure and has been much discussed; perhaps the easiest explanation is that women sellers naturally clustered together and sold articles mostly used by women; although, as we shall see, they sold practically everything. For the higher-class women to go shopping was thought highly improper,

---

[1] Aristoph. *Eccles.* 215; Poll. vii, 169.

[2] Acts xvi. 14. But Suidas (*s.v.*) records the word *porphyropolis*. Cf. also Cagnat, *Inscr. Graec. ad res Romanas pertinentes*, iv, 1071; Judeich, *Altertümer von Hierapolis*, No. 156.

[3] Plut. *Aem. Paul.* 8; Poll. iv, 125; Plato, *Rep.* 373 c. Cf. Lucian, *Rhet. Praecept.* 24.

[4] Dem. *in Eubul.* 31; Eupolis, *ap.* Athen. vii, 326 A.

[5] Ditt. *Syll.*³ 1250.   [6] *Char.* ii, 9.

[7] x 18.

although the Hetairae had no compunction on that score.[1] The rich lady stayed at home; her poorer sisters were busy selling their wares in the market, and doutbless enjoying themselves in the moving scene. To protect them against slander there was a law providing penalties for those guilty of evil speaking of respectable women.[2] Not that they were not fully able to look after themselves; the unlucky purchaser who incurred their wrath was likely to be assailed by a flow of the choicest "Billingsgate", and women sellers were notorious for their quarrelling and clamour.[3] They also, unfortunately, had a bad name for short-weighting and, no doubt, short-changing the unwary; but they were not unique in this; buying and selling was always a battle of wits.[4]

Their wares were varied; they sold practically everything. We hear of one stall where cream, honey and dried figs were on display.[5] Others sold wine,[6] and salt, at least so far as two inscriptions recording epitaphs seem to indicate.[7] They sold flour[8] and bread,[9] porridge,[10] figs,[11] vegetables,[12] honey[13] and sesame.[14] Pherecrates says that nobody ever heard of a female fishmonger, but Antiphanes alludes to an *ichthyopolis*, and there does not seem any particular reason why they should not have sold fish.[15] We have one reference to an incense seller,[16] and they certainly dealt in perfumes.[17] They wove garlands[18] and sold them in the market,[19] and evidently there were women in Athens engaged in weaving fishing nets.[20] Women also kept

---

[1] Dem. *in Neaeram*, 67 (but the reading is uncertain).
[2] Dem. *in Eubul.* 30.
[3] Aristoph. *Ranae*, 857; *Plutus*, 456; *Vespae*, 36; *Lysist.* 456.
[4] Aristoph. *Thesm.* 347; *Plutus*, 435. Cf. Plato, *Laws*, xi, 918 D.
[5] Aristoph. *Plutus*, 1120 et schol.
[6] Poll. vii, 193; Schol. *Plutus*, 426. Cf. Boisacq, *Dict. Etym. s.v.* Kapelos.
[7] *I.G.* ii, 3932, iii, 1456.   [8] Diog. Laert. v, 2, 168; Poll. vi, 37.
[9] Alciphron, *Epist.* iii, 60, 1 (at Corinth).
[10] Aristoph. *Plutus*, 427, et schol. *Lysist.* 562; Lucian, *Lexiph.* 34.
[11] *Lysist.* 564; Poll. vii, 198.
[12] *Vespae*, 497; *Thesm.* 387.   [13] Poll. vii, 198.
[14] Cf. Aristoph. *Lysist.* 457; *I.G.* ii², 1554, 40.
[15] *ap.* Athen. xiii, 612 B; Antiphanes, frag. 159; *Frag. Com. Att.* (ed. Kock), ii, 75. Cf. *ichthyopolaina*, Pherecr. 64.
[16] *I.G.* ii², 1576, 17.   [17] Aristoph. *Eccles.* 841; *Anth. Pal.* v, 180.
[18] *Thesm.* 448; Theoph. *H.P.* vi, 81; Athen. xiii, 608.
[19] *Thesm.* 446; Poll. vii, 199.
[20] Cf. Ziebarth, "Neue Verfluchungstafeln aus Attika etc.", *Berl. Sitz. Ber.* (1934), p. 5.

general stalls where they sold a variety of nicknacks (*pantopolis, gelgopolis*).[1]

Generally women did not work in the fields; Ischomachus wisely observes that nature had not designed them for such tasks.[2] But they were certainly busy at harvest time lending a hand.[3] They helped in the reaping,[4] stacking the cut grain into sheaves[5] and, like Ruth, were gleaners (*kalametrides*).[6] They also helped in weeding, as they do to-day.[7] There is some slight uncertainty as to what their work in the vineyards was, but there seems nothing improbable in supposing that they were busy during the harvest of the grapes.[8] The preparation of food was generally a domestic occupation, but as already noted cooked dishes were sold in the market; bread was certainly sold there.[9] Women cooks were held superior to men, at least by Socrates.[10] But the most famous were chefs, some of whose names are recorded in our chapter on Industry. There is only one reference to a female shoemaker.[11] As noted in the chapter on Industry there is one picture on a vase representing a potter's workshop where a woman is sitting painting a vase. Homer tells us of women workers in ivory in Caria,[12] and we hear of at least one woman who helped her husband in gilding helmets.[13] Women were innkeepers, or perhaps barmaids, not a very respectable calling.[14] As was natural, women were engaged as nurses.[15] Spartan nurses were considered superior; Alcibiades was nurtured by one.[16] They were exclusively employed as midwives.[17] Hyginus, a late writer, tells a curious story of one

---

[1] Poll. vii, 198–9. Gelgopolis, perhaps garlic seller. Cf. Cratinus, frag. 48; *Frag. Com. Att.* i, 26.

[2] Xen. *Oecon.* vii, 21; cf. Aesch. *Septem*, 200. Plato was shocked at the custom of the Thracians and other barbarous tribes of employing women in agriculture—*Laws*, 805 D.

[3] Hes. *W.D.* 602; cf. Theocr. xv, 80.

[4] Poll. vii, 150.   [5] Theocr. iii, 32.

[6] Hesych. *s.v.*; cf. *Anth. Pal.* ix, 89 (*akrologein*).

[7] Poll. vii, 148.

[8] Dem. *in Eubul.* 45; cf. Dio Chrys. i, 134 (260 R); Pliny, *H.N.* xix, 57.

[9] *Vesp.* 238.

[10] Plato, *Rep.* v, 455 C; cf. Athen. iv, 172 B, xiii, 612 B.

[11] *I.G.* ii², 1578, 5.

[12] *Il.* iv, 141.   [13] *C.I.A.* Appendix, 69.

[14] Aristoph. *Ranae*, 114; *Plutus*, 426. Ditt. *Syll.* 1951.

[15] Dem. *in Eubul.* 42; Plato, *Rep.* ii, 373 B, v, 460 D; and many others.

[16] Plut. *Alcib.* 1.

[17] Cf. art. "Medica" by Reinach in *D.S.*; Plato, *Theaet.* 149–50.

enterprising female named Agnodice, who disguised herself and attended the medical school of Herophilus to the scandal of the medical profession,[1] and Pliny tells of another innovator named Salpe.[2] Although the profession of nurse and midwife was looked upon as a lowly one, yet we find sepulchral inscriptions in their honour; so useful an occupation could not be despised.[3]

The Hetairae, as may be supposed, were occupied in what we may call the entertainment industry as flute-players, dancers, acrobats, fire-eaters and jugglers. We hear of one female trumpeter, Aglais, but all we know of her is that she wore a wig and had a prodigious appetite.[4] Although we are not expressly told so, we must infer that none of the arts of entertaining were followed by respectable women. Flute-player was evidently synonymous with *hetaira*, and such pictures as we have of feasts with musicians present leave little doubt on that score.[5] It was the task of the *astynomi* at Athens to see that they did not get more than 2 drs. for their services, and if more than one person was anxious to have the same performer at his house, they cast lots and gave her to the winner.[6] It would have been unthinkable to the Greeks that the daughters or wives of respectable citizens should mix so freely with men. It is needless here to expatiate on the laxness of morals prevalent in Ancient Greece; the case against Neaira, attributed to Demosthenes, presents a by no means favourable picture of society in Athens, and some of the comedies of Aristophanes are not exactly edifying reading.

That the whole status of women was unsatisfactory is clear, at least to some of the deeper thinkers.[7] Socrates was troubled on that score, and in the long discussion on education in the

[1] *Fab.* 274.

[2] *H.N.* xxviii, 7, 18, and others in same book. Salpe's remedies were strange and greatly astonished Pliny.

[3] In honour of Melitta, *I.G.* ii, 2729. Cf. Corinthian and Cytherean nurses, *I.G.* ii, 3097, 3111. Plato has a lot to say of the occupation of nurses—*Laws*, vii, 788 f.

[4] Athen. x, 415 A, B; Ael. *Var. Hist.* i, 26.

[5] The entertainers at the feast described by Athenaeus (iv, 129 D) were hardly respectable; but that was in Macedonia.

[6] Aristotle, *Ath. Pol.* 50.

[7] Mr Gomme's essay on "The Position of Women in Athens" in *Class. Phil.* xx (1925), republished in *Essays in Greek History and Literature*, p. 89, puts Greek thought with regard to women in the best possible light.

Laws has something to say on the training given to girls. He argues for what we may call equal opportunities for women as well as for men, and sees no reason why they should not do anything that men do, with the exception perhaps of active military service in the field. He is strongly attracted to the Spartan system of education, but condemns as barbarous the practice of the Thracians and many other tribes "who employ their women in tilling the ground and minding oxen and sheep and toiling just like slaves". On the other hand he has little liking for the custom of his own land where "we huddle all our goods together, as the saying goes, within four walls, and then hand the dispensing of them to the women, together with the control of the shuttles and all kinds of wool-work". The best system is the midway one of the Laconians, where "the girls share in gymnastics and music and the women abstain from wool-work, but weave themselves instead a life that is not trivial at all nor useless, but arduous, advancing as it were halfway on the path of domestic tendance and management and child nurture, but taking no share in military service".[1] Ischomachus, the model husband, seems to have realised that there had been something lacking in the education of his wife, whom he had married when she was fifteen, and who "had spent the preceding part of her life under the strictest restraint, in order that she might see as little, hear as little, and ask as few questions, as possible".[2] Socrates asks him whether it was not sufficient for her to be able to spin and weave wool and instruct the household slaves in their tasks, to which Ischomachus replies that her training had been too restricted and he had to instruct her himself in many things, which he did with exemplary thoroughness.

APPRENTICESHIP[3]

The practice of apprenticeship was well known in Greece. "If anyone wishes to have an individual taught the trade of a shoe-maker, a mason, a blacksmith or a horse-breaker, he is sent to a master capable of teaching him."[4] Certainly, Xenophon says, nobody can flatter himself that he can acquire skill in any trade

[1] Plato, *Laws*, 805 D, E.　　　[2] Xen. *Oecon.* vii, 5.
[3] Guiraud, *Main d'Œuvre*, p. 66.
[4] Xen. *Mem.* iv, 4, 5; cf. Plato, *Rep.* 467.

without receiving a training in it first.[1] But agriculture is not so difficult as other occupations, "the learners of which must wear themselves out before they can do enough in them to support themselves; but in agriculture, partly by seeing others at work, partly by listening to their advice, you may soon learn enough even to teach another, if you wish.... For those who practise other professions conceal to some degree the most important particulars which each knows in his own trade; but among husbandmen, he who plants trees best will be best pleased if another looks on while he is planting, and he who sows best will have the same feeling, and if you ask him about anything, he will have no concealment from you as to the way in which he did it."[2] Plato agrees with Xenophon that masters do not always impart the "mysteries" of the trade to their apprentices.[3] In several other passages he alludes to apprenticeship in the pottery, leather and weaving industries.[4] We hear of an apprenticeship of two years to a chef, which hardly appears long enough; but since this is from a comic poet, no doubt it implies that the person in question was a very bad cook.[5] The articles of apprenticeship were very carefully drawn up, specifying the premium paid, the length of service and the usual conditions on both sides.[6] So far as is known there was no state regulation of apprenticeship; it was an agreement between the two parties, and if broken on either side could be taken to court in a civil action for breach of contract.

Trade Guilds[7]

The Trade Union, as we know it to-day, is a product of modern industrialism, a child of the Industrial Revolution in Europe and the struggle of labour with the capitalistic system and large-scale production. There was never at any time in the Ancient World, nor indeed until the eighteenth century of the present era, any unions of paid workers banded together to protect their

[1] *Mem.* iv, 2, 2.
[2] *Oecon.* xv, 10, 11. [3] *Protag.* 16.
[4] *Rep.* iv, 421 E; *Gorgias*, 70; *Menon*, 27; *Cratylus*, 8.
[5] Philetairos, 14, in Kock, *Frag. Com. Att.*
[6] Xen. *de Equit.* ii, 2; cf. Plato, *Euthyd.* i; Isocr. xiii, 6; Theocr. viii, 35.
[7] M. N. Tod, *Sidelights on Greek History*, p. 78 ff.; E. Ziebarth, *Das Griechische Vereinswesen.*

interests in the face of the exactions of the employers. The Gild Merchant and the Craft Gild of medieval times were essentially associations of *entrepreneurs* for mutual benefits, the regulation of trade and the exclusion of unwelcome competition.

The reasons for the complete absence of anything resembling Trade Unionism in the ancient and medieval worlds are not far to seek. In the first place, so far at least as pertains to ancient times, the prevalence of slave labour made such impossible. Any associations of slaves aimed at bettering their conditions would have been promptly suppressed. Secondly, the limited scale of production and the smallness of industrial establishments would have made any association of free workers difficult. Unionism sprang from the conditions of large-scale production and great masses of workers in different trades in the cities and industrial centres who could, by combining together, bring effective pressure to bear upon employers. Unionism was impossible in a system of domestic economy when labourers worked very largely in their own homes.

The Trade Guild in Ancient Greece flourished in its greatest luxuriance in the Hellenistic Age; there are few records of such before Alexander. There is a reference to a guild of shipmasters (*naukleroi*) at the Piraeus at some time after 433,[1] and in 418–417 there is an inscription which records the resolve of all shipmasters and merchants (*naukleroi* and *emporoi*) to subscribe a drachma per ship owned by them for keeping up the temple which was dedicated to their worship.[2] We do not hear of this guild again until some time before 332, when we find an honour decree in the name of a Sidonian, Apollonides, who has done a service to the guild of shippers at the Piraeus.[3] Once more there is a long gap, and in 112–111 we hear of them petitioning the Boule or Council at Athens for permission to set up a statue of their *Proxenos*, one Diodorus, at the Piraeus.[4] Finally in 97–96 we find a funerary inscription in honour of another *Proxenos* of the society, Argaeus.[5] That is the last we hear of it, but it lasted, even from the information we have, for nearly 350 years. We hear of numerous guilds in Hellenistic times in the

[1] *I.G.* i², 127.
[2] *I.G.* i², 128³.
[3] *I.G.* ii², 343.
[4] *I.G.* ii², 1012 (*Syll.*³ 706).
[5] *I.G.* ii², 1339.

clothing trades, such as wool workers, weavers, wool washers, wool merchants, dyers, purple dyers, fullers, linen workers, linen weavers, linen sellers, tanners, cobblers, gold and silver smiths (the incident of Demetrius the silversmith who called together the members of his craft at Ephesus when their trade was threatened by the preaching of the Apostles, occurs readily to the mind) and a host of others of every conceivable trade were found,[1] especially in Egypt under the Ptolemaic régime where the system was more developed than anywhere else. Such guilds, so far as we are informed of their purpose, were primarily religious and did not seek normally to regulate working conditions or control trade practices. It is important to note that such guilds admitted both masters and workers, and some of them slaves. Even women and children were members, and it is interesting to know that they were admitted at half fees; but only got half portions at the feasts, as was eminently right and proper.

The part played by these guilds was a highly useful one. Mr Tod very appositely points out that one reason why the industrial history of the Ancient World, as distinguished from the political, was so peaceful can be found in these guilds, which fostered a spirit of brotherhood and common religious observance.

THE STATE AND LABOUR

The never-ending interference of the state with affairs of industry and labour is of very recent origin, and springs from the early Factory Acts of the beginning of the nineteenth century. Nothing like it was found in the Ancient World, except in so far as the laws protected the slave, more or less effectively, as will be seen later in the section that deals with that subject. There was no labour legislation, as we understand it to-day, no regulation of hours and holidays,[2] working conditions or wages. The state did not concern itself with the relations between employer and workman, except in so far as when once a workman agreed to enter the employment of a master, the law

---

[1] Cf. Ziebarth, *Das Griechische Vereinswesen*, p. 33 f.
[2] We do not even know for certain if the great religious festivals were legal holidays.

compelled him to fulfil his agreement[1]—and the law of Solon that forbade enslavement for debt.

There is extant only one known instance where a public official acted as mediator in disputes between workmen and employers.[2] In Paros a decree of honour was passed in favour of an *agoranomos* or market superintendent, who settled disputes as to labour conditions and wages, seeing that workmen did their work properly and employers paid the wages agreed upon. Plato in the *Laws*[3] saw the necessity for *astynomi* or city stewards regulating disputes "as regards wages due to craftsmen, and the cancelling of work ordered, and any injustices done to them by another, or to another by them, the city stewards shall act as arbitrators up to a value of fifty drachmae and in respect of larger sums the public courts shall adjudicate as the law directs". It will be noted, however, that the example from Paros of a market steward adjudicating in disputes over wages and employment does not presuppose any labour legislation, but rather the action of one who, by his official position, was able to compose altercations arising from such matters. It may be remarked that in England long before any workmen's compensation acts were in existence, a workman who was injured through the negligence of his employer could, under the common law, sue for damages, and in the same way in the Ancient World the courts were open to disputes arising from the conditions of employment.

We have no records of any strikes, at least on a large scale, in the sense of concerted action of all the workers in any particular trade; although no doubt the free labourers engaged on any job or in a particular workshop were quite ready to "down tools" if a dispute arose. In Ptolemaic Egypt the strike was a potent weapon in the hands of the overdriven peasantry who developed to a fine art—and this is a very modern touch—the "sit-down strike", much to the perturbation of large employers who spent a considerable time in trying to coax or drive them back to their work.

There are a few instances on record of the state commandeering labour in a public emergency; thus the Athenians rebuilt their

---

[1] Guiraud, *Main d'Œuvre*, p. 77; cf. Andocides, iv, 17.
[2] *I.G.* xii, 5, 129.   [3] viii, 847 B.

walls after Salamis in this fashion;[1] the people of Chalcis built a causeway between Euboea and the mainland;[2] the Argives built their walls and provided their soldiers with weapons.[3] When the great expedition sailed for Syracuse the Athenians "pressed" a number of bakers to go along with the fleet.[4] In this case we must suppose they were paid; but we do not know if in the other cases there was anything for the workers; probably it was looked upon as a patriotic duty.

THE METIC[5]

By the term Metic was designated that class midway between the full citizen and the slave. In it were included all foreigners found within the state and such ex-slaves as had been granted their freedom. It was the policy of all Greek states, except Sparta, to welcome such aliens and grant them, under restrictions of not too burdensome a character, considerable liberty to carry on their business. So important was this class that practically all trade and banking was in their hands and a large, even a preponderating, amount of domestic industry. It is a curious commentary on the attitude of the Greeks towards gainful occupations that to enter a trade a Greek had almost perforce to leave his own city, surrender his civic rights and privileges, and betake himself to another place, there to carry on his business on sufferance and without any voice in the government of the state. Although Xenophon calls them barbarians, Syrians, Lydians and Phrygians,[6] it is certain that the greater proportion were Greeks from practically every part of Greece and the islands of the Aegean. To be a Metic did not obviously mean that he was a barbarian, but merely he was not a citizen of the state in which he lived.[7]

---

[1] Thuc. i, 90.
[2] Diod. Sic. xiii, 47.
[3] Thuc. v, 82.
[4] Thuc. vi, 22.
[5] *Mélanges Glotz*, iii, 4; Clerc, *Les Métèques Athéniens* (Paris 1893); Guiraud, *Main d'Œuvre*, pp. 152 ff.; H. Hommel, art. "Metoikoi" in *P.W.*; Francotte, *De la Condition des Étrangers dans les Cités Grecques* (Louvain 1903); Busolt, *Griech. Staatsk.* i, 186, ii, 292 ff.
[6] *Revenues*, ii, 3.
[7] But it is notable that fourth-century inscriptions on tombs show a great number of non-Greek names. Cf. *I.G.* ii, 2723 ff., 2758 Bff. Mr Gomme's remarks on the status of the Metic are excellent (*Essays in Greek History and Literature*, p. 59).

Since the citizens were so much occupied with their civic duties, it was highly necessary that as many Metics as possible should be induced to live among them. Xenophon, in his proposals for the benefit of the city, suggests how life should be made more attractive for them. "It would be for our advantage and credit that such merchants and shipowners as are found to benefit the state by bringing to it vessels and merchandise of great account should be honoured with seats of distinction on public occasions, and sometimes invited to entertainments; for being treated with such respect they would hasten to return to us as friends, for the sake not only of gain but of honour. The more people settle among us and visit us, the greater quantity of merchandise it is evident would be imported, exported and sold, and the more gain would be secured and tribute received. To effect such augmentation of the revenue it is not necessary for us to be at any cost but that of philanthropic ordinances and careful superintendence."[1] Other suggestions he makes that would induce such foreign merchants to come to Athens are more expedition in the administration of the commercial courts, so that their business should not be unduly hampered by long delays of justice; the building of lodging houses for seamen and merchants and shops for retail dealers.[2]

Since Metics by law were forbidden to own land, agriculture was barred to them.[3] But in every sort of industry they were supreme. In masonry and the building trade, carpentry, the importing and selling of colours and varnishes they predominate. Textiles, leather, hides, the making of boots and shoes, and pottery they practically monopolise. The same is true in the metal trades, and in work in gold, lead and iron there is not a man mentioned in the accounts of public works who is not a Metic. It is somewhat startling to realise that the magnificent public buildings of Athens were for the most part built and adorned not by Athenian citizens but by foreigners! It is true that Pheidias, the greatest artist of Greece, was an Athenian, and was appropriately rewarded by his fellow citizens by being

---

[1] *Revenues*, iii, 3–6.   [2] *Revenues*, iii, 12–13.
[3] But Mr Tod, in *Annual of British School at Athens*, viii, 197ff., notes that eight freedmen Metics were classed as *georgoi*, farmers, or perhaps more likely, farm-hands (p. 205).

thrown into prison on a trumped-up charge of peculation; it was evidently much safer to be a Metic than a citizen.

Mining was generally denied to the Metic since he could not own land, nor by consequence excavate it. That the state would have done well to allow them this privilege was apparent to Xenophon, who advised that the mines of Laurium should be thrown open to them.[1] Since mining operations had languished, he evidently considered that the competition of Metics would be necessary to spur the citizens to greater efforts. We do hear of one Metic who was allowed to engage in work at Laurium—Sosias a Thracian—and he was evidently one of the largest and most successful of all the contractors.[2] Overseas commerce and trading were almost entirely in Metic hands. Particularly was this so in the grain and salted fish business. The most important merchants importing fish from the Euxine were Chaerephilus and sons, whose services to the state were so exceptional that they were rewarded by the grant of citizenship.[3] Chrysippus and his brother, large grain importers, came to the rescue of Athens at a time when wheat had risen to famine prices, and by munificent gifts of grain saved the situation.[4] Banking was practically entirely in the hands of Metics; the most celebrated, Pasion, was originally a slave and passed on the business to another slave, Phormio: both being freedmen they passed automatically into the Metic class.

There was no intellectual sphere in which Metics did not shine, or, perhaps better, outshine the citizen. They adorned the schools of rhetoric and philosophy, music and comedy.[5] They were prosperous and busy, cultured and generous, relieved from the burdens of statecraft that so oppressed the citizen. It is probably not too much to say that the Metic had a far better time than the citizen who, if he wished to prosper, had to leave his own city and seek fortune elsewhere.

Although they were welcomed to whatever city they went, yet the Metics suffered under some disabilities. First, they commonly lacked the right to bring lawsuits in the courts in their own name. Secondly, they were excluded from all public

[1] *Revenues*, iv, 22.　　　　　[2] *Ibid.* iv, 14.
[3] Alexis, *ap.* Athen. iii, 119f.　　[4] Dem. *in Phorm.* 38–9.
[5] Glotz, *Ancient Greece at Work*, p. 190.

offices and the priesthood. Thirdly, they had no voice or vote in the government. Fourthly, they were not legally allowed to marry a citizen, and the children of such a marriage were counted as illegitimate: a Metic woman marrying an Athenian citizen was degraded to the status of concubinage.[1] Fifthly, as already mentioned, they could not own land. And lastly, they could make no claims on the state for relief in distress; as, for instance, in times of famine they could not share in the distribution of grain, as was seen in 445 when, we are told, 5000 Metics, who falsely claimed citizenship, were struck off the rolls and sold into slavery.[2]

With regard to taxation there are some uncertainties. Undoubtedly Metics were subject to the capital levy or *eisphora*, and there is reason to suppose that it was assessed at a higher rate than for citizens.[3] Apparently they were free from the more onerous liturgies, since they were exempt from the trierarchy, and rarely had the expenses of the Choregia imposed upon them.[4] They were obliged to pay the tax imposed on strangers doing business in the market (*xenikon*)[5] and, in addition, they also paid a special Metic tax (*metoikion*) of 12 drs. a year for men, and 6 for unmarried women or widows who had not a son at work to support them.[6] Failure to pay this tax was severely punished by the culprit being sold as a slave. Plato condemned this tax and would not have it in his ideal state; where he would allow foreigners to live for twenty years only.[7] Diodorus Siculus states that Themistocles induced the Athenians to abolish this tax in order to attract more Metics to the city, but later it was reimposed.[8] Apparently Metics were liable for military service as hoplites but only within Attica. Doubtless this was a wise precaution, since if sent abroad such foreigners might be unreliable if the expedition were against their native country. On the whole, therefore, the position of the Metic, at least in Athens, was not unfavourable; indeed it is not too much to say

[1] *Ath. Pol.* xxvi, 4; Plut. *Pericles*, 37.
[2] Plut. *Pericles*, 37. The number is incredibly large.
[3] Cf. Dem. *in Androt.* 61; Andreades, *Greek Public Finance*, p. 279, n. 6. The point is obscure.
[4] Clerc. *Métèques*, p. 174.   [5] Dem. *in Eubul.* 34.
[6] For more on these taxes cf. p. 375.
[7] *Laws*, 850.   [8] xi, 43, 2.

that, with the exception of the disabilities mentioned above, they enjoyed very great privileges and were a welcome addition to the commerce and industry of the city.

Xenophon remarks: "We have granted to sojourners a certain equality with citizens; for the state has need of them through the great number of trades and for manning the ships."[1] Plutarch informs us that Solon even offered them full citizenship;[2] if this be so, it must only have been a passing policy and obviously not adhered to later. Isocrates warmly advocated every inducement to attract them.[3]

The explanation for such complacency on the part of the citizens is easy to find. As the Metics were allowed no political rights whatever, nothing was to be feared from them and everything to be gained from having them as numerous and wealthy as possible, as a convenient source of revenue by which the life of the citizen was made easy and pleasant. The anxiety to see that justice was expeditious for them was founded on their almost complete monopoly of the grain trade, the very lifeblood of the Athenian state.

Their number was considerable; at the beginning of the Peloponnesian war there were one-third as many Metics as citizens; at the end of the fourth century one-half.[4]

THE SLAVE[5]

It is curious to realise how the passage of time and the glamour of antiquity blunt our susceptibilities and soften the sharp

[1] *Govt. Athens*, i, 12.

[2] *Solon*, 24. Such, so far as Plutarch's statement goes, is the ostensible meaning of the passage, and has generally been so accepted. But for an entirely different view cf. Heichelheim in *Philol. Woch.* (1934), p. 126, in which it is argued that Solon's offer applied only to those foreign citizens who had been expelled for political reasons, and to aristocratic families, so that the law really made it more difficult, or even impossible, for foreigners to attain citizenship. The question is an open one and cannot be settled until further evidence accumulates.   [3] *De Pace*, 21.

[4] Busolt, *Griech. Staatsk.* i, 294; Guiraud, *Main d'Œuvre*, p. 157.

[5] Zimmern, *Solon and Croesus, Greek Commonwealth*; Oscar Jacob, "Les Esclaves Publics à Athènes", *Le Musée Belge*, xxx, 57ff.; Guiraud, *Main d'Œuvre*, vii; Francotte, *L'Industrie*, ii, cap. v; R. L. Sargent, "The use of Slaves by the Athenians in warfare", *Class. Philol.* xxii (1927), pp. 201ff., 264ff.; *ibid.* "The number of slaves at Athens"; E. Meyer, "Die Sklaverei im Altertum" in *Kleine Schriften* (1910), pp. 169ff.; Westermann, art. "Sklaverei" in *P.W.* Suppl. vi (1935), pp. 894ff.; Busolt, *Griech. Staatsk.* i, 272ff.; F. Oppenheimer, *System der Soziologie*, iii, 367ff.

outlines of what, on reflection, we must acknowledge, if we are honest, was a great evil—the slave system. It was universal in the ancient world; the Bible has innumerable references to slaves, albeit the word is softened into "servants" or the harsher "bondman" or "bondwoman".[1] But reading them we do not realise what they were, and in any case it was a long time ago. We are morally complacent about slavery. We know quite well that it is a bad system, economically as well as ethically, and we pride ourselves for having got rid of it, that is, so far as we are concerned. Our self-satisfaction may be a trifle tarnished when we are honest enough to acknowledge that a sweat-shop may be as bad, even worse, than any of the slave establishments of antiquity. We may also reflect that within the memory of living man slavery was highly developed in the southern portion of the United States, and that to-day there are thousands of slaves in the Orient.

But however true that may be, the fact remains that slavery was an integral part of ancient economy. We might even go so far as to say that without the slave the Ancient World could not have existed, or at least in the form it did. To those who look to Aristotle and Plato for guidance in the conduct of democracy, this reflection must come as an unpleasant shock to modern susceptibilities. It is hardly reassuring to appreciate that Plato's ideal Republic was founded and rooted in slavery. It is also somewhat startling to realise that actually Plato's laws with regard to slaves were harsher than those of Attica, for instance, where he provides that a slave who has killed his master in self-defence against a murderous attack shall be put to death.[2] Aristotle's grave discussion in the *Politics* as to whether or not a slave is capable of reason, although finally he decides he is, sounds curiously to modern ears.[3] His philosopher king was to rule, in his transcendent wisdom, over a society not of freemen alone, but also men and women accounted incapable and, therefore, unworthy of freedom.

It is difficult for us to-day to grasp that fact, much less to appreciate it. It arouses an uneasiness, a feeling that we would

[1] The word "slave" is only twice used, once in Jeremiah ii. 14, in the Old Testament, and once in the New, Rev. xviii. 13. Many references to bond-men and women.

[2] *Laws*, ix, 869 A, B, D.   [3] *Pol.* i, 13, 1259 B, 1260 A, B.

much rather it were not so, and yet it must be accepted with such equanimity as we can summon to our aid. We do not like, or rather we unequivocally condemn, slavery in any or all of its forms. The idea shocks our susceptibilities and outrages our finer feelings of what we conceive to be social justice; our repulsion thereto is genuine and deep-seated. And yet slavery was natural to the Greeks, who seldom bothered their heads about the ethical side of it. Just as the beasts were their four-footed servants and helpers in toil, so were the slaves their two-footed. Aristotle's phrase "animated property", tools or implements that were alive, as distinguished from inanimate things like ploughs or spades, puts the slave not far above the beasts of the field, if at all.

And yet for all their facile and apparently imperturbable acceptance and approval of the slave system, we may sometimes wonder whether, in their heart of hearts, they were altogether happy about it. No doubt the slave-driver, a familiarly repulsive figure in any age, never troubled his head about any "high-falutin" ideas; but every now and again we have an allusion that sets us thinking. The pathetic words of Eumaeus, the trusted and privileged slave of Odysseus, recur to the mind, who could not feel secure in the little comforts that a lifetime of faithful service had given him. "A little gift from such as we is dear; for this is the way with slaves who are in fear when young lords like ours rule over them."[1] And again: "Zeus takes away the half of a man's virtue when the day of slavery comes upon him."[2] Eumaeus, kidnapped in youth, was the son of a king, and over everyone from the highest to the lowest hung the horror of possible enslavement. Perhaps in that we find the source of Greek tragedy; the *Trojae* of Euripides is almost too poignant for our equanimity.

The institution of slavery is a phase of the evolution of human society; and, properly considered, a very distinct advance on the most primitive form. In earliest times, when one people or tribe conquered another, it was the almost invariable custom of the victors to slaughter the vanquished, or at least their male captives; the women might be reserved for the use of the conquerors. Such was merely a precautionary measure to guard

---

[1] *Od.* xiv, 56.   [2] *Od.* xvi, 323.

against further aggression. The next stage was when captives, both male and female, or at least such as were likely to be useful, were enslaved, in order to relieve the conquerors of the necessity of manual labour and leave them free to pursue the art of war and piracy. From that to a systematised slave trade was but a short and inevitable step, and a state of commercialised slavery came into being. It is essential to realise that slavery is always a natural part of a social system in which the male members of the tribe or nation are warriors, whose whole activities are taken up in fitting themselves for defence or aggression, and who in consequence have little time and less inclination for manual labour; such is left to the women and the slaves. To the Greek war was the portion of the free citizen and the slave a necessity of his condition. Such also was the destiny of the Roman in his task of conquering the world; when that was accomplished, and as soon as his empire started to crumble, slavery began to disappear, its severities to relax and eventually be replaced by serfdom. When the state is everything and political power omnipotent, the rights of the individual are disregarded and human liberty denied. But when, as in the third century in Greece and in the decadent Roman Empire, the state has failed and mankind has lost faith in it to solve all human problems, the thoughts of men turn back to the individual and the claims of humanity, and the right of domination by men over their fellows is called in question.

To the Greek, therefore, slavery was natural and necessary, and except by some of the deeper thinkers, never questioned as part of the social order. Both Plato and Aristotle accepted the system, although with some lurking misgivings. Aristotle argued that some were born with the servile spirit, too debased and spiritless to be anything else, and finding in it the best and only means of being useful members of society. That freemen should be enslaved by the ill-fortune of war was indefensible, and in any case the hope of freedom should always be the reward of faithful service.[1] Plato reluctantly accepts the system as inevitable, and in his ideal state the slave fills an important part and is the subject of contempt, although he deprecates illtreatment. The enslavement of Greeks by Greeks he condemns.[2]

[1] *Pol.* 1252 B, 1260 A.   [2] *Rep.* v, 469.

It may be remarked that Plato is totally inconsistent. He condemns kidnapping, and yet knows quite well that the one great supply of slaves came from that source. It is a curious instance of a really great mind being unable to transcend the circumstances of his age. He could not conceive of a world without slaves, and so they had to form part of his ideal state, whether they could be logically included or no. Euripides almost alone depicts the slave in a human light, and in several of his plays the faithful slave, grateful for the kindness of his master and honourable in his actions, bears a part.[1]

The supply of slaves came from various sources, of which hereditary slavery was almost the least general. As has been found everywhere, it did not pay to raise slave children; but as a reward for faithful service slaves were allowed to marry. Both Xenophon[2] and the writer of the Aristotelian *Economica* recommend this. "Good slaves when they have children become even better disposed towards their masters."[3] Hume, in his essay on the *Populousness of Ancient Peoples*, comments severely on this aspect of Greek morals. Secondly, there was, beyond all doubt, a certain amount of obtaining infants who had been exposed[4] by those who made it their business to rear them for the slave trade, or, even worse, for prostitution. Although not tolerated in Attica, free parents sold their children into slavery in other states. Enslavement for debt was stopped by Solon. Thirdly, prisoners of war were one of the greatest sources of supply for the market. Not only "barbarians" but Greeks were enslaved by their victors, and the armies were followed by dealers who bought the prisoners. It must be acknowledged, however, that the Greeks had a certain conscience on that score, especially Aristotle.[5] Fourthly, piracy and kidnapping, the most ancient and, even to-day, the most general of all methods of supplying the market. Kidnapping was by no means confined to "bar-

---

[1] E.g. *Medea*, 54; *Orestes*, 869; *Ion*, 854.

[2] Cf. Sargent, *Size of Slave Population*, cap. vi, pp. 122 ff.; Xen. *Oecon.* ix, 5; (Arist.) *Oecon.* 1344 B.

[3] For mention of slave children in wills cf. those of Aristotle and Lycon. Diog. Laert. v, 1, 9; 4, 9.

[4] Westermann, art. "Sklaverei" in *P.W.* p. 902.

[5] Plutarch tells us that Lycurgus passed a law forbidding Athenians to buy Greek war prisoners. *Vit. X Orat.* 842 A. Cf. Busolt, *Griech. Staatsk.* i, p. 276; Xen. *Hell.* i, 6, 14; *Ages.* i, 21.

barian" countries; children were stolen in every city in Greece, and the possibility of forcible enslavement was present to everyone. The trade was well organised, Syria, Pontus, Lydia, Galatia, Thrace, Egypt and Libya all supplying their quota. Chios was the most famous market, along with Cyprus, Samos, Ephesus, Athens and later Delos. In Athens we know that the market was held once a month, and the taxes levied on the trade were a source of considerable revenue.[1] On slaves purchased by foreigners the state levied a tax of 2 per cent on importation; a surtax of 1 or 2 per cent and an export duty of 2 per cent.

It is probably safe to say that, on the whole, and more especially in the case of domestic slaves and those employed in industry in the cities, the treatment accorded to them was humane; at least by ancient standards if not by modern.[2] In a well-known passage in the speech against Midias, Demosthenes cites the law whereby any personal outrage on free-born or slave was an indictable offence visited with heavy punishment, and in a fine burst of satisfaction as an Athenian goes on to say, "You hear, O Athenians, the humanity of the law which allows not even slaves to be insulted in their persons. By the Gods, let me ask— Suppose a man carried this law to the barbarians, from whom slaves are brought to Greece, and praising you and discoursing of Athens, addressed them thus—'There are certain people in Greece so mild and humane in their disposition—that although they have suffered from you many injuries, they permit not even those whom they have paid a price for and purchased for slaves to be abused, but have passed this law of state to prevent it, and have punished many already with death for transgressing this law.'" Then, somewhat naïvely, he imagines that, overcome by the humanity of the Athenians, these same barbarians would become allies, and presumably offer themselves gladly for slavery.[3] Xenophon has an eloquent passage on the treatment of slaves in Athens. "The licence allowed to slaves and sojourners in Athens is very great; it is not allowable to strike

[1] Apollodorus, in the first half of the third century, from whom Terence translated the *Phormio*, speaks, line 837, of a slave market at Sunium. Nothing is known of this.

[2] But the remarks of Plato on the somewhat perfunctory medical aid given to sick slaves are suggestive, *Laws*, 720. But cf. Xen. *Mem.* ii, 4, 3, ii, x, 1.

[3] *In Midiam*, 47–8.

them, nor will the slave yield you the way in the street. For what reason this custom is suffered to prevail in this country I will tell you. If it were usual for the slave or the sojourner or freedman to be beaten by the free citizen, he would often strike an Athenian born, imagining him to be a slave; for the people of the city wear no better dress than slaves or sojourners, nor are they at all superior in personal appearance. Yet if anyone feels surprised that they permit their slaves to fare luxuriously, and some of them to live even magnificently, they may be shown to act even in this respect with judgment; for where a naval power exists, it is necessary from pecuniary considerations to humour the slaves, that we may receive the profit from their work, and to indulge them in a liberal way of living. But where the slaves are rich, it is no longer expedient that my slave should fear you—in Lacedaemon indeed he does fear you—since if your slave fears me there will be danger that he will sacrifice all that he has in order to avoid peril to his person. On this account, accordingly, we have granted to slaves a certain equality with the free."[1] It is, of course, true that many slaves were "barbarians", more or less on a definitely lower scale of culture. The suggestion that for such slavery was a compulsory initiation into a civilisation higher than their own, while no doubt not without a certain amount of truth, yet arouses a somewhat uneasy feeling that the compulsion was probably unwelcome, not to say uncalled for. It recalls the ingenious and highly pious sentiments of the early English slave-traders who transported negroes to America for the purpose of saving their souls by bringing them under the blessings of Christianity. If they were also brought under the master's lash it was regrettable but doubtless under the circumstances unavoidable.

Zimmern in his *Greek Commonwealth* argues very persuasively that while there was "a sediment of slaves to perform the most degrading tasks", yet these were by no means typical of all, or even of the majority, who were rather "apprentices" brought in, albeit by force, to learn the arts of civilisation and, until they had won their freedom, to work under the direction of their masters. They were necessary in the economic conditions of their age, since the scantiness of the population made the

[1] *Govt. of Athens*, i, 10ff.

supply of free labour very small, and without the help of such "apprentices" trade and industry could not have been carried on at all. Manumission was easy and the slave could acquire money and even landed property, and so buy his freedom. Working conditions, except in the mines, were not hard; in fact master and slave worked side by side, sharing the same standard of living. In the erection of public buildings, of which we have records of costs and workmen employed, both slaves and freemen worked together on equal terms.

And yet, if the expression may be allowed, this is all very fine and large; there was an uglier side to slavery in Greece, as there always has been to slavery everywhere, of which we catch glimpses every now and again. It would be easy to collect a score of instances from cases in the courts and from the comic poets where slaves have been beaten unmercifully; we must suppose that the law as to corporal punishment was a dead letter, except for show purposes to permit a little self-satisfaction of the Athenians.[1] We have one or two pictures which suggest that the happy camaraderie of the workshop was not always unbroken. For instance, one shows work going on in a potter's shop, where one of the workers has been strung up by his hands and feet and is being lashed by his overseer; the other workers go on with their tasks unconcernedly—perhaps it was too usual a sight to arouse interest. In another a cat-o-nine-tails hangs suggestively on the wall.[2] These are from Phocis,[3] and we may charitably suppose that things were better in Athens. It has

---

[1] In the case argued by Lysias against Eratosthenes a slave girl is threatened with a whipping and relegation to work in a mill. Lysias, i, 18. The incident illustrating tactlessness in the *Characters* of Theophrastus (xii, 12) is hardly satisfying. Cf. also Xen. *Mem.* ii, 1, 16–17, iii, 13, 3.

[2] For pictures cf. Glotz, *Ancient Greece at Work*, pp. 205, 140.

[3] If we are to believe Timaeus in Athen. (vi, 264 c, d) the Phocians subsequently prohibited the keeping of slaves on economic grounds. Perhaps the severity of their treatment of them brought too great troubles with it. But doubtful cf. Heitland, *Agricola*; Oertel, *Anhang*, p. 527, n. 4. Zimmern, *Greek Commonwealth*, p. 265, says: "The vase-painters have left us many pictures of the homely interior of the potter's shop, with all the various processes going on in close juxtaposition. We can see the master working, as in the stoneyard, side by side with his apprentices, superintending and encouraging their own efforts at craftsmanship." The encouragement administered in this case at least must have been sufficiently drastic to insure satisfactory results! Attempts at toning down the brutalities of the slave system are not invariably successful.

been suggested that except under extraordinary circumstances no master could inflict more than fifty lashes on his slave, which corresponded with the maximum fine of fifty drachmae imposed on a freeman.[1] It may be remarked that a penalty of fifty lashes could be quite sufficiently severe under any circumstances. But one is left wondering as to those fine protestations of Xenophon and Demosthenes. It is only fair to remember, however, the wise counsels of Ischomachus who points out that severe punishments are of little use when careful training and strict discipline have failed to produce their salutary effects.[2]

Slaves in the law courts were invariably examined under torture. We need not suppose that it was always severe; perhaps in most cases it was a mere form or threat. But it is remarkable in reading many cases in the courts how often the master refused to allow his slave to be tortured. We may be generous and put this down to humanitarian grounds, or perhaps he did not want a valuable article to be badly injured, or perhaps out of fear of what might be revealed.[3] We do know of one case where a slave was induced under torture to implicate himself and his masters in a murder, and we may be sure that it must have been sufficiently severe to extract so grave a confession.[4] There is a particularly unpleasant passage in the *Frogs* of Aristophanes[5] in which Xanthias, in the role of Master of Dionysus, most cheerfully offers his supposed slave to be tortured, and reels off a gruesome list of the usual means employed, the lash, knots and screws, the rack, the water torture, fire and vinegar, "all sorts of ways", and insists that he be not treated leniently as a child but it be well laid on. The passage is, of course, in the comic vein, as Xanthias is really the slave and is deriving immense satisfaction in delivering his master to the tormentors. But all the same, as a catalogue of tortures to which any miserable slave could be subjected, it is hardly reassuring to the view that slavery in Greece was as innocuous as the humanitarians might wish.[6]

[1] Glotz, *Comptes Rendus de l'Académie* (1908), pp. 571ff. But doubtful.
[2] Xen. *Oecon.* vii, 41, ix, 5.
[3] Cf. Dem. *in Neaeram*, 124, where the challenger offers to pay damages if the female slaves to be tortured suffered any serious injury and their evidence was against his case.
[4] Antiphon, v, 47–8.   [5] *Ranae*, 616ff.
[6] Murray's remarks on the legal torture of slaves are worth pondering on (*Rise of Greek Epic*, p. 321).

The case from the orations of Antiphon where the slave con-
fessed to participation in a murder (he helped to dispose of the
body) was, we may hope, unusually scandalous, for his accusers
having extracted the confession then put the miserable wretch
to death, and this in flagrant contravention of the fact that
according to Attic law no master had the power of life or death
over his slaves.[1]

It is true that slaves were protected against *hubris*, which may
be translated as outrageous insult.[2] Demosthenes, in working
up the indignation against Midias, says that many have been
put to death for insult to a slave.[3] This is amazing to the modern
idea, but it must be remembered that the act of *hubris* was of
the nature of sacrilege; it was an offence against religion and
slaves did receive religious protection. It is curious to note
that they were more favourably situated in the religious community than in the civil. They were excluded from places where
citizens congregated like the gymnasia, but were admitted to
religious assemblies and public sacrifices. Plato, in a very fine
passage, warns against *hubris* towards slaves "for a genuine and
unfeigned reverence for justice and hatred of injustice show
themselves best in dealings with persons towards whom it is
easy to be unjust",[4] and for such a sentiment we may feel
sincere admiration. In another passage Plato says that a slave
is "one who, when he is injured or reviled, is without power to
help himself or anyone else for whom he cares".[5] We are even
a little doubtful about the laws against *hubris*; he was unable to
bring an action himself, it must be done by some kind-hearted
person, and since such an action was a very serious matter it
was seldom embarked on. In the case from Antiphon already
alluded to, the masters of the murdered slave are not prosecuted,
since action for murder was a private one, undertaken by the
relatives of the deceased, and in this case there was no one to

---

[1] Isocr. *Panath.* 181; Lycurgus, *in Leocr.* 65; Antiphon, *ut sup.* Also
Kahrstedt, *Staatsgebiet u. Staatsangehörige in Athen*, pp. 133, 139, 321ff.;
Busolt, *Griech. Staatsk.* i, pp. 273, 280, 982. The whole question is admirably
treated by Glenn R. Morrow in *Class. Philol.* xxxii, 3, p. 210 (July 1937).

[2] Dem. *in Mid.* 47.

[3] *In Mid.* 49. For more on criminal practice in the Athenian courts cf.
Gertrude Smith, *Administration of Justice from Hesiod to Solon*, cap. iv;
G. Calhoun, *Growth of Criminal Law in Ancient Greece.*

[4] *Laws*, vi, 777 D.   [5] *Gorgias*, 483 B.

avenge the death.[1] One defence a slave had, he could appeal to to sold to another master if he were maltreated, and he had the right of asylum by fleeing to the Theseum or the altar of the Eumenides on the Acropolis.[2]

The condition of the Helots in Sparta was, of course, notoriously bad; and in spite of the utmost precautions and at times wholesale massacres, their masters lived in constant fear of them. Slave rebellions were frequent, as, for instance, in Samos, when a thousand of them ran away,[3] and in Argos where they actually gained the mastery for some time until expelled, when they captured Tiryns.[4] In Sicily, always of ill repute for its treatment of slaves, and in Southern Italy, insurrections were constant.[5] Chios had more slaves than any other state except Sparta, and in consequence they were punished more severely than usual in cases of offence. When the Athenians invaded the island in 412 they deserted in large numbers and did much mischief to the country.[6] At the end of the second century we are told that the slaves employed in the mines at Laurium massacred their overseers, took the fortress at Sunium, and for a long time devastated the land.[7]

But however tarnished the brightness of the picture may be in detail, yet we may suppose that, on the whole, the slaves in Greece were well treated, more for the sake of the masters than for the slaves, as Plato quite candidly says.[8] A slave was a valuable possession, and it paid to keep him in good physical condition and tolerably contented; just as it pays a farmer to treat his horses well in order to get more work out of them. However we may excuse the system, the enslavement of human beings is always and under any circumstance bad and contrary to the elementary rules of humanity.

Again the picture is hardly true to life when we represent

---

[1] This fact explains the astonishment of Socrates when he hears that Euthyphro is bringing an accusation against his own father. It is not alone because he is shocked at the impious act.

[2] Art. "Asylon" in *P.W.*; cf. Eurip. *Suppl.* 268. Altar of Eumenides, Aristoph. *Frag. Com. Graec.* 567. Cf. *Equites*, 1312; *Thesm.* 224. A badly treated slave's appeal to be sold to another master, Poll. vii, 13.

[3] Athen. vi, 267. [4] Her. vi, 83.

[5] Plato, *Laws*, vi, 777 C; Diod. Sic. xxxiv, 2.

[6] Thuc. viii, 40. [7] Diod. Sic. xxxiv, 2, 19.

[8] *Laws*, vi, 77 C, D.

slavery as a mere prelude to freedom, and manumissions as easy and frequent; the records point to the contrary, and it is probably true to say that in the fifth century manumission was either very rare or non-existent. M. Glotz has found 1675 manumissions scattered among the inscriptions, of which the greater proportion were women.[1] Doubtless these represent only a fraction of the number actually set free, yet over a long space of time and in relation to the hundreds of thousands of slaves in Greece, it is an almost microscopical number.[2] In the twenty years from 340 to 320 there are records of 253 manumissions, or an average of somewhat over ten a year. Of these 142 are men and 111 women.[3] The Greeks were always poor; a slave was a highly valuable possession, and such acts of generosity were rare. Even Plato, who had five slaves, only freed one in his will, leaving four to his heirs, who might very well have objected to such altruism and have contested the will after his death. Even when manumission was granted it was rarely for nothing, or out of goodwill on the part of the master. It cost a large sum, 200 Alexandrian drachmae for a woman, 6 minas for a man.[4] This is hardly to be wondered at, since if a slave was able to save enough to buy his freedom, he must have been a good worker and a valuable possession to his master, and have reached the point where he had saved enough to purchase his freedom only after long training and expense. We must dismiss at once any idea that the Greeks, in the goodness of their hearts and as a reward for faithful service, were in the habit even on their deathbeds of freeing their slaves to any great extent. The view that slavery was little more than apprenticeship to free labour must therefore be accepted with caution.

Of the condition of the "chattel" slaves, especially those working in the mines, a far less favourable picture must be drawn. Here worked that "sediment" under conditions which were entirely bad. They were branded with their owner's mark and chained to their tasks. Labour was continuous in ten-hour shifts, and the conditions were so unhealthy that the death-rate

[1] Glotz, *Comptes Rendus*, pp. 199–200, 217–18. Cf. Calderini, *La Manumissione e la condizione dei liberte in Grecia*, pp. 70f., 80f.
[2] *I.G.* ii², 1553–78.   [3] Gomme, *Population*, p. 41.
[4] Zimmern, *Solon and Croesus*, pp. 162–3; cf. Jardé, *Céréales*, p. 138, n. 1.

was very high. We are told quite candidly that it did not pay to treat them well, but rather to wear them out and buy new ones.[1] It is fair to say that the conditions were recognised as scandalous. Plutarch remarks that "one cannot much approve of gaining riches by working mines, the greatest part of which is done by malefactors and barbarians, some of them too, bound and perishing in those close and unwholesome places".[2] We need not suppose that conditions at Laurium were so bad as the horrifying state of forced labour in the Nubian gold mines and the equally bad conditions in the Spanish silver mines described by Diodorus.[3] But that they were bad admits of no doubt whatever, and the picture of kindly and humane treatment of slaves in Attica is, at least in part, marred thereby. The high-class, intelligent slave in the home or the valuable craftsman in shop or factory is treated well and suffers little or nothing from his status. The low-grade slave, barbarous, sullen and resentful, untrustworthy except under the vigilant eye of the overseer; forced to his labour through fear of the lash, is treated like a brute, and only brutal taskmasters can manage him. The iron fetters found in the underground galleries at Laurium are grim reminders of the treatment such unfortunate wretches received. Slavery invites abuses; they are inseparable from the system, which stands condemned thereby in any age or under any conditions. And yet the principal method proposed by Xenophon in his *Revenues* for increasing the wealth of Athens was to purchase ten thousand of these unfortunates, and hire them out to contractors for work at Laurium. We are not told what the wastage might be through death and desertion, but it would be large, and we must regard Xenophon's estimate of a revenue of 33 per cent on the investment a highly optimistic one.

A slave was a risky investment, since if not employed or sick, he still had to be maintained and the same was true in old age. For that reason it was safer to hire gangs from contractors rather than sink money in their purchase. We, therefore, find in the fifth and fourth centuries a regular business in hiring out

[1] Athen. vi, 272.
[2] Plut. *Nic. et Crassus*, i; cf. Theoph. *de Lap.* 63; Xen. *Mem.* iii, 6, 12. Also Ardaillon, *Les mines de Laurion*, pp. 21 ff., 94 ff.
[3] Nubian gold mines, Diod. iii, 12. Spanish silver mines, v, 38.

slaves, not only for heavy manual labour, but as cooks, footmen, ladies' maids, dancers and flute girls. If a house or establishment were rented the slaves went with it. The practice of allowing slaves to work for themselves, giving a percentage of their earnings to their master, was very common. We hear of the labour market at Athens where all unemployed, slave or free, gathered to wait for jobs.[1]

Domestic establishments were small, on an average three slaves to a well-to-do household, and only the very rich had sometimes as many as 50;[2] the poor, of course, could not afford one at all, much to their discontent. Slave labour was little used in agriculture, since Greece was a country of small farms, and the intermittent labour on the soil made it bad business to feed slaves when not at work.[3] This was particularly so in grain farming, and in the cultivation of the vine and olive the skill necessary was so great that it could not safely be carried on except by the master himself. For oil-pressing gangs were hired who went from farm to farm, but these were mostly freemen with a few slaves. Aristotle remarked: "With the poor the ox takes the place of the slave."[4]

A numerous and well-treated class was that of the slaves belonging to the state. These comprised policemen, workers on the roads and street cleaners and minor officials in the Civil Service.[5] It is generally supposed that they were also engaged in the mint, but this is somewhat doubtful. The policing of Athens was in the care of the famous Scythian archers, public slaves maintained by the state at considerable cost. The commissioners of public works used slaves as well as freemen; in 329–328 seventeen public slaves worked in the yards of Eleusis under a slave foreman.[6] It seems fairly certain that most of the work of the permanent civil service was done by slaves, who by the nature of their work must have been educated and reliable, some of them occupying positions of trust and enjoying public

---

[1] Poll. vii, 133; Philochor. frag. 73, Müller, *F.H.G.* i, 396.
[2] Plato, *Pol.* ix, 578 E.
[3] Cf. Heitland, *Agricola*, pp. 44ff. The same was true in the Roman Empire. Cf. Barrow, *Slavery in the Roman Empire*.
[4] *Pol.* 1252 B.
[5] The employment of slaves by the state is treated more fully in the chapter on Public Finance.   [6] *I.G.* ii², 1672.

esteem. A most interesting but unfortunately somewhat obscure case is that of Epidamnus, on the coast of Illyria, where, if we understand the reference of Aristotle aright, all public works were carried on by slaves.[1]

DID SLAVERY PAY?[2]

As we have already remarked, a slave was a risky investment. When unemployed,[3] sick, or too old to work, he had still to be maintained; his death was a total loss to his owner. The prices paid varied widely according to the individual capabilities of each slave, and also according to the supply and demand in the market. After a war, when the number of prisoners was large, the price fell considerably. At the end of the sixth century the ransom for a prisoner-of-war was 2 minae; at the beginning of the fourth in Sicily it was 3. At the time of Alexander, along with the general rise in all prices, it was 5; in the third century the average price fell considerably.[4]

Generally speaking, an unskilled labourer, fit for only the roughest work and mostly employed in the mines, was worth from 130 to 150 drs. Skilled workers were much more valuable; a cabinet worker was worth 2 minae; an armourer from 3 to 6; a skilled builder's assistant 5 or 6;[5] while a slave exceptionally qualified to act as a foreman in the mine would fetch as much as a talent.[6] The prices paid for a string of slaves belonging to Cephisodorus, a rich Metic who was involved in the mutilation of the Hermae in 414 and had his possessions confiscated in consequence, are interesting as showing the values attached to the various nationalities. Two Thracian men fetched 170 and 130 drs. respectively; two Syrians 301 and 240; a Carian 105; two Illyrians 161 and 121; a Scythian 144; a Colchian 153; a man from Melitene 151; a Carian boy 124, and a little Carian

---

[1] Arist. *Pol.* 1267 B. The reference in this passage to the proposal of Diophantus to introduce the same system into Athens is unintelligible. For more on this obscure point, cf. art. "Monopole" in *P.W.* xvi, 150, by Heichelheim.

[2] Boeckh, i, 85; Francotte, *L'Industrie*, ii, 8 ff.; Guiraud, *Main d'Œuvre*, pp. 190 ff.; Calderini, *Manumissione*, p. 214.

[3] Cf. Aristoph. *Lysist.* 1204–5.

[4] Heichelheim, *Wirtsch. Schwank.* 112. Busolt, *Griech. Staatsk.* i, 200.

[5] Glotz, *Comptes Rendus*, 194–5; Andreades, *Greek Public Finance*, 283.

[6] Xen. *Mem.* ii, 5, 2.

boy 72. Of the women slaves, three Thracians fetched 220, 165 and 135 and a Lydian 170 drs.[1] Demosthenes, in the case against Spudias, says a farm slave was worth 200 drs., and in that against Nicostratus speaks of two others worth 125 drs. each.[2]

In reckoning the worth of a slave to his master, what he could earn must be set against the cost of food, lodging and clothing.[3] In 329 the cost of food to the state for a slave belonging to it was 3 obols a day, or 177 drs. a year.[4] A pair of shoes, with resoling, cost 6 drs. and lasted two years. A mantle cost 18½ drs., and a goatskin 4½. They were also provided with a tunic and a felt hat of which we do not know the prices. These were not renewed every year, but if we reckon the total expenses at about 200 drs., without anything for lodging, we should not be far wrong. To this must be added the interest on the money spent on his purchase, reckoned on the principle of amortisation, to cover his waning powers as he grew older and less able to work, and his eventual death when the entire sum invested in him was lost.[5] If we reckon everything at, say, 250 drs. a year, and that is a very low estimate, we can see that at a daily wage of 1 dr. for free labour the advantage of owning a slave instead of employing a free worker was very small indeed. When the risks of death, illness or accident, and escape are taken into account there was practically no advantage whatever.[6] When in later times the wage rose to 2 or more drs. a day, there was very distinct gain in owning a slave, provided he was industrious, healthy and faithful.

The risk of losing slaves through desertion was considerable; as for instance when 20,000 ran away when the Spartans occupied Decelea. The Athenians accused the Megarians of harbouring fugitives;[7] their return was stipulated in international

---

[1] *I.G.* i, 274, 275, 277; Hicks and Hill, *Greek Historical Inscriptions*, p. 72.

[2] *In Spud.* 8; *in Nicost.* 1.

[3] Guiraud, *Main d'Œuvre*, pp. 190–1.

[4] *I.G.* ii², 1672.

[5] Cf. Oertel on this point in *Rhein. Mus.* lxxix, 233.

[6] But on the other hand cf. Beloch's estimate that slaves in a well-conducted and profitable factory could bring in a net return of from 60 to 120 drs. a year; unskilled slaves in the mines a maximum of 60 drs., i.e. a return of from 20 to 50 per cent. The interest-bearing life of a slave he reckons at 25 years, certainly an overestimate for those working in the mines. *Griech. Gesch.* iii, 1, p. 319.

[7] Thuc. i, 139.

treaties;[1] an inhabitant of Chios was thanked in a public decree of Athens for restoring fugitives to their masters. The earliest case on record of insurance is contained in the business carried on by an ingenious person named Antimenes, a Rhodian who was in charge of the roads round Babylon under Alexander. For a premium of 8 drs. a year he would insure owners of runaway slaves at the price agreed upon. "Many slaves being registered, he amassed a considerable fortune. Whenever any slave ran away he ordered the satrap of the country in which the camp was situated to recover the runaway or else pay the price to the owner."[2]

An interesting confirmation of the view that slave and free labour were equal in value is afforded by the accounts of the building of the Erechtheum.[3] Laossoos, a contractor for fluting columns, had four workmen with him, one citizen, two slaves and another unidentified. Each of these earned 20 drs. for 35 days' work. If Laossoos paid 3 obols a day for food, clothing and lodging of his slaves, it would have cost him 17 drs. 3 obols, leaving him $2\frac{1}{2}$ drs. to cover every other expense connected with them, and to act as a reserve against unemployment or ill-health. Evidently the margin in favour of slave labour at that time was so small as to be non-existent.[4]

The case of Nicias, who owned 1000 slaves from whom he obtained a profit of an obol a day by letting them out to Sosias, the Thracian, for work in the mines of Laurium, is by no means clear. Boeckh supposes that the lessee clothed, fed and lodged the slaves, replacing any that died or ran away and paid an obol a day to Nicias for supplying them to him. Reckoning 350 days' labour a year and the average price of a mine slave at 140 drs., the return on the money invested in their purchase would be 47 per cent. This Boeckh regards as so enormous that he concludes the rent paid included that of the mine in which the slaves worked.[5] That is obviously one possible explanation; but

[1] Thuc. iv, 118.
[2] (Arist.) *Oecon.* 1352 B 33. Cf. A. Andreades, "Antimenes de Rhode et Cleomenes de Naucratis", *Bull. Corr. Hell.* liii (1929), p. 1.
[3] *I.G.* i², 372–4.
[4] Francotte, *L'Industrie*, ii, 15. Cf. also Ciccotti, *Il Tramonto della Schiavitù* (1899), p. 129.
[5] Boeckh, *Staatshaushaltung*, i, p. 377 ff.

there is nothing in the record to suggest that. On the other hand, it is also perfectly possible that Sosias paid, say, a drachma a day, and that Nicias paid all the expenses of upkeep and replacement, making a net profit of an obol per man. It is also quite uncertain how Xenophon meant to make the magnificent profit to the state which he so persuasively represents in his proposal for the purchase of slaves to work in the mines. It is to be observed that he makes no allowances whatever for lay-offs for accidents or sickness.[1] Again we ask, were these slaves to be leased to contractors at a flat rate of an obol, the contractor to pay all maintenance and replacement expenses? We can come to no definite conclusion on the point. Probably Francotte is correct when he concludes that small-scale craftsmen could hold their own against slaves, but in cases where gangs of slaves could be employed the free labourer was at a very serious disadvantage and could not successfully compete.[2]

The question as to how far slave labour depressed the whole wage scale in industry is very difficult to resolve, as anyone who has had experience in the complicated field of modern labour economics will readily appreciate. Only the broadest generalisations are possible, and these with the utmost caution. It would seem, however, fairly safe to say that, except when wages for free labour were high, slave labour had little or no advantage. If the slave and the free workman competed on equal terms, the latter was the superior and could beat the slave.

At the end of the fourth century the wage of the ordinary day labourer had risen considerably, the average standing at from $1\frac{1}{2}$ to 2 drs. a day, and at that figure it would appear that slave labour would prove a serious competitor. On the other hand the cost of maintenance of the slave had also risen, and it therefore remains doubtful whether even at so high a figure the free labourer was not able to hold his own. It is obvious that the work of slaves was of a low-grade order, where it generally did not compete with that of freemen. The free workers were elevated to the higher branches of industry where the scale of wages was better. It is open to question, however, whether or

---

[1] Xen. *Revenues*, iv, 22–4.
[2] Francotte, *L'Industrie*, ii, cap. 5 *passim*. For another view cf. E. Meyer, *Kleine Schriften*, p. 198 ff.

not this tended to overcrowd such occupations, and so through competition depress the wage scale. The example in our own day, where successive waves of immigration into the United States and Canada have tended to push up to a higher scale those who had preceded them occurs to the mind. Another interesting parallel might be found in Africa, where cheap native labour has overcrowded the "white collar" professions, much to their disadvantage.

It is, to say the least, unsafe to lay down any general principles in such a problem, except that slave labour is always inferior and except where it can be used in the simplest and least technical of tasks and in large numbers does not pay. Slave labour in the mines of Laurium, probably, if not certainly, was a paying proposition; just as gangs of slaves in the cotton fields of the Southern States paid before their emancipation. Probably also as an unskilled labourer in the city, as "a hewer of wood and a drawer of water", the slave if not a very lucrative investment was, at least, a useful possession. As a servant he was a luxury and need not be regarded on strictly economic grounds. That he was a demoralising influence in society is beyond all dispute. The prostitution of female slaves was an evil that assumed formidable proportions; the case of Neaira, argued by Demosthenes in the courts, reveals a state of affairs not only deplorable in any age on moral grounds, but distinctly subversive to public order and the stability of society.

Another aspect of slavery which cannot be regarded with equanimity was the deplorable insecurity that accompanied it in civil life. The treachery of slaves who informed against their masters was a constant source of danger. Such informers were actually encouraged to betray their owners by promises of emancipation.[1] How fruitful an incentive to treachery and false accusation that must have been is not difficult to imagine. Lysias remarks that a man whose slave knows of some crime he had committed is the unhappiest of men.[2] Opportunities of blackmail must have been eagerly sought for! A master who killed a slave for fear of such an accusation could be indicted for murder as if he had killed a citizen.[3]

[1] Plato, *Laws*, 932 D.   [2] Lysias, vii, 16.
[3] *Laws*, 872 C.

To the modern mind all this seems repugnant; but we must not forget that it seemed perfectly natural to the Greek, who accepted it as part of the natural order of things.[1] And so we leave it on the other side of that great gulf which lies between us and the Ancient World which we can never bridge.

It has often been alleged and there is much truth in it, that slavery, by providing the doubtful blessing of cheap labour, tends to stifle inventiveness. Why trouble to devise a machine which will do the work of six men, when half-a-dozen slaves are ready to hand, and especially when work must be found to prevent them "eating their heads off" in idleness? The point is an interesting one, and merits careful consideration. It must not be overlooked that the economic use of machinery is only possible under conditions of large-scale production. It does not pay to instal a machine that will do the work of a hundred men, if twenty can do the work required just as well; a fact that has been painfully apparent to many who have spent too much on equipment. Numbers were few in Ancient Greece; there was little or no need for production on a large scale. Hand labour can compete profitably with machine production in the luxury trades and where the cheapness of the product makes the payment of high wages impossible. Both of these were characteristic of the Ancient World and of Greece in particular. The Greeks were perfectly capable of inventing machinery; the genius of Archimedes is a case in point, but they did not need to. It was an economically sounder policy to rely on hand labour when cost of production was low through low wages; just as in the southern areas of the United States slave gangs in the cotton fields paid so long as production costs could be kept down and the price of cotton was high. With high wages and low prices such manual labour is uneconomical and the mechanical cotton picker has appeared to take the place of human hands. In the same way the reaper and binder, and now the gigantic "combine" that reaps and threshes, have been forced upon the farmers of the wheat areas, when the high cost of labour in the fields has made the harvest hand an expensive worker.

It is easy to expatiate upon the evils of slavery and prove,

[1] W. Weddigen, "Sozialpolitik als Schicksalsfrage der Antike", *Jahrb. f. Nationalökon u. Statistik*, xxxi (1929), pp. 374f.

apparently conclusively, that in the end it ruined every society that ever practised it. This is but a commonplace; and, broadly speaking, may be regarded as a truism. It is not so easy, however, to dismiss the whole question in such a summary fashion; nor can we attribute the decline of Greece to slavery alone. Far more deep-seated causes were the reason for the ruin of Greece, as we shall see later.

But be that as it may, the great fundamental fact remains that the Greeks possessed slaves in large numbers, and that much of the hard work was done by them, or by Metics and freedmen. In any study of the economic history of the Ancient World that stands out as one of the greatest factors, we may even say the greatest, in any appraisal of social conditions and economic progress. From age-long and bitter experience the world has learned that the slave system is bad from every point of view, spiritual and material, and we cannot, therefore, avoid the conclusion that, in the long run, slavery was harmful to Greece as it was to Rome. It is useless to speculate as to what would have been the destiny of Greece if there had been no slaves. The system was so part of Greek life that we can almost say that had there been no slaves there would have been no Greeks.[1] No such broad generalisation can, of course, be accepted in its entirety; but it is so nearly true that we may leave our brief survey of the subject on that note.

---

[1] "Greek civilisation itself was based upon and made possible by slavery" —Tarn, *The Greeks in Bactria*, p. 33.

CHAPTER V

INDUSTRY[1]

THE problems of industry and labour are inseparable; neither can be studied without reference to the other. In another chapter we deal with the Greek as a labourer; in this as a technician, and so far as our knowledge will permit us, his command over the processes of production are recorded.

The evidence is very scattered and often tantalisingly vague and allusive. The greatest care must be taken in drawing inferences which may, at first sight, appear justifiable but actually rest on the slenderest evidence or none at all. Particularly is this so in any attempt to relate Greek technical processes to those of Egypt, especially of Hellenistic Egypt, or Rome, of both of which our knowledge is far more complete. Generally speaking, the Greek was an inferior technician to either Hellenistic Egyptian or Roman. This may, perhaps, be too sweeping a generalisation; but all that can be said is that the evidence at our command seems to justify that statement. The Egyptian civilisation and its command over the arts was a far more ancient one than that of Greece; the Hellenistic and the Roman achievements were later and the accumulation of knowledge had proceeded farther. And more, the command over capital had vastly increased and it is, in the last analysis, that command which prescribes, retards or advances, the technical processes which mankind uses in the production of what is useful and necessary to his existence and ministers to his comfort.

Again and again we return to the same point; we cannot escape from it. The Greek was very poor and ill-equipped, and had to do his best with what he had. That his best was very good indeed, and that he was an amazingly dexterous artist does not alter the fact that his equipment was primitive and his processes imperfect. With all the resources of science at our hand, we are to-day capable of turning out from our factories and workshops

[1] Bluemner, *Technologie.* Old but still indispensable. The first volume was revised and enlarged in 1912.

products technically more perfect than ever the Ancient World was able to achieve. We reverence, and rightly so, the artistic genius that reared a Parthenon; but our builders to-day can rear a structure which will outlast it. The Greek potter was a supreme artist; the present-day one can beat him as a technician. The Greek metallurgist was severely hampered in his processes by his inability to produce very high temperatures in his furnace; the modern metallurgist is far superior to him—we may even say he is a greater artist.

Such reflections may appear derogatory to the Greek, but actually they are not so. It is characteristic of every age that it should deprecate its own achievements and reverence the skill and artistry of bygone times. Such is, within limits, a proper and becoming modesty; at least it keeps us humble. Much, far too much, that we do to-day is shoddy and unworthy of us, of which we may be heartily ashamed. But to say that the ancient workman was a superior craftsman is nonsense; he was not, simply because the means at his command were limited and his capabilities circumscribed. He worked with what he had, but he had not got very much; we have a great deal and so we can beat the Greek. Whether or not we may derive any satisfaction from that may be left to each of us to settle for himself.

Leather-Working

The art of the tanner has not changed very much since ancient days, and such scattered allusions as we have are perfectly recognisable at the present time. The green hide was first stretched upon a board or form (*thranos*)[1] and scraped on the under side with a bronze scraper fastened by rivets to a wooden handle; a long concave knife and a curved knife such as is used to-day by leather dressers were also employed. To take the hair off, the skins were first soaked in a solution of urine and mulberry leaves[2] or the berries of the bryony.[3] This solution, after it had accomplished its purpose, had so abhorrent an odour as to be the cause of frequent remark.[4] The numerous savage gibes and

---

[1] Aristoph. *Equites*, 369.
[2] Pliny, *H.N.* xxxiii, 140, xxiii, 16, xvii, 51.
[3] Diosc. iv, 181; Pliny, *H.N.* xxiii, 22.
[4] E.g. Theoph. *Caus. Pl.* iii, 9, 3, 17, 5, v, 15, 2.

coarse jokes of Aristophanes at the expense of Cleon the tanner need not be referred to here.[1] So disliked was the trade in consequence that it was carried on in a quarter by itself, outside the city, along with cheesemakers who followed another malodorous trade.[2] After the preparation of the hides, tanning was carried out with the agency of various sorts of bark, such as that of the alder, oak galls, and in Egypt with the juice of the acacia,[3] sumach[4] and oak apples.[5] Another method was with alum and salt,[6] and a third with oil or fat, as the scene in Homer very vividly depicts: "As when one gives men to stretch a great bull hide, swilled with grease, and they take it and stand in a ring and stretch it, and in a moment all moisture is gone and the grease sinks in."[7] It may be remarked that such a process would be unsuitable for tanned leather but rather for such things as harness straps. That it was used long after Homer is certain from an allusion in Lucian.[8] A fourth process, which cannot properly be classified under tanning, was that of parchment making.[9] Lastly, the leather was pounded with a mallet or club to obtain the requisite degree of firmness and solidity.[10] The skins were dyed with madder and vermilion (mercuric sulphide) or black with copper sulphate or vitriol.[11] But our information is very scanty on the subject. Polishing was done with smooth stones.

We have little information with regard to the different kinds of leather. Homer mentions only cowhides and goatskins; there is no reference to pigskin, but we must suppose that it was used. Pausanias tells us that in his time garments made of pigskin were worn by the poor in Euboea and Phocis; Pollux speaks of leather chitons and Plato of leather coats,[12] of what kind we do not know.[13] The supply of cowhide in Greece must have been

---

[1] E.g. *Equites*, 892; *Vesp.* 38, and many others.
[2] Schol. *ad* Aristoph. *Acharn.* 724.
[3] Theoph. *H.P.* iii, 8, 6, iv, 2, 8.
[4] *Ibid.* iii, 18, 5. [5] *Ibid.* iii, 8, 6.
[6] Aristoph. *Nubes*, 1237. [7] *Il.* xvii, 389.
[8] *Anacharsis*, 24. [9] Her. v, 58.
[10] Schol. *ad* Aristoph. *Equites*, 368.
[11] Pliny, *H.N.* xxxiv, 123; Diosc. v, 114; cf. Bailey's note, ii, 178.
[12] Poll. viii, 1, 2; Plato, *Crito*, 53.
[13] Theoph. *de Odor.* 62 mentions goatskins. There was probably a prejudice against them owing to the smell. They were worn by slaves.

limited and leather expensive. We know that the sale of hides from the animals slaughtered at the great public festivals was a valuable revenue to the state.[1] The soles of shoes were often made of wood.[2] Since the Greeks very generally went barefoot and only put on shoes for a journey or for ceremonial occasions, no doubt they kept their expenses down in that particular as much as possible.

The next stage in leather-working was carried on by harness-makers, shoe-makers and cobblers. Sometimes the various branches of the trade were combined; we hear of harness-makers who were also cobblers. Some specialised in particular things; for instance, there were those who made only bridles,[3] and shoe-makers who made only men's shoes, others who made women's. Xenophon says some shoe-makers did nothing but cut out the uppers, others the soles, while others stretched them.[4] Stitching was done with catgut,[5] at least in early times; we have no reference to such strong linen thread as shoe-makers use to-day. The soles were fastened on by iron nails.[6] Shoes were made over lasts, to which Plato refers in a simile in which he speaks of the shoe-maker stretching the leather on the last and smoothing out the wrinkles.[7] Cobblers were ready to repair footwear, as they are to-day. One of the characters of Theophrastus is a mean man who will stoop to having his shoes resoled.

We have several very realistic pictures of shoe-makers' shops. In one a lady is standing on a table while the master is about to cut the sole from the leather on which her feet rest with a "half-moon" knife. On the wall hang the lasts and implements of the trade, a pair of pincers, three awls and a knife. On the other side of the table sits a youth, evidently an apprentice, who holds in his hand a piece of leather from which the uppers are to be made. An elderly man, perhaps the father or husband, leans on a staff and gives directions. Evidently an argument is going on, perhaps as to the style or price, for the whole scene is animated.[8]

---

[1] Poll. vii, 70.   [2] *Ibid.* 87, 92.
[3] Xen. *Mem.* iv, 2, 1.   [4] *Cyrop.* viii, 2, 5.
[5] Hesiod, *W.D.* 544.
[6] Theophr. *Char.* iv, 13; cf. Pliny, *H.N.* ix, 69.   [7] *Symp.* 191 A.
[8] Bluemner, *Technologie*, i, 285, 287 (revised ed.).

There is an amusing scene in the seventh mime of Herodes, where three ladies (of course we know they are Hetaerae) come to buy from Kerdon, a shoe-maker and a rascal, who is quite ready to make more things than shoes for his customers, and cheat them into the bargain. There is a great bustle as the ladies arrive, Kerdon pretending to wake up his lazy slaves—he has thirteen working for him—bidding them set chairs and bring out the best in his stock. His salesman's patter as he shows them his finest wares is almost irresistible. One beautiful pair of shoes, painted with a flower pattern, he tells them cost him three gold staters. Everything has gone up in price now; the tanners are demanding much more for their leather; trade is bad; his workers are idle; really he does not know why he goes on in such a poor trade, and all the rest of his glib chatter. He bids Pistos, his slave, bring out a case of very special shoes and reels off the names of the various sorts, Sicyonians, little Ambracians, Nossians, Chians, Baucises, buttoned Ionians, bedroom slippers, ankle-high boots, Argive sandals, and a lot of others to which he gives fancy names such as parrots, crabs and scarlets. One of the ladies picks out a pair and asks the price, and after a lot of circumlocution Kerdon says a mina. The lady laughs at so enormous a price and then inquires about another pair. Euteris, the harpist, has been plaguing him to take five staters, but he dislikes her so that he won't let her have them at any price, so offers them for four darics. Then he offers both pairs for seven darics, and fits a pair on, praising the dainty foot and makes the sale at last by sheer force of "blarney". The scene ends with him asking his customer to return later for a fitting of a pair of "crabs", because they have to be stitched with extreme care.

CLAY AND POTTERY[1]

It is remarkable to realise that right up to the first century B.C. ordinary building was carried out with unbaked bricks. Pausanias gives a long list of temples built of such poor materials.[2]

---

[1] Art. "Figlinum Opus" by Jamot in *D.S.*; Lucas, *Anc. Egypt, Mats. and Inds.* pp. 316 ff.

[2] Paus. ii, 27, 6, x, 5, 4.

Certainly all ordinary dwellings were made of them,[1] and we must suppose the walls of cities in many cases. We are told that when the Spartans besieged Mantinea they turned the river so as to wash around the walls and so softened the bricks that it fell,[2] one of the few instances of success in capturing a walled city in the pre-Alexander period. It may be remarked in passing that the pre-hellenistic Greeks were singularly inept in siege works, and, as far as we know, never employed such engines as battering rams, although with the walls built of such flimsy materials their use would have been highly effective. The statement of Pausanias that the Philippeum at Olympia was built of baked bricks is open to doubt, since no traces of such have been found on the site.[3] The same author also speaks of a temple built of baked bricks at Argos, but this was probably of late Hellenistic times.[4] In any case discoveries of bricks and tiles in Greece are excessively rare. Our knowledge of brick-making is non-existent; we do not know if they were made by hand or in a mould,[5] nor the method of drying or later of baking them.

The trade of the potter[6] was, of course, of immemorial antiquity; we hear much of the potter and his wheel in Homer.[7] The earliest Greek vases were made by hand, but from the Early Minoan III and Middle Helladic I periods (i.e. about 2200) in certain places at least vases were regularly thrown on the wheel.[8] Apparently the wheels were turned by hand, the potter throwing the clay, a slave or boy sitting opposite to him

[1] Xen. *Mem.* iii, 1, 7. The remarks of Vitruvius on the use of brick (ii, 8, 16 ff.) are interesting. But traces of baked bricks have been found by the Johns Hopkins Archaeological Expedition at the site of Olynthus, which was destroyed in 348.

[2] Xen. *Hell.* v, 2, 5. A regular name for a burglar was "walldigger"—Athen. vi, 228 A.

[3] Pausan. v, 20, 10; Bluemner, *Technologie*, ii, 11, n. 4.

[4] ii, 18, 3.

[5] Bluemner, *Technologie*, ii, 16; cf. Pliny, *H.N.* xxxv, 170–1; Strabo, xiii, 1, 67 (c. 614); Vitruv. ii, 3.

[6] G. Richter, *The Craft of Athenian Pottery*. Miss Richter, in order better to understand Greek technique, learned the art of pottery making herself. The results are interesting and illuminating.

[7] *Il.* xviii, 600.

[8] Richter, *Athenian Pottery*, p. 9. The attribution to Anacharsis the Scythian of the invention of the wheel, as well as of the anchor, is obviously fanciful—Diog. Laert. i, 105.

making the wheel revolve.[1] There is only one reference in literature to the "kick-wheel", i.e. the wheel turned by the foot, that in the book of Ecclesiasticus of the second century, which speaks of "the potter sitting at his work and turning his wheel round with his feet".[2] There seems to be no apparent explanation as to why the invention of so simple a device as the treadle should have been so late. The larger vases, or those more difficult to turn on the wheel because of their form, were built up in sections, as they are to-day: a close inspection of many Greek vases will reveal where the sections were joined.[3] Another method practised to-day, that of building with coils of clay, was, so far as we know, not employed by the Greek potters. Moulding, where the plastic clay is pressed into moulds of burnt clay, was extensively used, many vases showing on the inside the finger marks where the worker pressed it into shape. The larger pots were built round wooden or wicker-work cores made in collapsible form, so that when the clay shrank through drying they might be taken out. A passage in Pollux, which had formerly puzzled writers, is thus easily explained.[4] Such technique is followed to-day, a wedge being put in the centre which can be knocked out when the building is completed so that the sides of the core fall in.[5]

After the pot had been thrown on the wheel it was left to dry until it became "leather hard" when it was "turned" or polished by means of wooden or iron tools of suitable shape; traces of the process of "turning" may be detected on many Greek vases. In modern pottery work the clay is twice fired, once when it is baked so as to produce the "biscuit" form, i.e. unglazed and undecorated; the second time when the composition to give the glaze has been applied. From evidences gathered from inspection of the vases, Miss Richter concludes that Greek craftsmen only fired once; the decoration and glaze were applied in the "leather-hard" condition. It is quite plain that the potters fired their wares at a much lower temperature than the moderns, probably not at a higher heat than 960° C. As is remarked in the section on metal work, the Greeks never seem to have been

[1] Richter, *Athenian Pottery*, pp. 64, 66. Cf. Plut. *de Gen. Socr.* 588 F; Athen. x, 449 B.
[2] Ecclus. xxxviii. 32.
[3] *Geop.* vi, 3, 4.
[4] *Onom.* vii, 164.
[5] Richter, *Athenian Pottery*, p. 94.

able to obtain very high temperatures, nor such perfect control over their heats as is possible under modern conditions. For this reason they were not able to make their clay "frit" properly, and so a glaze had to be put on to make them watertight, not always successfully, and bowls are wholly or in places porous, which explains a reference in Pollux: "Aristophanes says that a clay vinegar jar has leprosy, instead of saying that it is moist."[1] Actually it may be said that Greek potters, apart from the beauty of form which they achieved, were lacking in the technical skill of the moderns mostly because of this trouble of the heat.[2]

With regard to the glaze considerable uncertainty still remains. In general it may be said that Greek potters knew far less about glazing than the late medieval and early modern craftsmen. The ordinary modern salt glaze was beyond their powers because they could not command the necessary temperature (1300° C.). Although chemical analysis has revealed the secret of their composition, modern potters have failed exactly to reproduce the famous black glazes. These were made of 50 per cent magnetic oxide of iron, 27 per cent quartz and 23 per cent soda. A similar one could be made with iron filings, soda and marly clay. Probably the passage of time accounts for the change in the appearance of the colour which cannot be reproduced readily. A red glaze was put on with *miltos*, or red ochre. Miss Richter points out very pertinently that the *miltos* was not mixed with the clay, as certain references would suggest, as the clay would turn red in the firing in any case, but put on as a wash.[3] A reference in Athenaeus to the three hundred vases carried in the procession of Ptolemy Philadelphus would suggest an encaustic decoration; but of this little is known.[4]

The trade had many branches; the Kadopoios made water

---

[1] *Onom.* vii, 162.

[2] *Geop.* vi, 3, 5: "The firing is no small part of the potter's craft. Not too little or too much fire should be built under the pots, but just enough."

[3] Richter, *Athenian Pottery*, p. 53 ff.; cf. Pliny, *H.N.* xxxv, 152; Suidas, s.v. Koliades Keramees; Isodorus, *Etymolog.* xx, iv, 3. These passages are hard to explain except on the ground that the authors made a mistake and thought the miltos was actually mixed with the clay.

[4] Athen. v, 200 B. The whole question of encaustic decoration is obscure. Cf. Pliny, *H.N.* xxxv, 49, 122, 149; Ovid, *Fasti*, iv, 275. Also Bailey's note, ii, 222.

and wine jars; the Kothonopoios cups, the Chutreus pots.[1] Sometimes the potter decorated the vases himself, often crudely enough, but generally special artists were employed and the product signed by potter and painter.[2] It is curious to realise that the Greeks never achieved what we may consider to be the supreme work of the potter, the manufacture of porcelain; that was left to the Chinese.[3]

Although many remains of Roman kilns have been found, we have none of Greek potters. But we have several pictures of work going on, from which it is not difficult to make out the form of kiln and method of firing.[4] The kilns are domed and have three openings, one at the bottom for the fuel, another on the side for the insertion of the ware and to act as a spy-hole, and one at the top to let out the smoke and for the regulation of the draught. In one picture we see a figure about to climb up the kiln on a ladder, holding a hooked bar or poker with which he is going to manipulate the flue, from which flames are issuing at the top. Evidently the draught is too great and heat is being wasted. There are several more pictures that show workmen using a similar hooked bar attending to the flue; regulating the heat was of the greatest importance in a somewhat primitive kiln where accurate control was very difficult. Another picture shows the inside of a kiln, in horizontal section with two openings for the fire, each opening having two channels into the kiln. If this represents the usual Greek way of admitting the heat to the oven, it markedly differs from later Roman kilns where the floor of the oven is perforated to allow the heat to rise evenly all over.[5]

One particularly pleasing scene, which has been frequently reproduced, shows work going on in a potter's shop, where young men are busy painting vases while goddesses crown their efforts with wreaths. Two interesting points to be noted are that they all hold their brushes in their closed fist, in exactly

---

[1] Kothonopoios, Dinarch. fr. 89, 19; Chutreus, Plato, *Rep.* 421 D; Kadopoios, Schol. *ad* Aristoph. *Pax*, 1202; Poll. vii, 161, 2.

[2] Aristoph. *Eccles.* 995; Isocr. *de Permut.* 2.

[3] The supposition that the Latin *murrina* was porcelain is so doubtful that it must be rejected; probably it was either fluorspar or agate. Cf. Pliny, *H.N.* xxxiii, 5, xxxvii, 18, 204; and Bailey's note, i, 176.

[4] Richter, *Athenian Pottery*, p. 76 ff.

[5] Bluemner, *Technologie*, ii, 23 ff.

the same way as Japanese artists, and that at the extreme right is seated a woman's figure also busy at painting. This is of importance as showing that women workers, or at least one, were engaged in the trade, the only reference that we have of them being so employed in any industry outside of textiles and clothing. It is to be observed that she is not being crowned by a goddess! Another shows work going on in what was evidently a large establishment. A big pot is being thrown on the wheel; before it is crouched a boy who is twisting the wheel round with his hands. Some vases are still unfired; one is being carried away to dry; a man with a sack, probably of charcoal, on his back is approaching the kiln which is being fired by a man who is using a long poker. An elderly overseer with a long staff is watching the various operations. A third picture which is far less pleasing and we may suppose is of a comic character, shows what must have been a very ill-conducted potter's workshop with a slave strung up by ropes to the ceiling being whipped and another running away.[1]

It is curious to realise that the trade of the potter was looked down on as something far below the art of the sculptor or the painter. Isocrates says: "As if one should have the insolence to call Pheidias, who made the statue of Athena, a statuette maker, or to say that Zeuxis and Parrhasius had plied the same trade as that of the painters of vases."[2] Plato classes potters with blacksmiths and cooks.[3] It is practically certain that the quarter of Athens called Cerameicus was that in which potters carried on their trade, although Pausanias gives quite another explanation, that it was named after one Ceramos, but this may be fanciful.[4]

With regard to the distribution of manufactured articles, M. Francotte makes an interesting suggestion in supposing that many of the manufacturers of pottery and artistic wares worked for a "Patron", or perhaps we may call him a wholesale distributor, who undertook to dispose of their products on a large scale. Otherwise, as he says, it is difficult to understand how the

---

[1] Richter, *Athenian Pottery*, pp. 70ff.
[2] *De Perm.* 2. [3] *Euthyd.* 301 C, D.
[4] Paus. i, 3, 1. Cf. Judeich, *Topographie von Athen*, 2. Aufl. *s.v.* Kerameikos; and A. Newhall, "The Corinthian Kerameikos", *Amer. Journ. Archaeol.* xxxv (1931), p. 1.

output of individual workshops was distributed and went so far. It is perfectly possible that wholesalers did a large business in supplying containers for shipments of oil or wine; indeed it is reasonable to suppose that some such organised system must have been in existence; although as M. Francotte acknowledges, there is no evidence to substantiate this.[1] Sir Alfred Zimmern goes farther in saying that the merchants' marks on some Attic vases are evidence that the trader went into the workshop and scratched his orders on sample vases. These marks are often in Ionian characters, and show that previous to 480, during the most flourishing period of the Etruscan trade, this was in Ionian hands.[2] But again we must be careful not to suppose that such production and distribution was on a large scale. Except in a very small degree there was no large-scale capitalistic production, for one reason that capital was not readily available. Such capital as there was probably went into mining ventures[3] and sea loans.

Spinning and Weaving[4]

Although we possess no connected account of the various processes of spinning and weaving wool, yet, as is natural with so vitally important an industry which was carried on practically in every home, the references thereto are very numerous, and it is possible by piecing them together to obtain a very fairly accurate idea of its technique. With regard to sheepshearing we know little, although it seems fairly certain that in early times the wool was pulled out of the fleece and not cut off with shears; but in Pliny's time this was regarded as out-of-date.[5] The wool in the greasy state was washed by the *erioplutes*[6] with *strouthion* or soapwort[7] in hot water, after which the carder or *xantis* first beat it with a stick[8] and then combed it. The process

---

[1] *L'Industrie*, i, 308.
[2] *Greek Commonwealth*, p. 322, n. It may be remarked that this was certainly not a universal custom in all trades.
[3] Cf. F. Oertel, "Zur Frage der Attischen Grossindustrie", *Rhein. Mus.* lxxix (1930), p. 230. But cf. also another view by Schwahn, "Die Xenophontischen Poroi", *Rhein. Mus.* lxxx (1934), p. 253.
[4] Bluemner, *Technologie*, i, pp. 98 ff.
[5] Varro, *Res Rust.* ii, 11, 9; Pliny, *H.N.* viii, 191; Arist. *Probl.* x, 22, 893 A.
[6] Diosc. ii, 163.   [7] Theoph. *H.P.* vi, 4, 3, ix, 12, 5.
[8] Aristoph. *Lysist.* 575.

of combing is not perfectly clear; whether an iron comb was used or whether the tangled skein was unravelled with the fingers is not known.

The process of spinning is clearly seen in a figure from a Greek vase in the British Museum. A woman is holding up in her left hand the distaff in the form of a rod thrust through a ball of wool. With the fingers of her right hand she is twisting the fibres drawn from the ball. The yarn is attached below to the top of the spindle, a rod of wood or metal with a disc or whorl near the bottom to assist the rotation. The top of the spindle had a hook which facilitated the attachment of the yarn. When some quantity had been twisted it was cut away and wound round the body of the spindle, after which the twisting process recommenced. In the famous vision of Er, Plato likens the axis of the universe to the shaft of a spindle suspended by a hook of adamant, and the revolving starry heavens to a whorl made up of eight concentric rings, fitting one into another like boxes.[1] Extraordinary though such a simile may appear to modern readers, it was doubtless perfectly recognisable to his hearers, who must all have seen so familiar a sight in their own homes. It can readily be realised that such a process for producing yarn was very slow and tedious, far less efficient than even the old-fashioned spinning wheel. When the yarn had thus been roughly spun, the thread was reworked by being drawn over the out-stretched leg of the worker, when it was smoothed by the fingers and made more compact. Another method was to draw it across a wooden or terra-cotta instrument called the *epinetron* or *onos*, shaped like a greave so as to fit over the thigh and knee. Until a picture was found showing a woman at work drawing the thread across it, the use of this instrument was not understood, although several examples in terra-cotta were in museums.[2]

The Greek loom[3] seems invariably to have been vertical, no picture of a horizontal one being extant. The best presentment of such a loom is the well-known picture of Penelope at the web, whose non-completion kept the suitors waiting so long. A simile in the *Iliad* is illuminating on the point: "near as is the

---

[1] *Rep.* 616 c, d.
[2] Poll. vii, 32, x, 125; Bluemner, *Technologie*, i, 113.
[3] H. Ling Roth, *Ancient Egyptian and Greek Looms.*

winding rod to a well-girt woman's breast when she deftly
draws it with her hand as she pulls the spool past the warp and
holds it near to her."[1] It is quite easy to reconstruct the working
of the loom. The threads of the warp were fastened to a beam
from which they hung down, each thread being attached by a
loop to a weight to keep it taut. One cross rod, a "laze" rod,
serves to keep the warp threads in place and separate the odd
from the even so that the weft or woof thread may be passed
between them. The other rod is apparently a "heddle", that is
a bar of wood to which the odd warp threads are attached, but
the picture is not sufficiently clear to be certain on that point.[2]
Along the top of the loom there are nine pegs, on six of which
balls of coloured wool have been placed, evidently for working
out the designs. In Penelope's hand is held a spool, a piece of
stick round which was wound the thread that became the weft.
This spool was passed by hand between the alternate warp
threads; evidently it could not be thrown like a "fly shuttle",
and the simile quoted above becomes explicable when one
realises how close the weaver must have stood up to the warp
to be able to reach for this purpose to both sides of the loom.
It is also evident that the width of the web could not have been
greater than the span of the two arms. As each weft thread was
woven into place it was beaten upwards in order to keep the
weave compact and firmer. It may be remarked that Mr Ling
Roth made a model of a Greek loom on which a skilled weaver
demonstrated quite easily that it was a practicable instrument,
although clumsy and very slow to work. He also remarks that
Greek weavers were far behind Egyptian in skill, the Egyptian
loom being a much more advanced instrument and producing
a better quality of cloth.

Small "tapestry looms", held on the knee, were also used.[3]
Evidently· these were not mere embroidery frames for crewel-
work, as has been supposed,[4] but miniature looms very much of

---

[1] *Il.* xxiii, 761.

[2] Fragments of Greek woven cloth found in the Crimea were woven in
"haute-lisse", the warp of linen, the weft of wool. Haute-lisse is often
translated into English as "high warp", but is literally "high-leash".
Leashes are the strong loops of thread at the top of a vertical loom which
pull out the alternate threads of the warp, enabling the weaver to insert the
bobbins of weft.   [3] H. B. Walters, *J.H.S.* xxxi (1911), p. 15.

[4] Cf. remarks on this in art. "Phrygium Opus" in *D.S.*

the nature of those used to-day in the weaving of small rugs or mats.

Further details with regard to Greek weaving leave much in obscurity. There is much doubt if ornamentation was woven into the material, or, as seems more probable, either embroidered or painted on with pigments. The fragments of woollen cloth already mentioned found in Kertch in the Crimea were painted.[1] Herodotus says that the people of the Caucasus painted animals on their clothing with a vegetable pigment mixed with water.[2] The difficulty of washing such garments is obvious. One word, *polymitos*, presents a puzzle. This apparently refers to a form of damask in which several threads were taken for the woof in order to weave in patterns, that according to Pliny were called Alexandrian.[3] If this particular form of weave referred to the warp threads it would be easier to understand, since it is necessary to combine several threads together, otherwise hanging down as they did with weights they would quickly unravel themselves and fall apart. Helen "embroidered" battle scenes on the web she was weaving.[4] But Penelope seems to be weaving in the web tufts or rosettes of wool to form a pattern. Evidently Greek craftsmen were capable of the difficult art of weaving in various colours. The word *rhabdotos* probably means "striped", although it may mean "ribbed".[5] The word *enuphaino*, to "weave in", is unmistakable in its meaning. Athenaeus, quoting Menander, says: "They first weave in the purple to make the shadow, and after the purple comes this, which is neither white nor purple, but like a tempered beam of light in the wool."[6] Persian tapestries used as curtains, or perhaps rugs, were famous and costly. The Man of Petty Pride in the *Characters* of Theophrastus[7] boasted such. Doubtless they were the kind that scandalised poor Ezekiel so deeply.[8] Athenaeus also says that weaving in many-coloured textures reached its height when

[1] Abrahams, *Greek Dress*, pp. 97, 103.
[2] i, 203.
[3] *H.N.* viii, 19, 6. The word *poikilos* is not easy to understand other than woven with variegated patterns. Cf. Plut. *Reg. Imp. Apoph.* 185, 2.
[4] *Il.* iii, 126.
[5] Xen. *Cyrop.* viii, 3, 16. Cf. Athen. xii, 537 B, 215 C; also Q. Curt. iii, 3, 17.
[6] Athen. ii, 71 F; Arist. *de Mir. Ausc.* 838 A, 96; Theocr. xv, 80.
[7] *Char.* xxi, 5.   [8] Ezek. xxiii. 14.

the Cyprians Acesas and Helicon became the most renowned artists. There was a work of art at Delphi signed by Helicon of Salamis, son of Acesas. Another weaver, Pathymias the Egyptian, is also mentioned as a famous artist.[1]

Washing and fulling, as being impossible to do effectively in the home, was a distinct trade. The fabrics were put into large tubs and trodden with the feet in a solution of natron[2] when it was available, or more commonly in urine, allowed to stand for a fortnight until it had a strong ammonia content,[3] sufficient to take away the last vestiges of grease in the wool. Fulling was done with fuller's or Cimolian earth.[4] When this was not available, or too expensive, gypsum was used,[5] or earth from Lemnos or Samos.[6] Lastly the cloth was given a final washing in clean water.

The next stage was combing with a teasel to raise the nap,[7] after which the cloth was shorn by hand with a pair of shears.[8] Some cloths were not treated in this way but were left with the pile on both sides (*amphitapos*).[9] Others were shorn on both sides to produce *psilos*; *psilai persikai* are Persian rugs with no pile.[10] *Heteromallos* meant cloth with pile on one side only.[11] It is almost certain that no fabric like velvet was known to the Ancient World; it was probably an invention of the thirteenth or fourteenth century.

Although we have many references to felt (*pilema*) there is no information with regard to its manufacture, except that Pliny tells us that vinegar was used, which, rather surprisingly, made it so tough that it could resist steel.[12] It was used for making hats[13] and shoes;[14] we hear that Demetrius Poliorcetes possessed

[1] Athen. 197 B. [2] Poll. vii, 39, x, 135.
[3] Athen. xi, 484 A; cf. Pliny, *H.N.* xxviii, 66, 91.
[4] Poll. vii, 39; Pliny, *H.N.* xxxv, 195; cf. also Diosc. v, 152; Aristoph. *Ranae*, 711.
[5] Theoph. *de Lap.* 67; Pliny, xxxv, 198.
[6] Theoph. *de Lap.* 64.
[7] *Alc. Com.* 35; Schol. *ad* Aristoph. *Plutus*, 166.
[8] Athen. v, 197 B.
[9] Athen. ii, 48 B; cf. also xii, 538 D, 539 E.
[10] Athen. v, 197 B; Diog. Laert. v, 72.
[11] Strabo, v, 1, 2 (c. 218).
[12] *H.N.* viii, 192.
[13] *Il.* x, 265; Hesiod, *W.D.* 544; Athen. xii, 544 F; and many others.
[14] Hesiod, *W.D.* 540; Plato, *Sympos.* 220 B.

a pair of purple slippers.[1] Rugs or carpets were made of it,[2] also tents.[3]

It is not easy to affirm with certainty that Greek weavers produced both woollen and worsted fabrics, although it is by no means impossible that they should have done so. "Woollens" are those fabrics which do not show on the surface the intertwining threads of which they are woven. Woollens are woven, but fulling in which the cloth is given a felting effect and combing with the teasel, so that the surface is uniform, conceal the fact. "Worsteds" show upon their surface their woven origin. The description given of Greek methods would seem to suggest that woollens alone were made. But this is by no means certain, and it is quite likely that worsteds were also manufactured. Possibly Greek weavers made no distinction between the two.

There is no actual evidence that the Greeks ever used goat's hair in weaving, although there is no reason why they should not; there were plenty of goats in Greece. References in the Bible to goat's hair cloth are frequent[4] and the fabric was used by the Romans.[5]

LINEN AND SILK

One of the most curious and tantalising questions with regard to the manufacture of textiles among the Greeks is found in our ignorance of much that has to do with linen. The first difficulty arises in an almost hopeless confusion with regard to terms. What was the difference, if any, between *linon* and *othone*? Possibly the former was anything made of flax, e.g. nets, ropes, sails, etc., while the latter was fine linen made into garments; but this is pure conjecture. Then again what was that very mysterious substance *byssos*? It seems to have been a coarse form of linen which almost certainly came originally from Egypt, although Pausanias says it was grown in Elis, evidently an

---

[1] Athen. xii, 535 F; Plut. *Demet.* 41; cf. Poll. vii, 171.
[2] Xen. *Cyrop.* v, 5, 7.
[3] Strabo, vii, 3, 17 (c. 307). For a full treatment of the subject see B. Laufer, "The early history of felt", *Am. Anthrop.* xxxii (1930), p. 1.
[4] E.g. Exod. xxxv. 26, and many others.
[5] Pliny, *H.N.* viii, 203; Varro, *Res Rust.* ii, 11.

importation.[1] And lastly we are puzzled by the word *sindon*.[2] This is generally translated "muslin", and probably rightly so in the passages in Herodotus referring to India. But it is practically certain that no fabric made of cotton was woven in Greece, and other references to the word suggest merely a very fine form of linen cloth, loosely woven.

The only satisfactory account we have of the preparation of flax to make into linen yarn is in Pliny,[3] who gives a tolerably clear account of the processes of retting and hackling, and we can only conclude that the same procedure was followed in Greece. With regard to weaving we know little, two references in Pollux conveying little meaning to modern readers.[4] Curiously enough two references in Homer to linen weaving throw some light on the process followed and are of peculiar interest. The maidens in the palace of Alcinous are weaving "and from the close-woven linen the liquid oil runs off",[5] and the youths in the dancing place on the shield of Achilles wear tunics "well-spun, shining softly with oil".[6] Such use of oil is in line with the most modern practice when a closely woven cloth is required. In ancient times the yarn was certainly woven in the grey or raw unboiled state and so was harsh and difficult to work. Softening the weft yarn with oil would enable a greater number of shots of weft to be inserted in an inch of cloth, and this would result in a closely woven fabric. The pressure used in forcing the shot of weft home would thus tend to squeeze out the oil.[7] Bleaching on grass was apparently unknown; the general method seemingly was to stretch the material over a wickerwork frame, under which a brazier giving off sulphur fumes was set.[8] Theophrastus mentions a plant called *herakleia*

---

[1] Paus. v, 5, 2.

[2] Her. i, 200, ii, 95; Thuc. ii, 49; Soph. *Antig.* 1222; Theoph. *Hist. Pl.* iv, 7, 7; Michel, 832, 24 (Samos 4th cent.); Strabo, xv, 3, 19 (c. 734); Poll. iv, 181; *I.G.* ii², 1525.

[3] *H.N.* xix, 16–18; cf. Isaiah xix. 9.   [4] Poll. vii, 73, x, 176.

[5] *Od.* vii, 107.   [6] *Il.* xviii, 596.

[7] The problems connected with these two passages are discussed by Studniczka in *Beiträge zur Geschichte der altgriechischen Tracht* (abhl. des archäol.-epigraph. Seminares der Univ. Wien, vi, 1, p. 47). Cf. also Hertzberg in *Philologus*, xxxiii (1874), p. 8. Oil was also used in dyeing, Plut. *Alex.* 36, 2, and in cleaning clothes. Machon, *ap. Athen.* xii, 582 E.

[8] Poll. vii, 41; Pliny, *H.N.* xxxv, 175, 198. The sulphur dioxide thus produced acted as a strong reducing agent.

with a leaf like soapwort, which was used for bleaching linen.[1]
The use of linen for wearing apparel was undoubtedly later
than that of wool. We are told that Pythagoras wore woollen
garments, linen not having at that time come to those parts.[2]

Silk is first mentioned by Aristotle,[3] who, after describing
the changes undergone by the worm before becoming a moth,
says "some women undo the cocoons of this creature, winding
off the silk, and then weave it. Pamphile, daughter of Plateus,
is said to have been the first to weave it in Cos." Pliny[4] mentions
three kinds of silk—coa, bombycina[5] and serica. Apparently
the secret of getting the thread by unwinding the cocoon was
the discovery of the Chinese and was unknown to the Greeks
and Romans. The coa and bombycina, procured by piercing
and carding the cocoon instead of unwinding it entire, resulted
in a coarser and less brilliant yarn. In gathering the cocoons
of the wild silkworm after the emergence of the imago, the
filaments were severed so that they could not be unreeled in a
long continuous thread. To be utilised at all they had to be spun
and, as they lacked the properties essential to a firm spun yarn,
they were too fragile for anything but essentially decorative
uses; in effect they were a kind of coarse chiffon, which would
suit the description of the transparent materials of Amorgos.

The whole question of silk, *serica*, from China is very obscure
and it is more than doubtful if any reached the Mediterranean
until the Hellenistic era. It is quite clear that the Greeks had
heard of the Chinese, the Seres, but equally clear that they did
not know, except in the vaguest way, where China was. The
first mention is by Nearchus,[6] who was sent on a voyage of
exploration in the Indian Ocean by Alexander, and Pausanias
has a fabulous story of them living on the island of Seria in the
Red Sea, where there is an animal twice the size of a beetle
from which they get the thread for their Serican garments.[7]
There is a reference from Pherecrates which can be dated in
the second half of the fifth century to a substance called
trichaptos and explained by Photius as silk.[8] But this seems

[1] *H.P.* ix, 12, 5.   [2] Diog. Laert. viii, 19.
[3] *H.A.* v, 19, 551 B.   [4] *H.N.* xi, 22, 23.
[5] Cf. art. "Bombyx" by Mau in *P.W.*
[6] Strabo, xv, 1, 20 (c. 693); art. "Seres" by Herrmann in *P.W.*
[7] Paus. vi, 26, 6.   [8] Athen. vi, 269 B.

altogether too vague and cannot be accepted as indubitably referring to silk. Miss Richter suggests that the *amorgis* mentioned
in Aristophanes may refer to silk, but leaves the question open.[1]

Cotton was known to the Greeks, the first mention being in
Herodotus.[2] Theophrastus says that it grew on the island of
Tylos (Bahrein) in the Persian Gulf.[3] There is no evidence that
it was ever used in Greece.

THE CLOTHING INDUSTRY

In the clothing industry some made only cloaks, others exclusively the outer garment, or *chlamys*, worn by both sexes.
At Megara many were engaged in making *exomides*, sleeveless
vests commonly worn by slaves and the poorer classes.[4] At
Pellene in Achaea were made mantles of a rough hairy cloth.[5]
The *chlanides*[6] of Miletus were famous; Alcibiades, the fop,
wore one.[7] Costumes made of fabrics from Amorgos were
greatly admired and very expensive.[8] It is to be noted, however,
that probably neither place had a monopoly of these, but rather
the style of Miletus and Amorgos was copied widely in other
places.[9] Some costumiers and tailors were famous in Athens;
Xenophon tells us of Demeas, of the deme of Colyttos, who made
chlamydes, and Menon who was renowned for the cut of his
chlanides.[10] Athenaeus speaks of long robes of Corinthian make
called *kalasireis*.[11]

But again we must be careful to remember that the provision
of clothing for the family was one of the most important tasks for
the women of the household. The daughter was taught by her
mother; she had no other education, and when she married
she undertook the duty for her new home. The results must have
been fairly rough, but we may suppose that they were then sent

---

[1] *Am. Journ. Arch.* xxxiii, p. 27; Aristoph. *Lysist.* 735. For more on
ancient silk, cf. W. T. M. Forbes, in *Class. Philol.* xxv (1930), p. 22; W.
Rebel, "China als Ursprungsland der Edelseide", *Wien Beitr. zur Kunst u.
Kulturgesch. Asiens*, ii (1927), p. 47; art. "Serica" in *P.W.*; *Peripl. Mar.
Rubr.* 49; Procopius, *Anecd.* xxv, 14.

[2] Her. iii, 106; cf. Esther i. 6. [3] *H.P.* iv, 7, 7–8.
[4] Xen. *Mem.* ii, 7, 6. [5] Poll. vii, 67.
[6] *Chlanis*, an upper garment of wool worn by men and women.
[7] Plut. *Alcib.* 23, 3. [8] Aristoph. *Lysist.* 150, 735.
[9] Aesch. *in Timarch.* 97. [10] *Mem.* ii, 7, 6.
[11] xii, 525 D.

to be finished by professionals. There was also in Greece on patriotic, and to some extent on moral grounds, an aversion from the luxurious garments of the East, with beautiful embroideries and colours. We may shrewdly suspect that this feeling arose in some measure from an inability to produce anything as fine by their own somewhat primitive methods. The Greek dressed as he liked and hitched his clothes round him and pinned them as well as he could. Except for the young exquisite he was hardly a "dressy" and, if the truth be told, not an over-clean person, as many not too refined jokes in Aristophanes suggest. Woollen clothes are hard to wash, and the Greeks wore little of the much more expensive linen. But doubtless they were not less cleanly than our own ancestors of a century ago. The Man of Petty Ambition in the *Characters* of Theophrastus, who wants to push himself into the best society, often changes his clothes when they are not really dirty enough to go to the laundry and, perhaps even worse, cleans his teeth and gets shaved several times a month.[1] Aristophanes tells us that it cost three obols to have a dirty himation washed,[2] and Athenaeus mentions one Telanges who paid half an obol a day to have his cloak kept clean.[3]

We are not very well informed with regard to soap, although several references would seem to indicate that its manufacture from fat and lye from wood ashes was not unknown.[4] We do know that the usual cleaners were soda,[5] bran and pumice stone. Generally the Greeks washed in warm water, anointed themselves with oil and scraped their skins with a strigil. We know very little as to Greek baths. Athenaeus tells us they were a late innovation and formerly were not allowed within the city limits.[6] In Antiphanes, a poet of the Middle Comedy, who began to produce plays in 388, we have a fine old-fashioned outburst against the newfangled effeminacy of washing in hot

[1] Theoph. *Char.* xxi, 12; cf. x, xviii, 6, xxii, 8, xxx, 10.
[2] *Vesp.* 1127.   [3] v, 220 C.
[4] Plato, *Rep.* 430 A; Diog. Laert. iii, 27; Arist. *Probl.* xxv, 8, 938 B; Schol. Aristoph. *ad Lysist.* 470, *Acharn.* 18. Cf. also Pliny, *H.N.* xxviii, 191: in Bible Jer. ii. 22; Mal. iii. 2. Sonema was not soap, but an unguent rubbed on the skin after cleansing with water. Cf. Philox. *ap.* Athen. 409 E.
[5] I.e. Natron (sodium carbonate). Nitron, nitre or saltpetre frequently confused with natron.
[6] i, 18 B. Cf. excellent note on the Greek bath in Charicles, viii.

water.[1] But, on the other hand, we know perfectly well that public baths did exist, Athenaeus providing us with the remarkable story of Philoxenus who accustomed himself to eat hot food by gargling with hot water at the baths.[2] Xenophon tells us that some of the rich had private baths and dressing rooms, but the ordinary people went to the public establishments wherein "the vulgar have more enjoyment than the few and the wealthy".[3] Lucian tells us that the charge for admission to the public baths was two obols.[4] But this was in Roman times, and we must assume that prices had risen.

DYEING

Our knowledge of the technique of dyeing is a little more extensive than that of some other industries. Purple extracted from the murex[5] was very expensive. Athenaeus tells us it was worth its weight in silver,[6] not only because of the difficulty of making it, but because of the hard life of the fishermen.[7] The best was the Phoenician, after which came the Laconian.[8] The shellfish were mashed to a jelly[9] and boiled.[10] The most expensive fabrics were dyed twice (*dibaphos*),[11] first with the juice of the *Purpura murex* and then with that of the *Murex buccinea*, or trumpet murex. It was diluted with water or urine and often adulterated with other colours. From its excessively unpleasant smell those who used it were despised; dyers and perfumers were particularly disliked.[12] Experiments in modern times in making the dye from the actual shellfish have revealed that the product is of a dull and somewhat dingy reddish violet shade, in no way to be compared with the beauty of the modern aniline dyes. Many other agents were used in dyeing, as, for instance,

---

[1] Kock, *Frag. Com. Att.* ii, 118.
[2] Aristoph. *Plutus*, 535; Athen. i, 5 E. Cf. Sudhoff, *Aus dem antiken Badewesen*, p. 63; Isaeus, *de Haered. Phil.* 33.
[3] *Govt. of Athens*, ii, 10.   [4] *Lexiphanes*, 2.
[5] Bérard, *Les Phéniciens et l'Odyssée*, i, 407ff.; Arist. *H.A.* v, 544 A; Athen. iii, 88; Pliny, *H.N.* ix, 125; Bluemner, *Technologie*, i (revised ed.), p. 233.
[6] xii, 526 C; cf. Aesch. *Ag.* 959.   [7] Athen. x, 422 A.
[8] Paus. iii, 31, 6; cf. x, 37, 3. Chian and Ionian—Athen. xii, 539 F.
[9] Aristoph. *Acharn.* 381.   [10] Aristoph. *Eccles.* 215.
[11] Pliny, *H.N.* ix, 137; Cicero, *Litt. ad Att.* ii, 9, 2.
[12] Plut. *Pericles*.

Kermes,[1] or cochineal; madder;[2] saffron or crocus;[3] hyacinth;[4] orchil or litmus;[5] isatis or "woad".[6] There is some doubt as to whether indigo was known, but at least it is certain that the Greeks did not know how to dissolve indigo for use as dye.[7] Of inorganic dyes, yellow ochre (hydrated iron oxide)[8] was dug near Athens, but was very expensive and often adulterated; when heated it changed to a red colour.[9] Orpiment (arsenic trisulphide) and realgar (arsenic monosulphide) were also used as yellow and red dyes. The Athenian Colias is said to have invented an artificial form of cinnabar from a red sand that came from Ephesus.[10] Green was made from malachite, a basic copper carbonate which has been doubtfully identified with chrysocolla, a hydrous copper silicate.[11] Cinnabar, red mercuric sulphide, native vermilion from the common ore of mercury, the *kinnabari* of Theophrastus,[12] was probably applied to several distinct substances. Besides the large deposits at Laurium it came from Spain and Colchis.[13] Verdigris was made by soaking copper in wine lees. Black came from soot, and bone black was discovered by Apelles in 325 by charring ivory.[14] Vitruvius gives a long account of colours used by house decorators.[15]

WINE[16]

Wine, the ordinary drink in Greece in ancient times as now, was made everywhere, and the catalogue of different vintages as

[1] The error of supposing that the cochineal insect was a berry persisted for ages; Theoph. *H.P.* iii, 7, 3; 16, 1; Pliny, *H.N.* ix, 143, xvi, 32; Isaiah i. 18.

[2] Diosc. iv, 160; Her. iv, 189. Cf. also Athen. vi, 240 D; Pliny, *H.N.* xix, 47.

[3] Aesch. *Ag.* 239. Crocus, weld or luteum, a kind of mignonette—Vitruv. vii, 14, 2; Theoph. *de Odor.* 27.

[4] Hyacinth, uncertain, but perhaps the purple obtained from vaccinium or whortleberries—Xen. *Cyrop.* viii, 3, 13; Athen. vi, 255 E; Vitruv. vii, 14, 2.

[5] Theoph. *H.P.* iv, 6, 5; Diosc. iii, 115; Pliny, *H.N.* xiii, 136.

[6] Pliny, *H.N.* xxxv, 46; Vitruv. vii, 14.

[7] The question is discussed by Bluemner, *Technologie*, i, 54. Pliny, *H.N.* xxxiii, 163, says it was lately brought to Europe. Indigo is mentioned in the *Periplus Maris Eryth.* Cf. Bailey's note, i, 236.

[8] Arist. *Meteorol.* iii, 3, 11.

[9] Theoph. *de Lap.* 59.   [10] *Ibid.*

[11] *Ibid.* 26, 39. Bailey, ii, 205, discusses the point and identifies chrysocolla with malachite; cf. Athen. xii, 553 D.

[12] *de Lap.* 58.   [13] Strabo, iii, 2, 6 (c. 144).

[14] Cf. art. "Apelles" (13) in *P.W.*   [15] vii, 7–14.

[16] Art. "Vinum" in *D.S.*; "Torcular" by Hörle in *P.W.*

given in Athenaeus is quite prodigious although only a few became really famous. In Hellenistic times an important trade in Greek wines to Italy showed that they were appreciated there as being superior to the harsher products of the west. To-day Greek wines are inferior and do not leave the country. Generally speaking, ancient wines could not compare with the magnificent products of the present day, for the simple fact that the technique of making them was faulty owing to lack of knowledge of the chemical action of bacilli in decomposing. This accounts for the many quite remarkable compounds that were mixed with the wines in order to preserve them.

The grapes were put into a vat made of acacia wood and trodden out by the feet. When as much as possible had been extracted in this fashion, the skins and pulp were put in a sack of woven reeds or canvas which was twisted until the last possible moisture was extracted. The first juice that came from the untrodden grapes bruised by their own weight was drawn off to make a rare wine,[1] called in Mitylene *prodromos* or *protropos*.[2] The wine made from lightly trodden grapes was especially esteemed and counted best for its keeping qualities. Some new wine was drunk at once, after being clarified with vinegar,[3] but generally the must was taken to a cool cellar and put in earthenware jars. Wooden barrels were not used, perhaps from the scarcity of wood or perhaps because, as Pliny says, they were not suitable for warm climates.[4] Both the inside and out of these jars were coated with pitch and the containers sunk in the earth. After about six months of fermentation, during which the scum was constantly skimmed off, the wine was drawn off into smaller jars. The liquor was very impure and full of dregs, and had to be strained through a metal sieve or a piece of cloth.[5] The lowest kind of wine, fit only for slaves, was made by pouring water over the skins and pulp left after the last pressing.[6]

The struggle to correct acidity was a never-ending one and every kind of device was used to accomplish this end. Wine was mixed with sea-water, turpentine, pitch, resin, lime,

---

[1] *Geop.* vi, 16; Acts ii. 13.   [2] Athen. i, 30 B; ii, 45 E.
[3] *Geop.* vi, 15.   [4] *H.N.* xvi, 132.
[5] Poll. vi, 19, x, 75; Athen. x, 420 D; Aristoph. *Plutus*, 1085. Wine on the lees, Isaiah xxv. 6.   [6] Cf. Matth. xxvii. 48.

gypsum, burnt marble,[1] calcined shells and aromatic herbs and spices. Resin was a particularly favourite admixture, and resinated wine is still drunk in Greece; it was thought to give a bouquet.[2] To make the most highly flavoured and precious sorts costly unguents and perfumes were added,[3] which must have produced a kind of liqueur. Since distillation was not, so far as we know, practised the Greeks could not have had any form of brandy, although it is hard to imagine the potency of that really astonishing vintage that required to be watered to a twentieth of its original strength.[4] Nestor drank wine ten years old,[5] and Athenaeus speaks of some sixteen years old.[6] Many devices, more or less dishonest, were resorted to to make the wine appear older than it was, of which the favourite was to mix sea-water with it,[7] or heating it.[8] We know the name of at least one famous Athenian vintner, Serambus.[9]

OLIVE OIL

The extraction of olive oil is vividly depicted on a Greek vase. The olives are placed in layers between perforated or grooved boards, placed on a stand with a rim to catch the oil as it is pressed out. A press beam hinged at one end and heavily weighted with two stones at the other is being pulled down by a man and another to lend his weight has jumped on the beam. The oil runs over the outer sides of the wooden boards into the rimmed tray on which they stand, and from thence through a pipe with a tap into a container. Later a screw press was invented by Hero of Alexandria.[10] To preserve the oil it was mixed with

[1] Cf. Cato, *de Agri Cult.* 23; Prov. xxiii. 30; Cant. viii. 2; Psalm lxxv. 8.

[2] Plut. *Symp.* v, 3.

[3] Aelian *Var. Hist.* xii, 31; Theoph. *de Odor.* 10, 32, 44, 51; *C.P.* vi, 19, 2; art. "Drogen" by Schmidt in *P.W.* Suppl. v.

[4] *Od.* ix, 200; Athen. xi, 465 C. According to Athen. x, 426 B, the usual dilution was half and half. Neat wine was so potent that to drink it, Scythian fashion, unwatered was to risk madness. Cf. Her. vi, 84, and death of Chrysippus the philosopher, Diog. Laert. vii, 184.

[5] *Od.* iii, 391.   [6] xii, 584 B.

[7] Pliny, *H.N.* xiv, 78. Cf. Cato's recipe for loan wine, *de Agri Cult.* 24, 105, 112.

[8] Plut. *Symp.* v, 3; Athen. x, 429 C.

[9] Plato, *Gorg.* 518 B.

[10] *Mechanics*, iii, 20. Cf. A. G. Drachmann, *Ancient Oil Mills and Presses* (Copenhagen 1932); Cato, *de Agri Cult.* 64, 5, gives directions as to gathering and pressing the olives.

salt or gum and resin. The ethereal oils were not extracted, lacking an effective process of distillation.[1] Olive oil provided practically all the needs for which fats and lards are used to-day. A fat used as the basis of unguents was made from the natural fat of sheep's wool (*oisupe*, the modern lanoline).[2] It was, however, not much in favour as it decomposed very quickly. The trade in unguents was an important one, and we hear of a perfume market.[3] Dioscorides gives a lengthy list of perfumes.[4] As in the Middle Ages their use was very necessary when personal cleanliness was little practised.

Foodstuffs

We have already in our chapter on Agriculture described briefly the process of threshing the grain; it now remains to say something of milling. Strange as it may seem to-day the trades of miller and baker were not separated; the baker milled his own flour and used it there and then in making bread. Generally speaking, the entire process of preparing the grains of barley or wheat for the oven was carried on in the home; such bakers as there were seem to have been specialists or high-class confectioners, some of them quite famous. After threshing, a further process was necessary to separate the bran, which was done by roasting seemingly in a kind of machine like the modern coffee roaster. This was so important a duty in the home that it is said Solon ordered that a bride should carry one in the bridal procession as a symbol of her domestic duties.[5]

Apparently in early times the general method of milling was by pounding the grains in a mortar; and this primitive use was continued into historic times.[6] The results were evidently more of the nature of groats than flour. At the same time the far more efficient method of grinding with querns was well known,

---

[1] Distillation. How far distilling was understood is quite obscure. Aristotle seems to suggest that sweet water could be made from salt by boiling, i.e. distilling—*Probl.* xxiii, 18, 933 B. Dioscorides describes a very primitive apparatus, i, 72, v, 95; cf. Arist. *Meteorol.* i, 9, 11 (346 B), ii, 3 (356 B).

[2] Diosc. ii, 84. [3] Aristoph. *Equites*, 1375.

[4] Diosc. i, 52.

[5] Poll. i, 246; cf. also vi, 64, x, 108. Apparently this roasting or parching was only for barley; cf. Thuc. vi, 22, but the point is doubtful.

[6] Aristoph. *Vesp.* 201, 238.

and references to hand-mills in Homer are frequent.[1] Turning such querns was very exhausting work and generally given to slaves or criminals,[2] and the work went on night and day.[3] Athenaeus tells of Menedemus and Asclepiades who worked at night, and thereby earned two drachmas a shift to continue their studies in philosophy. Criminals wore a kind of halter or collar of wood which prevented them from eating the meal they were grinding.[4] Larger mills were turned by horses, donkeys or mules. We find a pathetic reference to the once famous race-horse that was condemned to spend his old age working in such lowly fashion.[5] As to whether or not the mill driven by a water-wheel was known in Greece before the Christian era there is no evidence, although this was by no means impossible. There is a charming little poem in the Anthology, by Antipatros of Thessalonica, who lived at the beginning of the first century A.D., in which the women who toiled at grinding are felicitated on their labour being eased by Demeter and the water nymphs who now turn the wheel.[6] This would seem to suggest that it was a new invention. Strabo mentions that Mithradates possessed a water-mill, evidently rather a wonderful thing.[7] The problem, in default of definite evidence, must be left unsolved. Wind-mills were a much later invention, probably fourth or fifth century A.D.[8]

To separate the flour from the bran the meal was sieved or "bolted".[9] According to the fineness of the sieve was the quality of the flour and the bread made therefrom, of which Athenaeus gives an impressive catalogue of different kinds.[10] Bread was generally leavened with yeast,[11] but unleavened made

---

[1] E.g. *Od.* ii, 355, vii, 104, xx, 106, and several others.
[2] Dem. *in Steph.* i, 33; Lysias, *de Caede Erat.* 18; Poll. iii, 78.
[3] Athen. iv, 168 B. The story of Menedemus and Asclepiades.
[4] Poll. vii, 20, x, 112; Schol. *ad* Aristoph. *Pax*, 14. Cf. the prohibition against muzzling the ox that trod out the corn—Deut. xxv. 4.
[5] *Anth. Pal.* ix, 19–21. At Olynthus has been found another form of small hand-mill in which the upper stone was pushed backwards and forwards by a wooden lever.
[6] *Anth. Pal.* ix, 418.
[7] Strabo, xii, 3, 30 (c. 556); Bluemner, *Technologie*, i, 46.
[8] Bluemner, *Technologie*, i, 49.
[9] Poll. vi, 74; Aristoph. *Eccles.* 991.
[10] Athen. iii, 108 F. Attic bread was the best—iii, 109.
[11] Arist. *Gen. An.* 3, 4, 755 A; Athen. iii, 113 B.

with soda was also known. References to kneading the dough are very numerous. We are told that Anaxarchos made his slaves wear gloves when engaged in this and have a kind of respirator over the mouth to prevent their breath from spoiling the dough, or perhaps their spitting in it.[1] By good fortune there have been preserved two terra-cotta groups representing the kneading of the dough.[2] In one two figures bend over a large trough and in another is a mass of dough. Another figure stands holding a sieve, and in the background is an oven. The other shows four women busy kneading while another blows on a pipe, no doubt to encourage them in their labour.

The oven seems to have been of the simplest description, an earthenware or clay structure standing on legs or with a space beneath for the fire. In one of the terra-cotta groups a woman is putting sticks underneath to feed the fire, while another is examining the loaves which are baking in the oven. One more little figure shows a man cooking at what is evidently a grill with a fire underneath, although it is impossible to say whether it is meat or cakes that he is busy with. All kinds of confectionery, fancy cakes, and pastry were made; we even know the name of one famous confectioner in Athens, Thearion.[3]

Any idea that the high thinking of the Greeks was accompanied by plain living, at least among the better-to-do, may be dismissed at once. The *Deipnosophists* of Athenaeus is a truly astonishing recital of the refined *gourmandise* of the rich; a super-cookbook that pours out endless accounts of dainties to be enjoyed by the gourmet. Earth and sea and sky are ransacked for delicacies, and the rival merits of this or that cooked dish are discussed at prodigious length. In rich households, where many slaves were kept, we hear of as many as a dozen cooks, each skilled in the preparation of a single dish, being employed in the preparations for a fashionable dinner party. Xenophon pities the poor man who has only one slave to do all the cooking and the household tasks. "The man who has only one servant to make his bed, lay his table, knead the bread and prepare the

[1] Athen. xii, 548 c.   [2] *D.S.* iv, p. 495, figs. 5694-5.
[3] Plato, *Gorg.* 518 B. Jardé, *Céréales*, p. 128, n. 1, has an interesting note on the use of various kinds of flour in cooking. Cf. also Arist. *Probl.* xxi, 927 A, where the differences between wheat and barley are discussed.

meal, must take everything as it is offered to him. But when each has his special task, one boiling the meat, another roasting, one doing the fish in spiced sauce, another frying it, and another making the bread in the fashion that best suits the taste of the master, it seems to me everything will be quite perfect." Cooked dishes were sold in the shops, and in the Agora was reserved a special place where chefs with their assistants and utensils[1] and waiters[2] were to be hired. Some of these cooks were famous for their special dishes and wrote cookery books. Among the most famous were Sophon, Simonactides of Chios, Tyndarichos of Sicyon, Sopyrinus, Mithaikos of Sicily,[3] Simos,[4] and Parmenion of Rhodes.[5] We also hear of Agis of Rhodes who was unrivalled in frying fish; Aphthonetos renowned for his sausages; Euthynos for his lentil soup, and Lamprias for his black puddings.[6] Curiously enough it is in cooking that we find, so far as is known, the only instance of a "patent" or temporary monopoly being granted to an inventor. At Sybaris, we are told, when a chef had invented a particularly fine dish, he was given the sole right of producing it for one year.[7]

Carpentry and Woodworking[8]

As we have repeatedly noted, Greece was lacking in good timber, such as there was being of poor quality. Practically all the timber used in carpentry was imported, and still more so that used in shipbuilding. Scattered all through the *History of Plants*[9] and in less degree in the *Causes of Plants* of Theophrastus are innumerable references to various kinds of timber, and incidentally to practices in the lumbering industry, building and carpentry. The fifth book of the *History* is entirely devoted to forestry, and from it we can pick up much of interest. The best

---

[1] Alexis, *ap.* Athen. iv, 164 F, vi, 229 B, xiv, 658; cf. Diog. Laert. ii, 72; Poll. ix, 48.

[2] Athen. iv, 170 D. [3] Plato, *Gorg.* 518 B.

[4] Alexis, *ap.* Athen. iv, 164 C. A very talented cook but a bad actor.

[5] *Ibid.* 662 C.

[6] Athen. ix, 379 E, xii, 516 C, where the names of eighteen famous cooks are given. Cf. also Xen. *Hiero*, i, 176.

[7] Phylarchus, frag. 45.

[8] Bluemner, *Technologie*, ii, 238 ff.

[9] Called in the Loeb edition "Enquiry into Plants". Vitruv. ii, cap. 9, has a good deal to say on timber used in building.

timber came from Macedonia, smooth, with a straight grain
and resinous. The second best came from Pontus, next from the
region of the Rhyndakos, a river flowing into the Propontis on
the Asiatic side, whose modern name is Edrenos Chai; fourth,
that of the country of the Ainianes, near Mount Oeta in Aetolia;
the worst was that of Parnassus and Euboea, which was knotty,
rough and quick rotting.[1]

Timber is either in the round, when it is debarked; squared,
when it is hewn with the lumberman's broad-axe; or it is split
with wedges or sawn into planks. There are careful instructions
with regard to splitting and sawing;[2] of the latter Theophrastus
remarks on the difficulty of sawing green wood which binds the
saw so that the teeth have to be set alternate ways in order to
clear the sawdust; green wood also blunts the saw which dry
does not.

There is a long discussion as to the woods most suitable for
different purposes, housebuilding or shipbuilding. The house-
builder, *oikodomos*, was at need a mason, bricklayer, carpenter
or shipwright. It is not quite certain with regard to the use of
nails; undoubtedly for heavy work iron ones were used, but
since iron was scarce we may suppose that wooden pegs were
more generally employed in the shape of trenails or dowels.[3]
Vitruvius gives a careful description of dovetailing.[4] Glue was
extensively employed, and Theophrastus gives directions as to
how it was to be employed with the various open or close
grained woods. It was made of animals' hooves, or a form of
fish glue, which Aelian says was made from the *oxyrhynchus*, a
kind of sturgeon from the Caspian.[5]

The usual carpenter's tools are mentioned—hammer; mallet
or beetle; lathe;[6] plane; auger and gimlet; spokeshave, etc.
There are detailed instructions for making "hinges" of elm
wood, which had to be seasoned in cow dung. It is to be noted

[1] *H.P.* v, 2, 1.
[2] *Ibid.* v, 1, 9, 10. There are some obscurities which need not be com-
mented on here; cf. note in Loeb, ed. i, p. 424.
[3] Cf. the description of the building of the ship or raft of Odysseus, *Od.*
v, 247. Cf. also Schol. *ap.* Aristoph. *Equites*, 463; Polyb. xiii, 7, 9.
[4] Vitruv. iv, 7, 4.
[5] *N.A.* xvii, 32; Her. ii, 86. Cf. also Arist. *Physica*, 227 A; *I.G.* ii², 1672,
68.
[6] *H.P.* v, 3, 2; cf. also Plato, *Critias*, 113 D.

that the word translated "hinges" does not convey the modern
sense of the word, but rather pivots turning in sockets.[1]

When the kings came to the help of Rhodes after the earthquake, Ptolemy sent ship's timbers enough to build 10 quin-
quiremes and 10 triremes of 40,000 cubits of pine planking,
Antigonus sent 10,000 pieces of timber from 16 to 18 cubits in
length to be used in housebuilding and 7000 rafters 7 cubits
long; Seleucus gave 10,000 cubits of timber.[2]

Pit-props, since the mines of Laurium were not dangerous,
were, we must suppose, not a particularly important item in
the timber trade. Most of them must have been imported; one
of the items in the attack upon Midias was that he used his
trireme for bringing timber for his silver mines.[3] Curiously
enough the only remains of such props as have been discovered
in the workings are of olive wood, obviously a local product.[4]
Small firewood for domestic use was plentiful; Phaenippus sent
six loads a day from his estate at Cythera, for which he got
12 drs. a day.[5] Theophrastus gives detailed instructions on
charcoal burning and the best wood to use.[6] Since coal was
certainly not used domestically, charcoal was a highly important
article, in the production of which the Acharnians were much
engaged.[7] Diitrephes made a fortune in making baskets and
crates.[8]

SHIPBUILDING[9]

It is tantalising to realise that our knowledge of shipbuilding
is very scant; we have no picture of work going on in a ship-
yard, a subject of sufficient interest to have attracted the eye of
an artist. Our lack of knowledge is so extraordinary that to this
very day such expressions as "quinquireme" elude exact definition. To suppose that such a vessel had five banks of oars one

[1] *H.P.* v, 3, 5; cf. also Vitruv. iv, 6; Plut. *Rom.* 23, 5.
[2] Polyb. v, 89: cubit about 1½ ft., but uncertain.
[3] *In Mid.* 167.
[4] Ardaillion, *Les mines de Laurion*, p. 56.
[5] Dem. *in Phaen.* 7; cf. also Alciphron, iii, 38, 1.
[6] *H.P.* v, 9, 1.
[7] Aristoph. *Acharn.* 181, 666.
[8] Aristoph. *Aves*, 798, 1440. According to Scholiast to be identified with
the Diitrephes of Thuc. vii, 29. Cf. Paus. i, 23, 2.
[9] Francotte, *L'Industrie*, ii, 104; art. "Seewesen" by Miltner in *P.W.*
Suppl. v.

above the other is beyond comprehension, and when we are told of enormous ships in the Hellenistic age with forty banks of oars, no conceivable explanation can be offered and we have to confess ourselves baffled.[1]

We have two accounts of a ship being built, the first that of Odysseus. The goddess Calypso at last lets Odysseus go and allows him to build a boat. The story is so lively that it is worth repeating at length. Calypso gives him a great axe of bronze, double-edged, with a heft of olive wood, and a polished adze, and shows him where the best trees grow, alder and poplar and tall pine, seasoned and already dry, so that when hewn they would float well. Odysseus cuts down twenty trees and trimmed and smoothed them with his axe. Calypso then gave him augers to bore holes with, and he joined them with trenails and dowels. "Wide as is the floor of a broad ship of burden, which some man well skilled in carpentry may trace him out, of such beam did Odysseus fashion his broad craft. And thereat he wrought, and set up the deckings, fitting them to the close-set uprights, and finished them off with long gunwales, and therein he set a mast with a yard-arm fitted thereto, and moreover he made him a rudder to guide the craft. He fenced it with wattled osier withies from stem to stern to be a bulwark against the wave and piled up wood to back them. Meanwhile Calypso the fair goddess brought him a web of cloth to make him sails, and these too he fashioned very skilfully. And he made fast therein braces and halyards and sheets and at last he pushed the craft with levers down to the fair salt sea."[2] It may be mentioned that the whole business only took four days; but since it was on a magic isle no doubt that was quite possible.

Many commentators have puzzled over this strange craft, and no very satisfactory explanation has ever been given of it. It is generally assumed that it was a raft; but can a raft have bulwarks and be steered by a rudder? The simplest explanation is that it was a clumsy flat-bottomed ship without a keel. Why the bulwarks should have been of withies is hard to understand, except that Odysseus was in a hurry to be off; but since he had already been eight years on the magic isle he might have given a little more care to the ship on which he was going to risk his

[1] Athen. v, 203 D.   [2] *Od.* v, 233f.

life. We can only conclude that in the Homeric age some such crude boat was about the best the Greeks could manage. It is quite clear they were far inferior to the Phoenicians in the art of shipbuilding, and it is easy to understand what an aversion they had to the sea if their ships were no better than that of the famous craftsman Odysseus.[1]

The second description of a ship being built is that of the famous and ill-fated monster *Syracosia* of Hiero of Syracuse. Unfortunately the description given in the *Deipnosophists* leaves very much to be desired as to actual construction of the hull, but a great deal is said of the wonderful fittings. That it was able to carry the enormous cargo, "ninety thousand bushels of wheat, ten thousand jars of Sicilian salt fish, six hundred tons of wool and other freight amounting to six hundred tons", is very much open to doubt and we are forced to suppose that the whole account is grossly exaggerated. But even at that the ship proved to be the *Great Eastern* of her day, unmanageable and unseaworthy, and after Hiero had given her to Ptolemy she seems to have been taken out of commission. The accounts given of other ships built by Ptolemy Philopator are similarly unsatisfactory: it is hard to imagine a ship that had four thousand rowers and four hundred sailors. As usual such figures are totally unreliable.[2]

In Athens the shipbuilding industry was highly organised. The building of the hulls, the making of the rigging, oars and sails occupied a great many workers. But unfortunately we have no information whatever with regard to the conditions of labour in the industry except from the administrative side. The number of ships to be built was voted on each year by the Assembly, which appointed the officers to superintend the work and the treasurer to disburse the sums voted. Ten *trieropoioi* were responsible for the completion of the work which was let to contractors, who, however, did not provide their own materials. These were under the care of the superintendents of the arsenals (*epimeletai*), who delivered the timber necessary for hulls and

[1] Cf. F. Brewster, "The raft of Odysseus", *Harvard Studies in Class. Phil.* (1926), p. 49; Köster, *Antikes Seewesen*, p. 69; T. D. Seymour, *Life in the Homeric Age*, p. 305.

[2] Athen. v, 204 E ff.; C. Torr, *Ancient Ships*; W. W. Tarn, *Hellenistic Military and Naval Developments*, p. 122; Köster, *Antikes Seewesen*.

oars to the *trieropoioi*. It is, therefore, quite evident that the contractors were simply carpenters hired to build the ships with the materials given to them.[1] In charge of these workmen was the architect (*architekton*), who was a trained technician. We know the names of some of these; for instance, Amyntas, who built a ship called the Euphoria, which was counted one of the best twenty-two ships ever launched.[2] Most of the ships were built in the yards at the Piraeus; others at Salamis. In the time of Strabo shipbuilding was carried on at Rhodes, Cyzicus, Massalia, Daton in Thrace, Cyprus and Cilicia. Cyprus, he says, has the unique advantage of possessing all the materials necessary in its own territory.[3] The logs destined for shipbuilding were squared and sawn where the trees were felled and exported unseasoned. For shipbuilding the timbers were never thoroughly seasoned as they then became too stiff to bend, and after the ship was built it was allowed to stand for some time before being launched.[4] We may surmise that this practice accounts largely for the rapid deterioration of a fleet, unless under perpetual care, and the length of time necessary for preparing the ships for the sea after being out of the water for a long period.

It also explains the great importance of materials for calking, such as tow, pitch, bitumen, resin and wax. Pitch or wood tar was distilled from hardwoods or beech in Macedonia, Turdetania in Southern Spain, and from the forests of Mount Ida and Syria.[5] The use of bitumen for calking was certainly general at an early date, as, for instance, in the account in Genesis of the building of the Ark, and was used by the Phoenicians who drew their supply from the Dead Sea, or perhaps from Commagene in South-west Cappadocia.[6] We have no certain knowledge that the Greeks used it or depended entirely on tar, but there is no reason why they should not; it would have been easy to get large quantities from several sources.[7] There is always the

---

[1] Arist. *Ath. Pol.* xlvi; *I.G.* ii², 1627.
[2] *I.G.* ii², 1612.
[3] Strabo, xiv, 6, 5 (c. 684).
[4] Theoph. *H.P.* v, 7, 4.
[5] Pliny, *H.N.* xvi, 21–2; Theoph. *H.P.* ix, 1 ff.
[6] Pliny, *H.N.* ii, 335. For more on use of pitch cf. Glotz, "Le Prix d'une Denrée", *Rev. des Études Grecques*, xxix, 281 f.; Tarn, *Hellenistic Civilisation*, p. 225.
[7] The provenance of bitumen or asphalt is dealt with at length in the chapter on Mining and Minerals.

difficulty in distinguishing between pitch and bitumen in the authors.[1] When Rhodes was destroyed by earthquake Antigonus gave 1000 talents weight of unboiled and 1000 amphorae of boiled pitch.[2] Wax for calking, a highly important article, was, we must suppose, fairly plentiful in Attica, famous for bee-keeping, but it was also imported.[3] Sails, made in early, and we may suppose often in later times, of hides sewn together, were generally made of linen or papyrus cloth, but we know little of their manufacture. Ptolemy gave Rhodes 3000 pieces of sailcloth; coming from Egypt they were probably made of byssus. Ropes were made of twisted ox-hide,[4] papyrus fibre,[5] hemp[6] or flax, the latter from Phasis and Colchis, and, according to Xenophon, from Carthage, where a fine variety suitable for making nets was grown. Resin, of which Theophrastus speaks,[7] was also used in shipbuilding; Seleucus gave 1000 talents weight of it to Rhodes after the earthquake.

BUILDING[8]

It is hardly to be wondered at that, although our knowledge of the construction of the great public edifices is sufficiently detailed, we know very little indeed of the building industry appertaining to more lowly purposes, and that for the simple reason that great stone-built edifices are lasting and we may study their construction to-day, while the humble houses of the people are swept away and nothing remains. As to the materials used for the ordinary Greek house we may be fairly certain. They certainly were not made either of stone, baked brick or wood.[9] Stone was too expensive except for the rich, and as we have already remarked, baked brick was unknown until quite late. There certainly are references to wooden houses, as, for instance, one of the accusations brought against Timotheus was that he had got wood from Macedonia to build his house at the Piraeus,[10] and the "Boaster" vaunts himself in a similar

---

[1] Cf. Vitruv. vii, 3, 8.   [2] Polyb. v, 89.

[3] Xen. *Cyneget.* ii, 4. From Colchis, Strabo, xi, 2, 17 (c. 498). From Pontus, Polyb. iv, 38, 4.

[4] *Od.* ii, 426; cf. Cato, *de Agri Cult.* 12.   [5] Theoph. *H.P.* iv, 8, 4.

[6] Athen. v, 206 F.   [7] *H.P.* ix, 2, 1.

[8] Bluemner, *Technologie*, iii. Description of Greek house by Vitruv. vi, 7.

[9] Vitruv. ii, 8; cf. Pliny, *H.N.* xxxvi, 171 f.

[10] Dem. *in Tim.* 26.

way in the *Characters* of Theophrastus.[1] We may infer, therefore, that such were the luxuries of the rich. We may be certain
that the ordinary dwelling of the less well-to-do Greek was
made of unbaked brick; it was easy enough to dig through them,
and a regular name for a robber was "wall-digger".[2] It is also
permissible to surmise that many of the more humble dwellings
were made of "wattle and daub". At least we know that such
was the case at Sardes,[3] but that was early. Vitruvius speaks of
that form of construction,[4] but disapproves of it as particularly
liable to fire.

Probably the walls were whitewashed, at least on the inside.
Apparently for a house to be plastered or covered with stucco
was a sign of great luxury.[5] The gypsum from which the stucco
was made came from Cyprus, Phoenicia and Thurii.[6] It was
burned in an oven, pulverised and then "slaked" in the manner
used now to make plaster of Paris.[7] It was employed for
plastering inside walls, for the making of mortar and for decorations, as, for instance, the adornment of the temple of Artemis
at Stymphalos.[8] The Greeks could make first-class mortar and
cement, as the large water cisterns at Laurium testify. These
reservoirs were finished with a cement surface on the inside
impervious to water, and the excellence of the methods used
have preserved them intact. M. Ardaillon gives a chemical
analysis of the constituents used in making a cement that cannot
be improved upon at the present day.[9] Alcibiades had his house
painted with frescoes by a celebrated artist.[10] Socrates disapproves of such luxuries.[11] The floors were made of plaster or
stone, seldom of wood.[12] Mosaics were naturally a great luxury
and evidently were first known in Greece in the fourth century;
houses with floors of a pebble mosaic have been found on the
site of Olynthus destroyed in 348. Demetrius of Phalerum had

---

[1] Theoph. *Char.* 23.
[2] Aristoph. *Plutus*, 565. [3] Her. v, 101.
[4] Vitruv. ii, 8, 20; cf. also Pliny, *H.N.* xxxv, 169.
[5] Plut. *Comp. Arist. Cato*, 4, 4. [6] Theoph. *de Lap.* 64.
[7] *Ibid.* 69; cf. Pliny, *H.N.* xxxvi, 182–3; Vitruv. vii, 2.
[8] Paus. viii, 22, 7.
[9] *Mines de Laurion*, p. 65; cf. Pliny, *H.N.* xxxv, 166f. Mortar mixed with
the bare feet, Aristoph. *Aves*, 839, 1145.
[10] Plut. *Alcib.* 16, 4. [11] *Mem.* iii, 8, 10; *Oecon.* ix, 2.
[12] Pliny, *H.N.* xxxvi, 184f.

such in his house, which were considered a great extravagance.[1] Roofs were made of tiles[2] or thatch; we have already mentioned that wooden shingles had been used when lumber was more plentiful in Attica.[3] Windows were unglazed; the use of thin sheets of talc or mica was of later introduction among the Romans.[4] Doors were of wood, turning on a pivot and socket, and secured by a bolt; the modern forms of locks and keys were unknown. Socrates had some sensible remarks to make with regard to building houses and particularly as to their aspect, to be warm in winter and cool in summer.[5]

METAL TRADES

Iron. The smelting of iron ore and the production of steel are difficult metallurgical processes, and it is only within very modern times that they have been reduced to an exact science. Steel, which is iron hardened by an admixture of carbon, has only been used in large quantities since Bessemer developed his process in 1856. Before that time the production of steel was a more or less hit-or-miss affair, according to whether or not the right proportion of carbon had been introduced through the agency of charcoal. Such accurate processes as the modern steel-maker uses were quite beyond the skill of the ancient metallurgists.

Since the Greeks were unable to produce temperatures in their furnaces sufficient to make pig-iron (1225° C.) they were only able to make it in the wrought form which requires a temperature of 700° C. Smelting was by the direct extraction process, using a furnace of the "Catalan" form[6] where ore

---

[1] Athen. xii, 542 D. Cf. description of Hiero's great ship, v, 207 C.

[2] K. A. Rhomaios, "Decorated architectural tiles", *Gnomon*, vii (1931), p. 648.

[3] Agesilaus was surprised to see roofs made with squared beams in Asia—Plut. *Apoph. Lac.* 210 E. The law of Lycurgus that roofs were to be made only with an axe and doors with a saw would only suggest very rough workmanship—*ibid.* 189 E, 227 C; *Life of Lycurgus*, 13.

[4] But remains of glass windows have been found in Pompeii and Herculaneum. Cf. Pliny, *H.N.* xxxvi, 160; Strabo, xii, 2, 10 (c. 540); also Juv. iv, 21; Seneca, *Ep.* xc, 25; Martial, viii, 14. Cf. also Pliny, *H.N.* xix, 64.

[5] Xen. *Mem.* iii, 8, 8.

[6] It is not strictly correct to describe the Greek furnace as "Catalan". In its most primitive form the Catalan furnace was built on the side of a hill where the wind provided the necessary blast. In medieval times this was generated by bellows driven by water-power. It was not until Smeaton in 1760 generated a blast by the compressed air pump that the problem of raising the temperature to a sufficient degree was solved.

mixed with charcoal is subject to a blast which melts the iron in the ore, causing it to seep down to the bottom, where it collects in the form of "bloom" covered with slag. The results are far from satisfactory because much of the "gangue", i.e. the stone or earth in the ore, remains and demands resmelting and re-forging before it can partially or wholly be eliminated, a long and expensive process. The bellows were worked by the foot both in Egypt and Greece; one very inconclusive picture suggests that they might in some instances have been worked by a lever, as the modern blacksmith works his forge, but the indications are too vague to be definite.[1] Charcoal was the only fuel used; the reference by Theophrastus to coal used by smiths cannot refer to smelting but only to its use in a smithy, for which the low-grade lignite found in Greece was not unsuitable.

References to iron in Homer are fairly numerous. Evidently it was mostly meteoric in form as the epithet "heavenly" is frequently applied to it. It was so scarce that weapons or armour were not made of it; indeed good bronze is superior to inferior iron. There are no references to steel, from which we may safely infer that either it was not known or was not distinguished from iron. The suggestion that *kuanos* refers to blued steel cannot be accepted. Later steel is certainly identified by the word *stomoma*, of which the best description is given by Aetius.[2] Tempering by plunging in water was known very early;[3] later tempering with oil was widely used.[4] A term used in connection with iron working which has given rise to discussion is *diploe*: it may mean twice-forged, or perhaps welded; no certain conclusion can be arrived at.[5]

In Hellenistic times Indian iron was held in high esteem,[6] and the temper of Spanish blades was famous. Celtiberian iron was buried in the earth until rust had attacked the impurities,

---

[1] Bluemner, *Technologie*, iv, 364, fig. 2.

[2] Aetius, x, 11; cf. Plut. *Def. Orac.* xli, 433 A; Muson, frag. 18 A; Arist. *Meteor.* iv, 6, 383 A; art. "Stahl" by Romel in *P.W.*

[3] *Od.* ix, 391. Cf. Plut. *Def. Orac.* xlvii, 436 C; *Quaest. Conv.* viii, 9, 734 A.

[4] Plut. *de Prim. frig.* xiii, 950 C.

[5] Plato, *Soph.* 267 E. Bluemner (*Technologie*, iv, 350) discusses the point inconclusively.

[6] *Peripl. Mar. Eryth.* vi; Pliny, *H.N.* xxxiv, 145, perhaps Chinese but quite uncertain. Cf. Bluemner, *Technologie*, iv, 349.

when it was dug up and reforged.[1] Bluemner points out that this practice has been described by the Swedish metallurgist Swedenborg, and was well known among famous sword-makers in Japan. Blades were sharpened on the whetstone, of which the best came from Naxos, famous for emery,[2] although Pliny preferred those from Crete.[3] The old problem as to whether or not the Greeks could produce cast-iron has never been settled; but Bluemner concludes that difficulties with their furnaces must have prevented them.[4] Pliny informs us that white lead, gypsum and pitch were used as a preventive against rust, apparently as a kind of paint.[5] The chasing of steel was well known, for which one Glaucus was famous,[6] and Strabo says that Cibyra in Phrygia was renowned for such work.[7] Doubtless the smith could turn his hand to making anything, but we hear of armourers,[8] shield-makers,[9] spear-makers, makers of farm implements such as sickles and pitch forks, sword- and knife-makers[10] and nail-makers. We have no evidence whatever that the Greeks ever made iron or copper wire; but they did know how to draw gold and silver threads for filigree work. The reference to the "net" made by Hephaestus is very vague.[11] Nails were hammered out by the smith on his anvil, as they were until a recent date in modern times.[12] The tools used by the smith, as seen in numerous pictures, were those familiar to modern days, hammers of various shapes, small and sledge, pincers and, in one picture, a hack-saw. As has always been the case, the smithy was a favourite meeting place for gossip on cold days; almost every picture shows one or more visitors watching the work go on. In one a woman is depicted who may be blowing the

---

[1] Diod. v, 33; Plut. *de Garrul.* xvii, 510 F. Cf. also Bluemner, *Technologie*, iv, 351, n. 2.

[2] Pindar, *Isth.* vi, 73.   [3] *H.N.* xxxvi, 164, xxxvii, 109.

[4] For various references cf. Paus. iii, 12, 10, x, 16, 1, x, 18, 6; Arist. *Meteor.* iv, 6; also Pliny, *H.N.* xxxiv, 146. Bluemner (*Technologie*, iv, 355) discusses the point at length.

[5] *H.N.* xxxiv, 149.   [6] Athen. v, 210 C.

[7] Strabo, xiii, 4, 17 (c. 631).

[8] Diod. xiv, 43; Plat. *Polit.* 280 D.

[9] Aristoph. *Aves*, 491.   [10] Eur. *Bacch.* 1208; Aristoph. *Pax*, 545.

[11] *Od.* viii, 273 f. Cf. Ex. xxxix. 3. Bluemner, *Technologie*, iv, 250.

[12] Nails or bolts, iron and wooden trenails—Xen. *Cyn.* ix, 12. Shoenails—Theophr. *Char.* iv, 13. For shipbuilding, wooden or bronze, sometimes iron—Polyb. xiii, 7, 9. Cf. I Chron. xxii. 3. Vegetius, *de Re Militari*, iv.

bellows, but this is very uncertain and may show the smithy of Hephaestus with one of the goddesses looking on.[1]

There are innumerable references to particular objects made presumably of steel which came from various places. For instance, swords from Chalcis, helmets from Boeotia[2] or perhaps helmets made in the Boeotian pattern; various weapons from Rhodes;[3] others from Argos, especially helmets. When Cinadon was plotting an insurrection in Sparta, on being asked where he was going to procure arms for the rebels, he pointed to the iron-market, where daggers, swords, spits, axes, hatchets and scythes were on sale, saying "all the instruments with which men cultivate the ground or hew wood or stone, would serve as weapons, while the greater part of the artificers had sufficient tools to fight with, especially against unarmed enemies".[4] Pollux tells us of a breastplate from Athens, a helmet from Boeotia, a knife from Laconia, a breastplate from Argos, a bow from Crete, a sling from Acarnania, a javelin from Aetolia, a dagger from Gaul and an axe from Thrace.[5] As mentioned already we know of several establishments in Athens, such as those of Lysias and Polemarchus, of Pasion and the father of Demosthenes, that made swords, knives, shields, and other warlike equipment. It is quite unnecessary to suppose that scattered references denote any large trade in such articles; it would be absurd to suppose that Gaul exported large quantities of daggers! In a warlike age weapons and armour were made everywhere and the blacksmith and the armourer were important craftsmen. It is not without interest at the present time to know that the international trade in war munitions was a flourishing one. Demosthenes tells us of a law proposed by Timarchus imposing the death penalty on anyone exporting weapons or naval supplies to Philip of Macedon.[6] Plato speaks of the same traffic and, surprisingly, justifies it as a necessity for the state; but on general principles considers such traffic should not be in the hands of private individuals for profit.[7]

Glaucus of Chios, at the end of the seventh century, imported

[1] Bluemner, *Technologie*, iv, 364, fig. 2.
[2] Xen. *de Equit.* xii, 3.
[3] Diod. Sic. xx, 84, 4 (but the evidence is late).
[4] Xen. *Hell.* iii, 3, 7. [5] Poll. i, 149.
[6] *de Falsa Leg.* 286. [7] *Laws*, 847 D.

or invented the art of iron-welding.[1] Metal-casting was of ancient origin; perhaps the invention of the Phoenicians or even earlier.[2] The earliest hollow-cast bronzes were made by what is known as the "sand-box" method; the *cire perdue* process was considerably later, probably not much before the middle of the fifth century.[3] The attribution of the art of hollow casting to Rhoecus of Samos, the architect of the temple of Hera on that island, and the development of the process by his sons Theodorus and Telecles, presents certain difficulties which need not be entered upon here.[4] Rhoecus is also credited with having first mixed tin and copper to make bronze, but that is quite fanciful. Pliny in Book xxxiv of his *Natural History* gives many details of Greek works in bronze and various alloys. Corinthian bronzes were particularly famous.[5] In Delos were made bronze feet and supports of dining couches;[6] Aegina was famous for its bronzes, "not indeed that the metal was produced there, but because the annealing of the Aeginetan products was so excellent". A curious fact is asserted in the sixth chapter: "Aegina was particularly famous for the manufacture of sockets for lamp-stands, as Tarentum was for that of the branches; the completed articles being produced by the union of the two." If this is correct, we have a surprising division of labour between two towns far removed from each other. It is, however, far more likely that the different parts of the candelabra were made according to patterns or in the style of artists who had once worked at Tarentum or Aegina. A long list of famous statuaries who worked in bronze is given in the same book.

[1] Her. i, 25. Not inlaying or damascening as sometimes suggested, but perhaps soldering. Pliny's narration of the various processes of soldering is quite vague (*H.N.* xxxiii, 94). Cf. Bailey's note, i, 209.

[2] I Kings vii. 46.

[3] Cf. Kluge-Lehmann-Hartleben, *Antike Grossbronzen*, i, 82ff. In the cire perdue method the figure is modelled in a mixture of clay and sand and covered with a layer of wax over which another outer covering of clay is placed, the whole being imbedded in sand as a support. The wax layer is melted, escaping through vents and molten metal poured in. The outer casing is then chipped off and the metal beneath worked upon. The inner core is usually left, or may be removed. This ancient method is still employed. For sand-box method cf. art. "Founding" in *Enc. Brit.*

[4] Paus. viii, 14, 8, ix, 41, 1, x, 38, 6; Pliny, *H.N.* xxxv, 152.

[5] The explanation that Corinthian bronze was accidentally discovered by various metals running together at the burning of Corinth by Mummius is fanciful. Cf. Bücher, *Beiträge*, p. 51.

[6] Cf. also Cicero, *Pro Roscio Am.* 133.

The attribution of certain works of art to various cities is always puzzling. For instance, we hear of metal vases in the temples of Athens which came from Chalcis and Lesbos, and in the temple of Delos from Teos, Miletus, Chios, Rhodes, Etruria and Laconia. We do not know whether these were made by native artists; they might just as easily have been made elsewhere and reached their final resting-place in the shrines through the places named.

Lead and Tin. Of working in lead we have only a few scattered references, for instance that of the use of iron dowels sunk in lead for joining heavy masonry.[1] Remains of lead water-pipes have been found on Delos,[2] and there are numerous references in Latin authors to lead containers for salves and medicines, and this use is mentioned by Athenaeus and Theophrastus.[3] We also hear of lead vases, lamps, weights, anchors, checks for entrance to the theatre and pencils.[4] Hiero's great ship, the *Syracosia*, was sheathed with lead.[5] Tin plating was well understood and very old.[6] Copper utensils were tinned, according to Pliny.[7] Aristotle says that tin was used for the containers of cosmetics,[8] and he also mentions a tin statue and tin money.[9]

Glass. There is no evidence that glass was made in Greece, although they knew all about it; probably difficulty in obtaining the materials stood in their way. Cast-glass was known from an early time[10] as an oriental product brought by Persian ambassadors.[11] Plato mentions it,[12] and Strabo has something to say about it.[13] It is always hard to distinguish between glass and rock crystal.[14] The manufacture of blown glass in Syria and Egypt, a Hellenistic invention, later became a valuable trade, and its use spread widely, bowls and cups being made of it.[15]

[1] *I.G.* i², 374.
[2] Vitruv. viii, 6, says lead pipes are poisonous.
[3] *de Odor.* ix, 41. Athen. x, 451 D, where litharge evidently means lead.
[4] Ardaillon, *Les mines de Laurion*, p. 120; Cratinus, fr. 180, 181; Diod. Sic. v, 36, 3; Catull. xxii, 9.
[5] Athen. v, 207 A.   [6] *Il.* xxiii, 561.
[7] *H.N.* xxxiv, 160, 162.   [8] *Soph. El.* i, 264 B, 24.
[9] *de Mir. Ausc.* lxxxi, 836 A; *Oecon.* 1349 A.
[10] Her. iii, 24; cf. ii, 69, glass earrings for crocodiles.
[11] Aristoph. *Acharn.* 73; cf. *Nubes*, 766.   [12] *Tim.* 61 B.
[13] xvi, 2, 25 (c. 758); cf. *Anth. Pal.* ix, 776.
[4] E.g. Theoph. *de Lap.* 49.
[5] Cf. Paus. ii, 27, 3; Athen. iv, 129 E; Achill. Tat. ii, 3; Job, xxviii. 17.

COMMERCE (I)

COMMERCE IN THE HOMERIC AGE

IN Homer we see the beginnings of Greek commerce. The Minoan thalassocracy had passed and the Aegean was anybody's sea, but mostly it was the Phoenicians', who traded everywhere. The "Greeks", if we may use that title loosely, had not yet taken to the sea as merchants and traders. They preferred piracy, and since they had little or nothing to give in return for what they wanted, they had to go and take it. This they did with considerable success, as the naïve boastings of Menelaus and Odysseus attest. Menelaus had roamed for eight years over Cyprus and Phoenicia and Egypt, had reached the Aethiopians and Sidonians and Erembi and Libya, "gathering much livelihood". Perhaps there may be more successful pirates than he, though he frankly doubts it.[2] Odysseus boasts that he made nine expeditions to gather his wealth.[3] "Of the booty I would choose out all that I craved, and much thereafter I won by lot. So my house got increase speedily, and thus I waxed dread and honourable among the Cretans." A mere trader was not a respectable character, as is amusingly shown by his indignation when Laodamas supposes him to be "such an one as comes and goes in a benched ship, a master of sailors that are merchantmen, one with a memory for his freight, or that hath charge of a cargo homeward bound, and of greedily gotten gains".[4] Evidently the Greeks had not yet "got the hang of the thing", if the expression may be allowed. The same spirit of adventure that had swept the "Dorians" into Greece

---

[1] General references: Hasebroek, *Trade and Politics in Ancient Greece*; Zimmern, *Greek Commonwealth*; Glotz, *Ancient Greece at Work*, cap. x; E. Ziebarth, *Beiträge*; F. Oertel, in Pöhlmann's *Geschichte der Sozialen Frage und des Sozialismus in der antiken Welt*, ii² (1925), pp. 516 ff., 572 f.; F. Heichelheim, in Schmoller's *Jahrbuch*, lvi (1932–3), pp. 1021 ff. in *Wirtschaftsgeschichte des Altertums*, pp. 320 ff.; E. C. Semple, *Geography of the Mediterranean Region, passim*; Knorringa, *Emporos, passim*; arts. "Seewesen" by Miltner (Suppl. v) and "Industrie und Handel" by Francotte in *P.W.*

[2] *Od.* iv, 80 f.   [3] *Od.* xiv, 229.   [4] *Od.* viii, 163.

was too strong for them, so they stole anything they could lay their hands on. But when we speak of early "Greek" traders we must confess that we do not know what proportion of the trade of the Aegean was in Greek hands and how much in Phoenician; all we can say is that certainly in Homeric times the lion's share belonged to the latter. The history of early commerce in the Eastern Mediterranean is highly obscure, and may possibly never be clearer. There is reason to suppose that much which hitherto has been labelled Phoenician was not in fact so, but rather Minoan.[1] It is certain, however, that at an early date the Phoenicians had established themselves in the delta of the Nile, where they had built trading posts, and traces of their activities are to be found all along the coasts of Asia Minor and probably, but not certainly, at Corinth. It is at least safe to say that the greater part of whatever sea trade there was in those troublous times went to Phoenicians, and Tyre and Sidon flourished.

They were detested for their tricky ways, and particularly for an unpleasant proclivity in the kidnapping line, of which many scandalous stories were told. They went with "countless gauds" and golden chains strung with amber beads to catch the fancy of the women,[2] silverware, cloths and carpets, glassware and such rarities as the apes and ivory and peacocks that Hiram brought to Solomon. From Thrace they carried wine, fine bronze swords and precious vases; from Lydia and Caria carved and painted ivories; from Cyprus copper. Herodotus tells us the methods followed by the Phoenicians in trading with the primitive peoples in the Libyan country beyond the pillars of Hercules.[3] Casting anchor a little way from land, they would go ashore, lay their wares on the beach, and having kindled a smoke to proclaim their arrival go back to their ship. The natives seeing the signal come down to the shore and lay beside the goods the amount of gold they are willing to give in exchange, and then retire in turn. If the Phoenicians are satisfied they take the gold, otherwise they wait until more has been produced. All this is done without direct contact between buyer

[1] Hall, *Ancient History of Near East*, p. 523, discusses the point at length.
[2] *Od.* xv, 409; or perhaps electrum. For further on early amber cf. note, p. 246.
[3] Her. iv, 196 ff.

and seller, on neutral ground which partakes of a sacred character over which the truce of the gods prevails.[1] Even to the most primitive mind it is apparent that, if any exchange is to take place, it must be on ground safe to all parties, and it is curious to note how this sacred character of the market place endured to much later times. Thucydides tells us of a market near Rhegium sacred to Artemis.[2]

The next step was to find a convenient landing place near a town where a fort could be built for permanent occupation, and a warehouse or depot maintained for the storage of merchandise; as for instance the "Milesian Fort" in Egypt, where the merchants of Miletus enjoyed some measure of extra-territorial rights; just as the Hanse merchants had their depot at the Steelyard in London.[3] Sidon was a warehouse through which passed merchandise from Cyprus, Egypt, Libya and Macedonia.

Rivals of the Phoenicians were the somewhat mysterious Phaeacians, or Taphians, dwellers in what are now known as the Ionian islands to the north-west of Greece. There is some uncertainty as to who these Phaeacians were; Ridgeway holds that they were "certainly not Achaeans".[4] They were evidently looked upon as rather curious people, who practised divination in a way not common to others. They boasted that their ships needed no rudders but understood the thoughts of the mariners.[5] They are referred to as "lovers of the oar",[6] and by their skill in navigation aroused the enmity of Poseidon, who did not like to have his terrors flouted by mortals.[7] Scheria, the modern Corfu, where Odysseus comes in his wanderings and is hospitably entertained by its king Alcinous, is a busy port which arouses the wonder of the stranger. "Odysseus marvelled at the docks and the ships lying there, yea, and the market places of the heroes and the long high walls crowned with palisades, a marvel to behold."[8] Evidently the Taphians went far afield, as far as

---

[1] Cf. *Enc. Brit.* (14th ed.), xxii, 345, for account of primitive markets in the Solomon Islands, where trading is to-day carried on under exactly similar conditions as described by Herodotus; trade with India, Paus. iii, 12, 4.

[2] vi, 44; cf. Hasebroek, *Trade and Politics*, p. 128.

[3] For further on Naucratis, see p.   .

[4] *Early Age of Greece*, i, 111.

[5] *Od.* viii, 556 ff.

[6] *Od.* i, 181.

[7] *Od.* xiii, 100 ff.

[8] *Od.* vii, 43 ff.

Sidon in the south to Thessaly in the north, where they varied trade with piracy and slave-running;[1] Eumaeus buys one from them.[2]

The whole geography of the *Odyssey* is utterly baffling, and no rational explanation of the wanderings of Odysseus is possible. The story of him braving the terrors of Scylla and Charybdis in the Straits of Messina may possibly point to a knowledge of that route whereby adventurous souls went to the western coasts of Italy and beyond. It is not impossible that early Greek sailors got to Sardinia; perhaps they got iron from Elba and possibly ventured as far as Spain. With regard to their penetration of the Euxine everything is obscure. It is not unreasonable to conjecture that the attack on Troy may have been an attempt to force the Dardanelles; in any case they must have known of the Black Sea, although there is no mention of it in the *Iliad*. Certainly the writer of this portion of the *Odyssey* was correct in placing on the borders of the Black Sea the lands of the Cimmerians, "people forever wrapped in clouds and mists",[3] and of the one-eyed Arimaspians who fought with dragons for gold[4] which, no doubt, refers to the gold in the Ural Mountains. But who were the Laestrygonians, with whom Odysseus had an unpleasant adventure? who dwelt in a land "where herdsman hails herdsman as he drives in his flock and the other who drives forth answers his call. There might a sleepless man have earned a double wage, the one as neat-herd the other as shepherding white flocks, so near are the outgoings of the night and of the day."[5] Undoubtedly they were not dwellers by the Black Sea, but evidently he is referring to the short summer night of some far northern country.

There seems to be little doubt that, in the story of the voyage of the Argonauts, we have an indication of an early attempt to reach the gold-producing country around Colchis. The Golden Fleece may refer to yellow-fleeced sheep;[6] but it is far more

---

[1] *Od.* xv, 426; xvi, 426.   [2] *Od.* xiv, 452.
[3] *Od.* xi, 14.
[4] Her. iii, 116, iv, 13. But Herodotus says he does not believe it; cf. Hennig, "Herodot's Gold-Hütende Greifen", *Rhein. Mus.* lxxix (1930), p. 326.
[5] *Od.* x, 80.
[6] I.e. the fat-tailed sheep of Arabia and Syria. If that explanation is accepted, then it was hardly possible the Argonauts went to Colchis to get some of these animals. The other is far more likely.

likely that it refers to the method described by Strabo[1] of putting fleeces into the streams to collect the drift gold, a practice which is perfectly recognisable. The legend was "improved" by later writers, notably Apollonius Rhodius, who showed a knowledge of the geography of the Black Sea far beyond what could have been known to the followers of Jason.[2]

CONTENT OF TRADE IN THE HOMERIC AGE

It is quite plain that trade other than in slaves consisted in articles of great value in small bulk. Gold probably came from Egypt, or at least the greater amount; that land with its great riches was a magnet for the hardy adventurer and pirate.[3] Silver came from the mysterious Alybe, "where the silver grows",[4] which was probably east of Paphlagonia, and may be identified with the silver mines of Taurus.[5] Copper came from Cyprus.[6] The legendary connection of Chalcidice with copper and metal working is a puzzle and is hard to substantiate.[7] Where iron, a very valuable metal at that time, came from is very difficult to say. When Athena takes the form of Mentes, king of the Taphians, she took a cargo of shining iron to Cyprus.[8] But there is no iron in Taphos and it must, therefore, have come in trade from elsewhere.[9] Sir William Ridgeway argues that the iron of the Achaeans came from Central Europe, or rather that the Achaeans brought it with them.[10] Iron, except as a rare curiosity, was not known, according to Sir Flinders Petrie, until

[1] Strabo, xi, 2, 19 (c. 499).
[2] Miss Bacon's *The Voyage of the Argonauts* discusses the whole problem excellently. Cf. also A. R. Burn, *Minoans, Philistines and Greeks*, cap. 9; Friedländer, "Kritische Untersuchungen zur Geschichte der Heldensage", *Rhein. Mus.* lxix (1914), p. 299; Wilamowitz, *Die Ilias u. Homer*, p. 362.
[3] *Od.* iii, 301.   [4] *Il.* ii, 856.
[5] Not, as M. Glotz supposes, the Iberian peninsula (*Ancient Greece at Work*, p. 60). Cf. Bury in *C.A.H.* ii, 492, also iii, 662; Leaf, *Troy*, p. 290.
[6] *Od.* i, 184; Bérard, *Les Phéniciens*, i, 381ff.
[7] Cf. art. in *Nature*, Dec. 31, 1932, "Bronze-Age mining round the Aegean" by O. Davies; Bérard, *Les Phéniciens*, p. 382.
[8] *Od.* i, 184f.; cf. Bérard, *Les Phéniciens*, i, 160ff.; F. B. Jevons, "Iron in Homer", *J.H.S.* xii (1892), p. 25ff.
[9] Seymour, *Life in the Homeric Age*, p. 77, identifies tentatively Ithaca with Leucas, and suggests that the home of the Taphians was on the island of Kalamo off the coast of Acarnania, where iron ore has been found.
[10] *Early Age of Greece*, i, cap. ix; cf. J. L. Myres, *Who were the Greeks?* p. 433ff.

800.[1] The Phoenicians certainly did not bring any iron with them when trading with the Greeks, or else it is certain we should have heard of it as part of their cargoes. But, on the other hand, we know the Greeks gave iron to the Phoenicians in exchange for wine.[2] There were large iron-ore deposits both in Cyprus and Crete, but there are no early objects of iron found there, or rather only such small objects as nails; large iron objects such as swords are of the Hallstatt type, undoubtedly not the product of Minoan workmen. The passage quoted above where the Taphians take iron to Cyprus would seem to substantiate Ridgeway's conclusion, and we may suppose that the iron came down the Adriatic from Europe and was distributed by "Taphian" merchants, which would account for their importance in the commerce of the day.[3]

The references to *kuanos*[4] are interesting and obscure. It has often been identified with lapis lazuli, and it is not impossible that this should be right. Lucas identifies it with an artificial frit, i.e. the material of which glass is made, consisting of a crystalline compound of silica, copper and calcium (calcium-copper silicate), made by heating together silica, a copper compound, probably malachite, calcium carbonate, and natron.[5] It probably reached Greece through Cyprus.[6] Lapis lazuli came from Badakshan, in the north-east corner of Afghanistan in the valley of the Oxus, perhaps through some Black Sea port;[7] or perhaps through Babylon and Egypt.[8] But the whole problem is quite uncertain.[9] Rock crystal, or quartz, and carnelian objects have been found in Minoan graves. These are both

---

[1] Very doubtful, cf. Heichelheim, Schmoller's *Jahrbuch*, lvi (1932-3), pp. 174f., in *Gnomon*, vii (1931), p. 588; G. A. Wainwright, "Iron in Egypt", *J.E.A.* xviii (1932), pp. 3ff.; Seymour, *Life in the Homeric Age*, p. 299.

[2] *Il.* vii, 472; cf. Bérard, *Les Phéniciens*, pp. 329ff. The Phoenicians found a ready sale for the wine they carried.

[3] For trade between Corcyra and the basin of the Danube cf. Myres, *C.A.H.* iii, 651.

[4] *Il.* xi, 24, 35; *Od.* vii, 87; art. "Kuanos" by Bluemner in *P.W.*; Bérard, *Les Phéniciens*, i, 397.

[5] Lucas, *Ancient Egyptian Materials and Industries*, p. 284.

[6] Trowbridge, *Philol. Studies in Ancient Glass*, pp. 11ff.

[7] Bacon, *Voyage of Argonauts*, p. 166.

[8] *Tell-el-Amarna Letters*, p. 21.

[9] The easiest explanation is that the artificial variety was mistaken for lapis lazuli; cf. Theoph. *de Lap.* 31, 37, 55; Pliny, *H.N.* xxxiii, 16, and Bailey's note, i, 234; xxxv, 47 and note, ii, 220.

plentiful in Egypt, and confirm once more the clear connection between Egypt and the Aegean. Ivory is frequently mentioned, but where it came from is quite unknown. Obviously it must have been brought by Phoenicians. Mr Childe remarks that the material of Minoan jewellery reflects the ramifications of the trade illustrated by the distribution of the beads. Silver may have come from the Troad, from Sardinia or from Spain. For gold we need not go outside the Aegean area. Rock crystal may come from the slopes of the Alps, but carnelian seems oriental. The "amber" from the early Minoan tomb of Koumasa is very doubtful. If genuine it may have come from the Baltic across Russia. In late Minoan times a regular traffic in this substance along the Elbe to the Adriatic had begun.[1] In conclusion it is quite evident that the Greek worker in precious metals was inferior to the Phoenician. Whenever a particularly costly article is mentioned it is almost invariably spoken of as Sidonian.[2] But perhaps the Greek of that age was as proud of something foreign as we are to-day. In any case we cannot doubt that the "cunning" Phoenician was more nimble-witted, a better craftsman and a more daring tradesman than the more stupid Greek.[3]

In conclusion, we may say that it is quite plain that we see in the Homeric poems a transition period between the semi-piratical conditions that accompanied the downfall of the Minoan power and the establishment of organised trade routes. It is very significant that in the *Odyssey* we meet for the first time the Greek word *emporos*,[4] meaning a passenger who pays a fare and does not go in his own ship, and, since such passengers were generally merchants, the word came to be applied to merchants generally.

---

[1] *Op. cit.* p. 39.

[2] E.g. the silver bowl in *Il.* xxiii, 740. The gold and silver bowl of Menelaus, *Od.* iv, 615–20.

[3] Odysseus, who was always supposed to be the very pattern of cunning, was easily outwitted by the rascally Phoenician who nearly sold him into slavery—*Od.* xiv, 288.

[4] *Od.* ii, 319, xxiv, 299.

GREEK COLONISATION[1]

In any study of Greek commerce we must, in order to grasp the main outlines, begin with a sketch of colonisation in the Mediterranean. If we know where the Greek colonies were, we know the main trade routes, for with their colonies the Greeks mainly traded. At a very early age, that is to say, in the last stages of the Homeric or "heroic" epoch, the inhabitants of Greece had begun to spread over the islands of the Aegean and the coasts of Asia Minor. No doubt this movement was accelerated largely by the invasions of the Dorians, but also no doubt it was caused by a spirit of adventure, a restlessness that craved for new scenes; and perhaps, although it is difficult to speak with certainty of so early a time, by population pressure. These early adventurers were "Achaeans" from Thessaly, who sailed probably from the port of Pagasae, and in the story of the Argonauts and their quest of the Golden Fleece we have an echo of such ventures. With these Achaeans went "Aeolians", if we are to distinguish the two and not regard them as the same people. Their first settlement was on the island of Lesbos, and thence to the shores of the mainland where they found places well suited for their colonies in the valleys of the Rivers Hermus, Granicus, Cayster, Caicus, Scamander and Maeander.[2] Farther south the new settlers could not go, as the Lycians, a warlike race, barred their way, and thus this fringe of Greek settlements on the western shores of Asia Minor was completed. One more settlement of this early time must, however, be recorded, that of Cyprus, an island rich in copper, iron and timber, and destined to be a battleground between European and Asiatic. How vital a part these early colonies were to play in the destiny of Greece was seen later; for it was in Ionia that the first stage of the great struggle between Europe and Asia was fought, when the colonists revolted against their Persian overlords and the Great King was drawn into the invasion of Greece.

Such was the first phase of Greek colonial expansion; a second was to follow which was to take them much farther afield. This second period, which may be said to have lasted from about

[1] Myres, *C.A.H.* iii, cap. 25, p. 631; Ciaceri, *Storia della Magna Graecia*, i, 2; Busolt, *Griech. Staatsk.* i, 173; Tozer, *History of Ancient Geography*, cap. 3, p. 43; Hasebroek, *Griech. Wirtsch. u. Gesellsch. Gesch.* p. 109 ff.

[2] Bilabel, "Die Ionische Kolonisation", *Philologus*, xiv (1920), p. 1.

750 to 550, may be classified as follows: First, on the north
coast of the Aegean from Thessaly to the Hellespont, bordering
on Macedonia and Thrace and including the peninsula of
Chalcidice, a region of great importance, since from it the
Greeks drew their supplies of timber and precious metals.
Secondly, the colonies on the Bosporus and Black Seas, which
were to become as time passed the granary of Greece. Thirdly,
in the west, Sicily and the mainland of Italy as far north as
Naples, where further expansion was halted by the warlike
Etruscans. And lastly, in the extreme west a scattered fringe
of colonies on what is now the Italian and French Riviera, westwards through Massalia, the modern Marseilles, and as far
south on the Spanish coast as Saguntum, where further expansion was checked by Phoenician hostility.

On their arrival on the Anatolian coast the new settlers found
the Hittite empire at the beginning of the first millennium B.C.
waning in power, but still strong enough to enforce vassalage
upon them. On its fall its place was taken by the Phrygian
kingdom, of whose ruler Midas marvellous stories of wealth
were told. Phrygia in its turn fell before incursions of barbarian
Cimmerians, until order was restored by the powerful Lydian
kings, who were able to impose their suzerainty over the Greek
colonies, to be followed by the Persians when they pushed their
conquests to the shores of the Mediterranean under the great
king Cyrus. Under the Persian kings they dwelt in peace,
singularly unmolested under their mild and enlightened rule,
until the great revolt at the beginning of the fifth century which
had such momentous results in the history of Greece. Agriculture and stock-raising, the cultivation of the olive and vine
were their principal pursuits. Wine became a famous article of
export; the soil of Anatolia, and the islands lying off the coast,
especially Lesbos, Chios and Samos, being favourable to the
manufacture of a product which was highly esteemed, especially
in Egypt where the vine could not be successfully cultivated.
Olive oil, a necessity in a region where butter was a rarity as an
article of diet and no other illuminant was known, was a highly
valuable article of commerce,[1] and the cultivation of the olive

---

[1] Cf. the interesting story recounted by Aristotle of the "corner" in olive
presses by Thales of Miletus, as a kind of demonstration of what a philosopher
could do if he really bestirred himself—*Pol.* i, 1259 A.

tree spread from Asia Minor to the mainland of Greece and the islands of the Aegean. On the Anatolian highlands, to the east of the Greek coastal colonies, flocks of cattle and sheep were raised, and from them supplies of leather and wool were abundant, in the working of which the inhabitants became expert, especially in woollen fabrics, for which Miletus was famous. The country was rich in minerals, iron, copper, silver and gold, and it is significant of their wealth that the invention of coined money was the accomplishment of the Lydians and Ionians. As their wealth and power grew they were strong enough to compete more and more effectively with the ancient traders of the Aegean, the Phoenicians, until they forced them to seek a new area, that of the Western Mediterranean, and Carthage took the place of Tyre and Sidon as the richest centre of commerce.

On the northern shores of the Aegean and round the Sea of Marmora and Black Sea, Greek colonies were widely scattered.[1] The peninsula of Chersonesus, the modern Gallipoli, was rich in minerals, and on it and on the shores of the Propontis, or Sea of Marmora, were many settlements, of which the most famous were Cyzicus,[2] Abydos,[3] Byzantium, Chalcedon and Cius.[4] On the Euxine, or Black Sea, were Heraclea, Amisus,[5] Sinope[6] and Trapezus (the modern Trebizond) on the southern shore; on the western shore were Apollonia, Mesembria, Tomi and Ister. At the mouth of the Dniester was Tyras; at the mouth of the Bug, Olbia, the modern Nikolaev; on the coast of the Crimea, Cercinites, Tauric Chersonesus and Theodosia, with Panticapaeum (the modern Kertch) and Phanagoria at the entrance of the Sea of Azov; Tanais at the mouth of the Don; Dioscurias and Phasis on the coast of Colchis. These were thriving agricultural colonies, later to become of supreme importance in supplying Greece with grain and fish. The tunny abounded in the waters by which they were founded, and

---

[1] v. Stern, "Griech. Kolonien des Schwarzmeergebietes", *Hermes*, l (1915), p. 209; Ebert, *Südrussland im Altertum*, p. 82; G. A. Short, "The siting of Greek colonies on the Black Sea coasts of Bulgaria and Rumania", *Ann. Archaeol. and Anthropol.* xxiv (1937), pp. 141 ff.

[2] Lehmann-Hartleben, *Ant. Hafenanl.* pp. 63 f.

[3] Strabo, xiii, 1, 22 (c. 590); Polyb. xvi, 29.

[4] Pomp. Mela, i, 19.

[5] Lehmann-Hartleben, *Ant. Hafenanl.* p. 242.

[6] Strabo, xii, 3, 11 (c. 545).

freshwater fish in the rivers flowing into the Black Sea. It is remarkable that colonies sent out other colonies, and we are told that the Black Sea group was largely founded by adventurers from Miletus, which is credited with no fewer than ninety settlements; probably an exaggeration, but sufficient to show its colonising activities.[1]

Turning now to the west, Southern Italy and the east coast of Sicily were thickly covered with Greek settlements; so much so that the former was called "Magna Graecia". Here were Taras, or Tarentum, Sybaris, Croton, Epizephyrian Locri, Rhegium, Elea, Cumae and Naples. In Sicily were Agrigentum, Gela, Syracuse, Tauromenium and Messana. Farther to the north the way was barred by the warlike Etruscans; in the west of Sicily Phoenicians prevented further expansion. Some of these colonies achieved fame and wealth as, for instance, Sybaris, which has given its name for all time to ease and luxury. Situated on a fertile plain, it raised wheat and vines, and its grazing grounds were so rich that its cattle were famous; we find their picture on the coins of the city. Near by were forests which supplied timber, resin and tar. On an open roadstead, it was an entrepôt for transit trade between the east and Laos and Scidros on the west. Taras, on the northern coast of the Gulf of Tarentum, was built on a rocky peninsula at the entrance of the only safe harbour in the gulf. It was a Spartan colony, founded by one Phalanthos,[2] and was set in a fertile district famous for its olive groves and sheep, which contributed to its wealth and fame for woollen fabrics, wine and oil, while the sea supplied its fisheries with a rich harvest and its dye works with the purple Murex. Cumae, on the west coast of Campania, twelve miles west of Naples, was probably the oldest Greek colony, having been settled by people from Chalcis at an early and undetermined date. It was always a centre of culture, and we are told that from Cumae barbarous Rome received its first lessons in civilisation.[3] How much wheat Greece received from the colonies on the mainland is unknown, but probably no very considerable quantity; timber on the other hand they supplied in

---

[1] Pliny, *H.N.* v, 31, 112.
[2] Cf. art. "Taras" by Philipp in *P.W.*
[3] Art. "Kyme (3)" by Weiss in *P.W.*

abundance, although they never equalled the principal source of Greek supply, Macedonia. Sicily was early one of the granaries of Greece, and continued to supply the Athenian market for centuries, and Rome for still longer. Syracuse became wealthy and fought off Carthaginian aggression; the disastrous expedition of the Athenians towards the close of the Peloponnesian war was undertaken to control the wheatlands of the island.

Still farther west the record of Greek colonisation becomes less certain, although it is clearly bound up with the quite remarkable achievements of the Phocaeans, Greek settlers in Ionia, who fled before the Persians.[1] It is uncertain if they ever obtained a footing in Sardinia, and their occupation of Corsica was short-lived, as they were expelled from that island by the Carthaginians in 535. Of all the Phocaean efforts at colonisation Massalia, the modern Marseilles, was the greatest and most successful. Here a flourishing and wealthy colony was planted which was to endure for centuries, until incorporated into the Roman dominions. In Spain the records of Greek settlement are very obscure, although it is fairly certain that small and possibly short-lived colonies were planted at Hemeroskopeion, the modern Calpe, at Mainake near Malaga and at Emporion, now Ampurias. Herodotus has two references to that lost and mysterious city Tartessus, the first telling how Phocaeans were kindly entreated by King Arganthonius, a somewhat mythical figure.[2] The second is the remarkable story of Colaeus of Samos having been blown there and returning with a fabulously rich cargo.[3] With the exception of Massalia, therefore, Greek colonisation west of Sicily in the face of Carthaginian rivalry was probably short-lived and unimportant.[4] As we have already

---

[1] Their track westwards may be traced by place names ending in *-oussa*.
[2] Her. i, 163.
[3] *Ibid.* iv, 152. The whole Colaeus incident is somewhat incredible. Hasebroek, *Trade and Politics*, p. 69, holds it to be clearly a fifth-century legend composed in order to give a historical explanation of the friendship between Samos and Cyrene; cf. also his *Griech. Wirtsch. u. Gesellsch. Gesch.* p. 270. But cf. also Heichelheim's comments in *Philol. Woch.* (1934), p. 127, in which he considers that the evidence in Herodotus is sufficient to warrant acceptance of the story. Cf. art. "Tartessos" by Schulten in *P.W.*; Knorringa, *Emporos*, pp. 21, 26; Cary and Warmington, *Anc. Explorers*, Index *s.v.* Colaeus; R. Hennig, *Terrae Incognitae*, i, 41 ff.; art. "Kolaios" in *P.W.* (Supp. iv).
[4] R. Carpenter, *The Greeks in Spain* (Bryn Mawr Studies).

remarked, we must not allow our sense of proportion to be deceived into thinking of a great network of populous and wealthy cities, each busy with manufactures for their export trade with their merchantmen in every port. These colonial settlements were very small, and at least at first very primitive.[1] Such stories as the wealth and luxury of Sybaris may be heavily discounted, and visions of beautiful cities fade before the cold light of archaeological discoveries. But in spite of that, we cannot doubt that these numerous colonies were prosperous, and on the small scale of the age rich. It is also evident that trade was extensive in that it was carried on both east and west. It is perfectly possible that Sybaris and the colonies on the Anatolian coast were more prosperous than the mother cities of Old Greece. It was not until Athens laid the colonies under tribute that the wealth of their rich lands and extensive trade began to flow back to Greece and the "golden age" of Pericles followed.

GREEK COLONISATION AND TRADE

It will now be fitting to consider briefly the causes which led to this outburst of Greek settlement beyond their own land. Dr Hasebroek very rightly protests against any idea that there was at such an early date a "colonial policy" which aimed at founding markets for the finished products of the homeland and sources of supply for raw products and foodstuffs. He points out that the Greek colony was not a trading one; nor was it national but cosmopolitan. It is true, he says, that Greek colonies often became centres of trade; but this is because they were not infrequently founded on sites which nature had marked out as centres of exchange, or which had been so used long years before by Phoenician, Greek or other private traders. In such places, no doubt, the agricultural settlers assumed control of the existing traffic as a source of revenue. Later, when there came an influx of foreigners who were debarred from holding land, it was these who took to trade.[2] It may be remarked in all justice to other writers that such a view by no

---

[1] Even the famous Sardes was mostly built of reeds, Her. v, 101.

[2] *Trade and Politics in Ancient Greece*, pp. 105–10. For another view cf. Grundy, *Thucydides and the History of his Age*, caps. iv, vii.

means originated in Dr Hasebroek.[1] He is rather protesting against the extreme position taken up by certain German historians of the present day who talk of a "colonial policy" founded upon far-seeing mercantile considerations.[2]

Archaeological evidence with respect to Greek expansion in the Western Mediterranean would seem to confirm this view and show that commerce with Sicily, Italy and Southern France predated colonisation. Mr Blakeway, before his lamented death, showed that Greek "geometric" pottery and its imitations, of a date earlier than the oldest "colonial" burials at Syracuse, have been found in no fewer than twenty-eight different sites from Syracuse and Apulia to Marseilles. From this he deduced a very old contact between Greece and the Western Mediterranean, trade going before colonisation.[3] He asked, whence came the necessary geographical knowledge that opened up the way to the planting of colonies? Such has always been attributed to Minoan, Mycenaean or "traditional survival" sources. But however that may be, undoubtedly trade was being carried on at a very early date, as shown by Hesiod. The argument that Greek wares were being carried to the Western Mediterranean by Phoenicians receives no confirmation from any Phoenician remains in early graves, and we may have to revise our ideas of a "Phoenician thalassocracy" and a "mare clausum". Mr Blakeway protested against neglect of archaeological evidence in favour of "tags" from the historians such as Herodotus and Thucydides. We may willingly agree that the point is well taken, and the historian will doubtless learn more and more from archaeological sources, as indeed he is already rewriting much of Greek history from inscriptions. It may be remarked, however, that "the flag following trade" is really no more than the reciprocal of "trade following the flag"; they are mutually

---

[1] Bury in his *History of Greece*, p. 86, had anticipated this view: "The cause of Greek colonisation is not to be found in mere trade interests...it satisfied other needs than desire of commercial profit. It was the expression of the adventurous spirit."

[2] E.g. Pöhlmann in his *Griechische Geschichte*, p. 46.

[3] A. Blakeway, "Prolegomena to study of Greek commerce with Italy, Sicily and France in the eighth and seventh centuries B.C.", *Annual of British School in Athens*, xxxiii (1932–3), pp. 170ff.; cf. Hasebroek, *Trade and Politics*, p. 50ff.; Bücher, *Beiträge*, pp. 65ff., 90, 95; Heichelheim, *Wirtschaftsgesch. d. Altertums*, p. 1006.

complementary, and where trade has preceded colonisation in one area it may very well have followed settlement in another.

Rather must we find the causes of Greek colonisation in growth of population and an unsound land system which drove "landless men" away from their mother country to find liberty and scope for their energies in new settlements overseas.[1] This was an invariable and inevitable economic development. For instance, Xenophon advised the Ten Thousand to go home and tell the people there that their poverty was their own fault. If they would send abroad those who were living in want they would soon see them living in plenty in their new homes,[2] while Plato remarked that the wise legislator always got rid of troublesome agitators by sending them to the colonies, a policy which has proved useful in later times.[3] We must, however, distinguish between two types of colonies, those which were founded by voluntary association of adventurers, and those sent out by a state under military leadership. The first, which the Greeks called *apoikiai*, were purely agricultural, and while loyal to the mother-city by bonds of sentiment and religion, were not in a strictly political sense dependent upon it nor necessarily in alliance with it. The second, or *cleruchies*, were planted systematically at strategic points to serve as garrisons for the subjection of barbarian inhabitants, and to keep open trade routes, particularly for the grain and timber supply. In the sixth century both Corinth and Athens sent out numerous cleruchies; those of the former including Corcyra, Leucas, Ambracia, Anactorium, Apollonia, Epidamnus and Potidaea;[4] while Athens secured Sigeum, Rhaecelus on the Thermaic Gulf and settlements on the Thracian coast, the Thracian Chersonese, Lemnos and Imbros.

THE EXTENT AND CHARACTER OF GREEK COMMERCE

Dr Hasebroek in his important and stimulating study, *Trade and Politics in Ancient Greece*, has roundly attacked many of the ideas that previous writers, notably Beloch, have put forward

---

[1] E.g. the colonising of Thera and Cyrene as recounted by Herodotus, iv, 147–51.

[2] *Anab.* iii, 2, 26.　　　　　　　　　[3] *Laws*, 736.

[4] Cf. J. G. O'Neill, *Ancient Corinth*, pp. 148 ff.

with regard to the character and extent of Greek commerce. His treatment of the problem is so important that it will be well to examine his thesis in some detail. He maintains that we should preserve a right perspective, and not magnify trade beyond the limits which the age and, more particularly, the peculiar viewpoint of the Greeks imposed. It is entirely fallacious, he argues, to think of Athens, Corinth or Miletus as the ancient counterparts of Venice, Florence or Genoa at the height of their commercial activity and power. The medieval Italian city republics were essentially commercial, and their whole policy was directed towards the extension and protection of their trade. Still less was there, as in Italy and the cities of the Hanseatic League, a class of rich merchants who were able to influence the policy of the rulers for the benefit of their own private ends. The very contrary was true in Ancient Greece. The state harried its rich men, and so far from favouring their business interests did all in its power to despoil them.

The whole Greek world lacked that stability and security which is indispensable to overseas trade. "The directing principle of the ancient state was utterly incompatible with the development of international commerce."[1] Athens, like Corinth, was not engaged in such peaceful activities but in "plain robbery and exploitation".[2] It was concerned with nothing except to fill its granaries and its treasury. National trade was foreign to its purpose. It was the intervention of the all-powerful state which hindered the growth and development of commerce.[3] The ideal of the city state was always isolation and self-sufficiency. If it had not in its own natural resources sufficient to maintain this isolation it must, however unwillingly, seek elsewhere for supplies of necessities. If these could be obtained by peaceful means, so much the better, but if not, or if the opportunity presented itself of obtaining them by force or plain piracy, then the state was quite ready to do so.

The policy of the state was not one of assistance to trade in general but of maintaining only one form of trade, that in the absolutely necessary essentials of grain and timber.[4] Such treaties as it made with other powers were aimed only at

[1] p. 139. [2] p. 140.
[3] p. 151. [4] pp. 139 ff.

securing these necessities. There was never at any time a commercial policy that influenced statecraft apart from this. There was no conception of favouring the industries of its own country by securing privileges for its exports in foreign markets. Oil or wine might sell readily abroad, but the state would not trouble itself in securing markets for these products. In a word the state was totally lacking in any form of "commercial sense". Trade grew and flourished in spite of, and often in opposition to it. In any case merchants were a despised class, nearly always Metics, petty hucksters who were beneath the notice of the state. They were useful, they paid taxes and customs dues, but they were not to be protected in any way except when the supply of the great staples was endangered.

To much that Dr Hasebroek has so persuasively put forward agreement must be accorded. Undoubtedly the extent and volume of Greek commerce has been exaggerated by many writers, and also undoubtedly motives and policies have been imputed to them which were alien and unknown to their genius. But when we have said that, we must also protest that he has in his turn overstated his case; he has gone as far in the other extreme as have the authors whom he criticises.

In the first place, he is trying to draw a distinction between a general policy favourable to trade, which he says the Greek city state never pursued, and one aimed solely at the provision of those staple commodities, wheat and timber, which were absolutely necessary to it. If that be so, and the point may be readily conceded, it may be not unfairly retorted that it is of little practical importance in our conception of Greek commerce and the policies of states regarding it. It may be perfectly true that we do not find anything like the elaborate trade agreements between nations, such as are found in modern times, with detailed schedules of various products which shall enter free or at preferential rates. Nor do we hear of the Athenian state sending envoys overseas to secure markets for Attic oil or wine. But we have numerous instances, as will be shown later, of the very greatest care being exercised to obtain preferential treatment abroad for the securing of timber and grain. It seems beside the point to draw a sharp distinction between such products and others of less importance to the national welfare.

Grain and timber had to be paid for, and certainly after the dissolution of the Delian League, with the cessation of the tributes of the allies and the falling off of supplies of silver from the mines of Laurium, these must have been paid for in exports. It is altogether too much to argue that the Athenian state was unconcerned with markets for its exports. We have no specific evidence of it, but we cannot doubt that every care was taken that Athenian exports should not be discriminated against in foreign markets.

Again, the state took very particular care that its nationals should enjoy privileges and protection abroad. The right of *Asylia*, to enter or leave a country by sea without being subject to seizure by privateers and without special treaty agreement in peace or war, and of *Ateleia*, exemption from duty on wares imported or exported, the right to enter or leave the country, and the treaties of *Symbolai*, whereby nationals were granted legal protection and equal status in the law courts with citizens in another country, all show that the state was deeply concerned in the welfare of its own merchants.[1]

To say that Athens, like Corinth, was not engaged in the peaceful activities of commerce and exchange but in plain robbery and exploitation,[2] is far too extreme a statement to pass unchallenged. The policy of the state was not of the "smash and grab" order; we must credit the ancient mind with some degree of intelligence. The appeal to Xenophon's *Government of Athens*[3] to prove this point is far from convincing. All that Xenophon is saying is that a powerful state can take care of its commerce and protect it against the rapacity of foreign rivals; which on the face of it is a simple statement of fact, and as true to-day as it ever was.

It is true that the costs and perils of commerce were very great. Warring powers and pirates, when piracy was not under control, made overseas trade hazardous at all times. Commensurate with the risks run were the rates of interest charged

---

[1] Arts. in *P.W.*, *s.v.*—Ateleia, Dem. *de Cor.* 90, 91; Symbolai, Dem. *de Hal.* 9, 11, 12; Arist. *Pol.* 1280 A; *Rhet.* 1360 A. Hasebroek, *Trade and Politics*, p. 112; Ziebarth, "Handelsgeschichte von Rhodos", *Mélanges Glotz*, ii, 918. (Hellenistic period, Miletus-Olbia, in *Milet, Ergebnisse der Ausgrabungen und Untersuchungen*, i, 3, 136, l. 6, Miletus-Cyzicus, i, 3, 137.)

[2] pp. 126–7.   [3] *Govt. of Athens*, ii, 11–12.

on "bottomry loans", i.e. loans to shipmasters on the hull and cargo of their ships.[1] But, as in medieval times, if the costs were high the returns from a successful voyage were great. The shipping season was short; only in the summer months could overseas trade be carried on safely in the frail ships of the time. Another drawback to trade, it is asserted, was the uncertainty of markets. A trader never knew where he could sell his goods and had no certainty of an acceptable return cargo.[2] This can hardly be maintained when it is remembered that the staples of Athenian export were wine and oil, both of which found a ready sale abroad on account of their excellence. A shipper who loaded at the Piraeus with a cargo of these commodities could be reasonably sure, or rather he could be perfectly certain, of disposing of them at one of the ports of South Russia, where the "corn barons" who had grain to sell would eagerly exchange their surplus for such highly acceptable luxuries. Not only was grain awaiting the arrival of the Athenian merchant, but another staple of trade, dried fish, for which an inexhaustible market could be found in Greece. The difficulties confronting the Athenian shipowner were not greater, if as great, as for the tramp steamer of to-day, which will go anywhere to pick up a cargo.

Nor were the troubles arising from the vagaries of the foreign exchanges any greater then than now.[3] It is true that the Greek shipmaster had to keep a very bright look-out against being cheated in the exchange of foreign currencies; but, on the other hand, the wide extension of the use of Athenian "owls", and later of Cyzicene staters, made such transactions easier. No doubt debased coinage, the difficulties of dealing with electrum coins and occasionally with local restrictions must have been harassing. We have one or two instances of "blocked exchange"; as, for instance, at Olbia where only the local coinage could be used in buying and selling;[4] also at Chersonesus.[5] But foreigners

---

[1] Cf. treatment of these loans in chapter on Money and Banking.
[2] p. 83.
[3] Ziebarth, *Beiträge*, pp. 82 ff.
[4] Olbia, Ditt. *Syll.* iii, 218; H. Schmitz, *Ein Gesetz der Stadt Olbia zum Schutze ihres Silbergeldes*; Ziebarth, *Beiträge*, pp. 82, 135; Hasebroek, *Trade and Politics*, p. 156; Heichelheim, *Wirtschaftsgesch. des Altertums*, p. 310.
[5] Chersonesus—J. Zingerle, in *Klio*, xviii (1927), p. 64.

were only too glad to get Athenian owls.[1] The Greek trader might be badly cheated, that was no peculiarity of the age; but we may be sure that the captain or super-cargo had, through bitter experience no doubt, acquired an entirely competent working knowledge of the perils of the exchanges, and could detect debased coins very readily. In any case the evils of clipping were effectively guarded against. Every merchant had his scales, and payments were regularly made against weight of silver or gold rather than face value of the coins used.

The statement that the Greek world lacked that security and stability which is indispensable to a commercial civilisation[2] needs a good deal of qualification. It is true that commerce was hampered by war, which was endemic; Athens was always at war with somebody. But what is very noticeable is that, in spite of it, commerce went on and flourished. To a very large extent war was an elaborate game carried on under strict rules and the merchant took very little notice of it. When the Spartans seized Decelea and cut the overland route from Oropus to Athens, to their dismay they watched the grain fleets safely rounding Cape Sunium and reaching port with impunity. Later, during the wars of the successors of Alexander, when the area of hostilities was immensely widened, commerce flourished more than ever. Admittedly the perils from piracy were very great and ever present. Athens policed the seas, and later the duty was taken over by the Rhodians, but do what they would they could never entirely get rid of the sea robber. The perils of piracy were lessened by merchantmen sailing in convoys and often under the guard of a squadron of warships. This was harassing and expensive, but it afforded protection and commerce went on. It was not until the pirates got completely out of hand, necessitating the highly effective measures of suppression carried out at a much later date by Pompey, that piracy actually brought water-borne commerce to a standstill.[3]

We are on much surer ground when it is pointed out that where the state by its constant levies upon capital and wealth harassed its richer citizens it was difficult, if not impossible, for

---

[1] Xen. *Revenues*, iii, 2.
[2] Hasebroek, p. 139.
[3] The subject of piracy is treated more extensively in another section.

a class of rich merchants to grow up.[1] Undoubtedly, as is seen very plainly in our treatment of the subject of public finance, the exactions of the state went beyond all reasonable limits, and capital was harried and plundered in a manner that made the lot of a rich man a far from enviable one. And yet it can reasonably be retorted, the state never succeeded in ruining all its wealthy citizens. There are innumerable examples of rich men— Demosthenes was one—who did manage to carry on. The art of evasion became highly developed, and the consequence was that capital was largely driven underground to find a refuge in the very employment that most favoured commerce, the sea loan. These transactions were difficult to follow and if the ever-active informer could be avoided, or perhaps bribed, the inquisitiveness of the state officials could be baffled.

We have followed these arguments in some detail because it is often through attacking or defending a thesis that the main outline, as well as many of the minor details, of any problem become most apparent. Although we may disagree with, or perhaps better demur at, many of the points, yet such treatment of a highly complex subject cannot be ignored nor lightly brushed aside. A most important service has been performed in pointing out many exaggerations and misconceptions which have crept into the work of previous authors, and it is safe to say that in the future authors will keep a wary eye on what they write. A polemical book does perform a very useful service and that has been achieved by Dr Hasebroek.

GREEK TRADERS

In our study of Greek commerce we must first understand the various classes into which the Greeks divided the merchants and traders.[2] The term *kapelos* was applied to the local dealer who sold in the home market, in other words the small shopkeeper. If he did not buy his stock-in-trade directly from the producers but from another middleman or importer, he was called *palinkapelos* or "dealer at second remove".[3] The merchant ship-

---

[1] Hasebroek, p. 152.

[2] Cf. Heichelheim in Schmoller's *Jahrbuch*, lvi, 1018, 1020–2; Hasebroek, *Trade and Politics*, pp. 1 ff.; Knorringa, *Emporos*, pp. 46–7, 51–2, 96–8, 113–18; Huvelin, art. "Mercatura" in *D.S.*; M. Finkelstein, in *Class. Philol.* xxx, 4 (Oct. 1935); Ziebarth, *Beiträge*, p. 45.

[3] Plato, *Soph.* 223 c, 231 D; *Pol.* 260 D; Dem. *in Aristog.* 46.

owner, or *naukleros*, sold his own wares overseas, generally going in his own ship himself, while the *emporos*, not possessing a ship, went as a passenger with his wares. Since the Greek merchant was not generally a shipowner, being in too small a way of business, the term *emporos* came to be the term in general use for all traders who were ready to sell either at wholesale or retail. The *naukleros* used his own ship for his business and, if he had room in his hold, he would convey the goods of others. But at no time was there a general shipping business for the conveyance of merchandise. Regular sailings from the Piraeus to other ports with tariffs for freight carried, or competition between shipowners for business, were entirely unknown to the ancient world.

It will be convenient at this point to mention briefly the office of *Proxenos*, which may roughly and within very strict limitations be identified with that of the modern consul. The proxenos was not, like the consul, an official despatched by a government to a foreign port to represent his country there and be of assistance to traders and fellow-countrymen in need of his services. He was a citizen of another country living in a foreign land, and was named *proxenos* by the government under which he lived. His appointment involved no diplomatic or extra-territorial status whatever, but he was recognised by the local officials as one who watched over the interests of his fellow-countrymen when they had commercial or legal dealings in the place where he resided. One definite duty that he performed was that he could introduce traders to the local bankers and payments made or received by them were made in his presence. It would be entirely unsafe to press the resemblance between the *proxenos* and the modern consul any closer; but it can be said that he undoubtedly performed a useful function in forwarding the general interests of trade and making the position of foreign merchants less difficult in the ports they visited.[1]

To engage in overseas commerce lent no distinction, in fact it was looked upon as a mean and petty business,[2] and Plato

---

[1] The whole problem of the proxenos is fully treated in the art. *s.v.* in D.S.; cf. also H. Schaefer, *Staatsform u. Politik, Untersuch. zur Griech. Gesch. d. 6. u. 5. Jhdts. v. Chr.* cap. 1.

[2] Xen. *Mem.* iii, 7, 6.

says that merchants were held in universal contempt.[1] Being in
so small a way of business they had little or rather no command
of capital; "neither ship nor shipowner nor merchant can put
to sea without the assistance of the lenders".[2] If a merchant
prospered he retired from the business as soon as possible, and
employed his small capital in the far more congenial manner of
lending to others.[3] Small-scale money-lenders were common in
Athens and other commercial centres, competing with the
large bankers and exacting extortionate interest from their
victims. Under such circumstances it is quite mistaken to
think of rich merchants who were able to influence the legislature
to make commercial treaties or impose tariffs in their favour.
Doubtless large fortunes were occasionally made. We hear of
Lampis of Aegina, a Metic to whom the Aeginetans would not
grant citizenship, although he was the largest shipowner in
Hellas and fitted out their city and their seaport.[4] But in
general the merchant was a small trader,[5] who peddled his
wares with little profit to himself and constantly in the clutches
of the money-lenders. Nor were the merchants invariably a
class to themselves; it was quite common for farmers and shopkeepers to take passage on a convenient ship to other ports to
get rid of their surplus wares. We know that the brother of
Sappho the poetess, who was a large farmer on the island of
Lesbos, took his wine himself to sell in Naucratis in Egypt.[6]
In one of the cases in which Demosthenes was engaged we hear
of a fisherman of Panticapaeum who came on board with a
stock of salt fish to sell in Theodosia.[7] On a larger scale was
Phormio the banker who, as his principal investment, leased a
shield-making business, and had his own ships by which perhaps
he sold his products in other lands and conveyed his raw
materials to Athens.[8] We must put out of our minds any idea

---

[1] *Laws*, 918 D.   [2] Dem. *in Phorm.* 51.

[3] Dem. *in Apat.* 4; *in Pantaen.* 54; cf. Cicero, *de Off.* i, 42.

[4] Dem. *in Aristocr.* 211; Plut. *Apoph. Lac.* 234 F, also *An Seni Respubl.*
787 A; Cicero, *Disp. Tusc.* v, 14.

[5] But at least they had one privilege—they were exempt from military
service, Aristoph. *Plutus*, 904.

[6] Strabo, xvii, 1, 33 (c. 808).   [7] *In Lacr.* 32, 34.

[8] Very doubtful; no conclusive evidence on the point. The vessels seized
by Chalcedon belonged to Phormio. We are not told he had leased them from
Pasion along with the shield factory. Dem. *in Steph.* i, 64.

of large and powerful shipping magnates or companies that ran lines of ships with regular schedules of sailings, systematised freight rates, etc. A shipmaster got a cargo wherever he could and sailed anywhere.

In examining the evidence of Greek commerce after the Persian wars, we find great difficulty in judging its extent and volume. Again and again we find chance references to various articles which, so far as we can judge, were objects of trade, or rather had found their way to other countries from their original homes. We hear, for instance, of Chalcidian swords and cups, Corinthian bronzes, Milesian woollens and garments, Amorgian articles of clothing, and Argive weapons. The Greeks were great fish eaters, since meat was of necessity a luxury and only to be found at the tables of the better-to-do, and so, as will be seen later, the commerce in fish was very great. Of luxuries we hear of garlic from Megara; game and fowls from Boeotia; cheese from Megara and Syracuse; that prized delicacy, silphium, from Cyrene and Carthage;[1] pork from Syracuse; raisins and figs from Rhodes; pears and apples from Euboea; acorns and almonds from Paphlagonia; dates and fine wheaten flour, a commodity greatly prized, from Phoenicia. Of relishes we hear of mustard from Cyprus; cardamom from Miletus; onions from Samothrace; marjoram from Tenedos; wine from Attica, Chios, Cnidos and Thasos. Aeschylus speaks of Syrian balm; a trumpet from Etruria; purple from the "far sea"; a sword from Pontus. Sophocles tells of electrum from Sardes and gold from India; Euripides of iron "from the land of the Chalybes", also from Sicily, by which possibly is meant Elba. We hear in the elegy of Critias of valuable chariots from Sicily; luxurious chairs from Thessaly; beautiful bedsteads from Miletus and Chios; golden bowls and bronze work from Thebes. Flax for making nets came from Phasis and Carthage; wool from

[1] There is some doubt as to the exact identity of the plant silphium, but probably, if not certainly, it was asafoetida, or a species akin to it, i.e. the African *Ferula Tingitana*, or *Thapsia Gummifera*. In any case the plant is now extinct in Northern Africa. Cf. *Zur Silphionfrage*, by Else Strantz; also *Bulletin of the Royal Botanical Gardens, Kew* (1907), p. 10; art. "Silphion" in *P.W.* and criticism of Strantz in Suppl. v; Theoph. *H.P.* vi, 3, 1-7.

Miletus, which probably came from Phrygia; cowhides from Cyrene; carpets and pillows from Carthage; tallow from Sicily. Syria exported incense, a highly important commodity for the use of the temples; Libya ivory; Crete cypress wood; Thessaly horses, and Epirus hunting dogs. To cap these Hermippus, a comic writer of the time of Pericles, adds a few more such as mackerel and salt fish from the Hellespont; spelt and beef from Italy; the itch from Sitalces of Thrace (a present for Sparta); shiploads of lies from Perdiccas of Macedonia; pigs and cheese from Syracuse; sails and papyrus from Egypt; pears and fat sheep from Euboea; slaves from Phrygia; mercenaries from Arcadia; slaves and branded rogues from Pagasae.[1] Pericles in praising Athens says: "Owing to the greatness of our city we draw from the produce of the whole earth, and it falls to us to enjoy the goods of foreign lands as readily as those of Attica itself".[2]

The list is certainly an imposing one and would suggest a rich and varied commerce, in which all countries shared, organised and financed on a large scale. But a little further examination will reveal that, after all, most of the articles enumerated are very distinctly in the luxury class, and many of them may be dismissed at once as rarities and costly *objets d'art*, which did not enter largely into the commerce of the day. It is needless to stress the obvious, but it is quite evident that there cannot have been any important trade in chariots and costly furniture, hunting dogs or pears and apples. We must be most careful not to magnify a chance reference to a particular object, included in the list, because it is a rarity and therefore worth mentioning, into an organised and extensive export of such things. Sailors since the world began have always brought home curiosities which have excited interest and wonder.

But putting aside such luxury articles as may occasionally, if not regularly, have been found in the markets of Athens, it is quite sure that there was an extensive overseas commerce coming and going to the Piraeus and other Greek ports. There is a significant passage in Pseudo-Xenophon's *Constitution of Athens* which is worth quoting in full: "The Athenians are the only nation among the Greeks and barbarians that can secure

[1] Athen. i, 27 E.   [2] Thuc. ii, 38.

wealth; for if any state is rich in timber for shipbuilding, where shall they dispose of it, unless they gain the favour of the rulers of the sea? Or if any state abounds in iron, bronze or flax, where shall they dispose of it, unless they obtain the consent of the lords of the sea? It is, however, from these very materials that our ships are constructed; for from one nation comes timber, from another iron, from another bronze, from another hemp, from another wax....I, without labour, have all those benefits from the land by means of the sea; and no other state has any two of these materials; for the same state has not timber and flax, since where there is abundance of flax, the ground is level and woodless; nor do bronze and iron come from the same state; nor are there any two or three other commodities found in the same state, but one state abounds in one and another in another."[1]

It is quite evident that, with the exception of the hides of Cyrene, none of the commodities listed are in any sense raw materials for industry, while the iron, bronze, hemp and wax are intended for the building of ships of war; and apart from these the only other import is grain.[2] From this it may be argued that we must not regard Athens as a large industrial centre, importing its raw materials in great quantities and exporting finished products. All we do know of Athenian exports is that they included olive oil, wool, wine and marble. It is a mistaken viewpoint to regard Athens and other Greek cities as large manufacturing centres. But, at the same time, with due regard to the relative size of both city and trade as compared with to-day, it is reasonable to conclude that commerce was quite considerable. We know that Athens was entirely dependent upon her imports of grain and timber for her existence, and we must suppose that she had something to give in return. She bought very large quantities of timber from Macedonia and wheat from Pontus, Egypt and Sicily, and these had to be paid for at least in part with olive oil, wine, marble and some manufactured articles such as pottery. More important still was the silver from the mines of Laurium, which Xenophon regards as the greatest source of Attica's wealth. Added to these were the

---

[1] *Const. of Athens*, ii, 11–12.
[2] Hasebroek, *Trade and Politics*, p. 92.

harbour dues which came to Athens from the trade in transit through the port of the Piraeus and, most important of all, the tribute from her allies. Athens obviously had a considerable "unfavourable balance" of trade, which when the tribute ceased after the break-up of the Delian League, told heavily against her.

AEGINA, CORINTH, NAUCRATIS

If we agree that Athens was not primarily a manufacturing city but a trade entrepôt, we must also take the same view with regard to Aegina and Corinth. Aegina, an islet off the coast of Attica, with an area of about 35 sq. miles mostly mountainous, was through its favourable position an early trading centre until conquered by Athens, its inhabitants being essentially itinerant hawkers. Through the poverty of its soil it was driven to trade by sea,[1] and was an early competitor of the Phoenicians. Undoubtedly it produced good earthenware, as Aeginetan pottery was famous. We also hear of its bronzes and candelabra,[2] perfumes,[3] paint, rouge, necklaces and glassware. But it is not necessary that all these things should have been actually made on the island itself, but rather they formed the stock-in-trade of Aeginetan merchants who peddled them about the Aegean, and who were always ready for a bargain, as when they bought the spoils that fell to the Helots after the battle of Plataea.[4]

Corinth, always called "rich",[5] had founded many colonies, Corcyra, settlements in Sicily, Acarnania, Aetolia, Epirus, and had influence in Ambracia, Leucas, Epidamnus, Apollonia and Potidaea. It was thus the centre of a wide sea empire and grew rich in tribute, market dues and tolls. Thucydides tells us that Corinth invented the trireme, fought the first sea battle and cleared the sea of pirates.[6] Pindar says that Corinth received many ancient inventions from the Muses.[7] It was famous for its pottery, Pliny telling us that Butades of Corinth was the first who mixed ruddle with the clay,[8] and that the potter's wheel

---

[1] Strabo, viii, 6, 16 (c. 375).
[2] Pliny, *H.N.* xxxiv, 11.
[3] Theoph. *de Odoribus*, vi, 27; Athenaeus, xv, 689 D.
[4] Her. ix, 80; Strabo, viii, 6, 16 (c. 375).
[5] *Il.* ii, 570. [6] i, 13.
[7] *Ol.* xiii, 24. [8] *H.N.* xxxv, 152.

was the invention of Hyperbius, a Corinthian.[1] We hear of Corinthian paintings[2] and terra-cottas. Evidently the Corinthians were highly gifted, but we may take leave to doubt whether *all* the things to which the term Corinthian was applied, such as earthenware jars, embossed terra-cottas, rugs, clothing and ointments, helmets and breastplates were made there. Indeed there are few traces of industry in the city itself and Francotte designates it as essentially agricultural.[3] Undoubtedly it received large revenues from the fact that it commanded the isthmus over which goods could be transported and ships hauled on a kind of tramway. But we can only suppose that such were light warships; we can hardly think of heavy merchantmen being got over the four miles with a rise of 160 feet.[4]

Mr Leaf has pointed out that the downfall of Corinth may be traced to economic causes. The defeat of Carthage by the Romans shifted the whole centre of gravity from the Eastern to the Western Mediterranean. With larger ships and bolder sailors the terrors of Cape Maleia were no deterrent. Delos, where the trade route from the Euxine to Italy crossed that from Greece to Asia Minor, became the emporium, and Corinth was sidetracked. It is to be noted, he says, that Carthage and Corinth were destroyed in the same year, and Corinth lay waste for a century simply because there was no need for her existence in the commercial order of the day.[5]

Naucratis,[6] the Greek settlement on the Canopic branch of the Nile in the delta, was the great entrepôt of trade between Greece and Egypt. Founded in the reign of Psammetichus I about 650, its site and peculiar privileges were given to the Milesians in return for their services as mercenaries in gaining the throne.[7] As time passed Naucratis lost its character of being exclusively Milesian and merchants from Samos, Lesbos,

[1] *H.N.* vii, 198. But cf. Hasebroek, *Trade and Politics*, p. 55, n. 5.
[2] Pliny, *H.N.* xxxv, 15; Strabo, viii, 6, 23 (c. 381).
[3] *L'Industrie dans la Grèce Ancienne*, p. 105. Lehmann-Hartleben, *Ant. Hafenanl.*, p. 18.
[4] Thuc. iii, 15; Strabo, viii, 2, 1 (c. 335).
[5] *J.H.S.* xxxv (1915), 165; cf. also Tarn, *Hellenic Civilisation*, p. 230.
[6] Her. ii, 178; H. Prinz, "Funde aus Naucratis", *Klio*, vii (1908); art. "Naukratis" in *P.W.*; E. R. Price, "Pottery of Naucratis", *J.H.S.* xliv (1924), p. 180; R. M. Cook, "Amasis and the Greeks in Egypt", *J.H.S.* lvii (1937), p. 147.
[7] Strabo, xvii, 1, 18 (c. 801).

Clazomenae, Cyrene, Melos, Corinth and Athens found their way to the city and set up their own establishments much like the "Steel-yard" of the Hanse merchants in London or the factories of the East India Company in India. How far Naucratis ever became a manufacturing city rather than a distributing point for the wares of other peoples is difficult to say. But undoubtedly there was a fairly extensive manufacture of earthenware, faience and alabaster, which competed with pottery from Greece, and was sold in Cyprus, Rhodes, Miletus, Pitane, Gordium, Olbia, Delos, Aegina, Athens and Etruria.[1] Under the Pharaoh Amasis, 570–526, who was a strong phil-hellene, the importance of Naucratis greatly increased, and it became the sole port of entry for trade passing up the Nile.[2] The Greeks were given practical autonomy in their own town, and the merchants of the various countries united together in maintaining sanctuaries of various religious cults. Such a sanctuary, the Helleneion, was founded jointly by traders from Chios, Teos, Phocaea, Clazomenae, Rhodes, Cnidus, Halicarnassus, Phaselis and Mytilene, while the Aeginetans had a sanctuary to Zeus, the Samians to Hera and the Milesians to Apollo. It is well to understand that these cults were purely religious in character and had no commercial aims whatever; as we shall see later. Such religious associations were common, and cannot be identified with any kind of trade union or commercial association for the furtherance of trade.

MILETUS[3]

The long history and outstanding importance of Miletus on the Ionian coast are so striking that they demand somewhat extended treatment. Situated at the mouth of the Maeander river, which was navigable for 150 miles inland, protected on

---

[1] Athen. xi, 480 E. The so-called Naucratic vases are of very doubtful provenance. Probably they are early Chian. Cf. E. R. Price, "Pottery of Naucratis", *J.H.S.* xliv (1924), pp. 139 ff.

[2] Her. ii, 179.

[3] T. Röhlig, *Der Handel von Milet*, Phil. Diss., Hamburg (1933); Haussoullier, "Etudes sur l'Histoire de Milet et du Didymeion", *Bibl. des Hautes Études*, 138 (1902); Wiegand, Th. (ed.), *Milet, Ergebnisse der Ausgrabungen und Untersuchungen seit d. J.* 1899 (1914–25); "Miletus", arts. in *P.W.* by Hiller von Gaertringen and Burckhardt; A. von Salis, "Die Ausgrabungen in Milet und Didyma", *Neue Jahrb. f.d.k. Alt.* xxv (1910), p. 2; Hasebroek, *Griech. Wirth. und Gesell. Gesch.* p. 120.

the coast by a series of islands, the site offered unrivalled advantages not only as an entrepôt of trade for the coasts of Asia
Minor, but also for the interior of the continent, the Black Sea
and as far south as Egypt, where Milesian merchants had early
established themselves at Naucratis.

An ancient city of Asia, it sent a contingent to the help of the
Trojans.[1] If we are to judge from the golden armour of their
leader, it was even then rich and prosperous. Undoubtedly, as
finds of pottery on the site testify, it had relations with Minoan
civilisation. At some unknown date it was supposedly conquered
and rebuilt by settlers from Pylos under Neleus.[2] Its early
importance as a commercial centre is shown from the fact that
it was second only to Sardes in minting coins of electrum on the
so-called Phoenician standard.[3] Fortunate in its situation with
regard to trade, it suffered from that very fact, as it was always a
rich prize of which the Mermnad kings of Lydia were covetous
but found too strong to conquer, until Alyattes, having been
outwitted by a somewhat transparent trick of Thrasybulus,
tyrant of Miletus, agreed to a truce.[4] Later the city submitted
to Croesus, under what circumstances is unknown, and on the
fall of that king passed under Persian rule. In the great revolt
of the Ionians against Persia in 500, Miletus led the way and
had a fleet of eighty ships.[5] Defeated at the battle of Lade, the
city was taken by storm in 494 and its inhabitants dispersed and
sold into slavery.[6] After the defeat of the Persians in the great
invasion of Greece, Miletus once more regained its liberty in
479 after the battle of Mycale.[7] It became a member of the
Delian League under Athens, but seized the opportunity offered
by the decline of the Athenian fortunes in the Peloponnesian
war to join the Spartans in 412,[8] who turned the city over to the
Persians. It was taken by Alexander in 334, and during the
struggles of the successors was fought over by Seleucids and
Ptolemies. During the Roman era it rose to wealth and was
particularly favoured by Trajan. The last mention that we have
in classical times is in the decree of Diocletian promulgated in

[1] *Il.* ii, 876.
[2] Her. ix, 97.
[3] Head, *Hist. Num.* p. 584.
[4] Her. i, 19–22.
[5] Her. vi, 8.
[6] Her. vi, 18.
[7] Her. ix, 106.
[8] Thuc. viii, 17.

A.D. 301, fixing the prices of various commodities in the Empire. During later times it became the seat of a Christian bishopric, but owing to the silting up of the harbour it was of no commercial importance, and to-day the site is occupied by the village of Palatia.

Such in brief was the history of Miletus; it now remains to speak of its commercial importance. Its site was highly favourable not only because of its harbour,[1] but the plain of the Maeander at its mouth provided rich wheatfields, the lower slopes of the hills excellent vineyards and orchards and the higher levels rich pasture lands for cattle and, above all, the flocks of sheep which provided the famous Milesian wool. Added to which the neighbourhood had excellent clay beds from which pottery was made. Although we know little or nothing of the city before the Persian war, it is certain that ships from Miletus ranged from the delta of the Nile in the south to the north shores of the Euxine and as far as Sybaris in the west. As Strabo testifies, Miletus was a great coloniser.[2] We need not credit the accounts given of the number of colonies founded, but we do have certain evidence with regard to several. For instance, Abydos on the Hellespont;[3] Cyzicus[4] and Cius[5] on the Propontis; Sinope on the south coast of the Euxine.[6] Farther west on the same coast was Amisus.[7] All these had excellent harbours and, we cannot doubt, served as outlets for the trade of Asia Minor.[8] What the extent of that trade was it is very difficult, if not impossible to say, but the finds of Milesian pottery[9] suggest that wine and oil and perhaps Milesian wool were exchanged in not inconsiderable quantities for the typical products of the countries bordering the southern shores of the Black Sea. Milesian colonies to the north on the coast of the Crimea were Chersonesus, Panticapaeum and Theodosia.[10]

---

[1] Glotz, *Hist. Grecque*, i, 276; Strabo, xiv, 1, 6 (c. 635).
[2] *Ibid.*   [3] Strabo, xiii, 1, 20 (c. 590).
[4] Lehmann-Hartleben, *Ant. Hafenanl.* p. 63.
[5] Pomp. Mel. i, 100.   [6] Polyb. iv, 56; Strabo, xii, 3, 11 (c. 545).
[7] Lehmann-Hartleben, *Ant. Hafenanl.* p. 242.
[8] Röhlig, *Der Handel von Milet*, p. 64.
[9] Prinz, "Funde aus Naukratis", *Klio*, vii, p. 132; Bilabel, *Ionische Kolonisation*, p. 6.
[10] Minns, *Scythians and Greeks*, p. 338; Rostovtseff, *Iranians and Greeks*, p. 61; Bilabel, *Ionische Kolonisation*, p. 26.

Farther west were Istros and Tyras.[1] Trade went up the Rivers Bug and Dnieper[2] and penetrated far inland into Rumania.[3] Evidences of this trade are found in the many Milesian jars found in South Russia which had contained oil and wine, both highly prized products in that region.[4] Besides their own products Milesian merchants took vases from Naucratis to their customers.[5] This trade with the Black Sea reached its highest point in the seventh and sixth centuries and with interruptions, as, for instance, on the destruction of the city in the Ionian revolt, continued until the wiping out of Olbia by the Goths in the third century A.D., that is to say, for a thousand years.[6] It must be understood, however, that Miletus had by no means a monopoly of this very valuable trade. Indeed, it is safe to say that Athens in the fifth and fourth centuries had by far the greater share, and in the Hellenistic age the trade of Ephesus eclipsed that of Miletus.

The connection of Miletus with Naucratis from an early time is beyond all doubt.[7] The destruction of 494 interrupted this trade, but it was resumed later and in Hellenistic times we hear of Milesian oil going to Egypt.[8] The close connection between Miletus and Sybaris in Southern Italy is shown by the account of the grief of the Milesians at the downfall of the latter city;[9] evidently there must have been trade between the two on a not inconsiderable scale.[10] The same is true of trade connections with Athens. For some reason which cannot be explained Miletus sent furniture, bedsteads and couches to Athens, where they were highly appreciated.[11] Milesian wool was famous, woven into garments or rugs,[12] and its popularity continued for centuries.[13]

---

[1] Bilabel, *Ionische Kolonisation*, pp. 19, 23.

[2] Rostovtseff, *Iranians and Greeks*, p. 64.

[3] Pârvan, "Pénétration Hellénique", *Bull. Sect. Hist. Roumaine*, x, 6, and note 4; Bilabel, *Ionische Kolonisation*, p. 19.

[4] Rostovtseff, *Iranians and Greeks*, p. 48.

[5] Ebert, *Südrussland*, p. 200.

[6] Minns, *Scythians and Greeks*, p. 440; Glotz, *Hist. Grecque*, i, 170.

[7] Her. ii, 178; Prinz, *Funde aus Naukratis*, p. 109.

[8] Pap. Cair. Zen. 59015; Edgar, *Zenonopapyri*, i, 30.

[9] Her. vi, 21.   [10] Glotz, *Hist. Grecque*, i, 185.

[11] Critias, *ap.* Athen. i, 28 B, xi, 486 E; Xen. *Anab.* vii, 5, 14. Cf. art. "Kline", in *P.W.*

[12] Aristoph. *Lysist.* 728; *Ranae*, 542; Plut. *Alcibiades*, 23.

[13] Horace, *Epist.* i, 17, 30; Verg. *Georg.* iii, 306, iv, 335; Amphis, *ap.* Athen. xv, 691 A.

Whether or not, as has been supposed, there was a dyeing industry there is open to doubt, and is supported by no evidence.
All that can be said is that there is no reason why there should
not have been.[1] That Alcibiades swaggered about, to the scandal
of the more staid citizens, in a cloak of Milesian wool dyed
purple does not necessarily imply that the garment was woven
and dyed at Miletus. But since among his belongings that were
sold after his expulsion from Athens were Milesian couches, it
is not unreasonable to suppose that they all came from the same
place and that the wool was dyed and woven there.[2] Of the
extensive relations of Miletus with other cities in Hellenistic
times, as shown by decrees appointing Proxenoi and granting
rights of citizenship to foreigners, revealed by excavations on
the site, it is unnecessary to speak here.[3]

TRADE ROUTES

We have already remarked that the Greek colonies were the
principal feeders of commerce. It now remains to trace the
principal trade routes of the Mediterranean area and the Black
Sea. To do this it is necessary to remember that the sailing
season was confined to the summer months and with the
approach of winter all water-borne commerce ceased.

Generally speaking the summer months were calm with
little wind, suitable for rowing across the Aegean and up the
Dardanelles to the Black Sea ports. With the approach of
autumn the prevailing easterlies began to blow, which sent
the heavily laden grain ships quickly back to port. But the
return must not be put off too late as we see in the Lacritus case
argued by Demosthenes. If the start homeward from the mouth
of the Dnieper was delayed after the rise of Arcturus, i.e. early
in September, the rate of interest on the "bottomry" loan on
ship and cargo rose steeply. Westwards to Sicily similar despatch was necessary. Rowing round Cape Maleia, or alternately
being hauled over the isthmus at Corinth, the voyage west was
made in the calm days of early summer and then with their

---

[1] Hasebroek, *Trade and Politics*, pp. 58f.; Beloch, *Griech. Gesch.* i, 1,
pp. 266ff.

[2] Plut. *Alcibiades*, 22, 23.

[3] Röhlig, *Der Handel von Milet*, pp. 45f.

heavy cargoes of grain they caught the Etesian winds, the north-westerlies which blew from about the third week in July to the middle of September. Southwards to Crete, Naucratis and the Syrian ports and Cyprus, the ships from the Piraeus ran down with the Etesian winds and then worked northwards, favoured by the northerly current along the Syrian shore to Cyprus and under the lee of Asia Minor to the islands and so back to Greece.[1] With their small ships, square-rigged and with a single mast, they could not sail into the wind, for beating up against a strong breeze requires fore-and-aft sails with two or three masts.[2]

Their ships were small, as we see from the Peace of Nicias, concluded in 421 between the Athenians and Spartans, in which it was stipulated that the Spartans could not sail along their own coast or those of any of their allies in any ship carrying more than 500 talents deadweight, i.e. something over 13 tons. These must have been little coasting boats, and the grain ships, no doubt, were much bigger. At the siege of Syracuse, six years later, we hear of the Athenians bringing up a vessel of 10,000 talents, or 262 tons, i.e. about 150 tons register.[3] From Demosthenes we hear of a twenty-oared ship with a cargo of 300 jars of wine.[4] The talent and amphora represent a cubic foot of water, the Greek foot measuring about 0·97 of the English. The talent and amphora would, therefore, weigh about 56 lb., and such a cargo of 3000 amphorae about 75 tons deadweight. It can easily be understood that no ship could be of great size if it had to be propelled by oars when there was a calm or the winds were contrary. Their warships were even smaller; "glorified racing-eights" in Mr Tarn's phrase. How fragile they were can be seen from the great destruction in any naval engagement.

Taking Athens and Corinth as centres, it will be found that there were four principal or "trunk" routes. First north-eastwards past the coasts of Macedonia and Thrace, through

---

[1] J. H. Rose, *Mediterranean in the Ancient World*, p. 11. The course taken by the big grain ship which was to carry St Paul to Rome, and in which he was wrecked, followed this route. Cf. Rose, pp. 166 ff.

[2] Cf. J. H. Rose, *Mediterranean in the Ancient World*, p. 171; Köster, *Antike Seewesen*, p. 143; T. R. Holmes, "Could ancient ships work to windward?" *Class. Quart.* iii (1909), p. 26.

[3] Thuc. vii, 25.   [4] *In Lacr.* 10.

the Dardanelles and Bosphorus into the Black Sea. This was the most important of all, for over it travelled a great amount of timber, grain, fish and slaves. The forests of Bithynia and the Danube valley supplied timber, charcoal and "naval stores" such as pitch and resin; Pontus and South Russia fish and wheat. The control of the Hellespont was therefore, as ever, a vital matter in keeping open the route to the Euxine. Up to the beginning of the fifth century it was held by Miletus. On its fall in the revolt against Persia, control passed to Athens from which it passed for a short time to Sparta. In the early fourth century it was held alternately by Athens and Persia and then passed to Rhodes. The importance of this route to Athens in securing grain from Pontus, and the efforts made to control it, are discussed at greater length in the section on the grain trade later in this chapter.

The second route, as has already been pointed out, went due south to Crete, thence to Egypt and back via Cyprus and Rhodes. At successive periods Rhodes and Delos were the entrepôts of this traffic, a highly important one because along it passed the trade of Asia, India, Arabia, Babylonia, Phoenicia and Egypt, while the grain, copper and timber of Cyprus also moved along this route. The important trade from Cyrene moved due north via Crete, and from thence a short voyage in open sea to Greece. Before the founding of Alexandria the cities of Phoenicia, Tyre and Sidon, struggled to monopolise the commerce between Asia and Europe against the rivalry of Greek traders in Miletus and Naucratis. But with the rise of Carthage their commercial importance waned and was finally almost wholly extinguished, the trade of the eastern Mediterranean being shared in the Hellenistic age by the newly arisen ports of Antioch and Alexandria.

The third main route, which was always largely in the hands of Corinth and her colonies, passed through the Gulf of Corinth by the coasts of Acarnania and Epirus to the ports on both sides of the Adriatic. The question of Greek trade in the Adriatic has been the source of considerable controversy. Beloch was the first to assert that their merchantmen avoided it, and since then it seems to have become invariable with all writers to find excellent reasons why the Greeks neglected that area. Upon further examination, however, it will be found that the evidence is scanty and more hypothetical than factual.[1] In the first place, it is asserted that the copious rainfall kept them away.[2] It is true that there are two rainy districts, Montenegro and Albania north of the Drin, and the north-east coast of the Gulf of Fiume. Otherwise the basin of the Adriatic is by no means excessively rainy, not more so than Southern Italy and Sicily. Secondly, it is alleged that the winds which blow down it are dangerous and the entrance is choppy enough to have deterred Greek mariners. While the sudden gusts of the winter wind, the *Bora*, are certainly dangerous, the Greeks were not winter seafarers, and the summer winds are by no means formidable.[3] Thirdly, it is alleged that the Illyrian pirates were so bad that merchants avoided that route. To this it may be replied that pirates only flourished where trade was, and that if merchants avoided the Adriatic there was no livelihood for marauders.[4] There seems, therefore, very little solid evidence for any deliberate avoidance of the Adriatic, nor is there any evidence that they were kept out by rivals, Phoenician or Etruscan. There is nothing to suggest that Phoenicians ever settled in Illyria, except an ill-defined legend as to the Phoenician Cadmus.[5] Nor is it possible to maintain that Etruscan hostility ever kept the Greeks away, since at no time were the Etruscans in command of the sea.

On the other hand the evidence with regard to a quite considerable Adriatic trade is very strong. First the Euboeans occupied Epidamnus, to be displaced by the Corinthians, in whose hands Adriatic trade remained. The valley of the Po was probably first reached by those hardy mariners the Phoenicians in their westward wanderings. The early trade of the Corinthians went up to Damastium in Southern Illyria for silver.[6] One important article of commerce was in the iris, which grew

---

[1] R. L. Beaumont, "Greek influence in the Adriatic", *J.H.S.* lvi (1936), p. 159.　　　　　　　　　　[2] J. L. Myres, *C.A.H.* iii, 633.
[3] But certainly it was regarded as stormy by Greek mariners. Cf. Paus. viii, 54, 3; Athen. xiii, 612 D.
[4] But evidently it was regarded as decidedly dangerous; a commercial venture, if successful, bringing in a profit of 100 per cent.—Lysias, xxxii (*in Diog.*), 25. *I.G.* ii, 809, 825; Hor. *Odes*, iii, 9, 23.
[5] Cf. Beaumont, *J.H.S.* lvi (1936), pp. 159, 196.
[6] Strabo, vii, 7, 8 (c. 326).

widely in Illyria, from which "orris root" and perfumes were made.[1] We know that Corinth was a centre of the manufacture. Little is known of trade with the Po valley which was begun by the Phocaeans in the sixth and reached its climax in the fifth century. Certainly tin from Bohemia came down the Adriatic after the Carthaginians had monopolised the Atlantic route. Amber, which in remote times had been an important article of trade, went out of fashion, and did not regain its popularity until the time of the Roman Empire.[2] Possibly grain came from Apulia, but this is highly conjectural. Later we have at least one evidence that a colony was founded on the Italian shores, although its position cannot be determined. A fragmentary decree of the Athenians, probably of the year 325, grants ships of war and the necessary equipment to a certain Miltiades "in order that the decree of the people in respect of the colony in the Adriatic be carried out without delay". Later there comes: "In order that for all time the people may have a market and a source of corn supply of their own, and may have an outpost against the Tyrrhenians by establishing an anchorage, and that Miltiades, the founder, and the colonists may have a fleet at their disposal, and that Greeks and foreigners, having an Athenian anchorage, may sail in safety into the Adriatic."[3] All that we can say with regard to the Adriatic is that it formed a less important trade route, and therefore did not attract Greek traders so much. It is quite unsafe, however, to say that the Greeks avoided it of any set purpose.

A fourth passed over the isthmus of Corinth or round Cape

---

[1] Pliny, *H.N.* xxi, 40; Theoph. *H.P.* iv, 5, 2; Athen. xii, 553 A.

[2] Provenance and early use of amber very obscure. That discovered by Schliemann at Mycenae not true amber (Lucas, *Ancient Egyptian Materials and Industries*, p. 337). Doubtful if electron of Homer and Hesiod amber or electrum (*Od.* iv, 72, xv, 459, xviii, 295; *Scut. Herc.* 141). True amber from the Baltic or coast of Friesland reached Mediterranean by various routes (Navarro in *Geograph. Journ.* (1925), p. 481). Pytheas of Massalia visited the amber isles of the North Sea (Diod. Sic. v, 23). Almost certainly he did not enter the Baltic. Abalus the amber isle is probably Heligoland (Pliny, *H.N.* xxxvii, 35). Confusion between amber and electrum (Theoph. *de Lap.* 29; Arist. *Meteor.* iv, 10; Pliny, *H.N.* xxxvii, 11, 46; Tacitus, *Germ.* 45; Her. iii, 115, river Eridanos). Subject treated at length by Bluemner in *P.W.*, art. "Bernstein", and in *Tech. und Term.* ii, 381; Jacob in *D.S.*, art. "Electrum"; Tozer, *Hist. Anc. Geog.* pp. 31 f., 164, and Cary's note, p. 7; Bérard, *Les Phéniciens*, i, 400.

[3] *Syll.*³ 305 = *I.G.* ii², 1629, 1, 217 ff.

Maleia to Sicily, and farther through the Straits of Messana, or by overland portage from Cumae to Laos and Scidros, to the west coasts of Italy, Sardinia, Corsica, Gaul and Spain. As far to the north as Cumae this route passed a continuous succession of Greek colonies as far as Gaul and Spain, where Massalia and Emporiae welcomed Greek merchants. Such daring ones as ventured so far reaped a rich harvest, and the story of the wonderful voyage of Colaeus to far-off Tartessus must have incited others to take the same risks. The Western Mediterranean, dangerous though it was from the jealousy of the Carthaginians and Etruscans, was always worth trying for; although in general the Greek merchants found Cumae the limit of safety. Wheat, cheese and timber from Sicily and the forests of South Italy were the staples of that route.

The Isthmic Theory

A theory which has attracted a good deal of attention and given rise to much controversy is what is known as the "Isthmic" with regard to trade routes. First put forward by M. Bérard,[1] it states simply that where possible early traders made a "portage" across an isthmus in order to avoid rounding a stormy cape or negotiating dangerous straits. Such an isthmic route is obviously that of Corinth which provided a short cut between the Saronic and Corinthian gulfs and avoided the stormy and pirate-infested Cape Maleia. Another such isthmic route was to be found between Sybaris and Scidros in Magna Graecia, whereby the Straits of Messana and the terrors of Scylla and Charybdis were avoided. A third was situated at the mouth of the Hellespont, where Troy dominated a convenient portage whereby the danger and fatigue of rowing up the narrow channel in the face of wind and current were avoided. Round Cape Sigeum the current rushes out along the Asiatic shore and there are no back eddies to counteract it. To row up twelve miles against a current running at five knots under a hot sun was a formidable task. Even if they struggled up those twelve miles, they met the final difficulties at the Narrows, where there are dangerous eddies. It was much easier to land at Assos in the

---

[1] *Les Phéniciens*, i, 69 ff.

Gulf of Adramyttium, and carry the cargoes overland past Troy to where above the Narrows calm waters were found once more.[1]

Generally speaking, it may be said that no doubt such portage routes were frequently used, more especially in the earlier age of Mediterranean commerce when ships were very small and mariners inexperienced. But that they were followed in historic times to any extent is more than doubtful. Greek merchant vessels were perfectly capable of making voyages that tested their seaworthiness and the skill of their navigators. The theory has been subject to very destructive criticism, more especially by Mr Gomme. It has been generally implied, he says,[2] that the close commercial relations that existed between Miletus and Sybaris were maintained by voyages across the Aegean to Corinth, where presumably it paid better to break cargo at the isthmus than to sail round the stormy coasts of the Peloponnese. If this were so, then the cargo would have been carried farther in Milesian or foreign ships through the gulf, up the north-west coast to Corcyra, or hurriedly across to Hydruntum, then following every curve of the coast past Tarentum and Metapontum to Sybaris. Thence, if goods must go farther, as so many did to Etruria, they must have taken another isthmus route overland to Laos or Scidros, and along the coast again as far as Massalia and Emporiae. Such cautious sailing routes would have put Corinth, Sicyon and Corcyra in complete command of trade with the .west; but Chalcis and Eretria, Miletus, Samos and Phocaea, and later Athens and Rhodes, were actively engaged in the western commerce and were quite independent of Corinth. Moreover, Mr Gomme says, farther west Massalia was founded not by Cumae or Velia or Syracuse, as would be expected by the "isthmus theory", but from Phocaea, and trade was maintained by the Straits of Messana and Corsica. Samos traded direct with Spain, and we may be sure their vessels did not hug

---

[1] Bérard, *Les Phéniciens*, i, 98ff.; W. Leaf, *Troy, a Study in Homeric Geography*, *passim*; H. Stier, "Dardanellen oder Besikabai", *Rhein. Mus.* lxxvii (1928), p. 113; F. Miltner, "Die Meerengenfrage in der griechischen Geschichte", *Klio*, xxviii (1935).

[2] "A forgotten factor in Greek naval strategy", *J.H.S.* liii (1933), pp. 16ff. Also criticism of M. Bérard's theory of an isthmic route across Boeotia in *Essays in Greek History*, p. 17.

the coasts of Africa, dependent on the goodwill of the Carthaginians. We can be certain that Milesian vessels did, in fact, sail to Sybaris round the stormy Maleian Cape[1] and across the Ionian Sea, and that Corinth and Athens traded direct with Etruria, not via Sybaris, and that Phocaean vessels were to be seen in Massalia.

The Greeks were no cowards; they were not afraid of the high seas, but they disliked venturing out of sight of land in their small ships.[2] It was easier and safer to hug the land, and if they exercised a cautious discretion in navigation we can hardly blame them for it. When we remember that they had no compass, and could only depend upon the rough method of calculating their position by "dead reckoning" on the day's run, or by reference to some landfall, or by the stars at night, our admiration for their daring and practical seamanship increases. It is true the Greeks seldom if ever ventured beyond the straits of Gibraltar on to the trackless Atlantic. But that was due mainly to Carthaginian control of the straits, and in any case such ventures would have been foolhardy.

Transport by Land

Overland commerce was of very small dimensions as compared with water-borne, for the very simple reason that it was much cheaper and easier to transport merchandise on shipboard than by road. Greek roads[3] were almost invariably bad; in most cases little better than narrow tracks along which strings of pack animals could be driven in single file. A few were good and suitable for wheel traffic, as will be seen later. The historic era of Greece fell between two epochs of good road-making, the Mycenaean and Roman, and approached neither in excellence of construction. Mycenaean technique, from such evidences as remain, was evidently first-rate, if very costly. Three roads

---

[1] The cape of Maleia was feared not only because it was stormy but because it was the haunt of pirates; cf. Strabo, viii, 6, 20 (c. 378). Livy, xxxiv, 29.

[2] Cf. also Toutain, *Economic Life of Ancient World*, p. 67.

[3] R. J. Forbes, *Notes on the History of Ancient Roads and their Construction*, cap. x; E. Curtius, "Gesch. d. Wegebaus bei den Griechen," *Abh. Kön. Akad. Wiss. Berlin*, 1854 (= *Gesammelte Abhandl.* i (1894), pp. 1 f.). Arts. "Via" in *D.S.*, "Cursus Publicus" in *P.W.*

ran from Mycenae to Corinth and a fourth to the Argive Heraeum, paved with polygonal slabs. With the downfall of the Mycenaean power the art deteriorated, or rather entirely disappeared; just as with the decline of Rome the magnificent road system fell into complete decay, and the art had to be re-learned a thousand years later.

Such sacred roads as there were, i.e. those leading to the sacred places for pilgrimages, were kept in good repair, at least spasmodically when a great festival was due. These highways were mostly, but not invariably, of that very interesting and, within limits, highly effective sort, which may be called "rut roads", that is, with grooves cut in the rock for wheels, wherever the track led over exposed rock. These ruts were usually about 4 in. deep and from 8 to 9 in. wide, with a gauge of 4 ft. 8 in. Some, where the traffic was heavy, had double tracks, e.g. those from Athens to the Piraeus and to Sunium, from Athens to Delphi, and from Sparta to Elis.[1] One very interesting feature on the road from Athens to Pyrgos has been found near the modern Stephani, where a barrier has been found right across the track. No explanation of this seems possible other than that offered by Curtius that it served as a kind of tollgate or customs barrier. At intervals bypasses (*ektropai*) were cut in order to allow two waggons or chariots to pass each other. The difficulties that arose on a single-track road can easily be imagined, and we have echoes of disputes when Oedipus met Laius on the "cleft way" to Delphi,[2] and the quarrel between Hercules and Cycnus when they met head on.[3] Transport roads in Attica, which were usually kept in good repair, led from the quarries at Pentelicon and another from the white marble quarries at Kamaresa. These had an average width of 16 ft., with double wheel tracks.

There were also roads constructed on a kind of macadam principle, although much inferior (*lithostrotos*), chippings from the marble quarries being rammed down into the subsoil. When they got into bad condition, which was frequent, a new layer was put down on top. Battos built such a road, still to be seen, in Cyrene.[4] In 310–319 the Agoranomoi constructed one of

---

[1] Cf. Eur. *Electra*, 775.
[2] Soph. *Oed. Rex*, 733.
[3] Hesiod, *Scut. Herc.* 357.
[4] Pindar, *Pyth.* v, 90.

this kind from Athens to the Piraeus.[1] The draining of these roads, lacking the proper macadam principle, was bad, and Strabo, speaking of such streets in Smyrna, infers that careful construction to insure proper drainage was either not understood, or not widely practised, until Roman times.[2] The track always followed the natural features it passed over, and few engineering improvements were attempted in the form of embankments, except where a suitable rocky subsoil was lacking as, for instance, on the sacred way from Daphnae to Eleusis; but very possibly this was due to later improvements by Hadrian.

The law of the Amphictyones in 380–379 provided that they should repair all roads and bridges.[3] But of bridges we know nothing. In Attica public officials (*Hodopoei*) were in charge of highways and their repair.[4] The construction or repair of roads seems to have been paid for sometimes by rich men; but whether this constituted a regular form of liturgy is not clear, and our information is very meagre on the subject.[5]

Pausanias has numerous references to the roads of Greece—few complimentary. One he did approve of ran from Tegea to Argos along the slopes of Mounts Parthenios and Hysiae, which he says was excellent for carriages.[6] One between Tithorea and Delphi was even longer, but unsuitable for vehicles.[7] The "cleft way" from Daulis to Delphi grew steeper as it went, and at last became difficult even for a traveller on foot.[8] From Cleonae to Argos there were two roads: one, a short cut, was a mere footpath; the other, over the path of Tretus, as it was called, was a narrow defile shut in by mountains, but was better adapted for driving.[9] The so-called roads along the slopes of Parnassus were no better than stony tracks so bad that foot travellers fared better on them than mules.[10] The track from Lerna to Anigraea was rough and narrow;[11] that from Chaeronea to Stiris was no better than a hill-side path, steep and stony.[12]

[1] *Syll.*[3] 313 = *I.G.* ii (2nd ed.), 380.

[2] xiv, 1, 37 (c. 646). Cf. also the same author's criticism in v, 3, 8 (c. 235).

[3] *Syll.*[3] 145 = *I.G.* ii[2], 1126.

[4] Arist. *Ath. Pol.* liv, 1; Plato, *Laws*, 761.

[5] *C.I.G.* 2570, 2782, 5141; Cagnat, *Inscr. Graec. ad Res Rom. pertin.* iii, 975, 1486 (Roman period).

[6] viii, 54, 5.   [7] x, 32, 8.   [8] x, 5, 2.

[9] ii, 15, 1.   [10] x, 32, 6.   [11] ii, 38, 4.

[12] x, 35, 8.

Between Sicyon and Titane the road was impassable for waggons owing to its narrowness.[1] The "Scironic" road from Megara to Corinth was first made passable by Sciron, but the emperor Hadrian had greatly improved it, so that even chariots could pass on it.[2]

The costs of land transport were almost prohibitive. The hauling of column drums from the quarries at Pentelicon to Eleusis, a distance of about 25 miles, was a terrific business occupying a waggon drawn by forty span of oxen 2½ days, each drum costing 342 drs. for cartage. Stones which cost 61 drs. in Corinth were worth 705 drs. laid down in Delphi.[3] Light goods were carried on pack animals, and the charges for transport were correspondingly heavy. Except for absolutely necessary carriage over short distances, as, for example, the Oropus-Decelea-Athens road, land transport was hardly used at all, very probably because of the scarcity of transport animals, at least in Attica.

ATHENS AS A COMMERCIAL ENTREPÔT

Although Athens may not have been a great industrial city in the modern sense of the word, yet its importance as an entrepôt for trade is beyond question. This was largely due to a number of causes which, taken together, made it almost unrivalled until, with the rise of Alexandria, the whole picture of Mediterranean commerce was changed. These causes may be summarised as follows:

First, the geographical position of the city and the excellence of its port, the Piraeus, which gave safe anchorage in its three harbours in all weathers and winds. No better description of these advantages can be found than in the panegyric of Xenophon.[4] "The traveller who desires to traverse the confines of Hellas from end to end, whether he travels by land or sea, will find that he is describing a circle, the centre of which is Athens. ...We possess the finest and safest harbourage for shipping, where vessels of all sorts can come to moorings and be laid up

[1] Paus. ii, 11, 3.   [2] i, 44, 6.

[3] Glotz, *Hist. Grecque*, p. 292, n. 1.

[4] *Revenues*, i, 6. For the port of Piraeus cf. W. Judeich, *Topographie von Athen* (2nd ed.), pp. 144 ff., 430 ff. Xenophon might also have mentioned that Athens lies outside the Mediterranean earthquake belt.

in absolute security as far as stress of weather is concerned. But farther than that, in most states the trader is under the necessity of lading his vessel with some merchandise or other in exchange for his cargo since the current coin has no circulation beyond the frontier. But at Athens he has a choice; he can in return for his wares either take away a variety of wares, or he can export silver." Isocrates echoes the words of the author of the *Revenues* and speaks of the debt of the whole world to those who had established the Piraeus as an emporium in the middle of Hellas where nations could dispose of their surplus products with ease.[1]

Secondly, the Athenians had deserved the gratitude of the rest of the world by effectually ridding the Aegean of pirates, and in return for an efficient policing of the main sea routes, other states submitted to Athenian regulation of their commerce as the lesser of two evils.

Thirdly, at least at the height of her power, Athens was able through what we may call her "navigation laws" to exert considerable if not complete control over the commerce of her allies. Such laws, which are very reminiscent of those of Great Britain under the Mercantilist régime, among other things forbade the lending of money to merchants not engaged upon the conveyance of goods to or from the Piraeus.[2] No inhabitant of the Athenian empire could transport grain to any place but the Piraeus, a law which ingenious traders found not too difficult to circumvent.[3] Athens was able to deal very drastically indeed with offenders when it suited her purpose. Thus the famous "Megarian Decrees", which were really the spark that ignited the conflagration of the Peloponnesian war, forbade the merchants of Megara to use the ports of the allies of Athens and the markets of Piraeus, a death-blow to the prosperity of the offending city.[4] Athens was wise enough to give privileges to her allies to help them in time of need and even to interfere on their behalf. For instance, at a time of famine, Methone was permitted to import

---

[1] Isocr. *Paneg.* 42.
[2] Dem. *in Lacr.* 50, *in Dionys.* 6. Cf. also Isocr. *Paneg.* 42.
[3] Dem. *in Phorm.* 37; Lycurg. *in Leocr.* 27. Conditions governing the control of the grain trade are dealt with more fully hereafter.
[4] Thuc. i, 39, 67, 144; Aristoph. *Acharn.* 533. Hasebroek, *Trade and Politics*, p. 122, discusses the motives of the decrees.

grain direct from Pontus, and a special embassy was sent to Macedonia to remonstrate when merchants from Methone were being shut out of Macedonian markets.[1] It is hardly to be supposed that Athens could have held her allies to her by force of arms alone; undoubtedly she gave substantial benefits in return for their allegiance.

Fourthly, the banking facilities of Athens were excellent and sufficient to finance any commercial venture. It was when the financial centre of the Eastern Mediterranean left Athens and the bankers of Alexandria, Delos and Rhodes took the business away from the Athenians that the final eclipse of the city came. And lastly, the commercial courts and laws of Athens gave to all justice and reasonable protection.[2] Not only could foreign merchantmen find fair dealing in the Athenian courts, but through commercial treaties the Athenian state had gained reciprocity in litigation whereby a decision of the Athenian judges would be respected elsewhere, and a merchant from Athens if sued in a foreign court would receive protection against injustice.[3]

Such were the foundations upon which the economic greatness of Athens was founded. It was, in fact, no idle boast that Athens was the "emporium" of Greece, and she held that position through all the storms that assailed her in the fifth and fourth centuries until she was finally ruined by the rise of Alexandria, the rivalry of Corinth, Rhodes and Delos, and the dynastic struggles of Alexander's successors.

It is exceedingly difficult to come to any conclusion with regard to the total amount of trade entering and leaving the Piraeus. We are told that in the year 401 the import and export duties levied at the port were leased out for thirty talents and next year for thirty-six.[4] If we can suppose that this covered everything, we arrive at the conclusion that the total inward and outward bound traffic was then worth between 1800 and 2000 talents, if the rate levied was 2 per cent. These figures have, however, for long been suspect, and it is very unsafe to accept

---

[1] *S.I.G.* 304.
[2] Ziebarth, *Beiträge*, p. 44. For more on the commercial courts see chapter on Money and Banking, p. 349.
[3] Dem. *de Hal.* 9, 11, 12; cf. Hasebroek, *Trade and Politics*, p. 127.
[4] Andocides, *de Myst.* 134.

them as conclusive.[1] As to the commerce of the whole Athenian empire, we know that in 413 the Athenians, in place of the usual tribute from the allies, put a tax of 5 per cent ad valorem on all merchandise entering or leaving the ports of the allies.[2] We also know that the tribute at that time amounted to about 1000 talents; and since the new 5 per cent tax must have been levied to increase the amount received from the allies, we may suppose that the total trade of the "empire" must have been at least 20,000 talents. But the trade of the Piraeus is not included in this, nor that of Chios, Samos and Lesbos, so all we can say is that the total trade must have been not far short of 25,000 talents a year, a very large amount for those times.

TAXES ON COMMERCE[3]

In general it may be said that, so far as is known, there was never any attempt in pre-Hellenistic times at any "protection" of industries through tariffs in the modern sense of the word.[4] This arose not from any "free trade" policy but because in pursuance of their ideal of self-sufficiency the Greek states only imported what they could not manufacture or were in want of themselves, wheat, timber, pitch, flax, dried fish and luxuries, the last on a very small scale. Tariffs were therefore entirely for revenue; the opening of a port to commerce was for the purpose of exacting tolls on the traffic entering it[5] and most cities depended upon them as their chief source of revenue. Very early customs duties made Corinth rich,[6] situated as it was on the isthmus and therefore able to take toll of all traffic between the mainland and the Peloponnese. The same was true of Megara which, as Isocrates says, became wealthy, although it had no fertile land, no silver mines and no harbours.[7] Olynthus, because of its command of the timber trade and the revenues derived from its many harbours and "emporia", became one

---

[1] Andreades, *Greek Public Finance*, p. 298, discusses the point inconclusively.
[2] Thuc. vii, 28, 4.
[3] Busolt, *Griech. Staatsk.* i, 613 ff. Cf. Schwahn, art. "Tele" in *P.W.*; art. "Schiffs-papiere" in *Rhein. Mus.* lxxxi, (1932), p. 41.
[4] G. Weicker, *Steuerpolitik in Altertum*, pp. 132 ff. (*Blätter für Freunde der Antik. Wien*, viii (1932)).
[5] Arist. *Pol.* 1327 A.   [6] Strabo, viii, 6, 20 (c. 378).
[7] Isocr. viii, 117.

of the richest cities of its time. Harbour dues from Macedonian ports amounted normally to 20 talents, which Callistratus increased to 40.[1] When Rhodes was at the height of its prosperity, Polybius says, its revenues amounted to a million drachmae.[2] Cersobleptes of Thrace drew not less than 200 talents from the taxes he imposed on commerce.[3]

Since trade by land was inconsiderable in comparison with that by sea, we know little of tolls imposed on such traffic. There seem, however, to have been "gate-tolls" (*diapulia*) of the nature of octroi, on goods entering or leaving a city, although the point is obscure,[4] and we are left to conclude that there must have been "customs zones" on the borders between Athens and Megara and Athens and Boeotia.[5]

In general it may be said that the most usual tax was the "fiftieth" or an impost of 2 per cent ad valorem.[6] In Athens there is reason to suppose that this had been raised from 1 per cent after the Sicilian disaster when the revenues of the city were in a serious state.[7] In the allied states the tax was 5 per cent on all imports and exports. This was also introduced after the Sicilian expedition to take the place of the tribute paid to Athens by members of the Delian League.[8] When Athens was in control of the Hellespont, she exacted what was then at least an enormous toll of 10 per cent on all traffic passing through the straits.[9] This was first imposed by Alcibiades in 410, and abolished after Aegospotami. It was reimposed by Thrasybulus in 389, and finally abolished by the Peace of Antalcidas in 386, to be later revived in the third century by Byzantium, which led to a war with Rhodes.[10] In other states we hear of dues on traffic by land recorded by some Cretan communities, as in the treaty between Olus and Latus.[11] In Crisa about 600 there was a

---

[1] Ps.-Arist. *Oecon.* ii, 1350 A, 16.   [2] Polyb. xxxi, 7.
[3] Dem. *in Aristocr.* 110.
[4] Cf. Andreades, *Greek Public Finance*, pp. 146, 295.
[5] *Ibid.* pp. 139, 295.
[6] Besides Athens this tax was imposed in Epidaurus, Troezen, Cyparissiae, Delos, Halicarnassus, Cnidos and Atarneus—Busolt, *Griech. Staatsk.* i, 614, note 4 for refs.
[7] Andreades, *Greek Public Finance*, p. 296, note 5.
[8] Thuc. vii, 28, 4.
[9] Xen. *Hell.* i, 1, 22; Ephorus, *ap.* Diod. xiii, 64.
[10] Polyb. iv, 38, 44, 46–7.
[11] Busolt, *Griech. Staatsk.* i, 613.

transit duty (*diagogion*) on all goods destined for Delphi, and extortionate exactions on pilgrims arriving on ships coming from Sicily and Italy.[1]

A point that remains in considerable doubt and is, perhaps, incapable of ever being definitely settled, is whether or not there was at the Piraeus a "free port" for transit trade. We know that there were harbour dues (*ellimenia*), which were evidently charged for the use of docking privileges.[2] Xenophon in the *Revenues* has proposals for providing improved dock facilities at the Piraeus to attract foreign merchants; which would be a source of revenue to the city.[3]

[1] Strabo, ix, 3, 4 (c. 419).
[2] Ellimenia, Poll. viii, 132, ix, 29. Cf. Busolt, *Griech. Staatsk.* i, 614, iv, 4; art. "Ellimenion" by Boerner in *P.W.*; Boeckh, i, 388. Lehmann-Hartleben, *Ant. Hafenanl.* in *Klio*, xiv (1923), p. 45, n. 1.
[3] Xen. *Revenues*, iii, 12.

CHAPTER VII[1]

COMMERCE (II)

GRAIN AND TIMBER TRADE

The Grain Trade

IN the chapter on Greek Agriculture we see that while the rest of Greece was occasionally in need of importing wheat, Athens was almost wholly dependent upon foreign grain. So vitally important was this trade to the Athenians, more vital to them even than the securing of adequate supplies of ship's timbers, that it is not too much to say that, in so far as the state may be said to have pursued an economic policy at all, it was centred on the grain trade. To insure a regular supply by keeping on good terms with the principal exporting countries, and to keep the main trade routes open against attacks by pirates and the seizure of cargoes by states in need of wheat themselves, was no small task, necessitating a large expenditure on squadrons patrolling the seas and the maintenance of garrisons at strategic points.

We do not know when Athens was first compelled to obtain wheat from abroad; but evidently by the time of Solon the problem of getting sufficient breadstuffs for the population was becoming acute, since we are told by Plutarch that he forbade the export of grain altogether.[2] As population increased, the preoccupation of the Athenians with the grain supply became greater, and during the fourth century it formed, according to Aristotle, a regular item on the agenda to be considered every month by the various assemblies at their meetings.[3] Demosthenes

---

[1] General references: Andreades, *Greek Public Finance*, pp. 238–45; Hasebroek, *Trade and Politics*, pp. 146–50; Tod, *C.A.H.* v, 11–20; Gernet, *L'Approvisionnement d'Athènes en Blé au Ve et au IVe Siècle*; Knorringa, *Emporos, passim*; Jardé, *Céréales, passim*; Grundy, *Thucydides and the History of his Age*, cap. iii; Ziebarth, *Beiträge*; Sauciuc-Saveanu, *Cultura*; Heichelheim, art. "Sitos" in *P.W.* Suppl. vi; E. C. Semple, *Geography of Mediterranean Region*, cap. xiii; Perrot, "Les Commerces des Blés au IVe Siècle avant Notre Ère", *Revue Historique*, iv, 1 ff.; Busolt, *Griech. Staatsk.* i, 431 ff.

[2] Plut. *Solon.*

[3] Arist. *Ath. Pol.* xliii, 4.

in various speeches refers to it as more pressing in Attica than in any other Greek state.[1]

In general it may be said that Athens got her wheat from whatever source was available. Barred from one market, she turned to another, and from time to time, if not always, supplies were obtained from Sicily, Euboea, Cyprus, Egypt, Thrace and, most important of all, in the fourth century Pontus.

Whether or not Athens got any considerable amount of wheat from Italy, or Magna Graecia, is difficult to say, although Gernet assumes that it was a regular source of supply, at least in the fifth century.[2] The only references which we have are obscure. Pliny quotes a line from the lost *Triptolemus* of Sophocles, "et fortunatam Italiam frumento canere candido",[3] and goes on to say that after the fourth century Greece no longer got wheat from Italy. The only other reference we have is that fragmentary decree concerning the colony of Miltiades on the Adriatic to which reference has already been made.[4] It is tantalising that so little is known of this colony; but the decree certainly does indicate a source of wheat supply and a protection against pirates in the Adriatic.[5] This decree refers probably to the year 325. It is hard to suppose that the supplies of wheat from Italy were in any case considerable; probably the timber trade was far more important.[6]

With regard to Sicily as a source of wheat supply in the fifth century, much uncertainty is apparent.[7] Undoubtedly wheat came thence to Greece early in the century, as Herodotus tells us that during the Persian wars Gelon, tyrant of Syracuse, offered to supply grain sufficient for the whole of Greece and a large army, if he were made commander-in-chief of the Greek armies, an offer which was refused.[8] That Athens received any supplies from Sicily in this century rests on no evidence whatever, and the theory of a "western policy" founded on keeping this trade route open cannot be substantiated. Undoubtedly

---

[1] *de Corona*, 87; *in Lept.* 31.
[2] *L'Approvisionnement*, 312–14.
[3] *H.N.* xviii, 65.   [4] Cf. p. 246.
[5] *Syll.*³ 305 = *I.G.* ii², 1629.
[6] Cf. p. 280. For further references to wheat from Italy cf. Thuc. vi, 103, vii, 14, 25.
[7] Hüttl, *Syrakus*, p. 20.
[8] Her. vii, 158. Cf. also Plut. *Coriolanus*, 16; Dion. Hal. iii, 1; Livy, ii, 34.

wheat was going to the enemies of Athens during the Peloponnesian war, and the Athenian expedition to Sicily in 427 to cut
off these supplies met with little success.[1] The great and disastrous
expedition to Syracuse twelve years later doubtless had as one
of its objects the stopping of grain supplies to the Peloponnese;
but since Athens was receiving sufficient for her needs from
Euboea and Pontus, it is hard to suppose that seizure of the
Sicilian wheatfields for her own supplies was in view, although
doubtless they would not have come amiss.

At the commencement of the fourth century with the invasion of the island by the Carthaginians, Sicily was too dis-
tracted by her own troubles to be a source of grain supply to
Greece; but by the end of the century trade had been restored,
as we know from various references. The case argued by
Demosthenes against Zenothemis, at an uncertain date but
after 355, deals with a shipment of wheat from Syracuse. We
also know from the case against Dionysodorus that it was the
arrival of grain ships from Sicily that broke the "corner" of
Cleomenes. Pliny tells us that Italian wheat was as popular in
Greece in the time of Alexander as it had been in the fifth
century.[2]

Turning now to Greece proper, we know that Boeotia was
rich in grain, and it is reasonable to suppose that Athens must
occasionally, if not regularly, have obtained wheat from that
source. Yet, curiously enough, we have no single reference to
Boeotian wheat reaching the Athenian market. Nor have we
any direct evidence of wheat from Thessaly, although we know
from Xenophon that, when Polydamas of Pharsalus asked
support from the Lacedaemonians, he referred to his country-
people "who from our abundance send out wheat to other
people".[3] The only other reference we have to wheat from
Thessaly is the incident of the Thebans when in need of supplies,
owing to the destruction of their own crops for two years in
succession, making a fruitless attempt to obtain ten talents
worth of grain from Pagasae, an attempt frustrated by their
enemies.[4]

---

[1] Thuc. iii, 86; cf. vi, 20; Diod. Sic. v, 2.
[2] *H.N.* xviii, 65. [3] Xen. *Hell.* vi, 1, 11.
[4] *Ibid.* v, 4, 56.

The place of Euboea in supplying Athens with grain and other foodstuffs was important, and it is unfortunate that we do not get a clearer view of it, since there are several obscurities which are very hard to clear up satisfactorily. Athens had early obtained a foothold in the island, which was subsequently strengthened by planting military colonies.[1] A revolt against Athens in 446 was promptly reduced by Pericles, and the island was finally lost in 411, after the seizure of Decelea by Agis of Sparta in 413. The loss of Euboea was a major disaster to Athens: "Euboea was everything to them...its loss caused a greater consternation than had ever been known before. For neither had the disaster in Sicily, though it had appeared a great one at the time, nor any other event yet alarmed them so much."[2] The reason for this intense alarm was the loss of the rich wheat lands and country estates.[3] Evidently Euboea had been exploited for all it was worth during the war, as a reference in Aristophanes shows where the demagogues promise 50 med. of wheat from Euboea for everybody, instead of the 5 of barley which was the best they could get.[4]

But how much of the wheat which ostensibly came from Euboea was actually raised on the island and how much came via Euboea from Pontus is impossible to say. The seizure of Decelea cut the land route from Oropus to Athens by which a considerable amount of grain reached the city.[5] Evidently Pontic wheat was freighted round the north of Euboea, via Histiaea, and landed at Oropus because, immediately after the seizure of Decelea, Athens fortified Cape Sunium, "that their wheat-ships might have a safe passage round",[6] and the Spartan commander Agis "when he saw many wheat-ships running into the Piraeus, said that it was no use for him and his troops to have been now so long a time excluding the Athenians from the command of their land, unless someone should also stop those from whom the sea-borne wheat was imported"; whereupon he sent an abortive expedition to seize the Hellespont.[7]

---

[1] Her. v, 77.   [2] Thuc. viii, 96.

[3] E.g. that of the son of Aristides, Plut. *Arist.* 27; Dem. *in Lept.* 115. Alcibiades kept his horses there and the Athenians sent their herds there on the invasion of Attica—Thuc. ii, 14.

[4] *Vespae*, 715–18.   [5] Thuc. vii, 28.

[6] Thuc. viii, 4. Bérard, *Les Phéniciens*, i, 41 f., discusses the question at length.   [7] Xen. *Hell.* i, 1, 35.

It is possible that this transport of Pontic wheat via Oropus was a war-time measure due to fear of enemy privateers way-laying the grain ships on the northern route. But that the Oropus-Decelea-Athens route was important at the moment is quite clear, and we have a tariff of transport rates which, although grain is not specifically mentioned, testifies to a close supervision on the part of the government.[1]

Evidently in the fourth century the trade in grain from Euboea was resumed, although on what scale is impossible to say.[2] There is an allusion in Demosthenes' speech on the Crown where he says that Philip had seized Thebes, Euboea and Byzantium, thus becoming "master of the wheat trade".[3] But, on the other hand, when in 376 Athens was blockaded by an enemy fleet cruising near Ceos, Andros and Aegina, we are not told that they seized Oropus, but that the Athenian ships could not get nearer than Geraestus at the extreme south end of Euboea.[4] It is probable, therefore, that the importance of the island either considerably declined or altogether disappeared as a source for wheat supply, its place being taken by Pontus and Egypt.

With regard to grain supplies from Cyprus, there are several obscurities which are difficult to clear up satisfactorily. How early this trade started is unknown, but it may reasonably be conjectured that the help given by Athens to the Cypriotes in revolt against the Persian conquerors in 450 was, partly at least, to secure the grain trade which had been interrupted; but this is quite uncertain in the absence of direct proof. We do know that, after the Sicilian disaster in 415, King Evagoras proved a good friend, and perhaps sent grain and ship's timbers.[5] In 386, at the close of the Corinthian war and the "King's Peace", the island was occupied by the Persians, and deliveries of wheat had been very irregular, leading to much distress in Athens owing to high prices, which occasioned the oration of Lysias in prosecuting the wheat dealers. In the great famine of 330–326 we have

[1] *I.G.* i², 40, 19ff. But cf. *I.G.* xii, 9, 1273–4. The whole question of the Oropus route is very obscure, and no satisfactory conclusion can be come to on it. Cf. Ziebarth, *Beiträge*, p. 123.
[2] Cf. Arist. *Rhet.* iii, 10, 1411 A.   [3] *de Corona*, 241.
[4] Xen. *Hell.* v, 4, 61; cf. Diod. Sic. xv, 34.
[5] Andocides, *De Reditu Suo*, 20, 21.

several references to the wheat trade from Cyprus. A Cypriote merchant named Heraclides had been captured by Dionysius of Heraclea, a city in the Black Sea, and his sails confiscated. Athens thereupon sent an embassy demanding return of the sails and non-interference with ships bound from Cyprus to the Piraeus.[1] In the same year the Athenians awarded a wreath of honour to a Cypriote trader and granted him diplomatic assistance, on the ground that, being the first grain merchant to reach Athens at the time of the famine, he delivered 3000 med. at a price of 5 drs. (the price in the open market having gone as high as 16); and furthermore had made a free-will donation of 3000 drs. to the city for the purpose of buying grain for the distressed populace.[2] It may be remarked, however, that we do not know for certain that this wheat actually came from Cyprus, but merely that the merchant was a Cypriote, which is quite a different thing. It is this very doubt that makes any decision with regard to Cyprus as a source of grain supply so uncertain. Did Athens use wheat actually grown in Cyprus, or was it wheat transhipped at Cyprus from Egypt or freighted via the island? It is very difficult to say, although we do know from Strabo that wheat was grown there.[3] Another inscription that belongs in the doubtful class in the fourth century refers to a convoy of grain ships from Cyprus.[4] It seems impossible to come to any definite decision on the point.

With regard to the Egyptian grain trade there is no doubt whatever. Supplies from Egypt were of long standing; but it is unreasonable to suppose, as has been suggested, that the founding of Naucratis was connected with that trade at so early a date when Greece, so far as we know, was not in a position to import wheat nor in any need of it.

The Persian wars interrupted whatever trade there was with Egypt, and in 460 a revolt against the Persian conquerors gave an opportunity to the Athenians to intervene. An expedition was sent up the Nile as far as Memphis, which was unsuccessful, and finally met disaster in 454. Nine years later, in 445, Psammetichus, a Libyan pretender to the Egyptian throne, anxious to secure the goodwill of Athens, sent a gift of 30,000

---

[1] *Syll.*³ 304 = *I.G.* ii², 360.   [2] *Ibid.*
[3] Strabo, xiv, 6, 5 (c. 684).   [4] *I.G.* ii², 407.

med. of wheat at a time of famine in Attica.[1] The whole episode
is far from clear and we know very little about it, except that
the reception of this gift was notable for the revision of lists
of citizens entitled to benefit therefrom, and the striking off of
5000 names from the register.[2] That both sides were receiving
grain from Egypt during the Peloponnesian war seems certain.
Dr Hasebroek's suggestion that the expedition to Cythera under
Nicias[3] was to intercept grain ships from Egypt and Libya is
very probably correct, if by Libya we understand Cyrenaica.
We know that in the last phases of the war, when the Spartans
had grasped the fact that the only way to bring Athens down was
to cut off her food supplies, and the help of Persia in money
and ship's timbers had enabled them to build fleets, one of the
strategic points seized was Cnidus, and that a squadron was sent
to cruise round Triopium, "to seize the merchantmen that were
approaching from Egypt".[4] The revolt of Rhodes in 411 was
also a serious blow, since it lay on the route from Egypt to the
Piraeus, a particularly favourable one since it, apparently, was
open in the winter when the Pontic route was closed.[5] In the
fourth century, as we have abundant evidence from Demosthenes, the grain trade between Egypt and Greece was active,
and the operations of the notorious Cleomenes brought not
only Athens but all Greece into great straits.[6]

With regard to wheat from Asia Minor not much is known,
but probably it reached Athens at an early date. We have a
decree of honour to some individual, whose name has not
survived, for sending wheat to Athens from that region in
319–318,[7] while another inscription speaks of importations of
wheat, probably from Mysia, in 349–348.[8] Athenaeus, quoting
Antiphanes, says that the finest sifted flour came from Phoenicia.[9]
There was wheat in plenty to be got from Thrace, "a country

---

[1] Philochorus, fragm. 90; Müller, *F.H.G.* 398–9.
[2] Plut. *Pericles*, 37; *C.A.H.* v, 102, 168.
[3] Thuc. iv, 53.
[4] Thuc. viii, 35.
[5] The point is not quite certain. Cf. Dem. *in Dionys.* 29, 30. Also Knorringa, *Emporos*, pp. 15, 94.
[6] This episode is dealt with at length hereafter, p. 275.
[7] *I.G.* ii², 398.
[8] *I.G.* ii², 207.
[9] Athen. iii, 127 B.

rich in agriculture".[1] The plain between the rivers Hebrus and Ergines was a rich one, and the grain could be expeditiously shipped from the port of Aenus. But the Thracian wheatfields were within the borders of the kings of the Odrysians, "too powerful to be coerced, too barbarous to be trusted".[2] Evidently towards the close of the fourth century Athens was getting wheat from Thrace, since Demosthenes tells us that Philip occupied the country as part of his plan to starve out Athens.[3] We also know from Lysias that wheat from the Thracian Chersonese (the modern Gallipoli) was being imported by one Diodotus, who had invested 2000 drs. in the trade.[4] Undoubtedly also we must suppose that grain supplies came to Athens from Chalcidice, a rich country which Xenophon says supported a large population through the fertility of its soil.[5] With Athens in control of Amphipolis it is reasonable that wheat as well as timber was exported, although we have no evidence of the fact.

The most important source of all, at least in the fourth century, not only for wheat but also fish, was the Pontic region of South Russia and the Crimea.[6] Wheat from that region was highly esteemed; it was harder than other varieties, made good bread and would last longer.[7] It is quite permissible to deduce from the anxiety of Peisistratus to maintain the tyranny of the Chersonesus, founded by Miltiades about 550, that he was quite aware of the fact, even at that early date, that control of the Straits was of prime importance;[8] another evidence being his seizure of Sigeum on the opposite shore at about the same time.[9] The capture of Lemnos and Imbros by the second Miltiades shortly afterwards was another step towards the complete control of the route from Pontus,[10] which, if Athens had been able to maintain it, would have put her in an extremely strong position. It does not seem, however, Athens made any attempt to monopolise the Pontic grain trade until much later.

---

[1] Isocrates, *de Pace*, 24; cf. also Ditt. *Syll.*³ no. 371.
[2] Adcock, *C.A.H.* v, 174.   [3] *de Corona*, 87.
[4] Lysias, *in Diog.* 15.   [5] *Hell.* v, 2, 16.
[6] Her. iv, 17. For Pontic wheat-growing cf. also Xen. *Anab.* vi, 4, 6; 6, 1; Theoph. *H.P.* viii, 4, 5.
[7] Arist. *Probl.* xiv, 909 A.   [8] Her. vi, 34ff.
[9] Her. v, 94. Cf. Busolt, *Griech. Gesch.* ii, 249, 316f., 374ff.
[10] Her. vi, 137, 140.

She was not strong enough to do so in any case until Aegina was subdued, and at the time of the Persian wars both Aegina and the Peloponnesus were drawing supplies from Pontus. As an example of conducting war "in the grand manner", the anecdote recounted with so much zest by Herodotus of the refusal of Xerxes to stop the ships sailing past Abydos laden with wheat for the Greeks, is inimitable.[1] It is significant that the earliest operations of the Greeks after the final defeat of the Persians at Mycale, was to free the Hellespont from their control and the seizure of Sestos in 479.[2] From that time onwards Athens was in virtual control of the Pontic route, and we may reasonably infer that the dismay caused by the decree in 432 that excluded Megara from the markets of the Athenian empire was very largely due to the closing of the Pontic ports to the Megarians and their allies. That every endeavour was made to keep on good terms with the Bosporian chiefs is evident. In 437 an adventurer Spartocus had become ruler of the Cimmerian Bosporus,[3] and Pericles seized the opportunity of gaining his friendship and impressing him with the might of Athens by going himself with a splendid squadron to visit the Propontis and Euxine. The embassy was a great success, as is evident from the goodwill which Spartocus and his son Satyrus showed to Athens. Athenian posts were established at Nymphaeum (the modern Eltegen on the straits of Kertch), which became highly prosperous, at Sinope, Amisus and Astacus on the Propontis. "So began a friendship which was to benefit both parties for a century. The corn-barons of the Crimea soon became amateurs of Attic pottery and terra-cottas, and from this time onwards Athenian wares are found in their houses and Attic writing in their inscriptions."[4]

Athens continued sedulously to cultivate the friendship of the Bosporian chiefs. In the middle of the fourth century a treaty was entered into with Leucon I, by which he granted freedom from duty to those carrying cargoes to Athens, and proclaimed

[1] Her. vii, 147. The incident is typical of the mentality of the Persian kings, another example being the gift of Myrcinus on the Strymon to Histiaeus, as recounted in Her. v, 23. This incident is further referred to on p. 280.
[2] Her. ix, 115; cf. Arist. *Rhet.* 1411 A, "Sestos the corn-bin of the Piraeus".
[3] Diod. Sic. xii, 31, 36, xiv, 93.
[4] Adcock, *C.A.H.* v, 174.

that merchants proceeding thither by sea should have priority in loading their ships.[1] He also established the port of Theodosia in the Crimea and made it free to Athenian ships,[2] a port so favourable for shipping, according to Strabo, that it was safe in the worst storms and could hold 300 ships at the same time.[3] The treaty was undoubtedly based on mutual concessions; but it is not perfectly clear what Athens gave in return. Evidently Leucon had had Athenian citizenship conferred upon him, and kept money on deposit in Athens.[4] We must, therefore, suppose that the Athenian government granted him exemption from taxation in the city.[5] The excellent relations with Leucon were maintained with his sons Spartocus II and Paerisades, who in 347–346 sent an embassy to Athens to announce that they would continue to see that wheat was sent thither as in the time of their father, and would at all times be ready to serve the needs of the city. The Athenians on their part granted them citizenship and freedom from taxation. High honours were paid to the envoys, and payment of money owing to the two sons of Leucon decreed.[6] Another treaty with the same Paerisades secured despatch of wheat duty-free from Bosporus.[7] With regard to this there seems some doubt as to whether wheat destined for Athens was entirely exempt from duty, since from another inscription[8] we learn that an export tax of $3\frac{1}{3}$ per cent was levied on all exports of wheat, but a drawback was granted to Athenian cargoes which reduced the rate to $1\frac{2}{3}$. The same privilege was granted to the Mytileneans up to a total of 100,000 med.; on all above that an additional tax of $1\frac{1}{9}$ per cent was added.[9]

To secure this route from the constant danger of pirates and seizure of the grain ships by other states, Athens occupied the islands of Imbros, Lemnos, Scyros, and maintained a large garrison on Andros. Constant patrol of the route was maintained by squadrons of warships,[10] at least 2000 sailors being on con-

---

[1] Dem. *in Lept.* 29 ff.　　　[2] *Ibid.* 33.
[3] Strabo, vii (c. 309).　　　[4] Dem. *in Lept.* 40.
[5] Hasebroek, *Trade and Politics*, pp. 113–14, discusses the question.
[6] *Syll.*[3] 206 = *I.G.* ii[2], 212.
[7] Dem. *in Phorm.* 36.　　　[8] *Syll.*[3] 212.
[9] For brief sketch of Greek trade with Pontus cf. Rostovtseff, *Greeks and Iranians in South Russia* (Oxford 1922), pp. 66 ff.
[10] Xen. *Hell.* i, 1, 36; repulse of the fleet from Megara by the squadron of nine ships "always on guard".

tinuous guard duty and, in times of war, twice or three times that number.[1] Officials called "Guardians of the Hellespont" (*Hellesponto-phylakes*) were stationed with guard ships in the Dardanelles to see that ships got through in safety, and inspect all cargoes. At the time of the Peloponnesian war Athens, so far as we know, "managed" the wheat supplies of her allies, as we see from an inscription with regard to Methone in the year 424–423.[2] This small town in South-west Macedonia, on the shores of the Thermaic gulf, had been in trouble with Perdiccas, king of Macedonia, and appealed to the good offices of Athens to intervene on its behalf. This Athens accordingly did, sending ambassadors to bid Perdiccas not restrict the trade of Methone by land or sea, nor to lead troops through its territory. A second decree records permission to Methone to import wheat from Pontus (the amount is uncertain owing to mutilation of the stone), upon giving notice to the Hellesponto-phylakes. The facts here are quite plain: Athens is protecting her ally, already having remitted some of the tribute due, and in token of further goodwill permits it to get some wheat which would otherwise have gone to the Piraeus. We may suppose that normally Methone was either self-supporting, or got its wheat from Macedonia; the trouble with Perdiccas had cut them off from this supply and they had to turn to the particular reserve of Athens to tide them over.[3]

Convoys (*Sitopompia*) of the grain fleets were provided by warships; Demosthenes speaks of a squadron of 20 such[4] and of another convoy which the Maroneans and Thasians claimed to join in.[5] In another passage he refers to payments received by the Athenian admirals from the Chians, Erythraeans and other sea-coast cities of Asia Minor for protection given.[6] The struggle against the pirates, and even states that seized the grain ships when faced with shortage, was a never-ending one. We know of Cimon's expedition against the Dolopians of Scyros, troublesome pirates, in 474.[7] Much later in the time of Demosthenes we have constant references to the necessity of

[1] Andreades, *Greek Public Finance*, p. 219, n. 2.
[2] *I.G.* i², 57.
[3] Cf. also *I.G.* i (2nd ed.), 28; ii (2nd ed.), 28.
[4] *de Corona*, 73.   [5] *In Polyc.* 20.
[6] *De Cherson.* 24 ff.   [7] Plut. *Cimon*, 8.

policing the seas. He speaks of decrees against those "violating the rights of merchants", and that the Melians had been fined ten talents because they had given harbourage to pirates,[1] and of a proposal of Philip of Macedon to co-operate with the Athenians in policing the sea.[2] That pirates were not alone involved in molesting the grain ships was seen in privateering, under state protection, of such cities as Byzantium, Chalcedon and Cyzicus, which seized grain ships in times of famine, in consequence of which prices rose considerably at the Piraeus.[3] The Rhodians, after the defeat of Athens at Chaeronea in 338, seeing a good opportunity for plunder, seized the grain ships on their way from Egypt to the Piraeus.[4] This led to so serious a situation in Athens that Demosthenes was appointed controller of the wheat trade, with what specific powers we do not know, but evidently they must have been extensive to cope with a national emergency.[5]

That these apparently high-handed seizures of grain by cities arose from real necessity and the actual fear of famine is attested by numerous instances. The difficulties of transportation were so great and the perils of the sea so frequent, that in numerous cases we find special measures being taken to insure the provision of grain to the inhabitants at prices not too exorbitant for them. Athens was successful through diplomatic means, when more high-handed methods were unavailable, in getting special privileges from the rulers of grain lands on the Euxine. The firm friendship that Pericles had established with Spartocus was repaid by permission to import grain from the Cimmerian Bosporus even in times of famine, when ships of other states had to leave empty.[6] Leucon was an even better friend in the fourth century, and is credited with the enormous gift of 2,100,000 med. of wheat, by which Athens made, characteristically, a profit of 15 talents.[7] We have already

---

[1] *In Theoc.* 53, 56.
[2] *De Halonn.* 14. A transparent trick to gain control of the seas according to Demosthenes.
[3] Dem. *in Polyc.* 6; (Arist.) *Oecon.* ii, 1346 B.
[4] Lycurgus, *in Leocr.* 18.   [5] Dem. *de Corona,* 248.
[6] Isocrates, *Trapez.* 20, 52.
[7] Dem. *in Lept.* 32, 33. The amount of the gift is incredible. Cf. Gernet, *L'Approvisionnement,* pp. 376 ff.; Kocevalov, *Rhein. Mus.* lxxxi (1932), pp. 321 ff.

mentioned the gift of Psammetichus in the fifth century, and in the fourth at the time of the great famine of 330–326, we find the city of Cyrene giving over 800,000 med. to be distributed among forty-three Greek states, of which 100,000 went to Athens.[1] A trader imported 10,000 med. which he sold at 5 drs. and donated a talent to the Treasury.[2] Such gifts, whether willingly given or under pressure, as is more likely, were common, and many other examples may be cited.[3] At a time of famine in Clazomenae, the government took vigorous measures for buying wheat in foreign markets, giving oil lent by private citizens as security for payment, and also hiring vessels to transport the grain.[4] Selymbria seems to have been guilty of particularly sharp practice, since a law had been passed forbidding the export of wheat at a time of famine, and, in consequence, found itself with a surplus. It then, at a price fixed by decree, bought all the wheat in the market, promptly repealed the law of export, and came out of the transaction with a handsome profit.[5] Byzantium seized passing grain ships, paid the owners 10 per cent on the price of the wheat it "commandeered", and when prices rose made a large sum on the sale.[6] An interesting inscription found at Teos, which seems to belong to somewhere about 470, gives a list of the curses which the magistrates every year pronounced upon wrongdoers. Such were poisoners, resisters of the law, magistrates guilty of brigandage or piracy or treasonable designs against the community, and those who prevent the importation of wheat into Tean territory or re-export it after it had been imported.[7]

ATHENS AND THE GRAIN TRADE

As has already been remarked, Athens was constantly preoccupied with the all-important problem of securing sufficient supplies of grain for her populace. So long as her navies were able to police the seas and keep the grain routes open, the

---

[1] For more on this cf. p. 277.   [2] Dem. *in Phorm.* 38.
[3] *I.G.* ii², 283, 342, 400, 407; vii, 42, 62 (Oropus); *Syll.*³ 354 (Ephesus), 493 (Histiaea), 495 (Olbia).
[4] Ps.-Arist. *Oecon.* ii, 1348 B, 16.
[5] (Arist.) *Oecon.* 1348 B, 33. The author delights in recounting such sharp practices.
[6] (Arist.) *Oecon.* 1346 B, 29.   [7] *Syll.*³ i, 37.

problem was no very difficult one. When her naval power declined, or when through famine prices rose to an exorbitant level, the matter became extremely serious and drastic measures were necessary. It is important to realise that the grain trade was always in private hands; and in spite of every endeavour to regulate it, the city was constantly in danger of being "held up". This led to outbursts of popular indignation against the grain merchants (*sitopolai*) and savage reprisals against their rapacity, actual or alleged. "These traders", says Xenophon, "from their desire of getting gain, sail in quest of it wherever they hear it is most abundant, crossing the Aegean, the Euxine and the Sicilian seas; and when they have got as much as they can, they bring it away with them, stowing in their own vessel in which they sail themselves. And when they are in want of money they do not dispose of their freight at hazard, or wherever they may happen to be, but wherever they hear that wheat will fetch the highest price and that men set the greatest store by it, they carry it thither and offer it to them for sale."[1]

If we are to believe what Lysias says in his speech against the wheat dealers, they had brought the business of the grain trade to a fine art, and were hated by the people in consequence. "Their interests are the opposite of other men's: they make most profit when, on some bad news reaching the city, they sell their wheat at a high price. And they are so delighted to see your disasters that they either get news of them in advance of anyone else, or fabricate the rumour themselves; now it is the loss of your ships in the Black Sea, now the capture of vessels on their outward voyage by the Lacedaemonians, now the blockade of your trading ports, or the impending rupture of the truce; and they have carried their enmity to such lengths that they choose the same critical moments as your foes to overreach you. For, just when you find yourselves worst off for wheat, these persons snap it up and refuse to sell it, in order to prevent our disputing about the price; we are to be glad enough if we come away from them with a purchase made at any price, however high. And thus at times, although there is peace, we are besieged by these men. So long is it now that the city has been convinced of their knavery and disaffection that, while

[1] Xen. *Oecon.* xx, 27–8.

for the sale of all their commodities you have appointed the market clerks as controllers, for this trade alone you elect special wheat-controllers by lot. And often you have been known to inflict the extreme penalty on these officials, who were citizens, for having failed to defeat the villainy of these men. Now, what should be your treatment of the actual offenders, when you put to death even those who are unable to control them?"[1]

This case is so interesting that it merits further attention. In 386 at the close of the Corinthian war and the "King's Peace", supplies of wheat from Cyprus had been very irregular, owing to the occupation of the island by the Persians. Consequently grain was scarce in Athens and prices so high that there was a great public outcry against the dealers responsible. Over the importers the state had no control; they could simply refuse to bring cargoes to the Piraeus.[2] But there was very strict control over the retailers, since it was decreed that only a specified amount could be bought at any one time, and the price to the purchaser should not exceed one obol per medimnus over the wholesale price. Although we have only the speech of Lysias to go on, it is not very difficult to perceive what had happened. Wheat was scarce and the importers were holding out for higher prices and, since the market was keenly competitive among the buyers, they were able to impose these exorbitant prices on them. Seeing what was happening, one of the magistrates, "that same sturdy old Anytus who had the misguided courage to bring Socrates to trial", had given permission to the buyers to form a combine to resist the exactions of the importers. This they did, evidently with good effect, since the importers engaged Lysias, the foremost advocate of the day, to prosecute the retailers on the ground of combination in restraint of trade, and with the further charge that they had taken advantage of the situation to raise the price to the public far above the legal maximum, making a profit not of one obol the medimnus, but one drachma, six times the amount allowed them by law.

---

[1] Lysias, xxii, 14–16 (Loeb translation). The case is discussed by Wilamowitz-Möllendorf, *Aristoteles und Athen*, ii, 374 ff.; cf. also Heichelheim's arts. "Monopole", p. 148, "Sitos", Supp. 6, pp. 837, 842 in *P.W.*

[2] E.g. one of the charges against Andocides was that although a shipowner he did not, like many Metics, bring grain to Athens after the disaster of Aegospotami. Lysias, vi, 49. Cf. Andoc. *de red. suo*, 11.

The speech by Lysias for the prosecution is a most interesting example of legal ingenuity. The plea that the retailers were acting on the orders of the magistrate is disposed of by saying that Anytus had only advised them not to compete among themselves so as to raise the price. What was an obviously wise counsel had been turned by them wickedly to their own advantage by buying in large quantities on common account, storing the wheat and then raising the price to the public. The specious argument "that it was in kindness to the city that they bought up the corn, so that they might sell it to you at as reasonable a price as possible", is brushed contemptuously aside by Lysias who says, "But I will give you a very strong and signal proof that they are lying. If they were doing this for your benefit, they ought to have been found selling it at the same price for a number of days until the stock they had bought up was exhausted. But in fact they were selling at a profit of a drachma several times in the same day, as though they were buying by the phormus at a time." The speech ends with a fine rhetorical flourish, accusing the retailers of being a set of rogues who fleeced the public at a time of scarcity and danger. It is always tantalising, as in the case of so many of the speeches of Demosthenes, that we have not the speech of the opposing counsel and the verdict. But it is quite evident that the whole case bristles with opportunities for the other side to put up an excellent plea for the defence.[1]

It is not exactly known when the *sitophylakes* were first appointed, but probably not till the fourth century.[2] "Formerly there were ten grain commissioners, elected by lot, five for Piraeus and five for the city; but now there are twenty for the city and fifteen for Piraeus. Their duties are, first, to see that the unprepared wheat in the market is offered for sale at reasonable prices; and secondly, to see that the millers sell barley meal at a price proportionate to that of barley, and that the bakers sell their loaves at a price proportionate to that of wheat, and of such weight as the commissioners may appoint; for the law requires them to fix the standard weight."[3] To

---

[1] Gernet, *L'Approvisionnement*, cap. iii, discusses the case at length.

[2] *Ibid.* pp. 365 f.; Glotz, "Die Zahl der Sitophulakes in Athen", *Klio*, xvi (1920), pp. 187 ff.; Heichelheim, art. "Sitos" in *P.W.*, Supp. 6, p. 842.

[3] Arist. *Ath. Pol.* li, 3.

prevent "cornering" of the market it was enacted that no dealer, under penalty of death, could buy at any one time more than 50 "phormoi" of wheat.[1] Lists were kept of the amount of wheat imported and in store, which were open to inspection, as Demosthenes tells us.[2] During periods of stringency extraordinary measures were made to control the supply under a board of managers (*sitonae*), who saw to the public distribution of wheat bought or seized by the state, selling from the public granaries at less than cost.[3] At a time of great national emergency a single controller was appointed, as was done in Athens after the battle of Chaeronea in the case of Demosthenes, as already noted. What his powers were and how successful he was in his office we do not know; but he was accused by Deinarchus of taking a bribe of 1000 med. of wheat a year from the Bosporian princes.[4] Further regulations included: (*a*) No inhabitant of the Athenian Empire could transport grain to any place but the Piraeus.[5] (*b*) "Bottomry" loans were permitted only on ships carrying grain.[6] (*c*) Only one-third of all grain brought to the Piraeus could be exported.[7]

With regard to taxation of imports of wheat it seems certain that the "fiftieth" or 2 per cent duty was levied upon it, since we hear in the speech against Neaera, attributed to Demosthenes, that one Xenoclides farmed the tax.[8] We do not know if this tax was removed at times of stringency, but it is reasonable to suppose so. As Gernet observes, it was a curious commentary on Greek public finance that the Athenians should have imposed a duty upon a commodity of such vital necessity as wheat. It is possible, however, that the tax may have been levied on wheat in transport and not on that destined for the city itself.

In conclusion, wheat was always, as it is now, greatly preferred to barley, and was invariably eaten when it could be

[1] Probably about 90 bushels. There is some doubt as to the exact amount of the phormus; cf. Gernet, *L'Approvisionnement*, p. 329; Sauciuc-Saveanu, *Cultura*, p. 125.

[2] *In Lept.* 32.

[3] Thuc. viii, 90; Dem. *in Phorm.* 37; *in Lept.* 32. Cf. Gernet, *L'Approvisionnement*, 375 ff.

[4] *Orat. in Dem.* 43.

[5] Dem. *in Phorm.* 37; Lycurgus, *in Leocr.* 27.

[6] Dem. *in Lacr.* 51.

[7] Arist. *Ath. Pol.* li, 4; cf. Gernet, *L'Approvisionnement*, pp. 370–2.

[8] Dem. *in Neaeram*, 27; cf. also Gernet, *L'Approvisionnement*, pp. 367–8.

procured. "We have no interest in barley since the town is full of wheat bread", says one of the speakers in the *Deipnosophists*.[1]

CLEOMENES AND THE GRAIN TRADE[2]

It would seem dramatically fitting that our survey of the grain trade before Alexander should end with a major disaster which brought Old Greece, and even a large part of the Aegean area, to the brink of starvation. Our knowledge of this event, while full in certain details, is imperfect in others. All that we can say with regard to the famine that occurred between 330 and 326 is that there is no certain evidence of a serious crop failure, but rather that the campaigns of Alexander not only interfered with the ordinary channels of trade but also drew away large supplies for the provisioning of his armies. The underlying cause of the scarcity therefore, so far at least as Attica was concerned, was the interruption of the regular deliveries of grain from the Bosporus.[3]

It is to be noted, however, that even before the situation became acute, Athens was having grave difficulties in obtaining supplies of grain owing to the unsettlement of the political situation, and that prices were rising very considerably. For instance we find a decree honouring two merchants of Heraclea who, in 335–334, brought wheat and barley from Sicily to sell in Athens at 5 instead of 9 drs. the medimnus.[4] Another honour decree concerns a Tyrian merchant, who also imported grain in 332–331,[5] and in 330–329 a merchant of Salamis in Cyprus is honoured for selling his grain at 5 drs. By 330 the shortage had become acute whether from crop failure or political disturbances,

---

[1] Athen. iii, 113 A; cf. also iii, 115 C.

[2] Dem. *in Dionys.* (lvi), *passim*; (Arist.) *Oecon.* ii, 1352 B; Ziebarth, *Beiträge*, p. 62; Jardé, *Céréales*, p. 180; Andreades, *Greek Public Finance*, pp. 243 f.; Arrian, *Anab.* vii, 23, 6; Andreades, *Bull. Corr. Hell.* liii (1929), pp. 10 f.; Van Groningen, *Aristote, le Second Livre de l'Économique*, pp. 183 ff.

[3] Rostovtseff, *C.A.H.* viii, 575. Cf. also Tarn, *C.A.H.* vi, 448; Westermann, "New documents in Greek and Roman history", *Amer. Hist. Rev.* xxxv, 17 ff., who also denies crop failures and attributes the crisis to price inflation, bad distribution and profiteering; Schwahn, *Rhein. Mus.* (1933), p. 255, n. 3. According to *I.G.* ii², 1672, the Attic crop of 329–328 comprised 363,460 med. of barley and 39,112½ of wheat, which was normal.

[4] *I.G.* ii², 408.   [5] *I.G.* ii², 342.

and the situation was seriously aggravated by the operations of Cleomenes of Naucratis, who had been appointed financial administrator of Egypt by Alexander. With a quick eye for the possibilities of the situation, according to the Aristotelian *Oeconomica*,[1] he bought up all the grain in Egypt and fixed his own price for it. He also perfected a system of obtaining early news with regard to prices in various markets, and through his agents could divert a cargo of grain to any port where it could obtain the highest price.[2] By these means he gained enormous profits but universal obloquy, which led to his downfall and execution after the death of Alexander,[3] who seems to have protected him.

A very interesting sidelight on the affair is cast by the case argued reputedly by Demosthenes against one Dionysodorus in the courts. Two partners, Darius and Pamphilus, had lent 3000 drs. to Parmeniscus and Dionysodorus on a ship which was to sail from Athens to Egypt and bring back a cargo of grain. On its arrival at the Piraeus both principal and interest were to be repaid. There was an express stipulation that no part of the cargo was to be unloaded at any intermediate port, which would be, in any case, contrary to Athenian law.

Parmeniscus sailed for Egypt, purchased his cargo of wheat and got as far as Rhodes on the return voyage. There he was met by a message from Dionysodorus to the effect that the price of wheat at Athens had fallen owing to the arrival of considerable quantities from Sicily. Parmeniscus, therefore, sells his cargo at Rhodes and, knowing that serious trouble would be awaiting him at Athens, does not return there, but spends the next two years getting freights wherever he can find them. Darius then sues Dionysodorus for the principal and interest on the 3000 drs. The defendant puts in a most ingenious defence, alleging that the ship had been badly damaged on the voyage from Egypt to Rhodes and could not safely continue to the Piraeus. He, therefore, offers to pay the principal and interest calculated as far as Rhodes, but denied further liability on the ground that the lenders were not entitled to recover anything unless the

---

[1] ii, 2, 39 (1352 A–B).
[2] Dem. *in Dionys.* 7 ff.; cf. Andreades, *Bull. Corr. Hell.* liii (1929), pp. 10 f.
[3] Paus. i, 6, 3.

ship arrived safely at the Piraeus. The plaintiffs reply that if the ship had been so seriously damaged as not to be able to continue her voyage, she could not have been repaired and continued in the carrying trade for the last two years. The whole affair was a piece of rascality they averred. "For you must know, gentlemen of the jury, that these men were agents and confederates of Cleomenes, the governor of Egypt, who from the time he received the government, has done immense mischief to your state, and still more to the rest of the Greeks, by buying up wheat and keeping it for resale at his own price, and these men have been acting in league with him." We do not know the verdict on the case, but the whole affair is so patently fraudulent, that we cannot doubt that it was for the plaintiffs.

In Athens very soon after Cleomenes began his operations, the seriousness of the situation got beyond private benefactions and the state was forced to take action. A commission was formed under the presidency of Demosthenes to raise subscriptions to a public fund for selling grain cheaply to the populace, Demosthenes himself giving a talent. It is quite evident that the situation became more and more serious until the operations of Cleomenes had to stop or widespread disaster through famine ensue. We know of help coming from Harpalus, the head of Alexander's civil administration.[1] But evidently the greatest assistance came from Cyrene, where an inscription records the despatch of the enormous amount of over 800,000 med. of grain to the various countries affected by the famine. As showing the extent of the shortage and the needs of the various peoples, it is worth recording the amounts sent to each. Epirus received 122,000 med.; Athens 100,000; Argos, Larissa and Corinth 50,000 each; Rhodes, Sicyon and Megara 30,000; Meliboea 28,500; Oetaea 21,400; Ambracia 16,500; Lesbos, Thera, Leucas, Ceos, Carystus 15,000 each; Cnossus 10,900; Aegina, Cythrus, Atragioi in Thessaly, Opis, Cydonia, Cos, Paros, Delphi, Tanagra, Gortyna, Elis, Acarnania 10,000 each; Cythera 8100; Phlius and Hermione 8000 each; Troizen and Plataea 6000 each; Astypalaea and Hyrtake 5000 each; Hiketyrioi 1000; Elyros in Crete 3000.

The whole episode is of great interest, and presents some

[1] Athen. xiii, 586, 596.

puzzling features, which our present knowledge does not allow us fully to clear up. The amount is so enormous as to suggest that the fertility and extent of agriculture in Cyrenaica was considerably greater then than in later times, and far beyond what is possible now, even though the shipments were extended over several years. We have no knowledge whatever of how the transaction was managed or financed, and must conclude that it was ordered by Alexander, who was alarmed at the distress of the various countries involved in the famine.[1]

THE TIMBER TRADE[2]

For a treeless country, or at least for one which, by nature or through deforestation, has little or no timber of sufficient size or quality for commercial purposes, the problem of securing adequate supplies of wood has always been, and still is, of paramount importance. Such was notably the case in Mesopotamia, a treeless country with the exception of the date palm, which is unsuitable for building purposes, where an age-long struggle was carried on for command of the timber growing in the foothills to the east of the Tigris.[3] Egypt, equally lacking in forests, was always striving to gain and hold the unrivalled timber reserves of Lebanon and Coele-Syria, from which the Phoenicians drew the materials for their naval and merchant marine.[4] To Greece, whose forests had early disappeared, the supply of ship's timbers was a matter of the gravest concern.[5] There were three articles of prime necessity in which the Greeks were not self-sufficient, slaves, grain and timber; and

[1] Cf. G. Oliverio, "La Stele dei Nuovi Comandamenti e dei Cereali", *Documenti Antichi dell' Africa Italiana*, ii, 1 (1933); Bickermann, *Phil. Woch.* (1930), p. 241; Westermann, *Am. Hist. Rev.* xxxv, 17ff.

[2] A. C. Johnson, "Ancient forests and navies", *Proc. Amer. Philol. Assoc.* (1927), pp. 199–209; Köster, *Das Antike Seewesen, passim*; C. Torr, *Ancient Ships*, pp. 31–7; Daremberg-Saglio, iii, pp. 1242–53, art. "Ligna", pp. 1626–33, art. "Materia"; E. C. Semple, "Ancient Med. Forests and Lumber Trade", *An. Ass. Amer. Geogr.* (1919), p. 13; Bérard, *Les Phéniciens*, i, 309.

[3] Cf. Köster, *Das Antike Seewesen*, pp. 51–4, for interesting pictures of timber transports with deckloads and rafts from palace of Sargon in Khorsabad 706 B.C.

[4] King Hiram of Tyre and his lumbering in the Lebanon—I Kings v. 9. For early export from Phoenicia to Egypt cf. H. Kels, "Aegypten", *Kultur-geschicte des Alten Orients*, i, 75, 111 n. 5, 114, 116ff.

[5] Cf. Arist. *Pol.* 1327 A, where he says the city must always import what timber it requires. For more on deforestation of Greece, see p. 82.

while we may suppose that the food supply was the most important of the three, yet we can see that adequate supplies of shipbuilding materials, especially timber, pitch, flax and wax, were vital to their existence, and that much of the strategy in war was directed towards securing these necessities and keeping open the trade routes along which they moved.[1]

Our knowledge of the sources of ancient timber supplies is fairly complete, owing to the writings of Theophrastus for the early period, and the *Natural History* of Pliny for the later or Roman era. Wood used for shipbuilding comprised fir, silver or white pine, Syrian cedar and Aleppo pine. Keels of triremes were usually made of oak or beech, a tough wood being necessary for the constant hard usage from beaching the vessels. For bentwood, Aleppo pine was used on account of its lightness, but mulberry, manna-ash, sycamore and acacia,[2] elm or white pine, were often preferred for their superior toughness. Plane wood was sparingly used because of its liability to decay. The cutwater and cathead were made of manna-ash, mulberry or elm; masts, yardarms and oars of silver pine.[3]

The chief problem was the supply of fir and Syrian cedar, of which the reserves were slender.[4] In Eastern Europe fir was found in abundance in parts of Thessaly and Macedonia, which accounts for their importance, the continuous attempts to obtain supplies from them and the efforts to conciliate the kings of Macedonia. In Asia shipbuilding supplies were obtained from Sinope, Amisus, Mysian Olympus, Mount Ida and Cilicia;[5] in the Euxine from Colchis, a territory, Strabo tells us, excellent for shipbuilding, with quantities of timber which was floated down the rivers to the coast.[6] The pines of Pontus were famous— "Pontica pinus, silvae filia nobilis".[7] In Phoenicia cedar came

---

[1] Mr Grundy, while justly stressing the importance of food supplies and their influence on the strategy of the Peloponnesian war, seems, curiously, to have almost completely ignored the importance of the timber supplies for the building of navies for both combatants.

[2] Sycamore and acacia were knotty and hard to work. The Egyptians had difficulty in using them, so built their ships of very short planks, 6 ft. long. Her. ii, 96; Köster, *Das Antike Seewesen*, p. 13.

[3] Theoph. *H.P.* iv, 1, 2, iv, 2, 8, v, 7, 1, 2; Ezekiel xxvii. 5–9.

[4] Theoph. *H.P.* iv, 5, 5, v, 8, 1–2.

[5] Hamascia in Cilicia grew fine cedars, which Antony gave to Cleopatra to build her fleet—Strabo, xiv, 5, 3 (c. 669).

[6] xi, 2, 17 (c. 498).   [7] Hor. *Od.* i, 14, 11.

from the forests of Lebanon. In Western Europe fir and silver pine of good quality were found in Latium, South Italy, and beech trees grew so large that a single log served for the keel of a Tyrrhenian trireme. Theophrastus considered the fir of Macedonia superior to all others because of its beauty, size and freedom from knots, which made it best for oars and masts.[1] Pliny in his *Natural History* says that the fir of the Alps and Apennines in his day was considered the finest. He also speaks of the fir forests of Gaul, and considers the Tyrrhenian fir superior to that of the Adriatic. Cedar from Crete, Africa and Syria was the best, but the biggest cedar logs came from Cyprus,[2] whose forests in the time of Strabo had been depleted for ship-building.[3] Liguria provided good timber, some of the logs being 8 ft. in diameter, and Pisa was famous for shipbuilding.[4] Sicily, in ancient times, was well wooded with pine and fir, especially on the slopes of Mount Etna.[5] The timbers for Hieron's "luxury liner", the *Syracosia*, came from the same well-wooded spot. The main mast was so enormous that a tree big enough for it could not be found until a swineherd by chance found one in the mountains of the Bruttei, and it was hauled down to the coast by the engineer Phileas of Tauromenium.[6]

The earliest ship's timbers for the Greeks probably, if not certainly, came from the Ionian coasts, where the Phaeacians and Taphians were famous seafarers, to be succeeded in later days by Corcyra. It was from this coast that Corinth got her ship's timbers, i.e. from Ambracia, Leucas, Epidamnus and Apollonia. The fleet that conquered the Persians at Salamis was built from timbers that came from this region, as well as from Sicily, Magna Graecia, or Southern Italy and Chalcidice. On a par with the complacency of Xerxes in letting wheat ships bound for Greece sail by him at Abydos was the proposal of Darius to reward Histiaeus, tyrant of Miletus, with the gift of Myrcinus on the Strymon, which was only prevented by the protests of those who pointed out that this port had splendid forests near by which could supply the Greeks with shipbuilding materials

[1] Theoph. *H.P.* v, 1, 7.   [2] *H.N.* xvi, *passim*.
[3] Strabo, xiv, 6, 5 (c. 684).
[4] Strabo, iv, 6, 2 (c. 202), v, 2, 5 (c. 223).
[5] Diod. Sic. xiv, 42.
[6] Athen. v, 206 F.

and oars.[1] At the battle of Salamis it is noteworthy that the squadrons in the Persian fleet came from countries where forests were plentiful, except Egypt, which got its ship's timbers from Phoenicia and Cyprus, and contributed a fleet next in size to the Phoenician contingent.[2]

After the Persian war Athens secured unrestricted access to the forests of Thessaly, Macedonia and Northern Asia Minor by driving the Persian garrisons from Europe and their fleets from the Aegean. As we have already remarked, the vital importance to Athens of food supplies and ship's timbers in the Peloponnesian war is apparent in the strategy displayed by both sides during that exhausting struggle. At the beginning of the war the enemies of Athens had little or no conception of fighting her at sea, but Corinth would doubtless have challenged the Athenian naval supremacy had not Athens by a master-stroke of strategy seized Naupactus, thus blockading the Corinthian gulf, and cutting off supplies of shipbuilding materials from the west. It was not until the Spartan allies got help from Persia and ship's timbers from Thessaly that they could effectually meet Athens on the seas.[3] The expedition of Brasidas into Chalcidice, and his capture of Amphipolis in 422, were designed primarily to cut off the supply of Macedonian timber from the Athenians, and give him materials for the construction of a fleet; a project rejected by the Spartans with that lack of the wider view of strategy which characterised them throughout.[4] Had Brasidas not been killed soon afterwards, it is entirely possible that the Peloponnesian war would have ended in the defeat of Athens eighteen years before the final catastrophe of Aegospotami. As Thucydides tells us, the capture of Amphipolis greatly alarmed the Athenians, and in 422 they made a treaty with Perdiccas of Macedonia[5] whereby Perdiccas agreed not to allow wood for oars to be exported to any other place than Athens, and that such timber, if sold to an ally of the Athenians, must be sent to Athens. This treaty was of very little help to them, since not long after Perdiccas quarrelled

---

[1] Her. v, 23.
[2] Her. vii, 89; W. W. Tarn, *J.H.S.* xxviii (1908), pp. 202 ff.
[3] Thuc. viii, 3; Xen. *Hell.* i, 24, vi, 1, 11.
[4] Thuc. iv, 107–8; Diod. Sic. xii, 68, 4.
[5] Thuc. iv, 132; *I.G.* i², 71; Hondius, *Suppl. Ep. Graec.* iii (1927–9), p. 14.

with Athens once more.[1] It was probably their failure to get adequate ship's supplies, of which pitch was of the greatest importance, that led Athens to turn to Sicily and Italy for timber. As Alcibiades told the Spartans, when he had deserted to them in 415, one of the objects of the Sicilian expedition was to obtain access to the forests of Southern Italy.[2] In the same year a Syracusan squadron burned a quantity of ship's timbers at Caulonia, on the east coast of Calabria, which had been got ready for the Athenians.[3] After the failure of the Sicilian expedition we may infer that the western sources of supply were definitely closed to Athens.

How important Macedonia was for its forests in the fourth century may be easily seen from the numerous references to treaties made with Macedonian kings. For instance, in 389, the cities of Chalcidice made a treaty with Amyntas of Macedonia whereby special permission must be obtained for the export of pitch and timber; this is particularly so in the case of fir timber, for which an additional permit must be obtained, which may be cancelled at any time.[4] Andocides asserted that King Archelaus of Macedonia had given him permission to cut as much wood for oars as he wanted and to export it, and Theophrastus[5] says that the "Boaster" brags that King Antipater of Macedonia had given him, as a special favour, permission to export duty free timber to build his house, evidently a great concession, and one to be boasted of. A similar permission given to the Athenian general Timotheus by Amyntas in 373 was one of the charges brought against him in the speech by Demosthenes.[6] The power in the hands of the rulers of Macedonia through their command of shipbuilding supplies was very great, as is shown by the rise of Olynthus when that city gained control of the trade in ship's timbers.[7] Demosthenes stressed the importance of keeping on good terms with Macedonia in order to have sufficient supplies of shipbuilding materials which, he said,

---

[1] Thuc. v, 80; cf. Heichelheim, art. "Monopole" in *P.W.* xvi, 156.

[2] Thuc. vi, 90.

[3] Thuc. vii, 25; cf. Schwahn, "Schiffspapiere" in *Rhein. Mus.* lxxxi (1932), p. 39.

[4] Hasebroek, *Trade and Politics*, p. 121; Andreades, *Greek Public Finance*, p. 142 (quoting Glotz); Ditt. *Syll.*³ 135.

[5] Andocides, *de Red. suo*, 11. Theophrastus, *Char.* 23.

[6] Dem. *in Timotheum*, 26.   [7] Xen. *Hell.* v, 2, 16.

could be bought at the cheapest price.[1] We can, therefore, easily understand that when Philip attacked Greece, Athens was unable to oppose him at sea, since its supply was entirely in his hands. When, at a later date, Demetrius Poliorcetes wished to re-equip the Athenian fleet, he sent enough material from the Syrian forests to build 100 triremes.[2] Athens made every effort to monopolise the trade in timber as part of her general commercial policy. The imports of such articles as entered largely into shipbuilding were under the control of the "Overseers of Commerce", and we are told by Pseudo-Xenophon that any country that possessed ship's timbers, iron, copper, wax, pitch or hemp was compelled to sell them to the Athenians, who would not allow them to be taken elsewhere or exported.[3]

Our knowledge of the transport of timber is imperfect.[4] We know that Hiram of Tyre used rafts,[5] but we can only suppose that for long voyages it was carried as a deck load. Theophrastus tells us that the Romans cut timber in Corsica and tried to get it away in the form of a great raft with fifty sails, but failed, since it broke up in open sea.[6]

---

[1] Dem. *On the Treaty with Alexander*, 28.
[2] Ditt. *Syll.*³ 334, i, 29–30. Plut. *Dem.* 10; Diod. Sic. xx, 46, 4. For further references to export of timber from Macedonia cf. Polyb. v, 89, 6; Pliny, *H.N.* xvi, 197.
[3] *Govt. of Athens*, ii, 11–13.
[4] Cf. Schwahn in *Rhein. Mus.* lxxxi (1932), p. 43.
[5] I Kings v. 9.
[6] *H.P.* v, 8, 2. For timber transport on Nile cf. M. Merzagora, "La Navigazione in Egitto", *Aegyptus*, x (1929), pp. 137f.

CHAPTER VIII

TRADE IN VARIOUS PRODUCTS. GREEKS AND PHOENICIANS. PIRACY

TRADE IN VARIOUS PRODUCTS

WHILE our knowledge of the grain and timber trades is fairly detailed because of their importance to Athens, we have only scattered references to various other articles which entered largely into the trade of Athens.

FIGS[1]

How far dried figs were an article of commerce is impossible to say, since our knowledge is very meagre. We do know that Solon forbade their export, a fact which Plutarch tells us was regarded with incredulity in his time, which seems to point to an export trade in them.[2] Since figs grew everywhere, it is hard to suppose that they were an important article of commerce. Athenaeus gives a lengthy catalogue of various sorts.[3] We hear of figs from Caria preserved in an earthenware crock, evidently a dainty, which the sailor brings home for his faithless love.[4] We also hear of Attic figs exported to Babylon,[5] where they did not grow.[6] The term "sycophant" puzzled the Greek etymologists. The explanation that it meant an informer who denounced an exporter of figs from Attica was doubted even in the time of Athenaeus.[7] In the Hellenistic era we hear of Amitraghata, king of India, asking Antiochus to send him figs, wine and a philosopher. Apparently he got the first two but no philosopher.[8]

OLIVE OIL

Olive oil, a prime necessity in all Mediterranean countries where animal fats were scarce, and serving as a lubricant,

---

[1] Art. "Feige" by Olck in *P.W.*
[2] Plut. *Solon*, 24.
[3] iii, 74 Cff.; Poll. vi, 81.
[4] Lucian, *Dial. Meret.* xiv.
[5] Plut. *Reg. et Imp. Apoph.* 173 C.
[6] Her. i, 193.
[7] Athen. iii, 74 E; Boeckh, *Die Staatshaushaltung der Athener*, i, 54.
[8] Athen. xiv, 652 F, 653 A.

emollient taking the place of soap, lard and butter, and as an illuminant, was an article of prime importance in commerce. The numerous references to it in the Bible are evidence of its indispensable character in Palestine, where the sale was a royal monopoly. In Attica, whose soil was unfavourable to grain culture, the olive tree found a congenial home, and the export of the oil and the manufacture of earthenware jars as containers was one of the principal industries. Solon was credited with having introduced the cultivation of the tree into Attica, but this is obviously mythical, as it was known for centuries before his time.

In a region in which the production of the commodity was so general, it is natural that we should find only scattered references, and those often dealing with extraordinary circumstances. For instance, in the Aristotelian *Oeconomica* we are told that Heraclea bought oil and other commodities on credit, and that Clazomenae bought wheat in foreign markets, giving oil in exchange which the city had borrowed from private citizens.[1] On the coasts of Anatolia, in the rich river valleys running down to the sea, the olive tree flourished. The oil of Miletus was famous from early times, Aristotle telling the story of Thales the philosopher who, as a practical object lesson on what he could do when put to it, anticipating in Miletus and Chios a large crop in the next year, bought up all the olive presses which he subsequently hired out, making a large profit on the transaction.[2] We hear again of oil from Miletus in the third century being imported into Egypt. One ship, belonging to Theon, was loaded with 255 big and 101 half jars of Milesian oil; the ship of Aeropus had 122 jars of Milesian and Samian oil and 140 half jars. Another smaller ship had 143 Milesian jars and 34 half jars. Under the Ptolemies there was a very strict oil monopoly, and the whole of this cargo had to be sold at the set price of 46 drs. the metretes.[3] Another reference from the same source tells of a ship coming to Alexandria laden with oil from Syria or Palestine.[4] In Cyrenaica the cultivation of the tree was most successful, Theophrastus saying that the fruit was excellent and oil abundant.[5] Later, in the second century, we have an

---

[1] *Oecon.* ii, 1347 B, 1348 B.   [2] *Pol.* i, 1259 A.
[3] Pap. Cair. Zenon. 59012.
[4] *Ibid.* 59077 (267).   [5] *H.P.* iv, iii, 1.

inscription of honour to an unknown Metic who, in 175–176 at a time of failure of the olive crop, had brought a cargo of oil to the Piraeus where he had sold it at a cheap price to the city, although offered a higher, instead of taking it to Pontus to exchange for a cargo of wheat. In the Hellenistic era there was an important oil market at Delos and the fluctuations in price were severe.

THE FISH TRADE[1]

Fish, as an article of diet, and the trade in fish were so important to the Greeks that they demand particular notice. Plato was the first to observe that, while Homer mentions fishing, he never says anything of eating fish,[2] and from that time onwards it has always been inferred that in the Homeric age fish as an article of food was despised. That view is, at least partially, confirmed by two passages, the first when the castaways on the island of Pharos have to betake themselves to fishing as a last resort,[3] and when Odysseus and his men were starving on Trinacria and were forced to snare birds and catch fish.[4] It must be observed, however, that these two instances are hardly convincing. It may well be that the Homeric Greeks, who were essentially landsmen and meat eaters, knew little of fishing and were unhandy in their efforts to catch fish, or at least the followers of Odysseus were, who, we may suppose, were unprovided with lines and nets. But the assertion that they despised fish, and would only betake themselves to such distasteful food when they could get no other, is hardly confirmed by two other passages. The man who fears the gods is blessed with the kindly fruits of the earth and the sea gives its store of fish to him.[5] Another tells of fishing, and affords the curious information that first the horn of an ox must be dropped in, presumably to attract the curiosity of the fish.[6]

---

[1] D. Bohlen, *Die Bedeutung der Fischerei für die antike Wirtschaft*; arts. "Fischereigewerbe" by Stöckle in *P.W.*, Suppl. iv, and "Thynnos" by Steier.

[2] *Rep.* iii, 401; cf. Plut. *de Iside et Osir.* 8.
[3] *Od.* iv, 368.   [4] *Od.* xii, 331.
[5] *Od.* xix, 113.
[6] *Od.* xii, 251; cf. Bluemner, *Griech. Privataltertümer*, p. 28, n. 3, p. 226, n. 2.

But if a fish diet was little resorted to in the Homeric age, in later times fish as an article of food was a passion with the Greeks, who ate anything and everything from barnacles to whales, including cuttle-fish, which were regarded as a delicacy. The third book of Athenaeus recounts an astonishing catalogue of every conceivable species that reached the tables of rich and poor, and the appropriate ways of cooking and serving were the especial care of the gourmet. They preserved every species and quality, from jars of precious pickle, which corresponded to caviar and anchovy, to dried lumps, answering to the modern stock-fish.[1] Sturgeon, beluga or white whale, mackerel, tunny and mullet were all sent to Greece, and later to Rome from the fisheries of the Sea of Azov and the Black Sea.[2]

Exports of dried or pickled fish from Pontus and Propontis were of great importance, for these were the fishing grounds for tunny and sturgeon. The Sea of Azov was, and is now, one of the principal breeding places for tunny from whence, swimming through the straits of Kertch, the shoals circle the southern shores of the Black Sea, making their way into the Sea of Marmora by Constantinople. It is evident that the breeding habits had been carefully studied, and Strabo has a good deal to say on these migrations.[3] All along the route were situated towns for whom tunny fishing was of prime importance. Demosthenes tells us of a peasant from Panticapaeum who had a supply of fish to sell in Theodosia.[4] On the coasts of the Chalybes fishing was carried on.[5] Fish curing was an important industry at Dioscurias, where salt was plentiful.[6] Phasis, on the coasts of Colchis, made fishing nets.[7] Trapezus[8] and Sinope were busy centres, more especially the latter, where curing was an important industry,[9] also Heraclea,[10] Chalcedon[11] and Byzantium. The last was so important that we have a number of references to fishing and curing there. It was called "the metropolis of

---

[1] Athen. iii, 116.
[2] E. H. Minns, *Scythians and Greeks*, cap. ii.
[3] vii, 6, 2 (c. 320).
[4] *In Lacr.* 31; cf. Strabo, vii, 6, 2 (c. 320).
[5] Strabo, xii, 3, 19 (c. 549).
[6] Strabo, xi, 5, 6 (c. 506).   [7] Xen. *de Venat.* ii, 4; Poll. v, 6.
[8] Strabo, vii, 6, 2 (c. 320).
[9] Diod. Sic. i, 91; Strabo, xii, 3, 11 (c. 545).
[10] Aelian, *Nat. An.* xv, 5.   [11] Athen. vii, 329 A.

the tunny".[1] On the north coasts of the Black Sea we hear of the fish trade at Olbia, where there was a big fish market.[2] The mouths of the rivers emptying into the sea were particularly favourable as fishing grounds and salt was plentiful for curing. There were the rivers Borysthenes, the modern Dnieper;[3] the Ister or Danube[4] and the Tanais or Don, flowing into the Sea of Azov.[5] Strabo tells of fishing through the ice in winter[6] and Aelian of fishing in summer from boats.[7]

Miletus had a flourishing fishing industry.[8] On the coasts of Greece we hear of tunny curing at Megara;[9] at Sicyon in Argolis;[10] of fishing off the coasts of Euboea[11] and at Chalcis[12] and Eretria.[13] The fisheries of Corcyra were so important that the city gave a thank-offering to Delphi for a good catch.[14] The western coasts of Italy were famous for the great shoals of tunny which swam southwards to the Straits of Messana, where they met the currents by Scylla which prevented them reaching Sicily,[15] although fisheries on the Sicilian coasts were numerous.[16]

Greek colonies in the Western Mediterranean were busy with the industry, for instance, Messana,[17] Tauromenium,[18] Syracuse[19] and Selinus,[20] while there are several references to fishing at Massalia.[21] Fishing along the coasts of Spain, for instance at Nova Carthago, the modern Cartagena, is frequently mentioned.[22]

---

[1] Archestr. fragm. 20 (21, 4). Cf. Athen. iii, 116 B, 118 C, vii, 307 B; Polyb. iv, 43, 44; Strabo, vii, 6, 2 (c. 320); Pliny, *H.N.* ix, 50f. Also art. "Byzant (3)", in *P.W.* p. 1142. Arist. *Pol.* 1291 B; Tac. *Ann.* xii, 63, 2. A back-eddy from the Bosporus current swirled the fish towards the shore. Cary's note in Tozer's *Hist. Anc. Geog.* p. ix.

[2] Ditt. *Syll.*[3] i, 506; cf. art. "Salsamentum" in *D.S.*

[3] Her. iv, 53; Pliny, *H.N.* ix, 45; Pomp. Mel. ii, 1, 6.

[4] Athen. iii, 119 A.

[5] Strabo, xi, 2, 2 (c. 493); Pliny, *H.N.* xxxii, 146, 149.

[6] Strabo, vii, 3, 18 (c. 307); cf. Her. iv, 53.

[7] *Nat. An.* xv, 5.   [8] Diog. Laert. *Thales*, 28.

[9] Athen. vii, 295 C.

[10] Athen. i, 27 D; vii, 288 D, 289 A, 293 F.

[11] *I.G.* xii, 9, 166.   [12] Athen. vii, 330 B.

[13] Athen. vii, 295 D, 284 B.   [14] Paus. x, 913, 4.

[15] Strabo, i, 2, 15 (c. 24).

[16] Athen. i, 4 B, C, iii, 116 F, vii, 302 A. Cf. Juv. v, 99.

[17] Athen. iii, 92 D, vii, 313 A.

[18] Juv. v, 93.

[19] Athen. vii, 300 E.   [20] Athen. vii, 328 C.

[21] Strabo, iv, 1, 6 (c. 181), iv, 18 (c. 184); Aelian, *Nat. An.* xiii, 16; Dio Cassius, xl, 54; Oppian, *Hal.* iii, 620.

[22] Strabo, iii, 4, 6 (c. 158); Pliny, *H.N.* xxxi, 94.

Look-out places (*Thunniskopeia*) were found at Volaterrae and Cosa,[1] and another on the coast of North Africa by the Syrtes.[2] Quoting Polybius, Strabo states that the tunny congregated in the Mediterranean on the coasts of Iberia outside the pillars of Hercules, feeding on the acorns of the "sea-oak" and the purple fish or murex.[3]

When ready for shipping the dried or pickled fish were handled by wholesalers (*Tarichemporoi, Tarichegoi*),[4] and then by retailers (*Tarichopolai*).[5] The making of jars as containers for pickled fish was an important industry, especially as we are told they had to be broken before their contents were extracted.[6] Pickled fish were cheap, the food of the poor, of slaves[7] and as military rations.[8] Sea fish was preferred to fresh-water, except eels from Lake Copais. Athenaeus gives us a long list of varieties sold in the Athenian market, such as mussels from Pontus, sprats from Carystus, sea bream, or braize, and crayfish from Eretria, smoked fish from Gades, conger eels from Sicyon, capros aper or boar fish from Argos, and a host of others. Fishmongers were a rough lot, cheats and cut-throats,[9] and a sharp look-out had to be kept on them by the police and market officials to prevent swindling. One ordinance forbade them watering the salt fish.[10] Smoked and dried varieties were wrapped in fig leaves.[11] Aristophanes tells of the market in the city where the best kinds were sold and a gentleman could with propriety make his purchases in person.[12] At the Piraeus was another market where the coarser kinds were on sale. Becker in *Charicles* has a spirited scene in the market. The Athenians were so enthusiastic over the trade in salt fish from Pontus introduced by Chaerophilus, a Metic, that they honoured his sons with citizenship,[13] and Alexis tells us the names of two famous fishmongers, Euthynus and Pheidippus.[14]

---

[1] Not the island of Cos as Dr Andreades states: p. 147, n. 8.
[2] Strabo, v, 2, 6 (c. 223); xvii, 3, 16 (c. 834).
[3] iii, 2, 7 (c. 145). "Sea-oak" not known; some form of sea-weed.
[4] Diog. Laert. *Vit. Bion.* iv, 46; *Alex.* 218.
[5] Athen. iii, 118 E, vii, 339 D; Plut. *Quaest. Conv.* ii, 1, 4; Lucian, *Vit. Auct.* 11; Poll. vii, 27. Cf. also Athen. 225 A, 226 B.
[6] Synesius, *Epist.* 147, p. 285.
[7] Poll. vi, 49.
[8] Aristoph. *Acharn.* 967.
[9] Athen. vi, 224 E.
[10] *Ibid.* 225 C.
[11] Suidas, *s.v.* Thria.
[12] *Vespae*, 789; *Ranae*, 1068.
[13] Athen. viii, 339 D, ix, 407 E.
[14] Athen. iii, 119 F.

MARBLE

Marble of various sorts is plentiful in the Mediterranean basin, and affords an important object of trade.[1] Among the natural resources of Attica, Xenophon speaks of marble. "Nor is the land superior only in things that grow up and decay every year, but also has permanent riches; for marble comes from it in abundance from which the most magnificent temples, the most beautiful altars and the finest statues of the gods are made, which many both Greeks and barbarians desire to have."[2] As a matter of fact marble from the quarries at Hymettus and Pentelicus in Attica was not of the finest quality.[3] Marble from the island of Paros was considered the best for sculpture,[4] and references to it are very numerous. It was a source of great wealth to the island, which was very rich, and among the members of the Delian League paid the largest tribute of 30 talents.[5] Pliny in his *Natural History* gives a long list of celebrated marbles. Parian marble was known as "Lychnites" because the quarries were underground and had to be worked by lamp-light. He mentions marbles from Thasos, Lesbos, Chios, the last supplying spotted and variegated varieties. The marble of Proconnesus covered the walls of the palace of Mausolus at Halicarnassus; marble from Carystus, and a black variety from Melos, which probably may be meant for Chios.[6] Naxos was and still is famous for its emery, and was noted for its sculptors. A beautifully variegated kind was found at Carystus at the foot of Mount Oche in Euboea; near by were the quarries of Styra and Marmarium, in which columns of Carystian marble were cut.[7] In the Troad was quarried a white variety at New Proconnesus.[8]

TEXTILES

The trade in textiles was considerable and the industries connected with their use widespread and important. Linen was

---

[1] Cf. art. "Steinbruch" in *P.W.* iii, 2241 ff.
[2] *Revs.* i, 4. [3] Plato, *Eryxias*, 6.
[4] Strabo, x, 5, 7 (c. 487).
[5] For other references to Parian marble, Athen. v, 205 F; Diod. Sic. ii, 52.
[6] *H.N.* xxxvi, 9 ff. [7] Strabo, x, 1, 6 (c. 446).
[8] Strabo, xiii, 1, 16 (c. 589).

expensive, the flax from which it was made being mostly imported from Colchis, Asia Minor and Egypt, but some was grown in Macedonia and Thrace. Byssus, which has been erroneously identified with cotton, was almost certainly a coarse cloth manufactured from flax; it is unknown when it was first introduced into Greece. Cotton was either unknown before the first century or very rare. Silk was first brought to Europe from Asia after the conquests of Alexander. Hemp was plentiful among the Scythians, and the Greeks probably got their supply for ropes from the Euxine.[1]

By far the most important textile product was wool, from which garments were universally manufactured. Originally a domestic industry, and always predominantly the work of the women in the home, there is, however, ample evidence that a flourishing trade was carried on in the finished products. Such woollen fabrics as did enter into international trade must have been luxury articles, special weaves such as those of Miletus or Amorgos, for which Greek exquisites like Alcibiades, or fashionable women, Hetaerae no doubt, were willing to pay a very high price.

Sheep were raised almost everywhere in the mountainous districts of Aetolia, Acarnania, Arcadia, Thessaly, Boeotia, the Megarid, Euboea, Samos, Cos, Cyprus, Sicily and Magna Graecia. Much wool was imported from Lydia, Phrygia and the shores of the Euxine. In Hellenistic times wool from Spain was famous, Strabo saying that the sheep of Turdetania yielded a raven-black product of surpassing beauty, and that rams were worth a talent apiece.[2] Gallic wool was rough and "flocky".[3] Wool from Italy was soft and fine from the district around Mutina and the River Scultenna (the Panaro in its lower course). Ligurian wool was coarse. A product of medium quality came from Patavium, the modern Padua, from which carpets and rugs were made.[4] Excellent wool came from Brundisium.[5] Gazelonitis in Cappadocia Pontica yielded a very soft wool, the sheep being wrapped in skins to prevent the fleece from becoming

---

[1] The use of these materials is more fully discussed under Industry.
[2] iii, 2, 6 (c. 144).
[3] iv, 4, 3 (c. 196), i.e. Transalpine Gaul.
[4] v, 1, 12 (c. 218).
[5] vi, 3, 6 (c. 282).

coarse, a practice still preserved in Mediterranean regions.[1] The country round Laodicea produced, he says, sheep that were excellent for the softness of their wool, surpassing even the Milesian in quality. From them Laodicea derived much revenue, as did also the neighbouring Colosseni, Colossian wool being dyed purple or madder red.[2]

Miletus was the most famous of all wool markets, producing fabrics renowned for their fineness[3] as well as tapestries for wall-hangings.[4] Fabrics from Miletus were greatly favoured at Sybaris which, we may suppose, afforded the Milesians so rich a market that when news of the destruction of the city came to Miletus the grief of the people was so great that they showed it, in a somewhat remarkable fashion, by shaving their heads.[5] Another famous place of manufacture was Amorgos, where a fabric, possibly but not certainly of wool, was made which was highly prized.[6] We hear of a valuable slave at Athens who was able to work the tissues of Amorgos and sold them in the market.[7] They were very expensive and rare, as the inventory of the temple of Artemis Brauronia shows.[8] Carpets came from Cyprus, evidently of artistic worth, since we hear of one at Delphi signed by its maker, Helicon son of Acesas.[9] Aristophanes speaks of a vestment from Crete,[10] and there is mention of one such worn by the king Archon at Athens.[11] Megara specialised in rough fabrics fit for slaves' clothing.[12] The woollens of Pellene were famous and sometimes given as prizes at the games.[13]

---

[1] Strabo, vi, 3, 6. Also in Attica and Tarentum, Varro, ii, 2, 18.

[2] Strabo, xii, 8, 16 (c. 578).

[3] Aristoph. *Lysist.* 724; *Ranae*, 542; Athen. i, 28 B. Cf. J. Röhlig, *Der Handel von Milet*, Phil. Diss. Hamburg (1933), pp. 12, 22, 37.

[4] Athen. xv, 691 A; cf. also xii, 519 B, 540 C. Verg. *Georg.* iii, 306, iv, 334; Aelian, *Nat. An.* xvii, 34.

[5] Her. vi, 21. Perhaps this interpretation of the passage attributes the sorrow of the Milesians to somewhat too sordid motives. Possibly the grief of the Athenians at the destruction of Miletus, with unpleasant consequences to the tactless Phrynichus, may also be attributed to regret at not being able to get Milesian fabrics as heretofore. Cf. *Od.* iv, 198; *Il.* xxiii, 141.

[6] Aristoph. *Lysist.* 150, 735; Poll. vii, 5, 7. The material of which these garments were made is uncertain.

[7] Aeschines, *in Timarch.* 97.

[8] *I.G.* ii², 1514–31.

[9] Athen. ii, 48 B.

[10] *Thesm.* 730.

[11] Poll. vii, 77.

[12] Aristoph. *Acharn.* 519; *Pax*, 1002; Xen. *Mem.* ii, 7, 6.

[13] Aristoph. *Aves*, 1421.

FURS AND HIDES

A question that has been discussed by several writers is whether or not the Greeks wore or trimmed their clothes with fur. Obviously in a warm climate furs were not necessary, but M. Besnier in his article "Pelles" in *Daremberg-Saglio* asserts that furs from Libya and Sarmatia were highly prized by the Greeks. To this Mr Minns retorts that none were exported from South Russia.[1] We need not doubt that furs were used by Greeks living on the shores of the Euxine, and very possibly they were an article of commerce on the north-eastern caravan routes to China.[2] Herodotus speaks of the Budini living in the Caspian region who hunted otters and beavers and, a very modern touch, sewed their fur on the borders of their cloaks.[3] *Serika Dermata* from the Himalayas and Pamirs are mentioned in the *Periplus of the Red Sea*. It is to be noted that Pliny has several references to *Pelles*, which he says were dyed by those mysterious people the Seres. But it must be acknowledged that his use of the word does not clearly indicate furs but possibly only leather.[4]

Hides were a highly important article of commerce for Greece, where a scarcity of cattle made leather a very desirable commodity. The most important sources were Cyrene and South Russia.[5] In the speech of Demosthenes against Phormio we hear of a deck-load of 1000 hides being shipped at Bosporus. The tanning business at Athens was an important one, at least two famous men belonging to it, Cleon, the demagogue, who had inherited it from his father, and Anytus, the accuser of Socrates, who had also inherited a tannery and a large fortune.

WINE

The wine trade, as affording the universal beverage of the Mediterranean, was most important, especially as the wines of Greece were highly to the taste of the Egyptians and the inhabitants of South Russia and the lands bordering on the

---

[1] *Scythians and Greeks*, p. 441.
[2] Cf. Speck, *Handelsgeschichte des Altertums*, i, 117; Ebert, *Reallex. d. Vorgesch.* viii, 146; Schwahn, *Rhein. Mus.* lxxix (1930), p. 326.
[3] Her. iv, 109.
[4] *H.N.* xii, 2, xxxiv, 145, xxxvii, 204.
[5] Strabo, xi, 2, 3 (c. 493); Minns, *Scythians and Greeks*.

Euxine. Thus we know from Demosthenes that wine was taken to Pontus from Peparethus, Cos, Thasos and Mende.[1] The stamps on the wine jars found about the Euxine are most frequently those of Thasos and Rhodes, those of Cnidus and Paros less numerous.[2] Thasos was a famous centre of the wine trade, and we have an inscription with regard to its regulation. The sale of the grape crop was forbidden before it was reaped in May and June; the purchase of wine was only legal if the jar was sealed; no Thasian ship might bring foreign wine between Athos and Pacheies.[3] From Thasos the Egyptian Zenon bought wine, also from Cnidus, Chios, Leucas and Lesbos. From the last the brother of Sappho took wine to Naucratis.[4] Naxos was rich in vineyards, and was the centre of the worship of Dionysus;[5] Cnidus had a flourishing transit trade in wine.[6] In the list of articles from which the island of Cos derived a revenue is wine from Calymnus, a dependency of Cos, and "wine at sea", an obscure phrase which may mean wine exported or perhaps wine mixed with salt water, so as to preserve it and give it the taste of old wine.[7] The wine of Corcyra was famous, so much so that the sailors of Mnasippus would drink no other.[8] These are, however, but scattered references where the cultivation of the grape was widespread, and where, if the crop was particularly abundant, the surplus was exported to other markets.

TRADE IN POTTERY

At a time when neither the wooden cask nor the modern iron drum was used, the earthenware jar and the more artistic vase were universally employed as containers not only for liquids, such as wine or oil, but for anything that required preserving, such as pickled fish and even threshed grain. Wherever the wine or olive oil of Greece or the islands went they were carried in

---

[1] *In Lacr.* 35; Athen. xi, 484 c. The coins of Mende bear a vine as their symbol. Those of Torone, Thebes, Corcyra, Chios, Opus and Melos show wine amphorae. Athenaeus, i, 28, gives a long list of Greek wines.

[2] Minns, *Scythians and Greeks*, p. 359.

[3] Ziebarth, *Beiträge*, p. 75.

[4] Strabo, xvii, 1, 33 (c. 808); Athen. xiii, 596 B.

[5] It is interesting to note that Naxos in Sicily struck coins with a head of Dionysus on one side and a bunch of grapes on the other.

[6] Francotte, *L'Industrie*, i, 54.

[7] A common practice; cf. p. 192 for more on adulterants.

[8] Xen. *Hell.* vi, 2, 6.

earthenware jars, or amphorae, and since trade in these commodities was very widely extended, Greek amphorae are found
everywhere round the Mediterranean and the Black Seas and
even farther afield. Along with these purely utilitarian containers went the products of the fine potteries, high-class
earthenware for use in the house, and the prized masterpieces
of the finest artists. Greek potters were renowned in the ancient
world, and their products were eagerly bought far from their
place of origin.

The whole question of the trade in pottery is highly complicated and bristles with innumerable difficulties; indeed no
problem has given rise to so much controversy and is more
obscure in its various aspects. To state the case in a few words,
it is this. An *objet d'art* may travel far, it may go anywhere,
passed on from hand to hand, to find its last resting place in the
collection of some connoisseur. But because some fine vase, or
even a number of them, is found in some locality, are we then
to speak of a "trade" in pottery from its place of origin with
the city or country where it is found? To that question an
answer is very difficult, in many instances impossible, and
definite conclusions are in the highest degree hazardous.[1] It is
by no means certain that all the "Greek" vases were made in
Greece; we know they were widely copied and many were
manufactured far from Greece.[2] We also know that potters
travelled about from place to place carrying on their trade, as
they do to this very day in some of the islands of the Aegean.
We even know the name of one potter, Xenophantus, who
travelled round South Russia making "Attic" pottery.[3] We
know also that imitations of Corinthian pottery were very early
made at Cumae in Magna Graecia and by the Etruscans,[4] and
Sir Leonard Woolley has found excellent imitations of Attic
pottery at Al Mina in Syria at the mouth of the River Orontes.[5]

---

[1] E. Pfuhl, *Malerei u. Zeichnung der Griechen*, i, 31; Bücher, *Beiträge*,
pp. 65ff. Cf. also Heichelheim, "Ausbreitung der Münzgeldwirthschaft"
art. in Schmoller's *Jahrbuch*, lv (1931), pp. 244ff.; V. Grace, "Stamped
Amphorae handles found in 1931–2", *Hesperia*, iii (1934), pp. 197ff.
[2] Bücher, *Beiträge*, p. 90.
[3] Hasebroek, *Trade and Politics*, p. 51; cf. S. Reinach, *Répertoire des Vases*,
i, 23.
[4] A. Blakeway in *Journ. Roman Studies*, xxv (1935).
[5] "The excavations at Al Mina", *J.H.S.* lviii (1938), 1.

There is no doubt whatever that Greek models were greatly admired and widely copied. But these were luxury articles and obviously could not enter very largely into trade.

But for all that a widely extended trade in pottery certainly existed; the archaeological remains attest that. First in the field were the Corinthians, who very early in the ninth and eighth centuries were making a crude but effective form of pot, in what is known as the Proto-Corinthian style, which went far afield. From about 650–550 they held the market, and their wares went to all parts of Greece, the islands, Asia Minor, except perhaps Miletus where they met an effective rival, to Syria, Cyrene and Carthage. Westwards Corinthian pottery went to the Etruscans of Italy, to the western Greek colonies and even to barbarous countries to the north and west of the Alps. The Corinthians were famous craftsmen and it is related that they were the first to mix *miltos*, or iron oxide, with their clay to give it a much admired colour.[1] But like others after them, they were spoiled by success. Having succeeded so long with their designs they took no trouble to improve them. The shapes and decorations which had been so admired seemed to them good enough always to hold their markets, and they did not see that in Attica a new school of potters was rising, that was destined by superior craftsmanship and more artistic form and decoration to beat them in the trade they imagined was their own particular preserve.

The victory of the Attic potters was overwhelming; the Corinthians could not compete with such masters as the Athenian Clitias and Ergotimus, whose signatures to fine vases made them prized everywhere.[2] Not long after 600 Attic products began to appear in Naucratis, in South Russia and Etruria, and by the middle of the sixth century they had penetrated everywhere, and the great Etrurian market was in the hands of a monopoly which they held undisputed for a century. Not that they did not meet with opposition, sometimes of a very formidable character, as, for instance, an attempt on the part of the Argives and Aeginetans to forbid their people drinking out of any but native wares.[3] So marked was the superiority of Attic pottery

---

[1] But doubtful. The point is discussed in the chapter on Industry.
[2] J. D. Beazley, *C.A.H.* iv, 600 ff.   [3] Her. v, 88.

that craftsmen from Ionia and the islands betook themselves to Athens, and it is more than probable that most of the Attic potters were in reality Metics, just as to-day so many renowned Parisian couturiers are not French. The superiority of the Attic product lay in the beautiful red vases with black figures, and later the black vase with red figures. They were more expensive than the Corinthian and never spread so widely; but they did capture the markets of the Euxine, Cyprus, Etruria, Liguria and the Iberian country. As early as the sixth century Attic vases in quantities went to Italy, and four-fifths of the extant Pan-Athenaic amphorae of archaic style have been found in Etruria. Later through the ports of Taras, the Latin Tarentum, and Adria Attic vases reached farther into the interior of Italy and to the barbarous regions of the north. Phoenician merchants took Attic products far afield down the West African coast to Cerne at the mouth of the Rio d'Oro.[1] Although the Persian wars while they lasted abruptly stopped the trade with the Euxine and there is a gap between the red-figure vases of severe style and the fine products of later times, yet the trade was resumed later when Athens was predominant in the Black Sea. We can well imagine how, when in search of a cargo of grain, the shipmaster would pack up a few choice specimens in order to tempt the wheat merchants of South Russia. In the necropolis of Panticapaeum, the modern Kertch, have been found many such works of art of the fourth century.[2] At the end of the fourth century Attic potters were still producing for this market, but it is notable that their products were more florid and lacked refinement. It is possible that this did not denote any actual decadence in the art but rather an adaptation to the less refined tastes of their customers; they were producing "trade vases". Another instance of such wares suited particularly for local markets were the Attic vases imported into Naucratis for the Ionian trade, which were lettered in Ionic characters. Attic potters were adaptable, and perfectly willing to please their customers in any way that would help sell their wares. When speaking of Naucratis, however, it is pertinent to remark that

---

[1] Peripl. Scylax; Müller, *Frag. Hist. Graec.* i, sect. 112; cf. Kaeppel, *Off the Beaten Track in the Classics.*
[2] Cf. Furtwängler and Reichhold, *Die griechische Vasen-Malerei*, ii, 42.

the local potters were themselves of high reputation[1] and, no doubt, imitations of Attic models were turned out for the trade to Asia Minor and Egypt. It may also be remarked that, in the earlier period when Milesian merchants were in control of Naucratis, they had been successful in keeping Corinthian pottery out of the city, and indeed until the downfall of Miletus they had kept them out of the Black Sea so effectively that not the smallest potsherd of Corinthian make has been found on the site of Miletus.

On the coast of North Africa Cyrene, at least in the Archaic period, was considered among the highest class of producers. The famous Arcesilas vase, with a picture of the king super-intending the stowing of a cargo of silphium, which was found in Etruria, came from Cyrene. It seems pretty clear that vases of the Cyrenaic pattern were made by itinerant potters who carried with them a light portable wheel and made the rounds of the islands. The pottery of Carthage was singularly poor, and the bulk of its wants was imported. In Punic cemeteries many Greek vases, mostly Proto-Corinthian and later Corinthian and terra-cotta figurines have been found. Probably, if not certainly, these were procured through Syracuse in the form of spoils of war, although Carthaginian merchantmen may quite easily have got them in trade.[2]

Massalia, the entrepôt of such purely Greek trade in the Western Mediterranean as was able to stand up against the Carthaginian quasi-monopoly in that region, did a large business in pottery. Many sites containing Rhodian, Ionian, Corinthian and Attic pottery in successive strata have been found in the vicinity,[3] and from it went Attic vases for trade with the Celts and Iberians. Finds of Greek pots and figurines have been made on the eastern coasts of Spain, pointing plainly to Greek in-fluence in those parts, in the earlier periods at least through those hardy mariners and colonisers the Phocaeans,[4] and later no doubt to Carthaginian traders who brought such ware to exchange for Spanish silver.

---

[1] Athen. xi, 480 E.
[2] Gsell, *Histoire ancienne de l'Afrique du Nord*, pp. 154, 162 ff.
[3] Cf. Toutain, *L'Économie antique*, p. 69.
[4] Rhys Carpenter, *The Greeks in Spain*, passim.

GREEKS AND PHOENICIANS[1]

EARLY PHOENICIAN TRADERS

We have already referred repeatedly to rivalry between Greek and Phoenician traders. From their strongholds on the coast of Canaan, these intrepid mariners and cunning merchants sailed into every sea known to the Ancient World and planted their colonies and trading posts. When their great cities of Tyre and Sidon had been overthrown, they lived on in their even greater second home, Carthage, and with Rome fought out the battle of Mediterranean supremacy to a finish.

Although it is probable that much of the trade of the Aegean attributed to Phoenicians in early times actually belonged to Minoans, it is certain that they far antedated the Greeks in the sphere of navigation and commerce. In Homer they are by all odds the traders of the time, and the references to their multifarious dealings, some of them none too honest, are innumerable. Until the rise of Greek commercial enterprise, they were practically in command of the trade of the Aegean, and were busy in exploring the Western Mediterranean, finding new sources of trade and jealously guarding their hard-won knowledge. We have in the Bible constant references to the wealth and power of Tyre and Sidon, and in Ezekiel a vivid description of their far-flung commerce.[2] The passage is so interesting and so illuminating in its details that it will be worth while to notice it at some length. Ezekiel wrote at the end of the seventh century and, therefore, we have here a picture of Mediterranean commercial relations which, allowing for a certain amount of poetic exaggeration, we may assume to be substantially correct. With the forests of Lebanon to the east, Tyre and Sidon were particularly well provided with shipbuilding materials. From Mount Hermon came fir planks for the hulls; from Lebanon cedars

---

[1] Ed. Meyer, *Geschichte des Altertums*, ii, 2 (1931)², pp. 77 ff.; Ebert, arts. "Phönikische Besiedlung", "Italien und der Orient, Gades, Sizilien" in *Reallexikon der Vorgeschichte*; I. L. Woolley, "Les Phéniciens et les Peuples Égéens", *Syria*, ii (1921), pp. 77 ff.; U. Kahrstedt, "Phönikischer Handel an der Italischen Westküste", *Klio*, xii (1912), pp. 46 ff.; F. Hasebroek, *Griech. Wirths. und Ges. Geschichte*, pp. 31, 269; Melzer-Kahrstedt, *Geschichte der Karthager*, i–iii; S. Gsell, *Histoire ancienne de l'Afrique du Nord*, i–x.

[2] Ezek. xxvii, *passim*.

for masts; from Bashan, which lay east of the Jordan, oak for oars; from Kittim, or Cyprus, boxwood, or perhaps more likely cypress, for the rowers' benches.[1] Rowers came from Sidon and Arvad, which lay to the north; the "wise men" of Tyre were pilots; calkers came from Gebal, called by the Greeks Byblos, which lay between Tripoli of Asia Minor and Beyrout. From Egypt came fine linen for sails; from "the isles of Elishah", by which probably were meant the coasts of Southern Italy, blue and purple; from Tarshish came silver, iron, tin and lead.[2] From Javan, by which is meant Greece, came slaves and vessels of brass, wool yarn probably from Miletus, wrought iron, cassia and calamus.[3] From Tubal and Meshech, by which the southern coasts of the Euxine are probably described, came the same products as from Javan, which seems to confirm the identification as referring to Greek colonies in that region. From Togarmah, by which is meant Armenia, came horses and mules; from Syria, emeralds, purple, broidered work, fine linen, rubies and coral,[4] or perhaps pearls, although the passage is obscure. From Judah came wheat, honey and oil; from Damascus, wine and white wool; from Arabia, lambs and rams, goats, spices, precious stones and gold.[5] A curious passage occurs in verse 26: "Thy rowers have brought thee into great waters: the east wind hath broken thee in the heart of the seas." Why the east wind is difficult to say; although we may perhaps conjecture that with ships laden with heavy cargoes coming back from the west, an east wind blowing off-shore was particularly dangerous.[6]

[1] Boxwood from Cytorus in Bithynia. Cf. Catullus, iv, 13. Verg. *Georg.* ii, 437. Theophrastus does not mention it as used for shipbuilding.

[2] Cf. Diod. v, 35. The identification of Tarshish with Tartessus cannot be sustained on etymological grounds. It is as mysterious a place as Ophir. Possibly by Tarshish the writers were referring to Carthage, since the word Tarshish is of Libyan or Berber origin; but probably no identification is possible. Presumably Tartessus was at the mouth of the Guadalquivir in Spain but all traces of it are lost. Cf. A. Schulten, "Tartessos", *Klio*, xxii (1929), pp. 284f.

[3] Cassia and cinnamon came from India. Possibly cassia and calamus, the aromatic root of the sweet iris, are confounded here. Cf. Exodus xxx. 23–4.

[4] Emeralds and rubies from India via the Asiatic caravan routes; coral from the Mediterranean, probably the coasts of North Africa or possibly from the Red Sea. Cf. Job xxviii. 18, but doubtful.

[5] Cf. also Her. iii, 107.

[6] Cf. also Psalm xlviii. 7: "With the east wind thou breakest the ships of Tarshish." Probably by east wind is meant any violent gale, the modern "Levanter".

They were certainly the most expert navigators of the Ancient World. It must have taken both hardihood and excellent seamanship to venture beyond the Pillars of Hercules northwards in search of tin across the Bay of Biscay, and the evidence that they reached Britain is pretty well established. The voyage of Hanno down the west coast of Africa, apparently as far as Sierra Leone and Cape Palmas, was a first-class achievement at the beginning of the sixth century. The only time we hear of a Greek penetrating beyond the Straits of Gibraltar was when a ship of Samos bound for Egypt was blown out of its course and arrived at Tartessus, from which it returned with great riches.[1] It is, however, only fair to say that the Carthaginians jealously guarded the straits,[2] and it was not only fear from the perils of a long sea voyage but also the danger of capture that kept the Greeks away from the Western Mediterranean, and in any case the trade of the Aegean and Pontus was sufficiently rich to satisfy them.

The excellence of their ships, far superior we may presume to those of the Greeks, is testified to by Xenophon who, in his *Oeconomicus*, tells how the indefatigable Ischomachus in the course of educating his wife in the ways of order and neatness, took her to see a Phoenician ship in the harbour of the Piraeus. "I once saw, I think, the most beautiful and accurate arrangement of implements possible, when I went on board that large Phoenician vessel to look over it; for I beheld a vast number of articles severally arranged in an extremely small space. For the ship is brought into harbour and taken out again by means of various tackle of wood and tow; it pursues its voyages with the aid of what is called suspended tackle; it is equipped with many machines to oppose hostile vessels; it carries about in it many weapons for the men; it conveys all the utensils such as people use in a house, for each company that take their meals together; and in addition to all this, it is freighted with merchandise, which the owner of the ship transports in it for the purpose of profit."[3]

Besides being great traders they were colonisers. At first we

---

[1] Her. iv, 152. The episode seems hard to credit; it was certainly a most remarkable voyage.
[2] Strabo, xvii, 1, 19 (c. 802).   [3] *Oecon.* viii, 11–12.

may suppose they established merely trading posts which later they made the nucleus of permanent settlement. Although the founding of Carthage is traditionally assigned to the era of the Trojan war, it is certain that it was later, probably in the ninth century. The same is true of the founding of outposts beyond the Straits of Gibraltar, which Strabo assigns to the same period.[1] All along the northern coasts of Africa, from Cyrenaica in the east to the Atlantic in the west, their sway extended from Leptis Magna to Tingis and Lixus: Gades in Spain, Corsica, Sardinia, Sicily and Malta all had their colonies and were at one time or another under Phoenician or Carthaginian control. Cyprus, with its riches of timber and copper, early attracted settlers and the mines of Tamassus[2] were exploited by them. Here colonisation was permanent and settlements established at Idalium, Lapethus, Larnaka and other places.

Although Phoenician genius excelled in trading and carrying the products of other nations, yet they were themselves considerable craftsmen; although it is to be noted that they never evinced any particular originality, but were content to copy the patterns of other peoples. There are many references in Homer to metal wares of gold, silver and electrum, which were presumably of Phoenician manufacture, although possibly the work of others and only traded in by Phoenician merchants. Their textiles, dyed with the famous Tyrian purple, were highly prized, and they also dealt in copper, iron and pottery wares, although of a definitely lower order of artistic merit than those of the Greeks.

GREEK AND PHOENICIAN RIVALRY

It was inevitable that Greeks and Phoenicians should clash; already in Homer we see the rivalry beginning, and the antipathy for those "greedy merchantmen" and sharp dealers, who stole women whenever they had a chance, becoming acute. The Greek islands lay right across the trade routes from Tyre and Sidon to west and north. As Greek colonisation spread and commerce with the Aegean islands and the Euxine increased, the clashes became more frequent and serious. Although there is no evidence that Phoenician traders ever actually penetrated

[1] Strabo, i, 3, 2 (c. 47).   [2] Or Temesa.

the Black Sea, yet we cannot doubt that such hardy mariners at one time or another must have ventured there. As previously mentioned, "Tubal" and "Meshech" are to be identified with the southern coasts of the Euxine, and Phoenician traders must have brought merchandise thence to Tyre and Sidon. It is to be noted that "Javan" is linked with the other two places, which certainly suggests that it is to the Greek colonies on the Euxine that Ezekiel is referring. It is certain, however, that any attempt to compete with the Greeks in the Propontis and Euxine must have met with very stiff opposition, and we can well imagine that getting by Abydos, Byzantium and Chalcedon must have been as hard for the Phoenicians as running the blockade of the Straits of Gibraltar was for the Greeks. As Greek commerce increased in the Aegean that of the Phoenicians declined, although it was always a serious factor.

But there was another chance left to them to regain all they had lost in the invasion of Greece by the Persians. The revolt of the Ionian colonies in 499 was crushed largely through the help given on the seas by Phoenician fleets. They did not love the Persians, from whom they had suffered much; but they hated the Greeks more, and the chance of beating their rivals was eagerly grasped. The colony of Byzantium was seized, the inhabitants expelled, and the Greek trading stations on the Propontis burned. When Xerxes made his great effort it was the Phoenician fleet that gave him greatest aid, and provided the best contingent that fought at Salamis. With the thrusting back of the Persian menace from Greece and the immediate recapture of the Hellespont, the struggle for supremacy between Greeks and Phoenicians was over, and the scene shifted westwards, where the last great struggle between European and Semite was to be fought out.

CARTHAGE

When the ancient cities of Tyre and Sidon decayed, the vigorous colonies to the west flourished and in Carthage the Phoenicians found their greatest stronghold. It is curious to realise that our knowledge of economic conditions in the Carthaginian state is extremely limited, especially when we reflect that it was, until its destruction by Rome, the greatest commercial power of the

Ancient World. Evidence from purely Carthaginian sources is almost non-existent, due to the fact that no literary remains are extant, with the single exception of a treatise on agriculture by Mago, which was so highly esteemed as to be translated into Latin by the order of the Senate in 146, as a guide to intending settlers in North Africa. It is very unsafe to say that Carthage produced no literature, philosophy or science; but all that can be said is that no traces of them have survived, we may presume destroyed along with the city on its capture by the Romans.

The colonists of Carthage exhibited all the characteristics of their racial kindred of ancient Phoenicia. Pre-eminently carriers and traders, their manufactures were inconsiderable and of poor quality, lacking in originality. Such wares as they did produce themselves were mostly of the luxury class of articles in gold, silver, ivory and precious stones. Textiles such as tapestries and rugs, some pottery, glass and lamps of inferior artistic merit, and a few raw materials such as timber and hides, make up the inconsiderable list of Carthaginian native products: the wares they dealt in were those of other nations.

In agriculture they excelled, and farming was practised on a large scale, the great estates of the nobles being worked by slave labour. That Carthage at the height of her power was the wealthiest city of the time is undoubted, and into it poured the treasures of the silver mines of Spain, the revenue from commerce and the spoils of conquest. In a predominantly commercial people it is curious to note that the monetary system was adopted at a comparatively late date. The first Carthaginian coins known are those struck in Sicily on Greek models in the fifth century for use among the colonists in that island, who had learned the art from the Greeks. The appearance of a domestic coinage in Carthage itself was even later, gold and bronze being first minted in the fourth, and silver from the mines of Spain not until the third century. There is no evidence of any specialised banking system, although it is hard to credit such a lack to a people of so essentially a commercial nature. Probably if the Carthaginians had dealt more with the Greeks and not so extensively with barbarian peoples on a purely bartering basis, their monetary and banking systems would have been more highly developed. But, in any case, the evidences that do survive are of so meagre a nature that any conclusions must be of an extremely tentative character.

GREEKS, CARTHAGINIANS, ROMANS

It is easy to see now that the rivalry between Greek and Phoenician in the Aegean must always, in the long run, have ended as it did in the downfall of the Semites. Situated as they were on a narrow strip of coast, it was a case in very truth of being between the devil and the deep sea; the devil being the enemies at their backs, Assyrians and then Persians, the deep sea the ceaseless rivalry of Greece and the Ionian colonies. Magnificent seamen as they were, their qualities and resources were not such as to insure a final victory in a long drawn-out struggle against wastage they were not able to replace. An interesting suggestion of Mr Holland Rose is well worthy of consideration on this score. The decline of Tyre and Sidon, he suggests, were probably due to their increasing difficulty in getting timber from Lebanon and Mount Hermon so soon as the neighbouring great monarchies held their hinterland. It is also possible that the perplexing collapse of the sea power of Carthage may have resulted from her inability to procure enough large timber after she lost Sicily, Sardinia and Corsica to the Romans.[1]

The attempts of the Phoenicians to keep the Western Mediterranean a close preserve for their own merchantmen was a failure. Beyond the Pillars of Hercules they were successful in an exclusion policy, as it was easy to guard the Straits of Gibraltar. But to keep other nations out of Sicily, Sardinia and Corsica, was an impossibility. Sicily was a prize for which Phoenician, Greek and Roman all strove, for not only was it a treasure house of riches in timber and wheatlands, but the strategic key of the Western Mediterranean. This the Athenians knew well when they staked everything on the supreme gamble of the Syracusan expedition, and it was in Sicily that the first great clash came between Roman and Carthaginian.

But long before Carthage and Rome were embroiled Carthaginian and Greek had struggled for the island. With the Carthaginians in the west and the Greeks in the east, with

---

[1] *Mediterranean in the Ancient World*, p. 23.

their great stronghold of Syracuse, the contest went on continuously with varying fortunes, but on the whole in favour of the Carthaginians who, although beaten back and almost entirely expelled for a time by the energy of Dionysius the Elder, tyrant of Syracuse from 405 to 367, yet always came back, and in the end defeated Dionysius. Syracuse baffled them, as it had the Athenians, and when Pyrrhus of Epirus, that romantic adventurer, turned from his fruitless campaign in Italy and came to Sicily, he was welcomed by the Syracusans as their king in 279. With a swift rush he drove the Carthaginians back until only Lilybaeum was left to them. But the old ineradicable fault of the Greeks made all his conquests in the island futile, the victors quarrelled among themselves and Pyrrhus left the island to its fate, to be the first battleground of Rome and Carthage. At first welcoming the Romans as deliverers from the Carthaginians, they soon found that Rome when she had vanquished their foes had no intention of leaving the island to the Greeks. From the moment that the first Roman army landed in Messina the fate of the Greek colonies was sealed, and Sicily became the granary of Rome, a province to be exploited and eventually ruined by such as Verres. The fate of the Greek colonies in Southern Italy and Sicily was but the prelude to the complete subjection of all Greek lands to Roman rule.

PIRACY[1]

The Mediterranean Sea has, from the most ancient times to the present day, been the home of piracy, and it has always been the task of the stronger maritime powers to suppress it, from Minos of Crete to the French who bombarded Algiers in 1830. The numerous islands of the Aegean, the inlets on the coast of Greece and Asia Minor, are ideal places for the pirate to lurk, from which he can sally out on plundering expeditions and run home before he is caught.[2]

---

[1] Ziebarth, *Beiträge*; Ormerod, *Piracy in the Ancient World*; P. Cloché, "Piraterie et Commerce", *Rev. Ét. Anc.* xxxii (1930), p. 25 f., a review of Ziebarth's *Beiträge*.

[2] In 1920 a Greek motor schooner was seized by a Turkish pirate in the Black Sea; cf. Ormerod, *Piracy in the Ancient World*, p. 14. The northern coasts of Africa are still unsafe for defenceless merchants; cf. Koester, *Antike Seewesen*, pp. 235–6.

We have already spoken of piracy in the Homeric age when it was looked upon not as an evil, but as a respectable and glorious career. The noble or chief who disdained to be a trader and found life dull at home if he had no convenient neighbours to fight, sought adventure on the seas in piracy and sudden onslaughts on other lands. At a time when commerce was almost non-existent, or at best on a very small scale, the only ready means of obtaining wealth or novelties from other peoples was to go and get them. The code was a simple one and, as far as it went, effective. If the other side was too strong to overcome peaceful trading ensued; if it was open to stronger methods, plundering was resorted to. Such was the method of the notorious traders and pirates of the earliest times, such as the Taphians and Phoenicians. If any power was strong enough to stop this and police the seas effectively, piracy ceased for the time being; only to break out again when the vigilance was relaxed. Along with, and indistinguishable from the individual pirate ship, went plundering by cities or states; often of necessity in order to obtain provisions when war or jealousy of other cities had cut their supply. Piracy was so deep-rooted and, except for short intervals, so ineradicable in the Ancient World, and for the matter of that in the modern as well, that it was accepted as a normal risk of commerce, to be encountered as frequently and escaped from as often as tempest or other perils of the sea.

No better description of the piratical ways of the early Greeks can be given than that of Thucydides.[1] After saying that Minos was the first to make an attempt to put down the pirates "for the better coming in to him of his revenues", he goes on to say: "For the Hellenes in olden times, and of the barbarians both those on the mainland who lived near the sea, and all who inhabited the islands, after they began to cross over more commonly to one another in ships, turned to piracy, under the leadership of their most famous men, both to satisfy their own greed and to maintain their own poor. Falling upon towns that were unfortified, and built in an open and straggling manner, they plundered them, making most of their livelihood by such means, this manner of life involving no disgrace but rather

[1] Thuc. i, 4–7.

glory." He then goes on to remark that until cities were built with sufficiently strong walls to resist attack from wandering marauders, they were always built at some distance from the sea, and also that the old custom of everyone carrying weapons showed how frequent was the danger of robbery.

As trade increased the necessity of making the seas reasonably safe for merchantmen became apparent. Corinth by her situation on the Isthmus was peculiarly favoured for commerce both by sea and land; therefore, according to Thucydides, the Corinthians were the first in historical times to make any attempt at putting down piracy.[1] During the Persian wars there was a serious recrudescence of the evil; most of it by fugitives from conquered territory, who took to piracy as the only means of making a living. Such were Histiaeus, tyrant of Miletus, who with the help of the Mytileneans seized Byzantium and captured ships sailing out of Pontus, and later captured Chios, massacring the inhabitants.[2] Dionysius of Phocaea, another fugitive, found refuge in Sicily, "and sallying out from thence established himself as a pirate, attacking none of the Greeks but only Carthaginians and Tyrrhenians".[3] So bad was piracy at this time that we find a curse laid on the magistrates of Teos if they wittingly permit it.[4] One of the first tasks that fell to Cimon after the defeat of the Persians was to deal with the Dolopians of Scyrus, "a people who neglected all husbandry and had for many generations been devoted to piracy; this they practised to such a degree that at last they began to plunder foreigners who brought merchandise into their ports".[5] We are also told that Themistocles helped to make the seas safe from pirates.[6]

With the command of the seas in the hands of Athens as leader of the Delian League piracy was effectually put down; but with the long-drawn-out Peloponnesian war it came to life again, increasing as the war continued. Andocides, speaking of the year 411, says: "As the war continued the warships were constantly at sea, and also the pirates, by whom many were captured to lose all their possessions and end their lives as

[1] Thuc. i, 13. [2] Her. vi, 5, 26.
[3] Her. vi, 17.
[4] Tod, *Greek Hist. Inscr.* 23. Ditt. *Syll.* (3rd ed.), 37, 38.
[5] Plut. *Cimon*, 19.
[6] Corn. Nepos, *Themist.* 2, 3. But the evidence is unreliable.

slaves."[1] It is significant that Lysander when he wanted the swiftest ship he could find to send to Sparta the news of Aegospotami, sent Theopompus, a pirate of Miletus.[2]

During the fourth century the allusions to the dangers of the seas from pirates are numerous. The Spartans never effectively controlled the seas, indeed did not try to, and confusion was supreme. Isocrates, in 380, declared that pirates ruled the seas and freebooters besieged the cities.[3] Aegina was a nest of robbers that preyed upon Athenian commerce. In 370 we hear from Demosthenes of the misfortunes of Lycon who was killed by pirates.[4] In the same year, or shortly afterwards, Nicostratus was captured and held for ransom.[5] In the Hellespont a regular war between pirates was going on; Iphicrates and Anaxibius sending out their privateers against each other.[6] The confusion in the Greek world with the successive failure of Sparta and Thebes to establish any lasting or effective hegemony is shown in such incidents as the raid of Alexander of Pherae and Philip of Macedon on the Cyclades and the capture of Peparethos.[7] Most daring of all, the same Alexander made a sudden raid on the Piraeus, plundered the money-changers' shops and escaped unharmed,[8] a sad commentary on the downfall of Athenian naval power. Xenophon's summary of Alexander's character is severe, "a naval ruler to the Thessalians, a violent enemy to the Thebans and Athenians, and an unprincipled pirate by land and sea".[9] As the confusion increased and the safe conduct of merchantmen became more difficult, even cities whose supplies were cut off took a hand in provisioning themselves by force, as did Byzantium, Chalcedon and Cyzicus in 362.[10] Philip of Macedon made use of pirates and privateers whose hiding places were in the islands of the north Aegean and in the inlets of Thracian Chersonese. We know the name of one of these freebooters, Charidemus of Oreus, a pirate who was ready to serve anyone.[11] Philip was playing a bold game, using pirates himself and pretending to take measures to suppress them, on

[1] Andocides, i, 138.
[2] Xen. *Hell.* ii, 1, 30.
[3] *Panegyric*, 115.
[4] *In Callippum*, 5.
[5] *In Nicost.* 6.
[6] Xen. *Hell.* iv, 8, 35.
[7] Diod. Sic. xv, 95.
[8] Polyaenus, vi, 2, 2.
[9] *Hell.* vi, 4, 35.
[10] Dem. *in Polyclem*, 6.
[11] Dem. *in Aristocratem*, 148, 166.

which plea he seized the islands of Halonnesus and Peparethos, strongholds of the robber Sostratus, which led to recriminations on both sides.[1] As the struggle with Macedon continued the confusion in the Aegean increased. The power of Athens on the seas was constantly waning, although she bent all her energies to keeping open the trade route from Pontus. But with her final downfall before Alexander the task became beyond her power and the whole centre of gravity in the commerce of the eastern Mediterranean shifted from the Piraeus. The subsequent policing of the seas by the fleets of Rhodes belongs to another epoch of the history of Greek commerce.

[1] [Dem.] *Letter of Philip*, 13.

CHAPTER IX

MONEY AND BANKING

MONEY

The Evolution of Money Forms[1]

IF we define money simply as a medium of exchange, used as a means of avoiding the inconveniences of simple barter, we have simplified our definition sufficiently to include anything that will serve as a medium, whether it be oxen, cowrie shells, wheat, beaver skins or any of the metals, gold, silver, copper or even iron. That these were in use at a very early date in the history of mankind cannot be doubted, and we may even go so far as to assume with good reason that such media, whatever they may have been—and probably they were various—were used in the fifth millennium B.C. in Mesopotamia and Egypt. This is, of course, conjectural; but we are at least on fairly safe ground when we say that in the second millennium, when the great Minoan civilisation was at its height, international trade was carried on, not in the modern sense on a monetary basis—there was no "money" as we understand it to-day—but on a basis whereby the precious metals and copper, and perhaps, but not by any means certainly, iron, were used as convenient media.

But from such use of the metals to a regular system of coinage was a great step which was not taken until historic times. The question as to which people first used minted coins has been much discussed; two, the Lydians and Ionians, both having claims to that supreme invention of human genius. The

---

[1] General references: Seltman, *Greek Coins*, caps. i–ii; A. R. Burns, *Money and Monetary Policy in Early Times*, caps. i–ii; G. F. Hill, *C.A.H.* iv, cap. v; K. Regling, art. "Geld", in Schrötter's *Wörterbuch der Münzkunde*; *ibid.* art. "Münzkunde", in Gercke-Norden, *Einleitung in die Altertumswissenschaft*, ii, 1, 4ff.; F. Heichelheim, "Welthistorische Gesichtspunkte in der Vormittelalterlichen Wirtschaftsepochen", in Schmoller's *Jahrbuch*, lvi (1932–3), p. 1004 (Bronze und Eisenzeit), p. 1010 (Alter Orient), p. 1016 (Griechenland); *ibid.* lv (1931), pp. 229ff. ("Ausbreitung der Münzgeldwirtschaft in Archäischen Griechenland"); Busolt, *Griech. Staatsk.* i, 591 ff.

ancient Greek writers gave the honour to the Lydians;[1] but
modern scholarship inclines more to the Ionians. In any case
it is a question involving so many complications as to be beyond
our purview, and there is a reasonable presumption that the
credit may be shared by both of them. It is probable that the
idea of marking pieces of metal with a seal or punch mark was
of great antiquity; but whether such marks denoted weight or
fineness, or were anything more than mere signs of private
possession, is difficult, if not impossible, to say; in any case the
point is too obscure for detailed discussion.[2] We may, however,
be fairly certain that the systematic marking of lumps of gold,
silver or electrum by merchants and bankers with crude but
recognisable signs, came into use in Ionia sometime before
the beginning of the seventh century. Such markings obviously
did not constitute any regular system of coinage,[3] but at least it
was a great advance, and the next step, that of systematic
minting of coins of guaranteed weight and fineness, was a not
very difficult one. Very likely the Lydian kings were the first to
do this; perhaps they learned how to do so from the doubtfully
historical King Midas of Phrygia. But Midas is a very shadowy
figure, and probably no more minted coins than he possessed
the golden touch or had ass's ears. In any case the practice
of minting coins, as distinguished from mere lumps or ingots
of metal, was well established during the seventh century, and
from that time forward takes its place among ascertainable
historic facts. It seems fairly certain that the first of such coins
were made of a natural alloy of silver and gold, *electrum*, probably so called as being of the pale yellow colour of amber.
Long before men had advanced enough in metallurgy to
separate the two, this electrum was regarded as a distinct
metal, and no attempt was made to determine the exact proportions of gold and silver in a particular coin or lump.[4] There
can never have been any ratio between electrum and the other

---

[1] Cf. Hall, *Ancient History of the Near East*, where the question is discussed. Also Seltman, *Greek Coins*, pp. 14 f.; Hill in *C.A.H.* iv, 126 f.;
Burns, *Money and Monetary Policy*, pp. 37 ff.

[2] Cf. Regling, art. "Geld" in Ebert's *Reallex. der Vorgeschichte*; art.
"Geld" in *P.W.* and in Schrötter's *Münzlexikon*.

[3] Cf. Arist. *Pol.* 1257 A.

[4] J. G. Milne, *First Stages in Development of Greek Coinage*, p. 5.

two precious metals; such a ratio would be impossible in any case, and attempts to discover one are futile. The first coins had no value in specie; like the Chinese Tael of to-day their value was determined by the market price of the bullion they contained in the city where they circulated, and so might vary from place to place. Their weight also varied considerably; it is probable that different cities of Ionia had different weights for their coins.[1] If the stamp guaranteed their fineness, it may be that it also guaranteed their weight; but in any case every merchant had his scales. We have such a scene described in Jeremiah where the silver is weighed before witnesses.[2] It is not difficult to suppose that from "coins" issued by merchants with their own private marks, the step to a regular royal mint with a monopoly of coinage was not a long one. In Lydia the working of the mines of precious metals was a royal monopoly, and by the time of Croesus[3] we have a royal coinage of a fixed and legal weight and fineness, and an abandonment of the clumsy and unsatisfactory electrum in favour of a bimetallic standard of gold and silver on a fixed ratio, although electrum coins persisted in various countries for centuries thereafter.

It was no accident that the invention of metal coinage was made in the seventh century when industry and commerce were fast advancing. At the beginning of the century the dynasty of the Mermnadae in Lydia was making Sardes a trading centre, and the Lydian merchants were middlemen between east and west.[4] Egypt, after a period of eclipse, was recovering her prosperity, and Greek traders were adventuring from the Crimea to Spain. It was also, be it noted, and the fact is significant, an era of intellectual alertness, and philosophers such as Thales, who is credited with a corner of oil presses at Miletus, were not so far removed from mundane affairs as not to be able to be of practical assistance to the commercial interests of their day. It was also the age of the tyrants, whose power was founded on a money economy.[5] It was another case of one being the

---

[1] J. G. Milne, *First Stages in Development of Greek Coinage*, p. 7.
[2] Jer. xxxii. 9 ff.　　　　　　　　[3] Her. i, 94.
[4] Keeping in mind Dr Hasebroek's protests against such phrases as "enormous strides", and Sardes being "one of the most important trading centres that have arisen in the world's history".
[5] Ure, *Origin of Tyranny*, pp. 1 f.

reciprocal of the other. A monetary system was necessary to a commercial development, and with the use of money, commerce and industry found a ready and convenient medium of exchange in place of the more clumsy barter of primitive times.

THE INTRODUCTION OF MONEY INTO GREECE[1]

Of money in Homer, in the modern sense of the term, there is no mention, although as a measure of value the ox was employed. It must be understood that the ox was seldom used as a medium of exchange, but rather as a unit with reference to which prices could be indicated, if indeed we can use the term "price" at all in so primitive an economy. Thus when Diomedes exchanged armour with Glaucus, "Zeus took away the judgment of Glaucus and he exchanged armour with Tydide Diomedes, the golden for the bronze, the worth of a hundred oxen for the worth of nine."[2] The task of reckoning the worth of gold in relation to bronze in terms of oxen was evidently too difficult for the somewhat limited intelligence of poor Glaucus. Again, in the funeral games of Patroclus, "a mighty tripod, to stand upon the fire, seemed to the Achaeans of the value of twelve oxen; and a woman servant, cunning in many tasks, was of the value of four oxen".[3] In the *Odyssey* we are told that Laertes had bought Eurycleia for twenty oxen.[4]

If we were to conclude that the ox was the sole unit of value, our picture of a system of exchange based thereon would be a simple and quite recognisable one. But the problem is severely complicated by the existence of another unit, the talent. Evidently by the time of Homer the old and clumsy ox unit was beginning to be challenged, and the idea of using a more exact and convenient method in reckoning by weight in terms of a precious metal, gold, was emerging. At the funeral games of Patroclus the first prize in the footrace was a silver bowl, the second an ox, great and very fat, and the third half a talent of gold.[5]

---

[1] Art. "Geld" by Regling in Ebert's *Reallexikon der Vorgeschichte*, also art. "Geld" in *P.W.*; Busolt, *Griech. Staatsk.* i, 587.

[2] *Il.* vi, 236.   [3] *Il.* xxiii, 705.

[4] *Od.* i, 421. No doubt she was a valuable slave at any time, but evidently the price of such had fallen by the time of the Trojan war, when captives were numerous in the camp.

[5] *Il.* xxiii, 740.

In the trial scene on the shield of Achilles, the prize for the best judgment was two talents of gold.[1] Odysseus, when a guest at the court of Alcinous, was presented with thirteen talents of fine gold.[2] Among the gifts to placate the wrath of Achilles were ten talents of gold.[3] It is quite evident, therefore, that the Homeric gold talent was a small one, and bears no relation whatever to that of historic times. Strong arguments have been advanced to suggest that this gold talent was a lump of metal weighing approximately 130 grains; but it is needless to enter here into the problem.[4]

At some time, conjecturally prior to the Homeric age, "talents" of copper were evidently introduced, weighing about 60 lb. Such were cast in shapes that strongly suggest cowhides from which the head and tail have been removed. One side mimicked the rough hairy outer surface of the hide, the other the raw inside with its edges curling inwards.[5] It has been suggested that such mimicry is fanciful, and that they were made in this form simply to facilitate tying together. But not many ingots weighing 60 lb. could be conveniently tied together, and the idea of simulating a hide is by no means impossible.[6]

As with all records of Greece, between the Homeric Age and definitely historic times, a period of almost complete obscurity intervenes, and the next we know of Greek money is that iron was being used, and, as far as we can judge, the gold and copper talents had completely disappeared. For this there can be no explanation other than that the "Dorians" brought iron "money" with them and preferred its use to the earlier and, we must think, more inconvenient forms, which they found on their arrival in Greece.[7] It must not be forgotten that iron at

---

[1] *Il.* xviii, 507.   [2] *Od.* viii, 393.   [3] *Il.* xix, 247.
[4] I.e. somewhat larger than the English gold pound, which weighs 123 grs., 11/12 fine. For detailed discussion cf. Lécrivain, art. "Talentum" in *D.S.*; Ridgeway, *Origin of Currency*, p. 8; Seymour, *Life in Homeric Age*, p. 289; Seltman, *Greek Coins*, p. 5. It should be noted that the word *talanton* signifies both the scales used for weighing and the thing weighed, e.g. *Il.* viii, 69, xvi, 658, xix, 223, and references cited above.
[5] Seltman gives an illustration of this in Plate I.
[6] A not inappropriate instance of what may be called a kind of metonymy, was found when the Hudson's Bay Co. introduced coins in place of beaver skins as units of value in trading with Indians. On such coins the figure of a beaver was placed.
[7] For the so-called iron money of Sparta see p. 321.

this-period was so scarce and valuable that it ranked among the "precious" metals. Its use as money, therefore, except for the fact that it rusted, was not at all extraordinary. Such iron money consisted of rods or "spits", or *obeloi*, of which six could be conveniently held in the hand, from which, conjecturally yet not unreasonably, the Greeks adopted 6 obols to the drachma.[1] There seems little reason to doubt that at some undetermined time between the eighth and sixth centuries[2] Pheidon, king of Argos, abolished this iron currency and introduced silver money.[3] Argos was then at the zenith of its power under the Temenid dynasty, and we are told that Pheidon "recovered the heritage of Temenos"[4] which included the island of Aegina, then the most important trading centre of Greece. It was, therefore, quite reasonable for Pheidon to select Aegina, as being so important a market, as the site of his mint. It is, of course, altogether possible that the introduction of state coinage by Pheidon may be legendary, as indeed Dr Hasebroek holds it to be,[5] but the legend is curiously substantiated by the discovery of a bundle of iron "spits" in the excavation of the temple of Hera at Argos, the story being that he had called in all such primitive forms of money and dedicated them to the goddess. It may also be fanciful to discern a settled and highly scientific system of coining the Pheidonian drachmas at a fixed ratio to the iron "spits", but Mr Seltman advances evidence to suggest that this ratio was 400 : 1.[6] The "Pheidonian" silver drachma, so far as can be judged from extant specimens, weighed slightly under 94 grains, and spread over most of Greece, as far north as Thessaly and through most of the Aegean islands to Crete, eastwards as far as Rhodes and Caria. After the fall of Miletus in the Ionian revolt the trade with the Black Sea fell to Aegina, and its unit was used in the Greek settlements on the Euxine.[7]

---

[1] *Drax*, a handful. For illustration of actual bundle of such iron spits cf. Seltman, *Greek Coins*, p. 34.

[2] Pheidon's date very uncertain; cf. H. Berve, *Griech. Gesch.* i, 160; Glotz, *Histoire Grecque*, i, 305 f.

[3] Her. vi, 127.   [4] Strabo, viii, 3, 33 (c. 358).

[5] *Griech. Wirtschafts- und Gesellschafts-Geschichte*, p. 285.

[6] *Greek Coins*, pp. 34 f. Cf. Regling in Schrötter's *Münzlexikon*, arts. "Äginetischer Münzfuss", "Pheidonisches Mass-Gewicht und Münzsystem".

[7] Burns, *Money and Monetary Policy*, 205–6; Gardner, *History of Ancient Coinage*, 169–71; *C.A.H.* iv, 131.

But although Aegina was in a particularly favourable position to control the silver market of Greece through her domination of the trade of the islands of the Aegean where silver was found, the use of the Pheidonian standard was not to remain unchallenged. To the west Corinth was geographically in a strategic position as regards the trade from Sicily, Southern Italy and the Adriatic ports. Silver could be obtained from the mines in the Albanian hills,[1] and we may not be far wrong if we date the first Corinthian coins at shortly after 650. These Corinthian coins were lighter than the Aeginetan, weighing about 65 grains instead of 94. The origin of this standard, generally called the "Euboic", is highly obscure and has given rise to countless discussions. Any suggestion that the island of Euboea was rich in copper, and therefore a "talent" of that metal, or more probably a bronze talent, was early evolved, thus differing more by accident than design from the iron basis of the Aeginetan or Pheidonian system, may be dismissed at once for the simple reason that there was no copper at any time in Euboea.[2] Although not so widely extended as the other, the Euboic standard was, as we have seen, early in use in Corinth, in the islands of Euboea and Samos, and finally was adopted in Athens as one of the so-called "reforms" of Solon in 594. The passage in the treatise on the *Constitution of Athens*, attributed to Aristotle, which has given rise to so much controversy reads: "During his administration the measures were made larger than those of Pheidon, and the mina, which previously had a standard of seventy drachmae, was raised to the full hundred. The standard coin in earlier times was the two-drachma piece. He also made weights corresponding with the coinage, sixty-three minas going to the talent; and the added three minas were distributed among the staters and the other values."[3] In other words 70 Aeginetan drachmas weighed roughly 6500 grains, and by reducing the weight to 65 grains Solon made 100 drachmas of the Euboic standard equal the mina. The weight of the talent he left unchanged, but was obliged to make it equal 63 of the new Euboic minas instead of

[1] Milne, *Development of Greek Coinage*, p. 15.
[2] The question is impossible of full explanation; for further discussion cf. Burns, *Money and Monetary Policy*, 206 ff. No copper in Euboea cf. p. 113.
[3] *Ath. Pol.* x.

the 60 Aeginetan. This readjustment necessitated also a change in the stater, which weighed 4 drachmas, from 260 to 273 grains.[1]

This new monetary policy of Solon had momentous effects in that it joined Athens to Corinth and Euboea in a common standard, which by reason of the commercial importance of the states using it, became not only a serious rival to that of Aegina, but soon almost completely triumphed over it in the commercial transactions of the Aegean, although the Aeginetan standard was never wholly abandoned.[2] Secondly, it stabilised the Attic drachma, embodying it in a national coinage, dealing a serious blow at the unconscionable exactions of the moneylenders who exploited the ignorance of Attic farmers in the intricacies of foreign exchange, and also giving to Athenian traders a definite basis for prices in a state-guaranteed currency.[3] That the Solonian standard was not entirely satisfactory is clearly shown from the fact that within fifty years Peisistratus raised the weight of the Attic drachma by 4 per cent, that is from 65 to $67\frac{1}{2}$ grains, and coined a tetradrachm of 270 grains. The reasons for this are obscure, but it has been suggested that it was designed to prove a corrective to rising prices owing to the output of silver from Laurium. It has also been suggested, not without plausible grounds, that Peisistratus did so in order to raise the pay of the mercenary soldiers who accompanied him back to Athens, who might very likely have objected to being paid in such light-weight coins. We may also surmise that the heavier coins were more suited to the eastern trade where they came into competition with Persian currency. It is certain, however, that both Euboea and Corinth followed suit in increasing the weights of their coins.[4]

---

[1] Busolt, *Griech. Staatsk.* i, 594, n. 1.

[2] E.g. Diphilus, *ap.* Athen. vi, 225 B, where a rascally fishmonger demands payment in Aeginetan currency and gives change in Attic. Theoph. *Char.* xxx, 11, speaks of a "Pheidonian measure" which was evidently smaller than the prevailing one.

[3] J. G. Milne, "Monetary reforms of Solon", *J.H.S.* l (1930), pp. 179 ff. and lviii (1938), p. 96. Mr Milne surmises that Solon procured supplies of silver for his mint either from Corinth or Euboea. It may be that he merely melted down existing coins and made a profit on his lighter ones.

[4] The whole problem is very obscure, and has been discussed at length in several places. Cf. Ridgeway, *Origin of Metallic Currency*, pp. 306–7, 748–50; Seltman, *Athens, its History and Coinage*, pp. 16–17; Adcock, *C.A.H.* iv, 39–40; Hill, *C.A.H.* iv, 34–5.

The earlier coins of Athens bore the image of an amphora or oil jar, thus, perhaps—but doubtfully—signifying the importance of Athenian olive oil in the trade of the city.[1] After the time of Solon, when the state was in the hands of oligarchs, the amphora type gave way to heraldic designs, presumably the badges of noble families.[2] But in 561 Peisistratus made himself tyrant of Athens, and to impress his power on public imagination and to appeal to the religious zeal of the people, struck the first coins bearing the head of Athena and her owl on obverse and reverse, the first of the famous "owls" which for centuries were the pride of the Athenian people.[3] Also, perhaps in order to make the coins more acceptable for foreign exchange, although this may be regarded as conjectural, he struck a tetradrachm, double the weight of the former standard didrachm, and from this the stater or four-drachma piece became the standard Athenian coin. The excellence of these pieces and the confidence inspired by their purity and unvarying weight made them widely acceptable; and it is to the credit of Athens that, whatever else she did and however straitened the state was for money in succeeding centuries, the currency was only on one occasion deliberately debased,[4] and from the Athenian mint, fed with immense supplies of silver from the great mines of Laurium, there poured these beautiful coins. Although the Confederacy of Delos had been established in 478, Athens did not begin her policy of compelling the use of her owls until about 445. While the reasons for this are not perfectly clear, we may surmise that the Athenian mint could not at first turn out a sufficient quantity for use among the members of the League, and secondly because

[1] Cf. Seltman, *Greek Coins*, p. 43.

[2] *Ibid.* pp. 46 f.; i.e. the so-called "Wappenmünzen".

[3] Cf. Ure, *Origin of Tyranny*, p. 51, who advances an interesting theory that the story told by Herodotus (i, 60, cf. Arist. *Ath. Pol.* xiv, 1) of how Peisistratus dressed up a maiden named Phye, who was six feet tall, but lacked three fingers, to represent Athena, placed her in a chariot and proclaimed that the goddess was bringing him back to Athens from his exile, is a misunderstanding on the part of the historian. Actually the head of Athena on the new coins represented the inducement to receive him. But this "most ridiculous story" as Herodotus calls it, seems extremely circumstantial, and it is just the kind of thing that an ingenious man like Peisistratus would do. We need not suppose the Athenians were fooled by it; doubtless they thought that anyone who could think up so diverting a "stunt" was worth having back.

[4] *Vide infra*, p. 326.

she was not strong enough to impose her monopoly, or quasi-monopoly, upon tributaries who were reluctant to abandon their own mints, a source of considerable local pride.[1] A decree of 423 imposes a severe penalty on anyone using foreign coins, weights or measures, and ordering that all such be paid into the mint.[2] The extreme rarity of silver coins of other cities of the League in the fifth century bears witness to the success of Athens in imposing her tetradrachms on others, a policy which was wholly to their advantage in obtaining so fine and universally accepted a currency. From Abydos to Theodosia no coins of any importance were issued during the domination of Athens. But as soon as the power of Athens was broken, the cities of the League hastened to strike their own currencies, with very poor results and quite cynical disregard for weight and fineness, which led to much confusion. But although Athens could no longer impose her owls on her subjects, the very fact that the coins of other cities were debased and so worthless that they circulated little beyond their own boundaries, enhanced their reputation. It is remarkable to realise that long after Athens had lost her independence under Roman rule she continued to issue her owls.[3] They acted as the "trade money" of the Aegean, very much like the Mexican dollar in China and the Maria Theresa dollar in the Persian Gulf. It was only the final exhaustion of the mines of Laurium that brought this famous coinage to an end in 25 B.C. For six hundred years Athens had minted her silver owls, from the archonship of Solon to the principate of Augustus.[4]

It remains but to mention one other standard, the "Phocaean", "Chian", or "Rhodian", as it is variously called. As early as 480 the island of Chios had struck tetradrachms of 240 grains,

---

[1] Cf. P. Gardner in *J.H.S.* xxxiii (1913), p. 287.

[2] Ditt. *Syll.*³ 87. Cf. on this passage Regling, *Münzkunde*, p. 116; Tod, *Greek Hist. Inscr.* p. 67.

[3] It must be observed, however, that the Athenian owls were imitated by other mints. Cf. C. F. Woolley, "The excavations at Almina", *J.H.S.* lviii (1938), p. 22.

[4] The view formerly held that there was an interruption of 30 years after the capture of the city by Antigonus Gonatas in 261 has now been abandoned. There is no numismatic evidence to warrant any idea that Antigonus either suppressed the mint or issued his own coins therefrom. Köhler's interpretation of *I.G.* ii.², 1534, in *Sitzb. Preuss. Akad.* (1896), p. 1092 and n. 2, is now generally rejected.

which gave a stater of 120 grains, about 8 per cent lighter than the Euboic. During the seventh century this light standard maintained itself in face of the Athenian, and indeed its maintenance at Cyzicus, Phocaea, Lampsacus and Mitylene suggests that Athens found it expedient not to interfere with it, since it fitted conveniently into the Persian system, being equal to two-thirds of the Persian Siglos.[1] After the revolt of Chios from Athens in 412 this standard began to spread rapidly with the waning power of Athens.[2] About 400 Rhodes adopted it, and it began with increasing rapidity to supplant the Euboic standard along the coasts of Asia Minor as far north as Byzantium, until in the fourth century this Chian or Rhodian standard became the dominant one, although the Euboic and even the archaic Aeginetan were never wholly displaced.

THE SPARTAN MONETARY SYSTEM

Brief mention may be made here of the so-called iron money of the Spartans. The legend that attributed this to the legislation of Lycurgus is patently without foundation, since it is quite evident that their use of iron as a medium of exchange was a conservative retention of the old system in use in other parts of Greece which was, actually or traditionally, discarded by Pheidon of Argos.[3] This "money" consisted of lumps of iron weighing about 1¼ lb., which, as Plutarch justly remarks, were "heavy and hard to carry",[4] so that "even small payments had to be transported in a cart drawn by a pair of oxen",[5] a sufficiently troublesome operation to discourage commercialism among the Spartan aristocracy.

These unwieldy iron "coins" seem to have been equated in weight with the Aeginetan mina, each being worth four *chalkeis*, or half an obol. If this be so, and it must be acknowledged that the point is very uncertain, we may arrive at a rough approxima-

---

[1] For further on the basis of this standard cf. Seltman, *Greek Coins*, pp. 29–30; Regling in Schrötter's *Münzlexikon*, arts. "Euboischer", "Phokäischer", "Rhodischer", "Kyzikener", "Lampsakener Münzfuss"; P. Gardner, "Financial history of Ancient Chios", *J.H.S.* xl (1920), p. 160.
[2] Gardner, *J.H.S.* xxxiii (1913), p. 287.
[3] Cf. Reinach, *L'Histoire par les Monnaies*, p. 28; Her. vi, 127; Wells, *Studies in Herodotus*, App. i.
[4] *Lysander*, 17.   [5] *Lycurgus*, 9.

tion of a ratio of iron to silver of 1200 : 1. Seneca talks of leather money used in Sparta;[1] but this is unsubstantiated from any other source. But we do know that bartering was largely resorted to.[2]

When we look a little closer into the alleged use of this extraordinary money we find some very puzzling problems which defy explanation. How far was it actually used by the Spartans? Certainly it was not by the government in the collection of taxes and public expenditures[3] nor by the Perioeci and Helots. We may even doubt whether it was actually used by the Spartans themselves, since we have a statement by Plutarch that along with the payments in kind to the messes, or Phiditia, each member contributed a small sum in money,[4] which is further explained by Dicaearchus as having consisted of ten Aeginetan obols.[5] Patently such a ponderous form of currency was impossible of ordinary use. Poseidonius tells us that rich Spartans kept their money on deposit in Arcadia.[6] This reference is illuminating, since it not only disposes of the traditional poverty of the Spartans, but also clearly indicates that their money was not iron.

A possible explanation, but by no means a probable one, is that the Spartans used these curious "coins" in the same way as the ingenious inhabitants of the island of Yap use their ponderous stones at the present time. Many of the stones are too heavy to move, but title to them passes without actual transference, a procedure which works with ease and despatch. It is not impossible that such a system, or something akin thereto, was worked out in Sparta; but of this we know nothing, and it is likely that if such had been the case we should have heard of it.

It is pertinent to remark that mere size or weight is not an insuperable objection to the use of any object, metallic or stone, as money. We have already spoken of the copper talents which simulated ox-hides and weighed 60 lb., and the heavy copper slabs that were in use in Sweden in the seventeenth century may be called to mind. The Swedish 2-dollar piece weighed $3\frac{1}{2}$ lb. and, we are told, had to be taken to market in a wheelbarrow.

[1] *de Benefic.* v, 14, 4.   [2] Polyb. vi, 49; Justin, iii, 2.
[3] *I.G.* v, 1.   [4] *Lycurgus*, 12.
[5] *ap.* Athen. iv, 141 C.
[6] Athen. vi, 233 F. Cf. Kirchhoff in *Sitzb. Preuss. Akad.* (1870), pp. 58 ff.

How far this extraordinary system of iron money contributed to the proverbial "seclusion" of the Spartans is hard to determine. The late Mr Blakeway suggested that such was the case on the ground that imports of foreign works of art ceased in the first half of the sixth century, a period coincident with the adoption of a precious metal standard by the rest of Greece.[1] It may, however, be reasonably objected that the iron standard of the rest of Greece did not consist of the heavy lumps of metal used in Sparta, but in the light and practicable "spits" or *oboloi*. As we have already remarked, it is extremely unlikely that any dealings with outside nations were ever conducted with the Spartan money, and in any case the merchants were Perioeci who, we know, never used it. Mr Blakeway's suggestion, therefore, is not capable of proof. The whole problem of this extraordinary form of currency must remain obscure, like so many others in connection with the economy and statecraft of the Spartans. Undoubtedly they did have some form of iron "money"; how it was used, and what its relation to other forms of currency may have been we do not know.[2]

GREEK MONOMETALLISM

It is well to understand that Greece was always on a monometallic silver basis. The only bimetallic system ever attempted was that of Croesus in Lydia as early as 564, whose task it was to get rid of the unsatisfactory electrum coinage of his father Alyattes. To his new silver currency the Persian gold system was adapted, which bore the long-established ratio of $13\frac{1}{3}: 1$.[3] This was done by reducing the weight of the gold stater and coining silver shekels, so that twenty went to the gold unit.[4] But since Greece proper was poor in gold but rich in silver,[5] it was natural that a silver standard should have persisted even in the face of Persian gold. In a highly interesting and often-

[1] *Classical Review*, xlix (1935), p. 185.
[2] Cf. Busolt, *Griech. Staatsk.* i, 596, n. 4; cf. also A. Ferrabino, "La Politica Zoppa", *Rev. d' Italia*, xxxi (1928), p. 469. Spartan policy was a struggle against capitalism.
[3] Following the view of Regling, *Münzkunde*, p. 4, who antedates the Persian by the Croesan system.
[4] Seltman, *Greek Coins*, pp. 60–1.
[5] Scarcity of gold in Greece, Athen. vi, 231, 13.

discussed passage Xenophon, in arguing for his scheme of state exploitation of the Laurium mines, remarks that no state or individual has too much money for when they are poor they want more to buy necessities and when they are rich to buy luxuries. He goes on to say: "If anyone should say that gold is not less useful for such purposes than silver, I do not dispute the truth of the assertion; but I am aware at the same time that gold, if it shows itself in great quantities, becomes much less valuable, but renders silver of a higher price."[1] This passage has been a stumbling-block to many commentators, and the general consensus of opinion has been that Xenophon here is guilty of an egregious economic "howler". Careful consideration will, however, reveal that this is somewhat too sweeping a judgment and that he is not quite so mistaken as it would seem. The key to the passage lies in the fact that Athens was on a monometallic silver basis and that gold, even so far as we know including Persian gold coins, was treated as bullion. If, therefore, there was a large increase in the amount of gold its value in terms of silver would fall, i.e. the purchasing power of silver over gold would rise, more gold could be bought for the same amount of silver. The mistake that commentators have made is in supposing that the purchasing power of silver would rise generally, i.e. the general price level would fall; but this Xenophon does not say, and the difficulty over the whole famous passage is thus resolved.[2]

Athens, however, did have recourse to issues both of gold and copper coins, but such were, at least when they were first issued, of an emergency character, and in the second issue of the nature of "trade money" to facilitate exchange with the gold and electrum using peoples of the Euxine. The first issue of gold, of which further notice is taken later, was minted according to a tariff based on the current price of the metal in the market, with no attempt to fix the value of the coins in terms of their equivalent in silver, but circulating as ingots of guaranteed weight and fineness. It is evident from the size of the gold pieces that they

[1] *Revenues*, iv, 10.
[2] J. H. Thiel, *Xenophontos Poroi*, p. 19. Karl von der Lieck, *Die Xenophontische Schrift von den Einkünften*, pp. 45 ff. Both Thiel and von der Lieck come to the same conclusion as the above. Cf. also Andreades, *Public Finance*, p. 387, n. 7; Beloch, *Griech. Gesch.* iii, 1 (2nd ed.), p. 338.

were not used commonly in ordinary commercial transactions but only for the settlement of large international balances. It seems fairly certain that at no time were Athenian silver pieces, or for that matter the silver coins of any Greek state, minted according to individual weight, but according to the number of pieces which could be made from a stated amount of silver, thus giving rise to the inexactness in weight of coins that has proved so tantalising to numismatists.[1]

We know from Xenophon[2] that local coinage had a very restricted area of circulation. "Merchants in most other cities must barter one commodity for another; for the inhabitants use money that will not pass beyond the limits of the country. But at Athens, while there is abundance of goods such as people require for exportation, still if merchants do not wish to barter, they may carry off an excellent freight by taking away our silver, for wherever they dispose of it, they will always gain more than its original value." There was not, in the modern sense, at any time a rate of exchange quoted between the currencies of any two countries. Coins were treated as bullion, and therefore extreme accuracy in their weight was not necessary.

It would not, however, be correct to state that bimetallism was unknown to the ancient Greeks; on the contrary the Persian bimetallic standard on a basis of $13\frac{1}{3}:1$, where 20 silver sigloi went to the gold Daric, was far more widespread than Greek monometallism. This system endured until Alexander abolished it by demonetising gold and setting up a silver standard. In Sicily and some other cities of Italy, attempts were made in the fifth century at a double standard of silver and bronze, the Syracusan silver Litra of $13\frac{1}{2}$ grains being equivalent to one pound of bronze. This standard remained more or less the basis of the Syracusan monetary system, working with tolerable efficiency as one-twentieth of a gold tetradrachm and one-tenth of a Corinthian silver stater.

These exceptions, however, have no bearing upon strictly Greek monetary standards, which were always on a mono-metallic basis, and such issues of gold or bronze coins were, at

---

[1] The man of "petty pride" in the *Characters* of Theophrastus "when he pays a pound of silver (i.e. a mina) has them pay it in new coin" (xxi, 5).

[2] *Revenues*, iii, 2.

least at first, strictly of an emergency character. Probably the oldest issue of gold outside of Persia was that of the Greek colony of Cumae in Italy in 474 when at war with the Etruscans. We know also that Syracuse issued gold coins at the time of the invasion of the Carthaginians in 397.

The most famous emergency issue of gold was that of Athens in 406 at the last crisis of the Peloponnesian war. In 413, under the advice of the renegade Alcibiades, the Spartans had seized and fortified Decelea,[1] a serious blow to Athens since it not only cut the overland route of supplies from Euboea, but also brought all work at the mines of Laurium to a stop. To make one last effort to fit out a fleet, the gold ornaments from the temple of Athena were turned into money. We do not certainly know how much this was, but evidently it was insufficient, for next year coins of yellowish copper plated with a thin covering of silver were issued from the mint. The shame of these miserable counterfeits was deeply felt by the Athenians, who for so long had been justly proud of the purity of their "owls", and Aristophanes refers bitterly to the "worthless pinchbeck coins of vilest die and basest metal".[2]

In the same year as this play was produced the culminating disaster of Aegospotami wiped out the fleet which had been built at such sacrifice, and the political power of Athens was ruined for ever. But while Athens lost her empire she did not lose her trade, and in a few years she was able to restore the purity of her currency. In 393 these base pieces were demonetised by public proclamation; of which event we have an amusing account by Aristophanes, where an unfortunate countryman, who had sold his grapes for the debased copper, went off with his cheek full of it to buy some barley, and was on the point of doing so when the herald proclaimed that only silver was legal tender.[3] The Athenians did their best to replace the gold taken from the goddess, and in 380 as a kind of earnest of good-will the instruments used in minting the gold were dedicated to

---

[1] Thuc. vi, 91. Cf. Regling, *Münzkunde*, pp. 12f.

[2] *Ranae*, 717–33.

[3] *Eccles*. 815–22. We are not told what the unhappy man did with his worthless copper, but perhaps he swallowed it in his mortification. The Athenian custom of carrying money in the mouth prejudiced them against copper money; in this case they were plated.

Athena in the Parthenon;[1] the whole amount was restored between 336 and 330.[2]

Once having learned the trick of issuing gold, Athens was not very long in doing it again. There is considerable doubt as to the exact date; the best that can be said is that probably it was before 375,[3] and in the absence of any compelling reason such as the desperate necessity of the first issue, we are led to conclude that the Athenians found the issue of gold a profitable and convenient measure. It is certain that the first issue was in large denominations, while the second was much more plentiful and varied, and was designed to circulate without any idea of its being a temporary or emergency issue. Indeed, after the political disasters the monopoly of Attic silver had been, more or less, destroyed and its place in the commerce of the Aegean was being challenged by the gold darics and staters of Cyzicus and the gold staters of Philip of Macedon. There was, therefore, no reason for Athens to abstain from issuing gold, and in self-defence she accordingly did so.[4] That the coins of the colony of Cyzicus on the Propontis should have become so important in the fourth century is explainable on the ground that much of the gold at that period came from the eastern shores of the Black Sea, Colchis and the Crimea, and was exchanged for manufactured goods in the Greek cities on the coast. The corn and timber of Pontus had to be bought with gold, and here Athens, which had the largest share of that trade, needed a gold currency, and so used the gold and electrum coins of Cyzicus, Lampsacus, Phocaea and Mytilene.[5]

Other than the emergency measure of plated coins issued after the disaster of Aegospotami, of which mention has already been made, there is no record of copper coins until Timotheus issued bronze at the time of the Olynthian war.[6] If the chronicler is correct this would seem to be a wartime inflationary measure, the coins not being of the nature of "token" money or small change. Undoubtedly bronze "tokens" were struck in Athens

[1] *I.G.* ii, 2, 665. Cf. A. W. Woodward in *J.H.S.* xxix (1909), p. 172.
[2] Cf. W. S. Ferguson, *Treasurers of Athena*, p. 123.
[3] But according to Regling much later, 338 or 295; *Münzkunde*, p. 12.
[4] Gardner, "Second issue of gold in Athens", *J.H.S.* xxxiii (1913), 187.
[5] *Ibid.* p. 154.
[6] Ps.-Arist. *Oecon.* ii, 2, 1350 A.

at the end of the fourth century, probably under Macedonian influence.[1] We hear of copper *chalkeis*, of which eight went to the obol or forty-eight to the drachma.[2] The silver obols were very small, and Aristophanes has an amusing scene where one of his characters is cheated by being given three fish scales, which he mistakes for obols, and puts them in his mouth only to spit them out again when he tastes them.[3] There was even a coin, the hemitetartemorion, one-eighth of an obol, hardly bigger than a pin's head, of which 192 went to the tetradrachm.

THE RATIO OF MONETARY METALS[4]

When mankind advanced from barter to the use of metals as media of exchange, a change of incalculable importance to the history of the race was effected. Exchange of commodities is always possible on a basis of simple barter and may be highly effective; but the advantages of a money medium are so great and obvious that once adopted it becomes an integral part of the life of the people, only to be abandoned when civilised existence breaks down. That the precious metals should be found the most convenient, as embodying great value in small compass, was natural; but with their adoption came difficulties almost if not as great as those inherent in a system of barter. Nature, unfortunately for man in his commercial dealings, has provided him with two metals which are both beautiful and precious, silver and gold, and still more unfortunately has fixed no stable or enduring value between the two. If gold were always and in every place say fifteen times more valuable than silver, the world would have been saved a great deal of trouble, and spared all the worries of shifting ratios between the two metals. But unhappily such has not been the case, and the very problems that confront us to-day were acutely pressing on the peoples of the Ancient World.[5]

---

[1] Cf. Regling in Schrötter's *Münzlexikon*, art. "Kupfermünzen".

[2] Dem. *in Phaen.* 22; cf. Vitruv. iii, 1, 7.

[3] *Vespae*, 791.

[4] Burns, *Money and Monetary Policy*, 473 ff.; Heichelheim, *Wirth. Schw.* p. 37; Regling in Schrötter's *Münzlexikon*, art. "Wertverhältnis der Münzmetalle".

[5] Cf. Ridgeway, *Origin of Metallic Currency and Weight Standards*, p. 338: "From first to last the Greek communities were engaged in an endless quest after bimetallism."

That ancient peoples could have adopted only one metal, either silver or gold, was impossible, since each nation used whatever metal was most convenient and of which it had the greater supply. Greece had silver but little gold, and therefore Greece was always on a monometallic silver basis; Persia had great stores of gold, and so used them freely as money. Ionia and Lydia had both silver and gold mixed, so used them in that form in the shape of electrum. Egypt had great copper deposits at its disposal and therefore used a copper currency. While such monetary systems worked well enough within their own borders, confusion arose and the foreign exchanges were hindered when merchants carried their money to other countries. Moreover, not only were foreign exchanges made difficult, but "Gresham's Law" functioned as inexorably in ancient times as it ever did in subsequent ages.

It is curious to note that in earliest times silver was more valuable than gold in Egypt. But with increasing discoveries of silver in other countries their values were reversed, and at the end of the third millennium gold was six times as valuable as silver in Mesopotamia. From that time onward gold appreciated still more, until in the last half of the sixth century it reached a more or less stable ratio of $13\frac{1}{3}:1$, at which figure it stayed for over a century. With the outbreak of the Peloponnesian war this stability was destroyed and subsequently its variations became extreme.[1]

In Greece, if we are to accept Pheidon's "reform" of the currency as a fact, and that he made his silver unit one-tenth of the gold, which is highly conjectural, it would seem that the ratio of silver to gold was $15:1$ in the eighth to sixth centuries. Towards the close of the Peloponnesian war, when Persian gold had helped the enemies of Athens, and the latter in 407 had been forced to turn into coin the gold ornaments of the temples, the ratio was quickly falling, and evidence after the war points to a ratio of $12:1$.[2] Not only was the diffusion of gold from the

---

[1] The gold daric weighed 124·1 grains, the silver siglos 82·7. At 20 sigloi to the daric the ratio was $13·33:1$. Her. iii, 95, says it was $13:1$. Cf. Regling in *Klio*, xiv (1914), p. 101; *id. Münzkunde*, p. 13; Köhler, *Zeitschr. für Numism.* xxi (1898), p. 11; Fox, *Num. Chron.* iv (1905), p. 1.

[2] Cf. Wade-Gery, "The ratio of silver to gold during the Peloponnesian War", *Num. Chron.* xxxvii (1930), pp. 16 ff.

Persian hoards having its effect, but also the output of the mines of Laurium had fallen off considerably, thus causing an appreciation of the price of silver in terms of gold. With the opening of the gold mines at Philippi in 356 the ratio fell further. In 338–337 in Delphi one Philippeus was reckoned as worth seven Aeginetan drachmae, which gives a ratio of 10:1.[1] We may reasonably suppose that in consequence of this drastic depreciation of gold in terms of silver, Alexander when he threw immense quantities of gold upon the markets abandoned any attempt at bimetallism and established parallel currencies of gold and silver. It is to be noted that towards the end of the fourth century gold began once more to appreciate. In 306 the ratio was 10·8:1; in 295 it was 12:1; in 280–270, 13:1 and in 258–257 it was back again to $13\frac{1}{3}$:1.[2] In explanation of this appreciation of gold it may be surmised that the impact of the immense gold supplies from Persian sources had spent its force and the output of the mines was falling off, while that of silver was continuing at about the same rate.

Since the proportions of gold and silver in the electrum coins varied widely, there never was any ascertainable ratio between electrum and the other metals, although there was what may be called a more or less rough ratio of 10:1. The temptation to increase the amount of silver in the coins was too much for such states as Lesbos and Achaea, and their electrum money fell into disrepute, while that of Cyzicus which contained from 30 to 35 per cent of gold was readily accepted, not only because the Cyzicene was superior in gold content, but also because it had become recognised as a convenient coin for international trade.[3] Especially was this so, since the Cyzicene stater accommodated itself admirably to the Attic standard. A Cyzicene electrum stater was generally equivalent to 24 Attic drachmae or 6 tetradrachms, and at the same time equal in purchasing power to the royal Persian gold daric.[4] Since the Cyzicene stater weighed about 247 grains and the Attic drachma 66, the ratio of silver to electrum in this case was about 3·7:1, much higher than the

[1] Regling in Schrötter's *Münzlexikon*, art. "Wertverhältnis", p. 742.
[2] Heichelheim, *Wirth. Schw.* pp. 10ff.
[3] Cf. Regling in Schrötter's *Münzlexikon*, art. "Elektron"; Heichelheim, art. "Monopole" in *P.W.* xii, 153f.
[4] Seltman, *Greek Coins*, p. 112.

conventional 10 : 1, owing to the high repute and considerable gold content of the coins of Cyzicus.

DEBASEMENT OF THE COINAGE[1]

A most difficult problem is how far the Greeks mastered the trick of debasing the coinage for the gain of the government doing so. It is not hard to suppose that the various tyrants of different cities were quite alert enough to seize upon such shady practices, and indeed the unknown author labelled "Pseudo-Aristotle" takes keen delight in recording such frauds practised upon the people. We are told Hippias of Athens in 512 "put up for sale the parts of the upper rooms which projected into the public streets and the steps and fences in front of the houses and the doors which opened outwards. The owners of the property therefore bought them and a large sum was thus collected. He also declared the coinage then current in Athens to be base and fixing a price for it ordered it to be brought to him, but when they met to consider the striking of a new type of coin, he gave them back the same money again." Several explanations of this somewhat drastic operation are possible. First, it may, of course, be the high-handed action of a tyrant to enrich himself; in which case nothing further need be said except that it is hard to believe that the people of Athens should have taken meekly so outrageous a proceeding. Secondly, a much more reasonable explanation can be found in the suggestion made by Mr Seltman[2] that the coins called in by Hippias were light-weight, pre-Solon pieces, stamped with the heraldic designs of powerful Athenian families against whom he had a grudge. Evidently he did not want to go to the heavy expense of re-minting these pieces, so contented himself with surcharging them with a stamp of a higher value, every 2-drachm piece re-appearing as a 4-drachm. He would by these means discredit the coins bearing the coat-of-arms of his enemies and make a substantial profit for himself in the process. It can also be argued with some show of plausibility that this inflation of the coinage was necessary to meet a serious fall in prices throughout Greece, due to the cutting off of the supply of silver from the

---

[1] Regling in Schrötter's *Münzlexikon*, art. "Münzverschlechterung".
[2] Seltman, *Greek Coins*, p. 77; cf. also Gardner, *J.H.S.* xxxiii (1913), 158.

mines in Thrace on their capture by the Persians in 512. But
the whole episode is so obscure that further conjecture is
useless.[1]

The same scandalous chronicle records the high-handed
action of Dionysius, tyrant of Syracuse, who, on the capture of
Rhegium in 387, if we are to believe Pseudo-Aristotle, seems to
have played a particularly mean trick. "Having borrowed money
from the citizens under promise of repayment, when they demanded it back he ordered them to bring what money any of
them possessed, threatening them with death if they failed to
do so. When the money had been brought he issued it again,
after stamping it afresh so that each drachm had the value of
2 drachms, and so paid back the original debt and the money
which they brought him."[2] Here again we find difficulties in
taking the story at its face value, since the extant coins of
Dionysius are not countermarked, and it is hard to suppose that
some specimens of them have not survived. According to
Julius Pollux of Naucratis,[3] the weight of the talent was halved
at about this time, and possibly Dionysius borrowed in talents
by weight and paid the debt back in the new standard. In any
case the whole proceeding seems to have been of a sufficiently
shady character to be up to the reputation of the tyrant in
question.[4] The stories of quite cynical debasement of the money
by Dionysius seem to be too many not to be true, at least in
part. The case mentioned by Diogenes Laertius of debasement
of the coinage of Sinope by Diogenes, son of Hicesius the banker,
is one of ordinary fraud on the part of the director of the local
mint.[5]

Merely to brush aside these cases of debasement of the coinage
as the dishonest expedients of tyrants does not by any means
cover the whole problem of the "management" of money in
Greece. Dr Hasebroek has apparently fallen into error when he
says: "The Greeks were accustomed to money which was constantly falling in value and had a legal purchasing power
considerably higher than its intrinsic worth."[6] Apart from such

---

[1] Cf. also S. R. Weil in *Corolla Numismatica*, p. 306.
[2] Ps.-Arist. *Oecon.* 1349 B.   [3] ix, 87.
[4] Cf. also Gardner, *J.H.S.* xxxiii (1913), 414.
[5] Diog. Laert. vi, 20.
[6] *Trade and Politics*, p. 84.

phrases as "legal purchasing power" and "intrinsic value" which provide puzzles for the monetary economist and may be passed over here, it cannot be accepted that the Greeks were accustomed to money which was constantly falling in value, i.e. to a continuous rise of commodity prices. Never at any time, not even when the mines of Laurium were at their highest point of production, was there enough money to warrant a rise in the price level until Alexander released the treasures of Persia. The output of precious metals at the best of times was never more abundant than was barely sufficient to keep pace with the production of commodities and the increase of population. The problem that constantly faced the Ancient World was that of low prices, which did not permit of a liquidity of capital enough to encourage productive enterprise in sufficient volume to insure against a low standard of living and allow the accumulation of further capital.

No doubt tyrants who wished to ingratiate themselves with the rabble could most easily do so by an inflation (i.e. debasement) of the currency whereby debtors are benefited and there is, at least temporarily, a redistribution of wealth. Debt, which could not readily or even over a long time be liquidated, was the plague-spot of ancient economy. Debts accumulate in a period of falling prices and are liquidated, wholly or in part, when prices rise. The Solonian "shaking-off of burdens" solved the problem more or less satisfactorily for Attica. It is significant to find that in the late Hellenistic period when prices were falling rapidly, the ugly spectre of enslavement for debt was found once more.

BANKING[1]

If we are content to use the word "banking" in a loose sense of the storage of valuables and the lending of money at interest

---

[1] General references: *P.W.* art. "Trapeza" by Ziebarth, "Banken" by Laum, Supp. iv, pp. 67–82. *Ibid.* art. "Giroverkehr" by Kiessling. Knorringa, *Emporos*, pp. 83–91; J. Hasebroek, *Trade and Politics*, pp. 85–8; A. Boeckh, *Staatshaushaltung der Athener*, i, p. 156 ff.; G. M. Calhoun, *Business Life in Ancient Athens*; F. Oertel in Anhang zu F. Poehlmann's *Gesch. der Soz. Frage und des Sozialismus*, ii, 2, 529 ff.; E. Salin, *Vierteljahrschrift f. Soz. und Wirthsgesch.* xxiii (1930), pp. 402 ff.; E. Ziebarth, *Beiträge*; E. Breccia, "Storia delle Banche e dei Banchieri nell' età Classica", *Riv. Stor. Ant.* vii (1903), 107 ff., 283 ff. Becker's chapter "The Trapezitae", in his *Charicles*, while old is still well worth reading.

to borrowers without any of the technique commonly associated with modern banking practice, it is safe to say that a primitive form of bank was found in the temples of Babylonia as early as the time of Sumer. Since they were recipients of the offerings of the devout, and because of their sacrosanct character were ordinarily safe from pillage, it is easy to see how this form of business naturally began. All through ancient times the temples were repository of valuables, and it is interesting to know that in the troublous times following the dissolution of the Western Roman Empire the monasteries were used for the same purpose.

Commercial banking unconnected with the temples was of much later date. With the extension of commerce and the evolution of a money economy under the Persians in the "Neo-Babylonian" period after 600, there grew up a much more advanced form of banking practice in private hands. We know of at least two famous banking houses in Babylon, the Egibi Sons and the Murassu, who evidently carried on a very large and, even according to modern standards, complicated business. Loans were made on a large scale both to governments and private individuals. Orders were accepted to pay from the account of one merchant to another, and the partners acted as commission men to buy on behalf of a client. They received deposits and paid interest thereon; acted as warehousemen and charged a fee for safekeeping. They lent money on mortgage and went into partnership with traders, making the necessary advances of capital, in such cases the borrowers taking the risks and the bankers dividing the profits with them.[1]

With the rise of commerce and a money economy in Greece, the same evolution in the practice of banking as had been seen in Babylonia followed there. The temples were the earliest treasuries, from which loans were made to states, and apparently, but the evidence is not perfectly plain, to individuals. The temple at Delos, when under Athenian control, lent sums for five years at 10 per cent, and that of Athena at Athens advanced money to the state between 433 and 427 at 6 per cent. Later the Athenians borrowed from the temple at $1\frac{1}{5}$ per cent, so low a rate as to suggest confiscation, but explainable on the ground that the

[1] W. L. Westermann, "Warehousing and trapezite banking in antiquity", *Journ. of Economic and Business History*, Nov. 1930.

money withdrawn had been deposited by the state treasury for safekeeping and so became technically the possession of the goddess. Great efforts were made after the close of the war to pay the entire sum back,[1] an evidence not so much of piety but rather a desire to accumulate once more a state reserve. It must, however, be emphasised that the temples never carried on what may be called a general banking business; that was left to private individuals of whose activities we have a fairly clear account from various sources.

BANKING IN ATHENS

So far as the evidence goes, and it must be acknowledged we are on very unsafe ground, the earliest banker in Greece proper of whom we have any evidence, is one Philostephanus of Corinth, who some time after the Persian wars of the fifth century, received the considerable sum of 70 talents on deposit from Themistocles.[2] When we consider banking as carried on in Athens in the fourth century B.C., it is essential to view the business in a right perspective and not to magnify it into a great international system, organised and carried on in the modern way, or even on the scale of the European banking of the Middle Ages. There were never in Athens great commercial banking houses such as the Fuggers and the Medici of fifteenth-century Germany and Italy. The incessant wars of ancient Greek nations, and the perils attendant upon foreign trade from pirates, made all international banking an impossibility. Indeed the laws of Athens were stringent in not allowing money to be lent on any ship that did not bring a cargo of grain to the city, or to anyone not a resident of Athens. Even between towns in the same state there were no banking facilities. The cheque and the bill of exchange were unknown.

The business of banking in Athens, like nearly all commercial pursuits, was largely in the hands of Metics. Pasion, the most famous and wealthy of all the Greek bankers, was originally a slave, his masters being Antisthenes and Archestratus, them-

---

[1] *Vide supra*, p. 326.
[2] Epist. Themist. 6, 7, in *Epist. Graec.* Ed. Hercher, p. 745 f. Cf. also J. Hasebroek, "Zum Griech. Bankwesen", in *Hermes*, lv (1920), p. 51.

selves bankers.[1] On being set at liberty he set up for himself, employing Phormio, a slave, and giving him in turn his freedom. Phormio also started for himself and on the death of Pasion married his widow, in accordance with Pasion's will. We have references to other Metic bankers, as, for instance, one from Cyprus, and another, a Phoenician.[2] Even in such a well-known house as that of Pasion, banking was only part of his activities, since he also owned a flourishing business making shields. When he died he was worth 70 talents, 20 of which represented landed property and 50 lent at interest through his banking business, 11 talents of which represented deposits profitably invested. We are told that the income from the bank amounted to a talent and forty minas, while that from the shield factory was only a talent. Yet Apollodorus, the elder son, chose the factory as his share of the inheritance, a wise choice Demosthenes says, "for that is a property without risk whereas banking is a business yielding a precarious revenue from other people's money".[3] Phormio, who succeeded his master Pasion in the bank and married his widow, became very wealthy, and we hear of him possessing ships which were seized at Byzantium and so presumably were in the grain trade.[4]

Although there were rich and famous bankers, yet the business of moneylending and foreign exchange was, in large measure, carried on by a swarm of individuals, who were notorious for their sharp practices and extortionate rates of interest, "money-sharks" of the worst description. So lowly and despised was the trade that Xenophon considers it one of the last refuges of the ruined farmer. "When agriculture becomes unprofitable many farmers, quitting their occupation of tilling the soil, betake themselves to the employment of merchants, or inn-keepers, or moneylenders."[5] Merchants who have retired from the perils of the sea employ the money they have saved in lending on sea loans. Parmenon says: "For a long time I occupied myself with commerce and encountered many dangers. It is not quite seven years since I left the sea, and as I have a small capital saved, I try to make it productive by lending it

---

[1] Dem. *pro Phorm.* 43, 48.　　　[2] Dem. *in Phorm.* 6.
[3] Dem. *pro Phorm.* 11.　　　　[4] *In Steph.* i, 64.
[5] *Revenues*, iv, 6.

out on loans to merchants."[1] A certain Nicobulus, another retired merchant, does the same in partnership with Euergus, and
lends money to the lessee of a silver mine at Laurium. But he
has not entirely left the sea, for immediately after making this
loan he has to go to Pontus on business, and during his absence
was swindled, he alleges.[2] In these cases the hatred felt towards
the petty moneylender is seen, both plaintiffs declaring they
are not the usual professional usurers, "who know no compassion, and for whom nothing counts except money-making".
We have an amusing letter from a countryman to his friend
describing a visit to one such moneylender.[3] "The usurers in
this city, kind friend, are a great nuisance. I do not know what
was the matter with me when I ought to have gone to you or
some other of my country neighbours at the time I was in need
of money for purchasing a farm at Colonus. On that occasion a
man of the city went with me to the house of Byrtius to introduce me to him. There I found an old man, looking wrinkled
and with brows contracted, holding in his hand an antique
paper, rotted by time and half eaten by moths and insects.
Forthwith he spoke to me in brusquest fashion, as though he
considered talking loss of time. But when my voucher said I
wanted money, he asked me how many talents. Then when I
expressed surprise at his mention of so large a sum, he forthwith
spat and showed ill-temper. Nevertheless he gave the money,
demanded a note, required a heavy interest on the principal,
and placed a mortgage on my house. A great nuisance these
men who reckon with pebbles and crooked fingers. Never, ye
Spirits, who watch over farmers, never may it again be my lot
to behold a wolf or a usurer."

In conclusion it would appear that in primitive times at least
the charging of interest was not formally recognised at all and a
legal fiction was necessary in order to protect borrowers.
Plutarch in his *Greek Questions* asks, "Why was it the custom
among the Cnossians for those who borrowed money to snatch
it?" He is not sure himself and suggests, "Was it that if they

---

[1] Dem. *in Apat.* 4.
[2] Dem. *in Pantaen.* 6. Cf. also statement that Zeno the philosopher lent
over 1000 talents on bottomry loans; Diog. Laert. vii, 13. The sum is obviously a gross exaggeration.
[3] *Letters of Alciphron*, i, 26.

defaulted they might be liable to the charge of violence, and so be punished the more?"[1]

MONEYCHANGING

Probably, if not certainly, the earliest activity of the bankers was moneychanging. We hear of a private bank at Byzantium to which the monopoly of changing money had been sold by the city; "no one else might either give money in exchange to anyone, or receive it in exchange from anyone, under penalty of forfeiting the money".[2] Moneychanging, a business which was never, so far as we know, undertaken by the temples officially, was certainly in bad repute at a time when the confusion in national currencies was so great as to give unlimited opportunities for sharp practice. The incident in the Bible of Christ driving the moneychangers from the Temple in Jerusalem on the ground that they had made it "a den of thieves" is illuminating in this connection. In any case in those uncertain times, when debasements of their currencies were far from unknown among the various Greek states, such an occupation must have been a risky one, Demosthenes remarking that anyone who keeps accounts of necessity always notes down the rate of exchange. There is even reason to suppose that the larger bankers would not trouble themselves with it, as apparently clients of the banking house of Pasion got their money changed elsewhere.[3] Undoubtedly we must suppose there were honest men in the trade, and we have references to such being called as expert witnesses in cases where the rate was in dispute.[4] In at least two instances the business of moneychanging was taken over by the state. By a decree of Athens about 423 it is enacted that "if any man in the allied cities coin silver money, or does not employ the Athenian coins, weights and measures, but foreign coins, weights and measures, he shall be punished according to the earlier decree of Clearchus.

[1] *Quaest. Graec.* 53, 303 B.

[2] (Arist.) *Oecon.* 1346 B. Cf. also Heichelheim in *P.W.* xvi, art. "Monopole", p. 155; B. A. van Groningen, *Aristote, le second livre de l'Économique*, pp. 60f.; E. von Stern, *Hermes*, li (1916), p. 427; Hasebroek, *Hermes*, lv (1920), p. 163; *Trade and Politics*, p. 156. A long controversy over the date of this monopoly to which no certain answer can be given.

[3] Isocrates, xvii, 40. Very doubtful. The meaning of the passage is not clear.

[4] Dem. *in Euerg. et Mnes.* 51; *in Dionys.* 15.

Private persons shall hand over their foreign money; the city shall change it...they shall pay it into the mint, where the superintendents shall receive it."[1] This exceedingly interesting inscription seems to suggest that Athens was trying to attain uniformity of coins and weights in the whole of the Empire, and to do so was calling in all other moneys. A similar decree is found in the city of Olbia, where, apparently in the early part of the fourth century, a decree was published to the effect that "whoever wishes to exchange gold or silver money shall do so at the stone in the Ecclesiasterium. Whoever shall do so elsewhere is liable to punishment". The rate of exchange is fixed at $10\frac{1}{2}$ Olbian staters to the Cyzicene stater, but no rate is fixed for other currencies, and no special tax is imposed upon foreign exchange transactions.[2] We have already spoken of the early monopoly sold by the city of Byzantium to a private banker. Such state monopolies in moneychanging can hardly be credited to any anxiety on the part of the authorities to protect their citizens and visiting merchants against fraud, but rather to a desire to keep for the city a particularly profitable business.

Besides moneychanging, which, as we have seen, the bigger banking houses possibly may have abandoned as too risky or too troublesome, the banks of Athens acted as intermediaries in payments between individuals. In the case against Callippus, attributed to Demosthenes, Lycon, a merchant from Heraclea, deposits a sum of money with the banker Pasion to be kept to the order of Cephisiades of Scyrus, who is out of the city, the said Cephisiades to be identified to Pasion by Archebiades and Phrasias. It would appear from this case that the payee could not claim the money merely on a written order; the business had to be done in the presence of witnesses. In the course of the case Demosthenes laid it down as the ordinary practice that "it is the custom of all bankers when any private individual deposits a sum of money with directions to pay it to any particular person, first to write down the name of the party depositing and the sum, then enter in the margin that it is to be paid to this or

[1] *I.G.* i², 295 and Tod, *Greek Hist. Inscr.* 67.
[2] Ditt. *Syll.*³ 218; cf. H. Schmitz, "Ein Gesetz der Stadt Olbia zum Schutze ihres Silbergeldes", *Studie zur Griech. Währungsgesch. des 4 Jahrh. v. Chr.* (1925).

that person, and if they know the face of the person to whom they are to pay, they do only that; but if they do not know him, they add the name of him who is to introduce the person who is to receive the money." In two cases, that against Euergus and Mnesibulus, and that against Dionysodorus, debtor and creditor must go together to settle the transaction at the bank. In another case Demosthenes exclaims, "Who would be so foolish as of his own free will to pay money on a written order?"[1]

This does not preclude, however, the use of the system known as "Giro", whereby transfers of sums in the accounts of the bankers could be made by a simple bookkeeping entry. No case is known to us in which two customers of a bank settled their indebtedness to one another by such means,[2] but the very simplicity of such a transaction makes it probable that this was the practice pursued.[3] That there was any clearing system between banking houses for the mutual cancellation of debts is still more unlikely, although here again it is very easy to imagine some primitive form of such practice. The waste of time and energy taken up in transferring cash from one bank to another may have struck the shrewd bankers of Athens and steps were perhaps taken to avoid it. The only safe conclusion we can come to is that all payments were made in person and in the presence of witnesses—in the case of foreigners unknown to the bank, apparently in the presence of the proxenos.[4]

Although, as remarked below,[5] the "bottomry" bond was to some extent a substitute for the modern foreign bill of exchange, yet it is safe to say that no system of foreign bills was in existence. But it is evident from the famous case[6] argued by Isocrates that the principle at least was not unknown. Here a young man, a native of the Bosporus, had been sent to Athens by his father

---

[1] *In Euerg. et Mnes.* 51; *in Dionys.* 15; *in Naus.* 12.

[2] Hasebroek, p. 85, n. 4; cf. also *ibid.* "Zum Giroverkehr im iv Jahrhundert", *Klio* (1923), pp. 375–8; Kiessling, art. "Giroverkehr" in *P.W.* Supp. v.

[3] Cf. Polyb. xxxii, 13; Dion. Hal. v, 28. The exact connotation of the terms *Diagraphe* and *Paragraphe* is a matter of considerable doubt. Cf. *I.G.* xi, 2, 287, A 135, referring to Delos in the third century, where the meaning is far from clear. It is certain, however, that the practice was well developed in Ptolemaic Egypt.

[4] Dem. *in Callippum*, 5.

[5] *Vide infra*, p. 345.

[6] *Trapeziticus, passim.*

with a cargo of wheat and to see the city and get some education. Evidently he was extravagant, because he got 300 gold staters from one Stratocles, who was going to Pontus, and he gave him a letter to his father Sopaeus. The proceeding was probably an unusual one, because Stratocles was careful to get a guarantee in case Sopaeus dishonoured his son's demand. In any case such dealings must have been rare and extremely risky owing to the impossibility of collecting from a foreigner once he had left Athens, as the Bosporian youth had. What is more, it was expressly forbidden by Athenian law to lend money abroad, or on a ship that did not bring a cargo of grain to Athens.

Deposits were of two kinds, cash and valuables lodged with the banker for safekeeping, and cash deposits on current account. As examples of the first class we hear in the case argued by Demosthenes against Phormio of valuables left with him by a business friend for safekeeping on going abroad,[1] and in the same case of another banker being the custodian of documents.[2] On such deposits, if in the form of cash, no interest was paid.[3] Deposits on current account bore interest,[4] and doubtless that part of his capital which the father of Demosthenes kept with bankers was of that class.[5] From such deposits the banker derived most, if not all, his funds for making loans, as we know from a remark of Demosthenes that a banker who traded exclusively with his own capital ran too great a risk, and was in danger of bankruptcy.[6] One of the questions asked in the Aristotelian *Problems* is why it is more blameworthy to embezzle a deposit than a loan, to which the answer is given that the man who steals a deposit robs a friend, for no man makes a deposit except with a man whom he trusts. A deposit is made for safeguarding and return, but a loan is made for profit. Obviously this does not refer to deposits made with a bank, but simply to the practice of leaving valuables in the charge of friends when called from home, perhaps on military service.[7]

Loans were of the sort usually made by modern bankers, commercial, accommodation, security and mortgage on private

---

[1] Dem. *in Phorm*. 31.
[2] *In Phorm*. 6.
[3] *P.W.* art. "Banken" (Laum).
[4] *In Aphob*. i, 11.
[5] *Pro Phorm*. 5.
[6] *Pro Phorm*. 51.
[7] Arist. *Prob*. xxix, 2, 950 A.

credit.[1] A large business was done in loans to lessees of silver mines at Laurium, and, as will be seen later, on shipping ventures. By the laws of Solon money could not be lent on security of the person of the borrower, although no such prohibition obtained in other states. Nor could agricultural instruments or arms or armour be taken in pawn as security for a loan.[2] We hear of a loan made on a stock of copper[3] and on silver cups and a gold wreath.[4] The father of Demosthenes had lent 40 minas on the security of 20 slaves.[5]

Although slavery for debt had been ended by the laws of Solon, yet he made no provision with regard to the rate of interest charged; the lender could demand whatever he wished,[6] with the single exception of a man separating from his wife and returning her dowry, when 18 per cent was fixed by law.[7] This same rate is mentioned by Isaeus[8] and also by Aeschines.[9] Sixteen per cent was common,[10] and Demosthenes speaks of 12 per cent as a reasonable rate.[11] Ten per cent was so low that it was charged on a loan between friends.[12] M. Homolle has drawn attention to rates of interest charged at Delphi in the first half of the fourth century, where it was decreed that not more than 3 obols per mina per mensem should be charged. Since it is not clear whether 70 or 100 drs. to the mina was the rule at Delphi at this time, we do not know whether the actual rate was 8·57 or 6 per cent.[13] We hear of some usurious rates charged by the moneylenders. Aeschines, when he wanted to go into the perfumery business, borrowed money at 36 per cent. Finding it impossible to carry on under such a burden, he was fortunate enough to get the money to pay it off from a friend at 18 per cent.[14] We hear of 33⅓ per cent being

---

[1] Oertel, "Zur Frage der Attischen Grossindustrie", *Rhein. Mus.* lxxix (1930), p. 230, denies that banking accommodation was ever given to manufacturing, except for mining. But cf. Schwahn, "Die Xen. Poroi", *Rhein. Mus.* lxxx (1931), pp. 253 ff., for another view.   [2] Diod. Sic. i, 79, 5.

[3] Dem. *in Tim.* 51.   [4] Dem. *in Nicost.* 9.

[5] *In Aphob.* i, 23.   [6] Lysias, *in Theomnest.* 18.

[7] Dem. *in Neaeram*, 52; *in Aphob.* i, 17.

[8] *De Hagn. Hered.* 42.   [9] *In Timarch.* 107.

[10] Dem. *in Nicost.* 13.

[11] *In Aphob.* i, 9, 18, 23, ii, 13; Aeschines, *in Ctes.* 104.

[12] Dem. *in Onet.* i, 7. Cf. Ps.-Arist. *Oecon.* 1346 B.

[13] T. Homolle, "La Loi de Cadys sur le prêt a l'intérêt", *Bull. Corr. Hell.* l (1926), pp. 3 ff.   [14] Athen. xiii, 611.

charged on small loans of a risky nature,[1] and Theophrastus writing at the end of the fourth century gives a most outrageous instance of a "loan shark" who exacted 25 per cent a day from "petty tradesmen, cookshops, fishmongers and fishpicklers".[2] The owls of Laurium certainly hatched some fine broods[3] when rates were so high and there were so many laws to restrain the avaricious. Compound interest was charged by creditors; Theophrastus tells us that the penurious man is given to distraining for a debt and exacting usury upon usury.[4] There seems to have been reluctance on the part of the courts to give facilities for collecting payment at high rates of interest by process of law. Cases involving loans at a rate of interest of less than 12 per cent could apparently be brought to trial more expeditiously than those at a higher. The point is not perfectly clear, but we may reasonably suppose that such was a device to discourage exactions and delay cases involving higher rates.[5] The Megarian revolutionaries are credited with the invention of "return interest" when they demanded from their creditors not only cancellation of debts but the return to them of all the money paid as interest.[6]

So far as we know there was no instance of the government of any state borrowing from private bankers, nor of any advice or assistance given by such in matters pertaining to public finance. The close connection between the government exchequer and bankers, which is so marked a feature of modern state finance, seems to have been entirely lacking: whether *demosia trapeza* denotes a state bank is discussed hereafter.[7] Even such a famous bank as that of Phormio or Pasion in Athens would hardly have been big enough to enter on any very large transaction.[8]

---

[1] Isaeus, fr. 23; *de Hered. Hag.* 42. [2] *Char.* vi, 9.

[3] Aristoph. *Aves*, 1105. [4] *Char.* x, 11.

[5] Billeter, *Gesch. des Zinsfusses*, pp. 26 ff.; Busolt, *Griech. Staatsk.* i, 185. For further references cf. Andreades, *Greek Public Finance*, p. 75, n. 1. Hasebroek's comment (p. 169) that "there was no legal rate of interest" is unnecessary. There is none to-day and the efforts of the Athenian courts to prevent usury were as successful, or not, as those in modern times.

[6] Plut. *Quaest. Graec.* 18, 295 D. [7] *Vide infra*, p. 350.

[8] But cf. Calhoun, *Business Life of Ancient Athens*, p. 104. Mr Calhoun considers that Phormio must have helped out the city by negotiating large loans on its behalf. Although his eminent services to the city are spoken of we are not explicitly informed as to what they were. It is just as likely that these services consisted in particularly splendid liturgies. Cf. Dem. *pro Phorm.* 39, 57.

Neither was there so far as our knowledge goes any system of syndicating banking business to allow of large-scale financing,[1] although there are instances recorded of inter-bank dealings. Thus we learn from Isocrates[2] that Pasion had dealings with another banker, Archestratus, when not able to furnish security for one of his own clients; and from Demosthenes[3] of further dealings with another, named Heracleides, Pasion giving security for a client when unable to lend the money himself.

It is unfortunate that in the cases argued, reputedly by Demosthenes and Isocrates, we hear only one side, and consequently we have the false impression that generally bankers in Athens were rogues. For instance, we do not know what was the outcome of the suit brought by the young man from Bosporus against Pasion. On the face of it the charges against the banker are very serious, and had they been proven would undoubtedly have ruined him. But since we hear later of Pasion doing a flourishing business, we must suppose that he successfully defended the case. Isaeus relates a highly edifying story of a banker named Sumathes, who, on hearing of a client's death, at once pays to the relatives the amount on deposit with him.[4] But perhaps this was so remarkable a case as to be worth chronicling for its peculiar interest. We must suppose that the reputable bankers conducted their business honestly; a rule of conduct that probably did not apply to the swarm of petty "loan sharks".

Banks, then as now, were highly vulnerable to panics, and runs might very well develop from rumours, or from uneasiness caused by a lawsuit against one of them.[5] We hear of one banker, Aristolochus, who was entirely ruined and had to surrender everything to his creditors.[6] Another, Heracleides, was obliged discreetly "to keep out of the way" after being involved in some very heavy losses.[7] The failure of Heracleides was evidently particularly bad, for some of the larger creditors had to form a

---

[1] Except perhaps for bottomry loans where syndicates would be formed to undertake large risks. But it is uncertain whether this was a regular banking practice or done through associations of private individuals. Cf. V. Brants, *Les Sociétés Commerciales à Athènes* (1882).

[2] *Trapeziticus*, 43. [3] *In Apat.* 7.

[4] Isaeus, fr. 18 (Loeb edition, p. 471).

[5] *Pro Phorm.* 51. [6] *In Steph.* i, 63.

[7] *In Apat.* 9.

sort of syndicate to take over the assets of the bank in order to realise as much as they could get out of them.[1]

SHIPPING LOANS[2]

Undoubtedly, of all banking and loan business, the most general and at the same time the most lucrative and hazardous were the loans made to merchants and shipmasters for the furtherance of commercial ventures in overseas trade. Such transactions have been generally described by the modern term of bottomry loans, but this is not strictly correct. A bottomry contract is in the nature of a mortgage on a ship, by which money is borrowed for the necessities of the ship to enable it to proceed on its voyage. Contracts of this kind "were invented for the purpose of procuring the necessary supplies for ships which may happen to be in distress in foreign ports, where the master and owners are without credit and where, unless assistance could be secured by means of such an instrument, the vessels and their cargoes must be left to perish".[3] This does not exactly correspond to the class of loan made by bankers, and often by private citizens in Greece, in order to finance a commercial venture. Where there were no large mercantile houses which owned or chartered vessels to carry on their business, and where the merchant or shipowner was in a very small way of business and had not sufficient capital to finance his operations himself, recourse was had to moneylenders who would advance the necessary funds. Thus there was, as in the modern bottomry contract, no desperate necessity to help the ship on its way which could only be met by hypothecating the ship. To describe such a form of loan by the term bottomry, therefore, is not entirely correct, although both were alike in form.

[1] Cf. Hasebroek in *Hermes*, lv (1920), pp. 168 ff. This explanation of the incident seems preferable to that of Calhoun, who speaks of guarantors or receivers who had become responsible for the bank's debts: *Business Life*, p. 111.

[2] H. Sieveking, *Das Seedarlehen des Altertums* (Leipzig 1893); G. M. Calhoun, "Sea loans in Ancient Athens", *Journ. Business and Econ. Hist.* (Aug. 1930), ii, p. 561; Knorringa, *Emporos*, pp. 92 ff.; Ziebarth, *Beiträge*, pp. 13, 48, 53, 58, 82, 119.

[3] Art. "Bottomry" in *Encyc. Brit.*; Sieveking, *Das Seedarlehen des Altertums*, p. 9. The case argued by Demosthenes against Dionysodorus is concerned throughout with a bottomry bond and gives an excellent summary of the questions involved therein.

Another form of sea loan, secured not on the hull but on the cargo, corresponded with the modern Respondentia contract. Evidently this was less common in Athens, as we have only two instances akin to it, and both contain peculiar features which make them hardly comparable with modern practice. In the case argued by Demosthenes against Polycles, a naval trierarch, or commander of a trireme, on whom fell the duty of fitting out the ship, the defendant had borrowed on the ship's furniture. Obviously since the hull belonged to the state he could not borrow on that, and the outfit of a ship of war can hardly be called its cargo. The other case, that against Lacritus, was a true Respondentia loan, since here it was secured by the cargo, but differed from the modern form of contract since it stipulated that, if the security was lost, the entire property of the borrower could be seized. This was undoubtedly an exceptional case, since in general in all contracts of sea loans it was provided that if ship and cargo were lost, either by tempest or capture by enemies or pirates, the lender lost all he had advanced and could not proceed against the borrower. That this was the general rule is shown clearly by another case, that against Dionysodorus, where the ship had been lost, scuttled the plaintiff asserted, and it was not until some time after that he discovered a fraud had been perpetrated and brought suit in the courts.

The terms of such sea loans were embodied in a contract (*syngraphe*), a most necessary document if the transaction led to a lawsuit.[1] Such shipping bonds served in place of Bills of Exchange, since the borrower might be required to pay the principal and interest to a creditor in a foreign port. Loans were contracted for a single or return voyage, the latter being much the more profitable to the lender, since if he got his money back by the middle of the shipping season he could lend it again to advantage. Thus Demosthenes says that moneylenders in Athens had no objection to receiving payment in Rhodes on loans on a voyage to Egypt, since they could easily get their money out again at once, the route from Rhodes to Egypt being open all

---

[1] Production of such contracts in court may be seen in several cases argued by Demosthenes, e.g. *in Apat.* 30; *in Dionys.* 15; *in Lacr.* 10. No law or regulation contrary to the spirit of the bond could be adduced against such a contract: *in Lacr.* 13, 39.

the year round; while if paid in Athens they might have to wait for the next season.[1] Those who lent money on a single voyage often went with the ship as supercargo, or sent a representative.[2] Loans had to be repaid within twenty days of the termination of the voyage, and were usually made only to 50 per cent of the value of the cargo,[3] a precaution necessary because of the severe fluctuations in the price of grain. In order to guard against fraud, loading was done in the presence of witnesses.[4] If any misfortune occurred during the voyage and part of the cargo was lost, the remainder went to the lenders, and no abatement was to be made in such case except for jettison made with the consent of all the passengers, or through seizure by pirates or enemies.[5] Ship and cargo must not be borrowed on twice for the same voyage, a type of sharp practice which seems to have been fairly common.[6] Withdrawal of the security by the borrower was looked upon as so serious a matter that the culprit was liable to the death penalty,[7] and for the sake of preventing such frauds the lender had the right to station guards over the security.[8] Repayment of the loan was made in the presence of witnesses.[9] The shipmaster must proceed to the destination named in the contract under the severest penalties.[10] No loan can be made for trade in foreign markets.[11]

With regard to interest charged and stipulations as to the conduct of the voyage, the case against Lacritus affords many enlightening details. Two Athenians, Androcles and Nausicrates, had lent 30 minas to Artemon and Apollodorus, on condition that they should sail in a certain vessel from Athens to Mende or Scione, and there purchase 3000 jars of wine. From thence they were to proceed to the Thracian Bosporus as far as the mouth of the Dnieper, and after selling their cargo of wine, purchase a return cargo to be brought in the same vessel to Athens. The loan was to be repaid with interest in case the cargo was brought safe to Athens within twenty days after its arrival, interest to be at 22½ per cent; unless they returned from

[1] *In Dionys.* 29.
[2] *In Phorm.* 8, 26.
[3] *In Phorm.* 6.
[4] *In Phorm.* 28, 29.
[5] *In Lacr.* 11.
[6] *In Lacr.* 11.
[7] *In Phorm.* 50.
[8] *In Apat.* 10.
[9] *In Phorm.* 30.
[10] *In Dionys.* 10.
[11] *In Lacr.* 50; *in Dionys.* 6.

the Euxine to Hierum in Bithynia early in September, in which case interest was to be at 30 per cent in view of increased perils owing to the lateness of the season. No abatement was to be allowed except for jettison made with the consent of all the passengers, or compulsory payments to enemies. The return cargo was to be delivered as security to the lenders to be held by them until all was paid. In default of payment not only the cargo could be sold, but the property of the borrowers could be distrained upon. If instead of entering the Euxine they remained in the Hellespont for ten days after the end of July and discharged their cargo there, which they were at liberty to do, or in any friendly port, it was agreed that a lower rate of interest should be paid. A declaration was affixed to the agreement by the borrowers that the security given was not encumbered by any previous hypothecation or engagement, and also an undertaking not to take up any further loan on it.[1]

There is some uncertainty as to the rates of interest generally charged.[2] In the Lacritus case it was $22\frac{1}{2}$ per cent; in the Phormio case 30 per cent. It has been suggested that since the Lacritus case arose sometime before 340 and the Phormio case sometime after 330, there had been a rise in interest rates during the ten or fifteen years that had elapsed, owing to increased piracy and disorder in the eastern Aegean.[3] But in another case[4] we hear of $12\frac{1}{2}$ per cent being charged for a single voyage from the Hellespont to Athens in war-time, a period when it would naturally be supposed the rates would be higher. A possible explanation is that the voyage would be made under convoy, but perhaps the most obvious one is that the interest was fixed on the principle of what the traffic would bear. Undoubtedly the business was an extremely hazardous one, but the returns were large if no losses were incurred. It was reckoned that, barring losses, anywhere from 40 to 66 per cent could be made in a season, and for particularly hazardous ventures in the Adriatic as much as 100 per cent was offered for accommodation.[5] It must be remembered, however, that a bottomry or respondentia

---

[1] Kennedy's translation and summary.
[2] Boeckh, i, p. 166 f., discusses the problems at considerable length.
[3] Calhoun, *loc. cit.* p. 576.   [4] Dem. *in Polyc.* 17.
[5] Lysias, *in Diogeit.* 25. But the point is not clear.

loan is, of itself, a peculiar one since, if the ship or cargo upon which the loan is made is lost, then the security for the loan and all means of exacting repayment are also lost. So hazardous were such investments regarded in Athens that the law forbade the money of orphans being used for them.[1]

There would seem to have been no system of marine insurance, as apart from the sea loans, in existence at that time, although it has been suggested that a form of insurance was practised by Greek traders, in that those who had sufficient capital to finance their own voyages without borrowing would take out marine loans for the purpose of insurance against risk. This is a possible procedure, but we have no evidence of such transactions.[2] It may also be remarked that apparently in the majority of cases the shipmasters or merchants seeking the loans were small men, who could not ordinarily finance the voyage themselves up to more than 50 per cent of the value of ship or cargo. According to the law of Rhodes, agreements in bottomry were forbidden in which the lender did not himself accompany the ship and so expose his own person to the dangers of the voyage. Boeckh explains that on the ground that the rates in bottomry bonds were regarded as so usurious that the lender was forced to run personal risk himself in order to profit by such rates, while in Athens, where no limit was placed on interest rates, there was no such stipulation.[3]

All cases arising out of sea loans and foreign commerce came before the court of the Thesmothetae.[4] They belonged in the category of "monthly suits",[5] since they had to be settled within a month. From a passage in one of the cases prepared by Demosthenes we hear that such cases were heard in the winter months (i.e. from Boedromion to Munychion).[6] But a recent writer[7] has given excellent reasons to suppose that this

---

[1] Lysias, *in Diogeit.* 25. [2] Cf. Calhoun, *loc. cit.* p. 580ff.
[3] Boeckh, i, p. 171.
[4] Dem. *in Apat.* 1; Lysias, *Orat.* 17; Arist. *Ath. Pol.* lv, 1.
[5] Dem. *de Hal.* 12. Evidently they were put in this category sometime between 355 and 342, i.e. between the time that Xenophon wrote the *Revenues* and the speech on the Halonnesus. Cf. Gernet, "Sur les actions commerciales en Droit Athénien", *Rev. Études Grecques*, li, 239 (1938), pp. 1 ff.
[6] *In Apat.* 23.
[7] E. P. Paoli, "Zur Gerichtsbarkeit der Dikai Emporikai im Attischen Recht", *Sav. Zeitsch. Rom. Abt.* xlix (1929), p. 473.

was not so, and that the names of the months have been transposed. On the face of it, it would appear to be more reasonable that pressing cases which arose during the season of navigation should be heard at once and not postponed till the winter.

It is not impossible that this expedition in hearing such cases was due to the advice of Xenophon, who says: "If we should propose rewards, however, for the judges of the tribunal of commerce, to be given to such as should decide points of controversy with the greatest justice and expedition so that persons who wished to sail might not be detained, a still larger number of people would by that means be brought to trade with us, and with greater pleasure."[1] To protect merchants against frivolous and oppressive cases a severe penalty involving *atimia*, or loss of civil rights, was imposed on the plaintiff on the subsequent withdrawal of the charge.[2] It is quite evident that the laws took very careful cognisance of all sea loans, since overseas commerce, especially in grain and timber, was vital to the Athenian state, which could not exist without it. It was necessary, therefore, that foreign importers should be treated with scrupulous justice and indeed encouraged in every way to bring their cargoes to Attica.

WAS THERE A STATE BANK IN ATHENS?

The problem as to whether there was a "state bank" in Athens is one of extreme difficulty. In the scholia to Aristophanes *Ranae*, 367, mention is made of the refusal of Archinus and Agyrrhius, managers or overseers of the *Demosia Trapeza*, to pay the prizes awarded by the state to certain comic playwrights on the ground that they had insulted them. The question is, was this *Demosia Trapeza* a "bank", or was it the state pay office, which disbursed the monies expended by the treasurers of the various state funds? Laum, in his article *Banken*, in Pauly-Wissowa, Suppl. IV, holds that it was "a bank which stood in close relationship to the state. It was not a 'state bank', but a private one which looked after the public monies and enjoyed a monopoly in doing the state banking business." This is mere supposition, and rests on no clear evidence whatever.

---

[1] *Revenues*, iii, 3.   [2] Dem. *in Theoc.* 10, 54.

It would seem far more likely that this *Demosia Trapeza* was the public treasury, and not a "bank" at all. The fact that both Archinus and Agyrrhius were public officials would seem to indicate that they had been regularly appointed to the managership of the state pay office rather than that they were partners in a private bank. But the problem must remain unsolved for lack of further evidence.[1]

[1] Cf. art. by Schmid in the *Philologische Wochenschrift*, Nov. 26, 1938 p. 1343. Boeckh, ii, p. 319, n. 2.

CHAPTER X

PUBLIC FINANCE

INTRODUCTION[1]

THE subject of public finance of the Greek city-state is one of very peculiar interest, which has attracted the attention of historians since the time when Boeckh wrote his monumental *Political Economy of Athens* to the present day when Dr Andreades has added so much to our knowledge. This is, assuredly, hardly to be wondered at, for as the Greeks very well knew, money was the life-blood of the body politic. "Money not men wins wars", said old Archidamus to the Spartans who affected to, but did not in reality, despise money. We must always remember that the Greeks were very poor; "Hellas and Poverty were ever foster-sisters." They had very little money and what they had they made go a long way. Always in the east was the menace of Persian gold, which the Greeks feared much more than Persian armies; a menace and a temptation, which sooner or later was to debauch the best of them.

The Athenian system of public finance presents some features of quite absorbing interest, which the present-day economist can ill afford to overlook. The whole subject of the incidence and effect of their taxation of capital called the *eisphora*, or capital levy, is one that merits careful consideration at the present day. And particularly may we study the means taken in Athens to relieve distress and the system of subventions to citizens for public services. The "dole" in Athens worked its own disastrous effects, as it did in Rome, and as it may, for all we know, in our modern world.

The system of public finance of the Athenian state was, beyond all question, essentially unsound. It rested on two main bases, the first being the tribute paid by the Allies. When the

---

[1] General references: Andreades, *History of Greek Public Finance*, i, translated by Carroll N. Brown, Harvard University Press, 1933. Boeckh's *Staatshaushaltung der Athener*, while old, is still indispensable. All references are to the third edition, revised by Fränkel in 1886 with many additions and corrections.

Delian League crashed after the defeat of Aegospotami, the greater part of the whole financial system went down with it. The second base was the taxation of the rich; and when the rich could no longer be squeezed, other sources of revenue were insufficient to bear the burden of expense. The Athenians greatly disliked and always avoided direct taxation. It was far easier to get the money out of the rich than out of the mass of the citizens, who were always ready to vote down any such proposal.[1] We cannot doubt that, essentially, the never-appeased enmity between rich and poor, oligarchy and democracy, was founded on and kept alive by the ceaseless attempts of the people to mulct the rich of their wealth. To be a rich man in ancient Greece was a dangerous thing; just as perhaps it may soon be in our present world. Lacking any system of raising money by public loans, the state had to do the best it could, and its expedients were almost invariably economically unsound.[2]

And lastly the Greeks, with the exception of Xenophon, never saw the fallacy of the "great illusion". They thought that war paid; and while they were plundering the Persians it certainly did. But despoiling each other was a different matter, and the ferocious treatment dealt out to conquered foes injured the conqueror as much as the wretched people they murdered and robbed. Nowhere is the genius of Xenophon shown more clearly than in the passage of his pamphlet on the *Revenues of Athens* in which he demonstrates the futility of wars. "If any-one still thinks that war is more conducive to the wealth of our city than peace, I do not know how he can better be convinced than by considering the effect of former events on our city. For he will find that in past times great sums of money were brought into the city during peace, all of which was expended during war. And he will learn that to-day many branches of the revenue are deficient through war, and that the money of those that have been productive has been spent on many urgent necessities; but that now, when we have peace at sea, the revenues are increasing and the citizens are free to make what-

---

[1] But Isaeus, v. 37, seems to suggest a general levy on all alike. The point is obscure; cf. also Dem. *Olynth.* 1, 20.

[2] Cf. Riezler, *Finanzen und Monopole*, pp. 56ff.

ever use they please of them."[1] Short campaigns, fought by citizen armies of small size, who served without pay, and in which the damage done on either side was not particularly serious, were not disastrous and soon recovered from. But as wars lengthened and became more serious; when the area of hostilities widened, and, as in the closing phases of the Peloponnesian war, the destruction of life and property became greater, the state of economic exhaustion became extreme and the "moral" of the people irretrievably lowered. Free citizens would not serve in the armies without pay, and to the already bankrupt exchequers of the combatants was added the impossible burden of paying their own citizens; or as the final phase of the degeneration of the democratic state, the hiring of mercenaries. The spectacle of economic decline in the fourth and third centuries is a melancholy one, marked by every characteristic that the world has come, through bitter experience, to recognise as accompanying national degeneration.

It is to be remarked that Athenian finance was always in a more or less precarious condition due to the city's "unfavourable" balance of trade. This arose from her inability to feed her own population without very heavy imports of grain, and at least at times of naval activity from the necessity of buying large quantities of timber for shipbuilding. Against these could be put what must have been fairly heavy exports of oil and wine, to a certain extent pottery and later marble and various forms of art ware and silver from the mines of Laurium. As "invisible" exports we must add first, by inference, freight payments for carriage of foreign merchandise by Athenian cargo ships, but of this we know nothing. Secondly, payments while they lasted of the tribute by the Allies. Lastly, we must add an item of which there is no hope of computation, in the profits made by Athenian bankers. Any idea of constructing a statement of the balance of Athenian trade is obviously out of the question; but it is equally obvious that as long as these sources of income could be kept up and utilised for payments abroad, so long were Athenian finances in a healthy condition. It is easy to realise how desperate was the situation when after

[1] *Revenues*, v, 11. (Referred to by many authors under the Latin title "De Vectigalibus".)

Aegospotami the tribute stopped, and exploitation of the silver mines, if it did not cease, at least fell off considerably. A careful perusal of the little pamphlet on the *Revenues of Athens* will reveal how clear a conception of these problems was in the mind of the author.

It was to the immensely valuable trade of the Piraeus that Athens owed her remarkable resiliency, as evidenced by the large revenues enjoyed when such capable financiers as Eubulus and Lycurgus took the public exchequer in hand, and even more remarkably when, at the end of the fourth century, Demetrius of Phalerum "liquidated" Athens, and put her on a sound financial basis, by eliminating all expenditure on armaments and cutting down all wasteful public services.

ATHENIAN PUBLIC FINANCE: THE BUDGET

Any study of the public finances of the Greek city-states in general must, of necessity, be based, in large measure, on our knowledge of those of Athens, for the simple reason that our information of Athenian finance is far more complete than for that of any other. Of that of the Spartans we know nothing and very little of any other. That being obviously the case, we will confine our attention to the financial system of Athens, with references, where pertinent, to similar practices in other states.

In the first place it is well to inquire as to whether or not there was in Athens that most important adjunct of modern statecraft, the budget. Broadly speaking, there was not a unified single budget presented yearly to the legislature by a minister of finance. But at the same time they did have what essentially amounted to a budget; they foresaw their expenditures and their revenues, and tried to strike a balance between them, just as they clearly distinguished their regular from their extraordinary outlay.[1] At the same time we must be careful of our use of the word budget. There were, as a matter of fact, a number of budgets which dealt with funds paid into the receivers. The system was to vote a tax for a specific purpose, and to use the proceeds for that purpose and none other. Whatever may be said in favour of this system, it had one great drawback, it

[1] Andreades, p. 365; Boeckh, i, p. 253.

obscured a general view of the national finances as a whole and led to extravagance along certain lines.[1] If a surplus were found in one of the treasuries, for instance in that of the "Theoric Fund", or of that designated for building warships or public works, the temptation to dissipate the balance on some perhaps frivolous object was very great. Doubtless if there had been a single unified budget, presented by a responsible minister of finance, many financial troubles and extravagances might have been avoided. It was not till late in the fourth century that a competent financial expert was found in Eubulus and, a little later, Lycurgus, who was able to gather the surpluses from all the various funds into one, and so save them from being severally dissipated.[2]

TAX FARMING

The system of selling the right of collection or "farming" the taxes, so universally condemned at the present time, was general in the Ancient World, and regularly followed in Athens and other Greek city-states. From long experience such a system has been found wasteful and peculiarly liable to abuse and injustice on the part of the farmers. Consequently it has now been everywhere abandoned, as it was in the later Roman Empire, in favour of collection by a permanent civil service.[3] In condemning the system we must not, however, allow our modern ideas nor yet our Biblical prejudices to obscure the real use of the tax farmer. The frequent condemnation of "publicans and sinners" in the New Testament gives us a view of the system which is not altogether fair. At a time when banking and the mechanism of finance had developed only to a small degree, and when the state treasury was unable to anticipate the receipt of taxes by issuing treasury bills or borrowing from the banks, the practice of selling the taxes beforehand to the highest bidder was the only practicable one to obviate the difficulties of the exchequer. That auctioning the taxes was liable to lead to serious abuses is quite plain. In the first place,

---

[1] The practice is not unknown in modern municipal finance and the consequence just as mischievous.

[2] Cf. A. Motzki, *Eubulos von Probalinthos u. seine Finanz-politik.*

[3] As late as 1840 small towns in Canada, lacking adequate machinery for the collection of rates, sold the right to collect the taxes to the highest bidder.

the higher the sum bid the more necessary was it for the farmer to extract more from the taxpayer. Secondly, as was found in Athens, it was by no means difficult for the tax farmers, a small class since large capital was necessary, to form a "ring" whereby bidding-up the price of the tax was avoided.

The tax farmer was hated and feared as in all ancient nations, and modern ones for the matter of that. Demosthenes in the case against Androtion[1] speaks of respectable citizens hiding under beds and climbing over neighbours' roofs to escape the tax gatherer who has called to collect the few paltry drachmae owing. But all the same there was sturdy stuff in the Athenian citizen that would not submit to excessive exactions, as is seen, for instance, in the edifying story of the beating administered to a tax gatherer by Lycurgus, who had arrested the philosopher Xenocrates of Chalcedon.[2] They were invariably despised and disliked, as several contemptuous references to them testify,[3] and the trick played by Alcibiades on them by putting up a dummy bidder to run the price up and then be bought off by the dismayed professionals, was evidently highly relished and conduced to his further popularity.[4] The farmers were put under heavy bond, and formed themselves into syndicates, over which a farmer-general (*Telonarches*) presided.[5] They were armed with considerable powers, to seize contraband goods and lay information against smugglers, which involved severe penalties.[6] Considering the fluctuating nature of public receipts of which notice is taken later, the business was a hazardous one, and we may be sure that the experts in buying the taxes beforehand gave themselves a good margin for possible failure of the anticipated receipts. In any case the system was, if unavoidable, extravagant and open to grave abuse.

THE ATHENIAN CIVIL SERVICE

In the detailed account given by Aristotle in the *Athenaion Politeia*[7] of the various boards and commissions which dealt

---

[1] *In Androt.* 53.
[2] Plut. *Lycurgus*, 16; also *Vit. X. Orat.* 842 B.
[3] E.g. Andocides, *De Myst.* 133-4; Lycurgus, *in Leocr.* 19; Poll. ix, 29.
[4] Plut. *Alcibiades*, 5.
[5] Dem. *in Phorm.* 7, *in Midiam*, 133; Poll. viii, 47.
[6] Dem. *in Timocr.* 144; Andocides, *de Myst.* 173.
[7] Caps. 41–60; Boeckh, i, p. 200 f

with the collection and expenditure of taxes, we find a good deal of overlapping and lack of co-ordination which led to confusion and extravagance. We have the Hellenic treasurers (*Helleno-tamiae*), whose duty it was to receive and administer the tribute of the Allies. With the dissolution of the Delian Confederacy their office ceased. There were also the treasurers of Athena and the other gods who administered the revenues of the temples, and the treasurers of the other non-sacred revenues which came to the state. Secondly, commissioners for public contracts (*Poletae*), whose duty it was to lease the mines and sell the collection of taxes to the farmers. They also sold the property of those who had fled the city, or whose goods had been confiscated, and leased the sacred enclosures or lands of the temples. Thirdly, there was the board of ten receivers-general (*Apodectae*), who received the instalments on the taxes paid in by the farmers and paid out the funds to those appointed to administer them. Fourthly, there were ten auditors (*Logistae*), and ten examiners of accounts (*Euthuni*), with two assessors (*Paredri*) for each examiner, whose duty it was to receive accusations against any magistrate suspected of misappropriation of public funds.

For the carrying on of the business of the city there were a number of elected boards, in almost all cases of ten members each, one from each tribe, these having as assistants expert slaves, who as a matter of fact, formed the only non-elective and permanent Civil Service. First, there was a board of ten commissioners for repairs of temples, who received thirty minas from the receivers-general for that purpose. Second, ten city commissioners (*Astynomi*), five in the city and five in the Piraeus, whose duties varied, for instance, seeing that female flute, harp and lute players did not receive more than two drachmae for their performance and deciding by lot between disputants for their services. They also had to see that "no collector of sewage shall shoot any of his sewage within ten stadia of the walls. They prevent people from blocking up the streets by buildings, or stretching barriers across them, or making drain-pipes in mid-air with a discharge into the street, or having doors which open outwards; they also remove the corpses of those who die in the streets." Third, ten market commissioners (*Agoranomi*), five for the Piraeus and five for

Athens, whose duty was to see that all articles offered for sale in the market were unadulterated. Fourth, commissioners of weights and measures (*Metronomi*), whose duties are implied in their title. Fifth, thirty-five grain wardens (*Sitophylakes*), who superintended the sale of grain, meal and bread. Sixth, ten superintendents of the market, whose chief duty was to see that merchants did not re-export more than one-third of all grain imported.[1] Seventh, a special police, called the Eleven, had supervision over the public gaols, the lists of farms and properties claimed as belonging to the state, and informations lodged against magistrates. Eighth, five introducers of cases (*Eisagogeis*), who brought up the "monthly cases" to the law courts.[2] Ninth, a board of forty magistrates to decide petty cases where the sum at issue did not exceed ten drachmae. Tenth, a board of arbitrators who decided upon the lists of those liable for military service.[3] Eleventh, a board of five commissioners of roads (*Hodopoei*), commissioners of public worship (*Hieropoei*), and a board of ten annual commissioners to offer sacrifices and administer all the quadrennial festivals except the Panathenaea, which was under the supervision of a board of ten commissioners of games (*Athlothetae*) who held office for four years, and had as their special care the provision of oil for the athletes from the sacred olives.[4] It is not necessary here to speak of the nine senior magistrates, of which six were termed Thesmothetae, one archon, one king archon, and the last polemarch;[5] nor of the military officers, the ten generals (*strategi*), the ten commanders of infantry regiments (*taxiarchs*) and the same number of cavalry officers (*phylarchs*), with the treasurer for the two sacred despatch boats for state uses. Besides these elected officers there were the members of the legislature and the jurors who received pay for their services. Members of the Assembly received a drachma a day, and for special occasions nine obols; members of the Council received five obols. The nine archons drew four obols and were allowed the services of a herald and a flute player.

---

[1] For more on these officials *vide supra*, p. 273.
[2] For more on these cases cf. p. 349.
[3] Cf. *Ath. Pol.* liii, 4–7.   [4] *Ath. Pol.* lx, 1.
[5] For the duties of these magistrates cf. *Ath. Pol.* lv, 59.

Control of finance was in the hands of the Boule, or Council, but the Ecclesia, or Assembly, was also kept informed by reports submitted every month by the chief clerk of the finance department (*Antigrapheus*), detailing current receipts and expenditures. These were provisional estimates, and when the final accounts of the year were made up the entire balance sheet was scrutinised by the board of Auditors.[1] As in all democracies the system of accounting and auditing was highly developed; when an official went out of office he had to submit to a searching examination of his books, with unpleasant consequences if he was found to have helped himself to the public funds.

EXPENDITURES OF THE STATE

As in modern states, the cost of government may be divided into three main categories: expenditures on public safety through police and standing army; those on civil administration and lastly payments for relief of destitute citizens and for services to the state.

Public order in the city and country was maintained by a police force, the so-called "Scythian" archers, a body of public slaves of uncertain number,[2] who apparently acted as city policemen and also as mounted constabulary in the rural districts and as forest and game wardens.[3] In addition to these were slaves at the disposition of the "Eleven", who were attached to the government direct, and charged with the keeping of the prison and dealing with offences against the state, particularly with regard to the treasury.[4] There were also, but later, a kind of "police des mœurs" or *Gynaikonomoi*.[5] We have no means of computing the cost of all these services; the police must have

---

[1] Antigrapheus, Aesch. *in Ctes.* 25; Boeckh, i, p. 226. Provisional accounts, Lysias, xxx, 4, 5. For system of public accounting cf. Boeckh, i, p. 253; Andreades, p. 371.

[2] The numbers of the policemen are hopelessly confused, being computed at from 300 to 1200. Miss Sargent reviews the controversy (*Size of the Slave Population at Athens in the 5th and 4th centuries* B.C. pp. 114 ff.) without coming to any definite conclusion but suggests that the police numbered 300, other public slaves 700, making 1000 in all. Cf. also O. Jakob, "Les Esclaves Publiques à Athènes", *Musée Belge*, xxx (1926), pp. 57 ff.

[3] Arist. *Pol.* 1321 B. Their upkeep cost the state 3 obols per diem, *I.G.* ii,[2] 1672.

[4] Arist. *Ath. Pol.* lii, 1.

[5] Athen. vi, 245 Aff., counting how many guests at a dinner party.

cost, for maintenance and replacement, at least 40 talents a year.[1]

With regard to military expenses, it is to be noted that, certainly down to the outbreak of the Peloponnesian war, the armed forces of the state were composed of citizens who provided their own equipment and maintained themselves while on active service. Since campaigns were short and arranged so as not to interfere with seed-time or harvest, it was quite possible for the state to bear little or no expense in that matter, especially when it was a cardinal principle in all wars that they should pay for themselves by plunder or indemnities from the enemy. We are ignorant, however, of how campaigns of long duration overseas, as for instance the disastrous expedition to Egypt from 459–454, were paid for; except on the reasonable supposition that there must have been a constant rotation of troops serving for a few months.[2] But even then if the citizen soldiers served without pay, we cannot doubt that, at least for the poorer members of the army, there must have been a subsistence allowance for families left at home, of which we have no account, although we do know that orphans of soldiers killed in the wars were maintained at the public expense.[3]

Besides the voluntary citizen army of war-time, there was maintained, or at least there was in existence in 420 at the time of the Peace of Nicias, according to Aristotle,[4] a regular standing army of 1600 archers, 1200 cavalry and 550 guards of the Acropolis and docks at the Piraeus, or 3350 all told, which comprised the garrison of Athens. The upkeep of the archers cost probably 3 obols a day, which on a whole-time basis would amount to 48 talents a year for the entire force of 1600. The cost of the cavalry is uncertain, and it is not easy, for several reasons, to come to a satisfactory conclusion thereon. In the first place, we do not know how many of them belonged to the class of "knights" (*Hippeis*), who provided their own horses and arms,

---

[1] Andreades, p. 215. Boeckh's estimate is 36 talents a year. (Nor do we know how efficient they were in their duties although we may suspect they left a good deal to be desired, if we are to believe the tales of high-handed offences we hear in cases in the courts. It adds to the mystery of the incident of the mutilation of the Hermae when we ask how such a thing were possible if there had been any patrol of the streets at night.)

[2] Very doubtful; no evidence on the point.

[3] *Infra*, p. 368.   [4] *Ath. Pol.* xxiv, 3.

and how many had these provided for them at the expense of the state. Indeed we know that this was done; either a payment being made for the purchase of a horse or one provided (*katastasis*).[1] Since horses were scarce and very expensive, this must have been a heavy item of expenditure.[2] As pay the cavalryman received 1 drachma a day, out of which he had to pay for feed for his horse and the keep of a groom, if he employed one, which is hardly likely for the poorer members of the regiment. Xenophon states that the expenditure on the cavalry amounted to about 40 talents a year,[3] which, as Dr Andreades observes, is a very low estimate, since 1200 cavalrymen at a daily wage of 1 drachma would cost 73 talents a year, exclusive of the cost of remounts. No definite conclusion can be arrived at, and we can only suppose that many of the soldiers provided their own horses and perhaps drew no pay while they served in the regiment. With the upkeep of the archers and regular pay of 3 obols a day to soldiers on garrison duty, we may reasonably estimate the cost of the permanent army at from 120 to 140 talents a year. But this must be regarded as a minimum; it probably cost a good deal more.

Besides the Athenian garrison the state maintained in constant commission two fleets of twenty ships each, one to act as guardians of merchantmen against pirates, the other to overawe the "allies" and collect the tribute. The number of sailors and marines necessary to keep the crews at full strength is doubtful, and has been reckoned at from 4000 to 6000.[4] Reckoning the pay of the sailors at 3 obols, and the heavily armed marines or hoplites at 4 obols, we may estimate that 174 talents were needed to keep the fleets at sea for six months every year. It is,

---

[1] The point is obscure. Cf. Andreades, p. 218. Boeckh, i, 319. Cf. art. "Theten" by Schwahn in *P.W.* (1936), p. 202.

[2] Jardé, *Céréales*, p. 127, reckons the price of a horse at 1200 drachmae, an enormous price. The extreme care taken of horses is notable in Xenophon's *Oecon.* and *Hipparch.*

[3] *Hipparch.* 1, 19. Xen. *Oecon.* ii, 6, lists the keeping of horses as among the financial burdens of the rich farmer. This would seem to suggest that they were raised and kept available for the use of the army by private individuals. The phrase in the same passage "so much to pay for men to serve" also suggests that cavalrymen were horsed and paid while on active service by wealthy men, who perhaps thereby secured exemption from military service. Cf. also *Hipparch.* i, 11.

[4] Cf. Andreades, p. 219, n. 2.

therefore, clear that in actual pay the permanent forces cost well over 300 talents a year, and since we have no figures for the annual cost of building ships and the provision of arms and rigging, although we do know the average cost of the hull was one talent, we must conclude that the total expenditure was very considerable, how much it is unsafe to conjecture.[1]

INTERNAL ADMINISTRATION

Turning now from expenditures on defence to those on internal administration, we find that the principal items in the budget were those allotted, first, to what we may call, for lack of a more exact term, educational, intellectual and religious activities of the state; second, public works; third, relief of destitution, pensions to disabled soldiers,[2] widows and orphans; fourth, in times of famine the public distribution of grain; fifth, salaries of officials and payments by the state to private individuals; sixth, a state medical service.

As regards the first, it must be realised that at no time was there in Athens a system of free public education for the children of citizens; that was the duty of the parents, although Aristotle considered it essential that this should be the function of the state.[3] Primary school teachers charged highly for their services, a grammar-school teacher received 20 drs. a year for each pupil, an instructor of gymnastics 100.[4] Poor people could not pay for good teachers, and had to be content with wretched specimens.[5] Although we may suppose that all that could afford it had their children taught, yet we must conclude that the greater proportion of the inhabitants of Attica, and of every other Greek state as well, especially those living in the rural parts, were illiterate. The picture we so often have in our minds of every Athenian citizen as highly educated is entirely erroneous; after all the number of those who delighted in art, philosophy and literature was very small indeed. Such as could afford education given in the schools of philosophy, rhetoric and

---

[1] Boeckh, i, p. 340 ff.
[2] H. Haessler, *Veteränensfürsorge im Griech. Alt.* Jena 1926.
[3] *Pol.* 1337 A.　　　　　　　　　　[4] Athen. xiii, 584 C.
[5] K. J. Freeman, *Schools of Hellas*, p. 278, does not give a very attractive account of Greek primary education.

music, using the latter term in the wider Greek sense of a study of the Muses, paid large fees for entering the classes of the more famous instructors. We are told that Isocrates was supposed to teach Athenians without a fee, yet was not above accepting gifts, and that foreigners had to pay the quite enormous sum of 1000 drs. for admission to his classes.[1] But, while the state did not concern itself with the formal education of its children, it did provide a highly effective, indeed unique, form of intellectual training in the numerous religious festivals and presentations of dramatic performances, for attendance at which citizens received a payment. That anyone should be paid to witness a performance in the theatre seems, at first sight, an extraordinary thing to the modern mind; but if we look upon it as a state subvention for public education it assumes a more rational aspect. We know very little about it, and it would be easy to exaggerate the point. It is more than probable that the system was abused; and it is not hard to imagine innumerable old men, like the professional jurymen that Aristophanes derides, who were more than willing to slumber peacefully through any number of dramas at so much a day. We do not even know if school-children were taken to the theatre as a part of their regular curriculum; but at least we may give the Athenians the benefit of the doubt, and suppose that such was the practice; and at all events it is pleasant to think so.

Education to the Greek consisted not only in literature and music but in the training of the body and athletic contests, and the provision of the great games in which Greeks from every state took part was a very costly affair. In Athens there were many religious and athletic festivals, in fact the practice of athletics had a religious significance, and Plato remarks that such festivals were more numerous and costly than in any other state.[2] Great numbers of animals were sacrificed, although the flesh of the victims was used for feeding the people and the hides formed a valuable perquisite of the state. Much of the expense of these festivals was borne by individuals, rich men upon whom were laid the duty of "liturgies", but even then the

---

[1] Diog. Laert. in his *Lives of the Philosophers* gives many instances of large fees charged by instructors.

[2] *Alcibiades*, ii, 148.

cost to the state must have been very considerable. It is not possible to arrive at any estimate of this item of expenditure; Boeckh puts it at from 25 to 30 talents a year,[1] and it may very well have been considerably higher. In any case we cannot doubt that they formed a large part of the annual budget, as large proportionately, or perhaps even larger, than the cost of public elementary education in our own time. It is a moot point which is the better system.

With regard to state medical services there is much obscurity. That certain doctors were paid by the state seems certain;[2] but we have no information as to their duties. Perhaps they were army surgeons. In Delphi and Cos apparently a tax was levied to provide a public medical service.[3] It is much to be regretted that our knowledge on the point is so scanty.

PUBLIC WORKS

All the world knows that the Greeks excelled in the building of public edifices. It is unnecessary in this place to expatiate on the glories of the temples and other buildings reared by the artistic genius of that wonderful people. It is a strange reflection to realise that, so far as poor mortal man can know it, perfection of its kind had been reached by Greek architects nearly two and a half millennia ago; just as the portrayal of the emotions of the human soul reached heights in their tragic drama which no later writer can ever hope to surpass. It was in the "golden age" of Pericles that the greatest activity in the adornment of Athens took place, although after his death work still went on. It is difficult to estimate what was the total cost of these. Temples and other public edifices included the Parthenon, the Propylaea, the Odeum, other temples and monuments such as the temple of the "Wingless Victory" (*Nike Apteros*), together with the chryselephantine Athena of Phidias. Of more strictly utilitarian character were the long walls to the Piraeus and the docks in the harbours. Estimates of the total cost of erecting these buildings vary from 6000 to 8000 talents;[4] but whatever the cost may have been, it was undoubtedly

[1] i, p. 284.
[2] Cf. Xen. *Mem.* iv, 2, 5; Plato, *Gorgias*, 23.
[3] Ditt. *Syll.*[3] *s.v.* Iatrikon; Busolt, *Griech. Staatsk.* p. 611, n. 3.
[4] Cf. Andreades, p. 234; Boeckh, i, p. 254 f.

enormous, sufficient to arouse the protests of the "allies" against the spending of the tribute, ostensibly levied for the protection of the Delian League, in adorning the capital city. Plutarch voices this indignation in no uncertain language: "Greece considers that she is enduring the most dreadful affronts and is being tyrannised over most egregiously, when she sees us expending the money, which she has been forced to contribute for the sake of carrying on the war, in order to gild and adorn our city; which, like a wanton woman, decorates herself with costly jewels, with statues and temples on which thousands of talents are expended."[1]

From the point of view of the allies who were paying the tribute the point is doubtless well taken. Such use, or misuse we may even call it, of funds collected for a definite purpose can hardly be defended. If there was an annual surplus after the expenses of maintaining the defences of the League had been adequately defrayed, either the tribute should have been lowered, or the whole surplus put aside as a reserve against future contingencies. It is plain that there were two motives actuating the policy of Pericles in this matter. First, a purely artistic one in the building of these deathless masterpieces, which in his own words conferred "everlasting glory" on the city. We may also suppose, and the supposition is by no means an unworthy one, that he was very shrewdly aware that to make the capital of the League impressive to the allies would heighten their respect for the might of Athens. The second motive, of which we can have no doubt whatever, is that through these works he provided employment for a considerable number of labourers and the circulation of large sums of money, that would otherwise have lain idle in the treasury. For, as Plutarch remarks, "the employment scattered and spread prosperity everywhere", and gives a long list of the various materials and labourers employed.[2] In this activity no doubt some of the allies shared, and in any case the money was better expended than in, perhaps, the far more doubtfully useful payment of Athenian citizens for public services and attendance at religious ceremonies. On each count, therefore, the policy of Pericles in carrying out a large programme of public works cannot be

[1] *Life of Pericles*, 12.   [2] *Ibid.*

condemned. In an age when "productive" expenditure was small, or non-existent, such undertakings put money into circulation when the failure of money to circulate or "turn-over" owing to lack of opportunity for investment was one of the most serious problems underlying the whole economic structure of society.

EXPENDITURES OF THE STATE ON ITS CITIZENS

Turning now to expenditure of the state on its individual citizens, we find that they may be divided into three categories: the purchase and distribution of grain at times of famine and high prices; pensions for disabled soldiers and orphans; and most important of all, the payment of salaries for services to the state. With regard to public expenditure on grain and the attempts, not invariably successful, to control the price of imported wheat, much is said in our chapter on the grain trade, which it is unnecessary to repeat here. It must, however, be emphasised that these distributions were not a regular feature of public economy, but were only resorted to at times of distress. In a somewhat different category were the distributions of meat from the victims at the sacrifices at the great religious festivals. Since, as we have already noted, the number of such festivals was large and the sacrifices often on a big scale, the cost to the state must have been considerable; we hear, for instance, of a "hecatomb" of 109 animals costing over 8400 drs.[1] Some part of this expenditure was, however, recovered since the state sold the hides.[2] As the diet of the poorer Athenians was mainly vegetarian, we may assume that these feasts were a pleasant change, providing them, perhaps, with a substantial meat dinner once a week or so.[3]

Athens was generous to her disabled veterans and to the

---

[1] Boeckh, i, p. 94. It is to be noted that "Hecatomb" did not necessarily denote 100 animals. Cf. art. by Stengel in *P.W.*

[2] Revenue from sale of hides (Dermatikon) was considerable; we hear of over 5000 drachmas being received from this source in 7 months in 334–333 (*I.G.* ii (2nd ed.), 1496). Cf. art. "Dermatikon Telos" by Caillemer in *D.S.*

[3] It is interesting in this connection to note the constant prohibitions in the New Testament against the early Christians partaking of flesh offered to idols. Not to share in these public distributions must have entailed severe self-denial, and also rendered those who refused very conspicuous. High price of meat in Athens, Xen. *Mem.* iii, 14, 1.

orphan children of those who fell in her wars. According to Plutarch[1] these pensions were instituted in the time of Peisistratus and amounted to 2 obols a day. Aristotle[2] tells us that later all who were incapacitated by sickness, accident or old age from earning their living also shared in these pensions, if they did not possess 3 minas, the first mention of a "means' test" in history. The hard feelings occasioned thereby are illustrated by the case of the cripple presented by Lysias,[3] who bitterly complained that he received a pension insufficient to keep a slave to help him about. Orphans of fallen soldiers were maintained at the public expense till their eighteenth year; males on coming of age were given their military outfit free,[4] and penniless girls, if sufficiently comely, a dowry.[5] We have no idea what the cost to the exchequer of these benefactions may have been, but undoubtedly it was heavy as we know that, owing to the numerous wars, the number of orphans was very large.[6] Since Metics served in the army and had no share in public benefactions, their orphans presumably received no help nor their disabled soldiers any pension. But of this we have no information.

SALARIES FOR PUBLIC SERVICES[7]

It is when we come to the subject of payments by the state to its citizens for service in the law courts, in public office and for attendance at festivals, that we are confronted with a problem that has been most hotly contested. It is, of course, obvious that a well-conducted machinery of state requires an efficient, paid civil service. It is also to be remembered that attendance on juries in our own day is rewarded with a slight remuneration. But to compensate a jury of twelve quite inadequately for loss of time in attending a case and paying juries of 500 a regular

---

[1] Plut. *Solon*, 31.   [2] *Ath. Pol.* xlix, 4.
[3] Lysias, xxiv.
[4] Aristoph. *Aves*, 1362.   [5] Dem. *in Neaeram*, 113.
[6] Isocr. viii, 82. Cf. O. Jacob, "Les Cités Grecques et les Blessés de Guerre", *Mélanges Glotz*, ii, pp. 461 ff. Busolt, *Griech. Staatsk.* i, p. 209, n. 1. Boeckh, i, p. 308. Polycrates of Samos solved the problem of making provision for the mothers of soldiers killed in the wars by handing them over to rich citizens to look after. Duris *ap.* Zenob. v, 64.
[7] W. Schwahn, "Gehalts und Lohnzahlung in Athen", *Rhein. Mus.* lxxix (1930), pp. 170 ff.; Boeckh, i, p. 287 f.

maintenance fee of 3 obols a day is a very different thing. We cannot doubt that the system was flagrantly abused, as Aristophanes so amusingly shows in the *Wasps*. We also cannot doubt that such payments were looked upon not so much as compensation for services rendered as subventions to those lucky ones who could claim full Athenian citizenship. It seems almost incredible to the modern reader, but we have the authority of Aristotle for saying that the number of jurymen (*dicasts*) reached the extraordinary total of 6000.[1] Although the courts did not sit every day, nor the whole 6000 attend, their pay of 3 obols a day must have amounted to at least 100 talents a year.[2] To these must be added 500 senators at 5 obols a day, or a total expenditure of about 20 talents, and 1400 permanent civil servants at home and abroad,[3] who cost the state about 70 talents.[4] With regard to the pay of the Assembly men no estimate can be made, as we have no means of telling what their numbers were.

THE THEORIC FUND[5]

We have already spoken of the system of paying citizens for attendance at religious festivals. The "cult budget" was one of the greatest drains upon the public treasury, and was financed through a special fund. It must be understood that this "theoric" fund was a surplus left over when all other public expenditures had been provided for, and it is in the ineradicable idea of the Greeks that surpluses should be divided between the citizens that we find the explanation for the spending of the money in giving pay for attendance at festivals. Once it is admitted that a surplus should be used for the immediate benefit of the people and not set aside for future contingencies, the system becomes intelligible. Indeed when we consider that the invariable practice of every modern finance minister is to remit taxation when his receipts have exceeded his budget, a

---

[1] *Ath. Pol.* xxiv, 3.

[2] Aristoph., *Vesp.* 660ff., reckons the total expense at 150 talents, but this is an over-estimate. Cf. Boeckh, i, p. 295 f.

[3] *Ath. Pol.* xxiv, 3. If we accept the statement that there were 700 in Attica and the same number abroad. Doubt has been cast on these figures: the 700 abroad may be a mistake on the part of the copyist; the number would seem to be enormous.

[4] Andreades, p. 252. This amount is quite conjectural.

[5] Boeckh, i, p. 274 ff.

plausible but highly erroneous argument might be advanced that not to take money from the taxpayer is not very different from giving it back to him in the form of favours or subventions. We must also remember that direct taxation of the great bulk of the citizens was shunned, or rather very greatly disliked, in Greece. The surplus was created from the tribute of the allies, the receipts from the mines of Laurium, customs duties and harbour dues, and taxes on Metics and foreigners, none of which stood in any need of reduction whatever in the opinion of the tax-voting citizens. If such a surplus might be used for the advancement of art and literature, and the education and amusement of the citizens, and no pressing necessity for any other use presented itself, it is not hard to excuse what, to the mind of the Athenian, must have appeared a perfectly natural and praiseworthy expenditure of public funds.

But when we have said this we have said everything that can be advanced in its favour, or urged as an excuse. The system, as we have already remarked, was recognised as vicious by the best thinkers. Aristophanes did not fail to thrust a bitter jibe at the whole system. "If two orators should speak before you, and the one should tell you to build warships and the other to draw a lot of salaries, the one that proposed the salaries would win the victory over the one that talked about triremes."[1] That this was the literal truth was seen nearly a century later when, as Plutarch tells us, Demades, a finance minister of undoubted ability, if doubtful patriotism, gave the people the choice of spending the money on a grand festival or of building triremes; they chose the former.[2] The pay was 2 obols a day, and Aristotle condemned it completely: "The wickedness of men is insatiate; at first the diobol alone is enough, but when this has become a matter of habit, they always ask for more, until they end in what is limitless....What is left over the demagogues distribute, and the people take it and at once ask for as much again, for such aid to the poor is like using a jar with holes in it."[3] It speaks much for the influence of Demos-

---

[1] *Equites*, 1349.

[2] *Quaest. Plat.* x, 4 (*Praec. reip. ger.* xxv, 818). But obviously it was the policy of Demades to prevent the city from helping those who had revolted against Alexander. Plutarch in the *Life of Phocion* is violently prejudiced against him. [3] *Pol.* 1320 A.

thenes that he was able to persuade the Athenians to spend the
Theoric money on military purposes to oppose Philip of
Macedon in 339.[1] It is quite impossible to make any estimate
of the sums thus distributed; no doubt the amounts varied
from year to year as the surplus was large or small. It is probable, however, that 40 talents was the lowest amount in any
year, and possibly much more when times were good.[2] The
trouble with such a system of public distributions was that once
it was begun it could not be dropped, and the populace looked
upon it as a right to be enjoyed every year, instead of a "share-
out" of a surplus that had accrued in a particularly prosperous
time.

THE TOTAL REGULAR EXPENSES

Is it possible, therefore, to come to any conclusion with regard
to the ordinary expenses of the state? With so many conjectural
features such is clearly impossible with any degree of accuracy,
but we may conclude, with the utmost possible caution, that
perhaps 700 talents a year might be reckoned as the expenses
for the year 420. Of these 300 talents went for the upkeep of
the permanent military and naval forces; 250 for the civil list,
and 150 for the "cult budget", public works and other current
expenses.[3]

REGULAR INTERNAL REVENUES[4]

It must be remembered that all Greek city-states had large
public possessions in the form of lands, forests, mines where
there were any, and slaves. In fact, to a certain degree, there was
a system of state socialism which made the state the dominant
factor in economic affairs in a time when private capitalism was
still not fully developed. We must, however, be careful not to
use the term "state socialism" in too literal a sense. As a
matter of fact, the state, while retaining its extensive possessions,
did not exploit them itself, but either sold them or rented them

---

[1] Dem. *in Neaeram*, 4. Philochorus, fr. 139 (Müller, *Frag. Hist. Gr.* 1, 406).
[2] Kahrstedt, *Göttingen Nachr.* (1929), p. 156ff., reduces the estimate to 40,000 drs., a very small sum.
[3] Andreades, p. 266.
[4] Boeckh, i, p. 366 ff.; Busolt, *Griech. Staatsk.* i, 609ff.

out to lessees.[1] Except for the public slaves, of which there was not a very great number, the state was not a large employer of labour. By far the most valuable possession of the Athenian state was the mining field of Laurium. Since we deal with this at some length in another chapter, it is unnecessary to say much on this subject in this place. As we note elsewhere[2] there is considerable uncertainty as to the revenues derived from the system of selling mining leases, and we are also not perfectly clear as to the annual tax on the output.[3] Besides Athens the islands of Thasos and Siphnos derived large public revenues from their gold mines while they were productive,[4] and the returns to the Macedonian kings from the gold and silver mines of Pangaeus and the state forests were enormous. Unfortunately we have no information whatever as to whether the marble quarries of Pentelicus were leased on a similar system; nor do we know anything about the returns from leases and sales of public lands and forests.[5] Indeed, with the exception of the mines of Laurium, of which our knowledge is fairly extensive, we are not even certain whether the state leased such public lands as it owned, or whether, when such came into its possession through confiscation of enemy property, it did not sell them at once, which is more probable. We do know, however, that such came under the jurisdiction of the board of officials known as "the Eleven", of which we have already spoken briefly.

REVENUES FROM THE LAW COURTS[6]

Every state, ancient or modern, has always derived a certain revenue from court fees and fines. But in general, except under a corrupt government, this has been moderate and the judicial

---

[1] The whole subject is obscure. Cf. Ps.-Arist. *Oecon.* 1345 B–46 A. Also Andreades, 101–2; Boeckh, i, p. 372 f.

[2] Cf. p. 105 f.

[3] Andreades, p. 270; Boeckh, i, p. 377. Thirty to forty talents a year in the time of Themistocles according to Boeckh. But cf. Arist. *Ath. Pol.* xxii, 7.

[4] Perhaps as much as 200–300 talents a year; but the passage in Her. vi, 46 is obscure.

[5] Xen. *Revenues*, iv, 19, speaks of consecrated grounds, temples and houses. Cf. Busolt, *Griech. Staatsk.* i, 604 ff.

[6] Boeckh, i, p. 415 ff., treats the subject extensively. Cf. also H. Grant Robertson, *Administration of Justice in the Athenian Empire* (Univ. of Toronto Studies, 1924).

system never pays its own way. The Athenians, however, with their genius, or perhaps it would be better to say their vice for litigation, derived considerable revenue from their law courts, especially when their allies or subjects were forced to bring their suits to Athens. So profitable was this that when Alcibiades was urging the Spartans to seize Decelea, he mentioned the loss of revenue from the law courts likely to follow on the blockade as one of the severest blows to Athenian finance.[1] Court dues consisted principally of deposits made by both parties to a case (*prytaneia*) for the costs of the trial, the successful litigant receiving his deposit back and the loser then paying both.[2] Another form of deposit was called *parastasis*, which was made by an accuser who denounced someone of a crime against the state or morals. If successful, the deposit was returned and the accused paid both the *parastasis* and a fine; if not the deposit was forfeited.[3] The amount of the *prytaneia* varied according to the sum involved. In suits of 100–1000 drs. the deposit was 3 drs.; from 1000–10,000, 30 drs., with larger sums in proportion.[4]

Money penalties imposed by public vote on individuals consisted of *timemata* or fines and *demioprata* or confiscations.[5] The *timemata* go back to the time of Solon, although whether he was the first to introduce them is doubtful.[6] It is certain, however, that in the earlier epoch such fines were moderate in amount; but later, in cases involving treason against the state, they were enormous. The most usual was 1000 drs., but we hear of quite outrageous fines such as that of 50 talents imposed on Miltiades; 50 or 80 talents, it is uncertain which, on Pericles; 10 talents on Demades; 50 talents on Demosthenes. Obviously such enormous sums could not be paid, and they therefore amounted to complete confiscation of the property of the condemned. It is noteworthy that these fines were imposed often on what we must regard as frivolous grounds, or even more

[1] Thuc. vi, 91.
[2] Dem. *in Euergum*, 2; Poll. viii, 37f.
[3] E.g. when Aeschines failed in his accusation against Ctesiphon he not only lost his deposit but was condemned to so large a fine that he had to flee from Athens.
[4] Boeckh, i, p. 416.   [5] Cf. Arist. *Ath. Pol.* iv, 3.
[6] Aristoph. *Vespae*, 657; Poll. viii, 95.

often in vexation at the ill success of a general. Thus Miltiades, the hero of Marathon, was fined because the expedition in 479 against Paros was a failure; Pericles because the Spartans had invaded Attica.[1] Demosthenes was convicted in the Harpalus case of accepting bribes;[2] but the fickle populace forgave him the penalty;[3] Demades was fined because he proposed divine honours for Alexander.[4] Doubtless such fines were often of a vindictive character against the rich and sometimes abused. Perhaps the most outrageous instance of all was the case of Diphilus, counted the richest man in Greece, who was impeached by Lycurgus sometime between 345–325, and his entire fortune confiscated and divided among the people, who got 50 drs. apiece "or as others say 100".[5] Aristotle condemned them,[6] and accuses the demagogues of slandering the rich in order to have their property seized. It is fair to say, however, that outrageous instances of fines and confiscations were far fewer in Athens than in other Greek states, of which the author of the Pseudo-Aristotelian *Oeconomica* gives some scandalous examples. In Athens banishment was in some instances effected by ostracism, which did not involve confiscation of property, and in any case there is reason to suppose that there was a certain amount of calculated laxity in the collection of such fines as were imposed. Added to which, as Boeckh remarks,[7] the populace was often soft-hearted and remitted part or all of the fines if it imposed hardships upon widows and orphans. His opinion is that, in Athens at least, revenue in fines was comparatively small.

DIRECT TAXES[8]

As we have already observed, the Athenian populace had a rooted objection to any form of direct taxation on themselves;

---

[1] The Greeks demanded a high standard from their generals which they, poor men, amateurs at best, were frequently unable to attain. An unsuccessful battle often entailed execution or banishment on the defeated leader; which accounts for their marked disinclination to return home. Miltiades, Her. vi, 136; Plut. *Cimon*, 4; Corn. Nepos, *Cimon*, i. Alcibiades, Thuc. ii, 65.

[2] Plut. *Dem.* 26.   [3] *Vit. X. Orat.* 846 D.

[4] Athen. vi, 251.

[5] Plut. *Vit. X. Orat.* 843 D. But there are numerous obscurities in this case which cannot be satisfactorily explained.

[6] *Pol.* v, 4, 3, vi, 3, 2.   [7] i, p. 467; e.g. Dem. *in Aphobum*, i, 65.

[8] J. H. Lipsius, "Die Attische Steuerverfassung u. das Attische Staatsvermögen", *Rhein. Mus.* lxxi (1913), pp. 161, 584.

but had none with regard to imposts on Metics, foreigners, slaves and sundry other classes of a less reputable description. We have frequently spoken of those resident aliens called Metics, who played so large a part in the economic affairs of Greek city-states, and especially in those of Athens, and it is therefore unnecessary to say anything further on that subject here. A poll tax (*metoikion*) of 12 drs. a year was imposed on all males, and 6 drs. on women who had no husband or son at work, and who presumably supported themselves. Since we are in considerable doubt as to the number of Metics in Athens at any time, it is impossible to estimate the total amount accruing to the treasury from this tax. Of another tax on "foreigners" (*xenikon*) we have even less knowledge. It may have been one levied on transients, or as a passage in Demosthenes suggests,[1] it may have been a license fee for the privilege of doing business in the market. We have no information with regard to the amount of this tax nor the revenue collected therefrom. Whether or not there was a poll tax on slaves has been a matter of considerable controversy. Boeckh, following a passage in Xenophon,[2] has assumed its existence, but later writers have rejected it. Dr Andreades leaves the whole subject open, neither denying nor affirming the possibility of such a poll tax being levied.[3] We know for certain that the import of slaves was heavily taxed; 2 per cent ad valorem on importation, 1 or 2 per cent (the amount is doubtful) as a surtax (*eponion*) and 2 per cent on exportation. The evidence with regard to a tax on prostitutes (*pornikon*) is quite clear,[4] although whether it was a poll tax on individuals, or a percentage of their earnings, is doubtful. There is no information with regard to its amount.[5]

THE LITURGIES[6]

Although the system of Athenian taxation was essentially an indirect one, yet the mulcting of the rich through heavy exactions

---

[1] *In Eubul.* 34.
[2] *Revenues*, iv, 25; Boeckh, i, p. 402.
[3] Pp. 281–4. There was also, apparently, a tax levied when a slave was set free, but of this nothing is known. The reference in Aristoph. *Eccles.* 1007 to one-fivehundredth is not very illuminating.
[4] Aeschines, *in Tim.* 119; Poll. vii, 202, ix, 19.
[5] Cf. Boeckh, i, p. 404. Art. "Meretrices" in *D.S.*, "Hetairai" in *P.W.*
[6] Andreades, 130f., 291f.; Boeckh, i, pp. 533, 623 ff.

was very much to their taste. The whole question of these taxes,
or *liturgies*, is exceedingly interesting, and a great deal has been
written upon it. Originally they were, we may suppose, free-
will expenditures of wealthy citizens who desired to bring glory
to their city by paying for religious festivals, dramas, choruses
and dances. Even much later this honourable desire to serve
the state was not entirely lost. Aristotle says: "Of these expenditures there are some that we call honourable; such are
the offerings to the gods, buildings and sacrifices; likewise such
as pertain to everything divine, or whatsoever may appertain to
the good of the state, as when men consider themselves serving
gloriously as chorus leaders, or in fitting out warships or in
entertaining citizens."[1] But from a praiseworthy desire to
glorify their city to an attempt to win public applause by
ostentatious expenditures is a very short step, and human
nature being what it is, it is not surprising to find other writers
protesting against vulgarity and unworthy rivalry in the pro-
digality with which such services were performed.[2] Alcibiades
was accused of buying public esteem in this manner.[3] In
Isaeus we hear of an accusation of meanness in not spending
enough on a Liturgy,[4] and Isocrates laments the time when
such services were performed not in a spirit of vainglory or
snobbishness.[5] Some of these voluntary liturgies had little or
no artistic or religious value, as for instance the torch race
(*lampadarchia*) and "useless and expensive expenditures on
choruses", as Aristotle calls them.[6] It is uncertain how often
such services were performed by citizens; but we may suspect
that often such free-will offerings were made by Metics, from
the simple fact that most of the wealthy residents belonged to
that class, and it is hardly likely that citizens would pay for such
if aliens could be found to do so.[7] How burdensone these
exactions from the rich could become and what immense sums
were paid out by them over and above what was legally demanded, is vividly portrayed in a speech on behalf of an
unknown plaintiff written by Lysias.[8] "I passed my *doki-*

---

[1] *Nic. Eth.* iv, 5. [2] *Ibid.* iv, 6. [3] Plut. *Alcibiades*, 16.
[4] Isaeus, v, 44. [5] *Areop.* 53. [6] *Pol.* 1309 A.
[7] But we know that Demosthenes did so, and was insulted by Meidias in
the performance of his solemn religious duties. *In Mid.* 156.
[8] Lysias, *Oration* xxi.

masia[1] in the archonship of Theopompus,[2] and being appointed choregus for tragedies, I expended 30 minae, and two months later 2000 drs. in winning a victory at the Thargelia with a chorus of men; in the archonship of Glaucippus[3] I spent 800 drs. at the great Panathenaea on the Pyrrhic dancers. In the same archonship I won a victory at the Dionysia with a chorus of men, expending on it, inclusive of the expenses of setting up the tripod, a sum of 5000 drs.; when Diocles was archon,[4] at the lesser Panathenaea 300 drs. on a cyclic chorus. In the meantime I served as trierarch for seven years and expended 6 talents. While I was spending these sums and was daily incurring danger in your behalf away from the city, I was subjected to two eisphorae, one of 30 minas and one of 4000 drs. When I returned to Athens in the archonship of Alexias[5] I was chosen gymnasiarch at the Prometheia and won a victory with an expenditure of 12 minas. Later I became the choregus for a chorus of boys and spent more than 15 minas. In the archonship of Eucleides[6] I was a choregus for Cephisodorus in comedies and expended 16 minas, including the dedication of the furnishings. At the lesser Panathenaea, with beardless Pyrrhic dancers, I spent 7 minas. In a trireme race off Sunium I won a victory at a cost of 15 minas. Furthermore, I have expended on sacred missions, processions and the like, more than 30 minas. Now if I had performed my liturgies according to the letter of the law, I should not have spent more than a fourth part of all these sums I have listed." We therefore see that in the space of nine years this wealthy citizen expended 63,000 drs., an enormous sum. Another mentioned by Lysias, named Aristophanes, expended 57,000 drs.[7] We have to agree with Mr Ferguson when he says: "We have to adjust our ideas to a financial dominance of the Athenian state over private individuals unparalleled in modern times."[8]

But although originally, and always to a certain degree, such liturgies were of a voluntary nature, yet later they became a regular imposition on the wealthier classes from which there was no escape. Such duties were either "regular" (*encyclic*),

---

[1] Dokimasia. Scrutiny for admission to citizenship.
[2] 411.   [3] 410.   [4] 409.
[5] 405.   [6] 403–402.   [7] Lysias, xix, 42–3.
[8] *Treasurers of Athena*, p. 166.

that is to say recurring at regular intervals as the times for the various festivals came round, or "irregular" (*prostactic*), which consisted in expenses on fitting out warships (*trierarchies*). The regular liturgies included the choregia, or presentation of plays and musical performances. This entailed considerable expenditures on training and costumes, the payment of musicians and dancers. The *gymnasiarchia*, or provision for the expenses of the torch races, was exceedingly heavy; according to Lysias amounting at the Panathenaea to as much as 1200 drs. Not only had the cost of training the runners to be defrayed, but also that for decorations and illuminations, although whether or not the state provided the oil for the lamps is a moot point.[1] And lastly, considerable expense was incurred by individuals in paying for public dinners to the "tribesmen" at the various religious festivals. It is uncertain how many times a year these feasts took place, or what they cost, although Boeckh supposes about 700 drs. As an additional expense, we understand from Isaeus that the wives of the tribesmen were also entertained by the wife of the giver of the feast.[2] Socrates, while congratulating Ischomachus on his fortune, shrewdly remarks that no doubt he paid heavily for it, and recites a long list of expensive public duties that fall to the lot of a rich man.[3]

THE TRIERARCHY[4]

We have so far dealt with the regular or encyclic liturgies; it now remains to speak of the irregular, of which the most famous was the duty of maintaining in good repair a trireme when on active service. It must first be understood that the cost of building and rigging the ship was borne by the state,[5] and a lump sum of 30 minas for the provision of rations and pay for the crew.[6] All other expenses were met by the trierarch and undoubtedly the burden was a very heavy one, especially if the ship and rigging were handed over in bad condition.[7]

---

[1] *I.G.* ii², 1138; Boeckh, i, p. 548.
[2] Isaeus, iii, 80. [3] Xen. *Oecon.* ii, 6.
[4] Trierarchy, Andreades p. 322; Boeckh, i, p. 628 ff.
[5] Thuc. vi, 31. The word "empty" here means without crew, not without rigging or equipment.
[6] Dem. *de Trier. Coron.* 11.
[7] Cf. Aristoph. *Equites*, 912f. The case against Euergus and Mnesibulus, argued by Demosthenes, turns upon this point.

Naturally the expense varied with the fortunes of the vessel and the damage it received from tempest or battle, and we therefore have no means of estimating an average year's cost to the trierarch.[1] The system was of long standing, before the middle of the fifth century, but with the Peloponnesian war became of prime importance and also of crushing weight to those whose possessions laid them open to it. In the last few years of the war when so many wealthy men had been ruined, the expense had to be divided and the *syntrierarchy* instituted by which two or more were associated in the upkeep of a vessel. Later, probably in 357–356, by the law of Periander a new system altogether was introduced, whereby 1200 of the richest inhabitants were formed into 20 *symmories* of 60 members each, sub-divided in turn into a number of *synteleiae* or groups of members responsible collectively for a certain number of ships.[2] Designed to expedite the performance of the duties of the trierarchy and spread the expense more evenly, it was, if we are to believe Demosthenes, a failure and worked badly, accentuating the abuses it was designed to remedy and leading to every sort of evasion, corruption and injustice.[3] In 354 Demosthenes was successful in passing a law which he hoped would remedy the more glaring defects of the system.[4] It is not perfectly clear whether the symmories were retained, but there was an attempt to return, more or less, to the older system whereby individuals were made responsible. The richer members were given two triremes to maintain. If they possessed enough to take care of one trierarchy but not enough for two, the surplus above one was contributed to the fund for helping out the contributions of the poorer. While this law was designed to spread out the burden, yet the effect seems to have been bad, and in the end to have laid almost the whole weight on not more than 300 people.[5]

Looked at from the modern viewpoint of scientific taxation,

---

[1] Cf. D. F. Robertson, "The duration of a trierarchy", *Class. Rev.* xli (1927), pp. 114ff.

[2] Boeckh, i, p. 647 ff., discusses the question at length. Synteleia, Dem. *in Lept.* 23, *in Mid.* 155, *in Euerg. et Mnes.* 78.

[3] *De Corona*, 102ff.; *in Mid.* 155; *On the Navy Boards*, 16ff.

[4] I.e. *On the Navy Boards*.

[5] Cf. Aeschines, *in Ctes.* 222; Hyperides, *in Harp.*

it is impossible not to condemn the whole system of liturgies. It worked badly because it was founded on a polite fiction, once a reality we must suppose, that the more fortunate citizens should delight to honour their city by freewill offerings, and in war to defend it on the same patriotic grounds. Actually, as we have seen, the freewill character entirely disappeared and the whole system simply became a means for mulcting the rich. It has always been and is now, more so than ever before, a cardinal principle of taxation that the rich should pay more than the poor, not only proportionally, but "progressively" more as incomes increase in size. This, of course, supposes that an even-handed justice is done, and that the wealth of the taxpayer can be ascertained with reasonable certainty. As we remark elsewhere wealth in the Ancient World "went to earth" in order to escape the depredations of the tax collector,[1] and not being in the shape of real estate but almost exclusively in cash, it was very hard to find and so hoarding was unduly prevalent. As the means of replenishing the revenues of the state through customs duties and, after the downfall of the Delian League, from the tribute of the allies became smaller, the drive for raising money at any cost became greater and what we may call a "dead set" against the rich was intensified. "When I was a boy", says Isocrates, "it was not dangerous to be called rich and a man was proud of it; to-day he does all he can to hide the amount of his possessions, for it is more dangerous to pass for wealthy than to break the law."[2]

The allocation of the liturgies was patently a fairly "hit or miss" business, and the task of extricating himself from a ruinous position if a liturgy was imposed beyond all possibility of performance was left to the individual, by means of what, to modern minds, must appear the extraordinary procedure known as *antidosis*, which was briefly as follows. Should one on whom a liturgy had been laid consider himself unjustly treated or unable to afford it, he could name another individual and challenge him to take it over from him. Should the second party

[1] Cf. Isaeus, vii, 40, xi, 47; Lysias, xx, 23. Zimmern, *Greek Commonwealth*, cap. ix, speaks enthusiastically of the "constant stream of generosity" wherewith the rich delighted to do honour to their city. The reality was somewhat different and the bright picture decidedly tarnished.

[2] xv, 159.

decline to do so, pleading poverty, he could be challenged to an exchange of property and if he still refused, the liturgy was transferred to him.[1] Dr Andreades characterises this as "a clever and unique institution".[2] We may readily agree as to its unique character; but may very well demur as to its cleverness, while the imagination becomes confused as to the manner in which the respective properties were exchanged and the consequences attendant upon it. The whole system was, beyond all argument, bungling, amateurish and bad, and it is not hard to imagine the endless disputes between individuals which it must have engendered. We also cannot doubt that the notoriously litigious character of the Athenians must have arisen, or perhaps have been intensified, by just such a system which, by its unscientific character, made recourse to the law courts practically inevitable.

THE EISPHORA[3]

That form of taxation in Greece termed *eisphora* may be defined as a capital levy, or a special tax on capital intended to cover a definite urgent national need.[4] The whole subject bristles with innumerable difficulties and has been the source of protracted controversy, with sharp divergence of opinion among scholars from the time of Boeckh to the present day. Into the various controversies it is impossible to enter here, and we must content ourselves with a somewhat superficial survey of the whole problem. In the first place, it must be understood that it was not a regular tax, like the modern income tax, levied every year, but only on the occasion of a special need. In order that it should be imposed special and somewhat lengthy legal forms had to be gone through even before a vote on the subject was

---

[1] Boeckh, i, p. 673, treats the whole subject at length. Cf. arts. "Antidosis" in *D.S.* by Caillemer and in *P.W.* by Thalheim.

[2] P. 294.

[3] Cf. art. "Eisphora" in *D.S.* by Lécrivain, and "Tele" in *P.W.* by Schwahn. Andreades, p. 326 ff. and "The capital levy in ancient Athens" in *Econ. Hist.* ii (1931), p. 155 ff. Schwahn, "Die Attische Eisphora", *Rhein. Mus.* lxxxii (1933), p. 247 ff. Wilhelm, "Untersuchung zu Xenophon's Poroi", *Wiener Studien*, lii (1934), p. 18 ff. Boeckh, i, p. 555 ff. Van Groningen, "De Tributa quod Eisphora dicitur", *Mnemosyne*, lvi (1928), p. 395 ff.

[4] Andreades, p. 327.

sought in the Assembly.[1] Undoubtedly an *eisphora* was regarded as a very serious affair, in which we may heartily agree. Where a people will readily agree to a tax on income, even of a crushing weight, a levy on capital is something very different, and far too suggestive of an attempt to kill the goose that lays the golden eggs. The difficulties in the way of apportioning such a levy in any reasonable manner are obviously formidable. In the first place, we are confronted with the question of the exact connotation of the term "capital", and to that no universally satisfactory answer can ever be given. In the second place, as regards the system in Attica, we have to solve the problem as to whether the levy was made wholly on immovable wealth, that is to say, land and houses, or whether movable wealth, money and slaves was included. Although the question is incapable of precise solution, we may reasonably surmise that this was the practice. This conclusion is in part confirmed from the undoubted fact that Metics, who by law were unable to hold landed property, paid their share of the *eisphora*, amounting to one-sixth of the entire sum raised, if we are to accept the reference of Demosthenes in his speech against Androtion.[2] It must, however, be admitted that the point is excessively obscure, and although Dr Andreades argues that one-sixth of the total sum thus collected represented a heavy exaction from the Metic class, from the very fact that their wealth was wholly in movable property, there is still a reasonable doubt on the point.[3] If the Metics were far more wealthy than the citizens, surely on their movable wealth alone a greater proportion than one-sixth would have been raised? It is, however, needless to pursue the point further.

The next problem that arises is as to the system of apportioning the levy. We do not know what this was during the period of the Peloponnesian war, but we have some evidence that throws a certain amount of light upon it in the reforms introduced during the archonship of Nausinicus in 378–377. By this enactment the total number of individuals liable to the levy was

[1] A special authorisation, called *Adeia*, from the people as a whole had to be obtained before the proposal was presented to the Assembly. Cf. art. "Adeia" in *P.W.*

[2] *In Androt.* 61.

[3] Cf. Andreades, p. 279, n. 6, and p. 329, n. 2.

divided into *Symmories*,[1] in such a way that the assessment of the members of each Symmory was approximately equal. To the symmory was then left the task of raising the amount of the *eisphora*. At a time when the number of treasury officials was small and the task of collecting the taxes a difficult one, such a system certainly would work well, since obviously it was entirely to the interest of the members of each symmory to see that they all fairly paid their share. Again we may remark that the necessary prying into each other's affairs must have been a sore trial of the patriotism and goodfellowship of the members, and the extraordinary number of lawsuits arising out of accusations of bad faith can hardly be wondered at. We cannot doubt that the concealment of wealth must have been a fine art and formed a constant pre-occupation for the wealthy.

In order that the amount capable of being raised by the imposition of an *eisphora* could be calculated beforehand, a valuation (*Timema*) was made of the wealth of those liable to the levy. We do not know how this was done, nor do we know on what basis it was reckoned, and the problem is hopelessly obscured by such references as are available. Thus we are told by Polybius[2] that in 378–377 the total wealth of Attica liable for the *eisphora* was found to be 5750 talents. If we are to take the passage in a speech of Demosthenes at a later date (354–353) as referring to a new valuation, he puts the taxable wealth at 6000 talents at that time.[3] Are we then to assume that this constituted the entire wealth of those liable to the tax? Great as were the losses suffered by the rich in the Peloponnesian war, it is almost incredible that their wealth had been reduced to so small a sum. On the other hand, in another speech[4] Demosthenes suggests an entirely different view. "The amount of the property is, therefore, evident from this; three talents is the timema on 15; this was the Eisphora they thought it right to pay." Are we to suppose from this that the *eisphora* was levied on only one-fifth of the valuation? If that is so, then from the figure of 6000 talents previously given by Demosthenes we must assume that

[1] Not to be confused with the Trierarchic Symmories which were entirely separate. Cf. Boeckh, i, p. 609 ff.
[2] Polyb. ii, 62, 6–7.
[3] Dem. *On the Navy Boards*, 19.
[4] *In Aphobum*, i, 9.

the total taxable wealth was 30,000 talents, which seems as incredibly an over-estimate as the other was an under-estimate. The point is hopelessly obscure and has led to a sharp divergence of opinion, into which it is needless to enter.[1]

But indeed the obscurities involved are many and baffling. For instance, how many of the inhabitants of Attica contributed to the capital levy, and was it of a proportional or progressive nature, i.e. did the richer contributors pay at a higher rate than the poorer, or was the same percentage of their wealth demanded from all alike? Isocrates in his speech on the Antidosis says, in referring to his opponent, "You reckon yourself among the 1200 persons who pay the *eisphora* and discharge liturgies."[2] From this we would infer that only the wealthier were liable. A capital levy on the poor would bring in very little indeed and the difficulties of collection would be enormous. And yet Isaeus seems to say that everyone was included, rich and poor alike. "So many Eisphorae have been made towards the war by all the citizens."[3] Again Demosthenes says, "It is necessary then, it seems to me, that if there is great need all should contribute largely, if there is little need only in small sums."[4] More doubtful evidence is provided in the Aristotelian *Oeconomica* as follows: "The Athenians who dwell in Potidaea, being in need of money to carry on the war, ordered all the citizens to draw up a list of their property, each man enrolling not his whole property collectively in his deme, but each piece of property separately in the place where it was situated, in order that the poor might give in an assessment; any one who possessed no property was to assess his own person at 2 minae. On the basis of this assessment they contributed each in full to the state the amount enjoined."[5] Obviously there are obscurities in this passage, yet the general meaning seems fairly clear—an *eisphora* was collected from everyone, rich and poor alike. It is, of course, entirely possible that the circumstances at the moment in Potidaea were so exceptional that a desperate measure was

[1] Andreades discusses the problem at length; cf. pp. 334–7, 342–8. Ferguson, "after much vacillation", accepts the total of 5750 talents. Cf. *Treasurers of Athena*, p. 166. For other views cf. Lécrivain, art. "Eisphora" in *D.S.*; Wilamowitz, *Staat und Gesellschaft*, p. 111.

[2] Isocr. *On the Antidosis*, 145.   [3] Isaeus, v, 37.

[4] *Olynthiac* i, 20.   [5] Ps.-Arist. *Oecon.* 1347 A.

necessary; in any case it is quite unsafe to draw any conclusions from this source. Some writers, basing their theory upon a passage in Diodorus,[1] are of the opinion that those with capital of less than 2000 drs. were exempt; but the reference is very late, in the time of Antipater, and it is hard to draw any safe conclusion therefrom. But we can be quite sure that, in the usual Athenian fashion, the rich must have borne a heavier burden proportional to their wealth than the poorer contributors. We know that by a system of prepayments, termed *Proeisphora*, the 300 richest citizens were saddled with the task of "underwriting" the whole capital levy and had then to collect what they had advanced to the treasury from their fellow taxpayers.[2] The declaration of property was on oath, a source of endless trouble in the courts.[3]

We have already spoken of the practice of rich citizens, and Metics probably more frequently than citizens, giving large freewill offerings and incurring heavy expenses for the sake of the city.[4] These freewill gifts or "benevolences" (*epidoseis*) were for many purposes, but most frequently for military needs. Thus we know that individuals gave substantial sums to pay for military equipment and war vessels. For instance Demosthenes gave 8 talents to help outfit expeditions to Euboea and Byzantium; Aristophanes gave 5 talents for the expedition to Cyprus; Nausicles paid 2000 hoplites in Imbros. We know also of most generous contributions of rich grain merchants, both in kind and money, at times when the scarcity of wheat had raised prices in Athens to a dangerous height.[5] There were also gifts recorded to pay the expenses of public sacrifices and the repair of temples. While we may suppose that in many, if not most, instances these "benevolences" were prompted by entirely patriotic motives, we may also shrewdly surmise that a certain amount of pressure upon rich men to show their generosity was not lacking, and in any case the public honours in the shape of crowns and popular acclaim were an incentive, as they have been in every age and are now.

---

[1] xviii, 18.   [2] Cf. Boeckh, i, pp. 613, 620.
[3] Cf. Isaeus, vii, 38; Dem. *in Aphobum*, i, 7–8, *in Aph.* ii, 4, 11, *in Aph.* iii, 59.
[4] Cf. Boeckh, i, pp. 657, 685 f.; Dem. *in Midiam*, 156; Plut. *Alcibiades*, 10; Theophrastus, *Char.* 22.
[5] Such gifts are noted elsewhere; cf. pp. 270, 275.

INDIRECT TAXES[1]

We have already in our chapter on Commerce mentioned customs duties. There is reason to suppose that before the disasters of the Peloponnesian war began to create serious financial difficulties for Athens, there had been a tax of 1 per cent (*hecatoste*) on both imports and exports at the Piraeus,[2] and that when it became necessary to raise further revenues this was doubled (*pentecoste*),[3] and that thereafter this 2 per cent tax was permanently retained. Among the allies of Athens a tax of 5 per cent was imposed to take the place of the tribute when further sums were required after the Sicilian disaster.[4] We have no certain knowledge of how much the 2 per cent tax brought in, except that according to Andocides[5] in the year 400–399 the "fiftieth" produced 30 talents, and that it had been farmed out for 36 talents for the next year. On this basis the total trade of the Piraeus could only have amounted to about 2000 talents in that year, which seems so small a sum that the figures given by Andocides appear, in some not perfectly clear manner, to be wrong. It is, of course, possible to suppose that in that year, shortly after the close of the Peloponnesian war, the trade of the Piraeus had sunk to an extraordinarily low level. The point is too obscure for further inquiry in this place.[6]

A sales tax (*eponion*), apparently, but far from certainly, of 1 per cent was imposed.[7] With regard to this tax there are great difficulties. We do not know if this was levied on sales in the market place alone, in which case it corresponded to the "market dues", or whether it was collected on all sales, whether transacted in the market or not. If the latter, the task of collection must have presented extreme difficulties. We are also uncertain whether it was a uniform 1 per cent on the sale of all articles, or whether the term *hecatoste* was rather a generic term

---

[1] Cf. Schwahn, art. "Tele" in *P.W.*
[2] Xen. *Resp. Ath.* i, 17.
[3] Cf. Beloch, *Griech. Gesch.* iii, 1 (2nd ed.), p. 443; Boeckh, i, p. 382 f.
[4] Thuc. vii, 28, 4.   [5] Andocides, i, 133.
[6] The figures of Andocides have been suspect from the time of Boeckh and few scholars have been willing to accept them at their face value. Cf. Andreades, pp. 298–9, for a discussion of the difficulty.
[7] Boeckh, i, p. 395.

which covered a good many differences. The reference by Aristophanes in the *Wasps*[1] to "many hundredths" merely makes the difficulty greater. There is reason to suppose that there was a tax on sales by auction, but of this our knowledge is very meagre.[2] There were also gate tolls (*diapylia*), which seem, although our evidence is not very clear, to have been a kind of octroi.[3]

In other cities, but apparently not in Athens, there were a variety of taxes or fees termed *encyclia*. There were in Delos taxes on pasturing cattle; on purple; harbour and exchange dues; fishing licenses and ferry charges. In Cyzicus, there were taxes on slave dealing and horse trading, one probably for the use of the public scales and several others for which no explanation can be found (*nausson* and *tetarte*).[4] In Cos, much later than in Cyzicus, probably in the second century, there were taxes on bread, wheat, wine of Calymnus, barley, wool, frankincense sellers, beans, salt fish, "wine at sea", house lots, and *obelia*.[5] So far as we can surmise there were also taxes on cultivation of the temple properties, on rents, on draught oxen, vineyard workers and female slaves.[6] From an inscription at Teos[7] we hear of other taxes on wood selling; woven goods; animals of all sorts, oxen, sheep, swine and bees; and on "gardens", by which is probably meant vineyards, olive groves and market gardens as distinct from arable land.

THE TRIBUTE OF THE ALLIES[8]

The greatest single item in the budget of the Athenians, the tribute received from their "allies", we have reserved for the last. Originally designed as a contribution from each ally for

---

[1] *Vespae*, 658.   [2] Cf. art "Auctio", in *P.W.*

[3] Hesychius, *s.v.* The reference in (Arist.) *Oecon.* 1348 B, 25, to a tax on corpses taken for burial outside the city is not very illuminating on the subject of this tax. Boeckh, i, p. 394.

[4] Ditt. *Syll.* 464.

[5] For "wine at sea" no adequate explanation can be given other than wine exported, or possibly wine mixed with salt water (Athen. i, 32). The tax on "house lots" does not convey very much except possibly a tax on sales of urban sites. "Obelia" probably means a peculiarly shaped loaf of bread carried in religious processions, Poll. vi, 75.

[6] Cf. Andreades, pp. 150 ff.   [7] *Supp. Epig. Graec.* ii, 579.

[8] Literature on this subject is very extensive. Cf. bibliography in Andreades, p. 307, n. 4.

the upkeep of a fleet to guard them against the Persians, it had later become quite undisguisedly, with the transfer of the treasury of the Delian League to Athens, tribute paid by subject states and cities to the Athenian overlord. Fixed at first at 460 talents by Aristides, whom the allies trusted as an honest man,[1] the amounts levied varied from time to time. Why the sum of 460 talents was settled upon at first is not perfectly clear, but Dr Andreades, with the aid of hypothetical figures, suggests that it is not unreasonable to calculate it upon the basis of a fleet of 200 ships. Thus, with a crew for each trireme of 188 men, drawing 2 obols a day during the seven months of the cruising season, the entire rations for the fleet would cost 439 talents; and with 21 talents for repairs and replacements we arrive at the sum of 460 talents.[2] This ingenious explanation, however, is far from explaining everything, since we know that by 453 a surplus of 3000 talents had been collected, and the conclusion we must arrive at is that the Athenians were making considerable savings and not expending the whole tribute on the object for which it was ostensibly collected, although it is perfectly possible that this reserve was accumulated with the consent of the allies. Later Pericles quite cynically used large amounts of the tribute money for beautifying Athens, much to the discontent of the tributaries. The amount of the tribute levied at various times differed considerably, and it is excessively difficult to come to any precise and definitive conclusions with regard to it. If we are to trust Plutarch and Thucydides in 478 the amount was 460 talents. Just before the Archidamian war in 431 it had fallen to 415 talents.[3] Cleon raised it to 1200 talents according to Aeschines.[4] Inscriptions, however, do not bear out these figures, and according to a series of studies by Meritt and West the amounts have to be considerably modified.[5] At the beginning of the Peloponnesian war the tribute had fallen to 415 talents; in 425 it was raised to 1460 by quadrupling the original contributions and adding new allies; but actually the receipts did not reach more than 900 talents.[6] At the Peace of Nicias in 421 it was put on a peace-time basis of 575 talents, with

[1] Plut. *Aristides*, 24; Thuc. i, 96.　　　[2] Andreades, p. 308, n. 4.
[3] Thuc. ii, 13, 3.　　　[4] *De Leg.* 175.
[5] *Harvard Studies in Class Philol.* 1926; *Amer. Journ. of Archaeol.* 1925.
[6] *Ibid.* The Athenian assessment of 425 B.C. Univ. of Michigan Press.

an additional 100 from the Euxine allies. On the eve of the Sicilian expedition it was raised again to 1200 talents. Immediately after the Sicilian disaster the method of collection was changed and an import and export duty of 5 per cent substituted. With the downfall of Athens in 404 the tribute was entirely wiped out, but with the founding of the second Delian League in 378–377 payments began once more. These were no longer termed "tribute" (*phoros*), but by the gentler term "contributions" (*syntaxeis*). But with the surprising success of the second hegemony of Athens very soon these contributions became tribute once more and the old discontent of the "allies" was renewed. In 357 Chios, Cos and Rhodes revolted, and although not all the allies deserted Athens, their contributions fell to a very small sum, about 50 talents.[1]

At the close of the war with the allies in 355–354, the expenditures on the war and the loss of tribute had reduced the revenues of Athens so greatly that when Xenophon wrote his pamphlet on the *Revenues of Athens* in the same year, something drastic had to be done to restore the public finances.[2] It is not the place here to speak at length of this small treatise; suffice it to say that Xenophon recognises that any hope of reimposing Athenian hegemony by force has gone. Athens must do all in its power to attract merchants to her markets and pursue the ways of peace. But principally must she exploit her own natural resources by intensive working of the mines of Laurium through an elaborate programme of purchase of slaves for labour in the mines. We have no idea what reception was given to these proposals; but so far as we know they were not acted upon. And yet there is evidence to show, as will be seen later, that less than twenty years later the revenues of the city had very markedly increased; from what causes, other than peace, it is hard to say.

TOTAL REVENUES OF THE CITY

Like every state that has to finance costly and protracted wars, Athens suffered from violent fluctuations in her revenues.

---

[1] Dem. *de Corona*, 234, says 45. Aeschines, *de Leg.* 71, says 60.

[2] Schwahn, "Die Xenophontischen Poroi u. die Athenische Industrie im Vierten Jahrhundert", *Rhein. Mus.* lxxx (1931). Schwahn characterises the pamphlet as the party programme of Eubulus.

Thus about the year 433, on the eve of the Peloponnesian war, Xenophon says: "For we Athenians came into the war against the Lacedaemonians and their allies at a time when there was an abundance of money in the Acropolis, and annual revenues from the internal taxes and from those abroad of not less than a thousand talents."[1] Eleven years later, Aristophanes in the *Wasps*[2] says, "First of all, to calculate roughly, not with pebbles but on one's fingers, the tribute that comes in as a whole from the cities, in addition to the separate duties, the numerous hundredths, the prytaneia, the metals, the markets, the harbours, the salaries, the sales of confiscated goods, the sum total of them all comes to nearly 2000 talents." Doubtless between 433 and 422 the exigencies of the war had made the pressure of taxation much greater and it is not to be wondered at that the increase of the annual income was as great as Aristophanes makes it out. What the national revenues fell to at the end of the fifth century is impossible to conjecture, but we may be sure they were at a very low ebb.

The next direct evidence we have is in the speech of Demosthenes against Philip in 340.[3] "The time is not long past when not more than 130 talents was the revenue of our city....Later, fortune being more favourable to us, many changes have come about, and now 400 talents come in instead of 100." We may infer that the first figure refers to the desperate straits into which Athens had fallen after the war with the allies in 355. We have no exact information with regard to how the increase was effected, but undoubtedly it was due to the financial genius of Eubulus, who at least gave Athens peace. In 338, when Lycurgus became "finance minister", the revenues had recovered still further, and during the twelve years that he was in charge he is said to have raised them to 1200 talents a year. In the life of Lycurgus attributed to Plutarch, it is stated that during that time he collected, according to some, 14,000 talents and according to others 18,650, and that he spent 18,900 talents.[4] These are very wide discrepancies which require a good deal of ingenuity to reconcile, but in any case it is plain that the annual

---

[1] *Anab.* vii, 1, 27.   [2] 656 ff.
[3] *Phil.* iv, 37–8.
[4] *Vit. X. Orat.* 841 B.

revenue during these twelve years must at the lowest estimate have been over 1100 talents, and at the highest considerably more.

CONCLUSION

We have now, in an imperfect and all too cursory a fashion, sketched the main outlines of public finance as practised by the Athenians. During the course of our survey we have had occasion to criticise the various policies and expedients which were characteristic of the raising and expending of state revenues, and it is, therefore, unnecessary to repeat them in this place. It may, however, be useful to attempt a general appraisal of the whole subject, at least so far as it contrasts with modern practices of public finance.

In the first place, it must be acknowledged that the Athenians showed a financial "toughness" of no small order. To have carried on so prolonged and expensive a struggle as the Peloponnesian war, and to have shown so striking a power of recuperation immediately afterwards, argues not only a resilience of the national character but a practical ability in finance for which the Athenians have had too little credit paid them. Obviously they were far superior as financiers and administrators to the Spartans and Thebans who succeeded them.[1] Although their exactions from their "allies" were heavy, and although their tributaries grumbled and protested, as tributaries always have, yet on the whole it is evident that their Athenian overlords gave them services in return which were worth the money broadly speaking.

Secondly, at a time when there was a very imperfect diffusion of wealth and the amassing of considerable fortunes by a favoured few was as easy, or perhaps even easier than it is to-day, the system of exactions from the rich in the shape of special levies, such as the Liturgies and Eisphorae, was really a species of excess profits tax, which ought to have worked with reasonable fairness. In the absence of death duties and inheritance taxes, of which we have no record and which almost

---

[1] If we are to believe the stories told in the Pseudo-Aristotelian *Oeconomica* (1346 A ff.) of the practices of other states, we must conclude that the Athenian system of public finance was far superior to that of other governments.

certainly did not exist, we may agree that the Athenians took the only way open to them to obtain from the richer individuals their share of the financial burdens of the commonwealth. We must not forget that the indirect taxes, in the form of customs duties and other taxes, must have borne heavily on the poor.

But when we have said that we have said all that is favourable to the system. Did the system of exactions from the rich work fairly? We are forced to the conclusion that only too often it did not. How incessantly do we hear of that sinister class of informants, the sycophants, who made it their business to denounce the rich! We may, to some extent, discount the evidence of Isocrates who had himself been condemned in a suit of Antidosis and forced to assume a trierarchy very much against his will, but we can accept his diatribes against the demagogues and sycophants as being substantially true. "Athens is rife with lamentations. For some are driven to rehearse and bewail amongst themselves their poverty and privation, while others deplore the multitude of duties enjoined upon them by the state—the liturgies and all the nuisances connected with the symmories and with exchange of property; for these are so annoying that those who have means find life more burdensome than those who are continually in want. I marvel that you cannot see at once that no class is so inimical to the people as our depraved orators and demagogues. For, as if your other misfortunes were not enough, their chief desire is that you should be in want of your daily necessities, observing that those who are able to manage their affairs from their private incomes are on the side of the commonwealth and of our best counsellors; whereas those who live off the law courts and the assemblies and the doles derived from them, are constrained by their need to be subservient to the sycophants and are deeply grateful for the impeachments and indictments, and the other sharp practices which are due to the sycophants. Wherefore these men would be most happy to see all our citizens reduced to the condition of helplessness in which they themselves are powerful. And the greatest proof of this is that they do not consider by what means they may provide a livelihood for those who are in need, but rather how they may reduce those who are thought to possess some wealth to the level of those who are in poverty."[1]

It would, perhaps, be going a little too far were we to find in the exactions of the state from the rich the whole explanation of the never-ending quarrel between oligarchy and democracy. To the violently political Greek the wrangles of the various parties were the very breath of life; they would have fought and harried each other anyhow if both had been penniless. But it is perfectly clear that the chance of currying favour with the irresponsible masses by offering them the means of plundering the rich was in Greece, as it is to-day, the best policy for the demagogues, and a source of livelihood for that most sinister of all the figures of history, the informer.

The whole theory and practice of public finance was unsound, and we may agree with Dr Andreades in his final summing up when he says it was the financial system "which should in fact be branded as, in all probability, the real cause of the destruction of the noblest of all states known to history".[2]

---

[1] *de Pace*, 128–31 (Loeb). For further complaints against the informers cf. Xen. *Symp*. iv, 30; *Mem*. ii, cap. 9; Lysias, xxvii, 1; Plato, *Rep*. viii, 551 D. Class hatred, Busolt, *Griech. Staatsk*. i, 210 ff.
[2] *History of Greek Public Finance*, p. 363.

SELECT BIBLIOGRAPHY

Abrahams, E. B. *Greek Dress*. London, 1908.
Andreades, A. M. *History of Greek Public Finance*, i, Eng. trans. by C. N. Brown. Cambridge, Mass., 1933.
Ardaillon, E. *Les Mines de Laurion dans l'Antiquité*. Paris, 1897.
Bacon, J. R. *Voyage of the Argonauts*. London, 1925.
Baily, K. C. *The Elder Pliny's Chapters on Chemical Subjects*. London, 1929–32.
Becker, W. A. *Charicles*. (8th ed.) London, 1889.
Beloch, J. *Griechische Geschichte*. Berlin-Leipzig, 1913–23.
—— *Bevölkerung der Griechisch-Römischen Welt*. Leipzig, 1886.
Bérard, V. *Les Phéniciens et l'Odyssée*. Paris, 1902–3.
Billeter, G. *Geschichte des Zinsfusses im Griechisch-Römischen Altertum bis auf Justinian*. Leipzig, 1898.
Bluemner, H. *Technologie und Terminologie der Gewerbe und Künste bei den Griechen und Römern*. 2 vols. Leipzig, 1875. Revised ed. of vol. i, 1912.
—— *Gewerbliche Tätigkeit der Völker des klassischen Altertums*. Leipzig, 1869.
Boeckh, A. *Die Staatshaushaltung der Athener*. 1817.
—— Revised edition by Fränkel. Berlin, 1886.
—— English translation, *Public Economy of Athens*. Cornewall Lewis, London, 1828.
Brendel, O. *Die Schafzucht im alten Griechenland*. Würzburg, 1934.
Bücher, K. *Beiträge zur Wirtschaftsgeschichte*. 1922.
—— *Industrial Evolution*, trans. by S. M. Wickert. New York, 1907.
Buechsenschütz, A. *Besitz und Erwerbe im Griechischen Altertum*. Halle, 1869.
Burns, A. R. *Money and Monetary Policy in Early Times*. London, 1927.
Busolt, G. and Swoboda, H. *Griechische Staatskunde*. 2 vols. Munich, 1926.
—— *Griechische Geschichte*. Gotha, 1893–1904.
Calderini, A. *La Manumissione e la Condizione dei Liberti in Grecia*. Milan, 1908.
Calhoun, G. M. *The Business Life of Ancient Athens*. Chicago, 1926.
—— *The Growth of Criminal Law in Ancient Greece*. 1927.
Carpenter, R. *The Greeks in Spain*. New York, 1921.
Cary, M. and Warmington, E. H. *Ancient Explorers*. London, 1929.
Casson, S. *Macedonia, Thrace and Illyria*. Oxford, 1926.

Cavaignac, E. *Études sur l'histoire financière d'Athènes au Ve Siècle.* Paris, 1908.

—— *Population et Capital dans le Monde Méditerranéen Antique.* Strasbourg, 1923.

Ciccotti, E. *Il Tramonto della Schiavitù nel Mondo Antico.* Turin, 1899.

—— *Le Déclin de l'Esclavage Antique.* French translation by G. Platon. Paris, 1910.

Clerc, M. *Les Métèques Athéniens.* Paris, 1893.

Davies, O. *Roman Mines in Europe.* Oxford, 1935.

Drachmann, A. G. *Ancient Ore Mills and Presses.* Copenhagen, 1932.

Drumann, W. *Arbeiter und Communisten in Griechenland und Rom.* Königsberg, 1860.

Ferguson, W. S. *Hellenistic Athens.* London, 1911.

—— *Greek Imperialism.* Boston, 1913.

—— *The Treasurers of Athena.* Oxford, 1932.

Francotte, H. *L'Industrie dans la Grèce Ancienne.* Brussels, 1900.

—— *De la Condition des Étrangers dans les Cités Grecques.* Louvain, 1903.

—— *Les Finances des Cités Grecques.* Liège-Paris, 1909.

Gardner, P. *History of Ancient Coinage.* Oxford, 1918.

Gercke, A. and Norden, E. *Einleitung in die Altertums Wissenschaft.* 3 vols. Leipzig, 1914.

Gernet, L. *L'Approvisionnement d'Athènes en Blé au Ve et au IVe Siècles.* Paris, 1909.

Glotz, G. *Le Travail dans la Grèce Ancienne.* Paris, 1920.

—— *Ancient Greece at Work.* Eng. trans. by M. R. Dobie, London, 1926.

—— *Histoire de la Grèce.* Paris, 1925.

Gomme, A. W. *The Population of Athens in the Fifth and Fourth Centuries.* Glasgow, 1933.

—— *Essays in Greek History and Literature.* Oxford, 1937.

Groningen, B. A. van. *Aristote, le second livre de l'Économique.* Leyden, 1933.

Grundy, G. B. *Thucydides and the History of his Age.* London, 1911.

Guiraud, P. *La Main d'Œuvre industrielle dans l'Ancienne Grèce.* Paris, 1900.

—— *La Propriété Foncière en Grèce jusqu'à la Conquête Romaine.* Paris, 1893.

Haeseler, H. *Veteränensfürsorge im Griechischen Altertum.* Jena, 1926.

Halliday, W. R. *Growth of the City State.* Liverpool, 1923.

Hasebroek, J. *Griechische Wirtschafts- und Gesellschaftsgeschichte.* Tübingen, 1931.

—— *Staat und Handel im alten Griechenland.* Tübingen, 1928.

Hasebroek, J. *Trade and Politics in Ancient Greece.* Eng. trans. by Fraser and Macgregor, London, 1933.

Hassinger, H. *Geographische Grundlagen der Geschichte.* Freiburg-i.-Br., 1931.

Hatzfeldt, J. *Les Trafiquants Italiens dans l'Orient Hellénique.* Paris, 1919.

Head, B. V. *Historia Numorum.* Oxford, 1911.

Heichelheim, F. M. *Wirtschaftliche Schwankungen der Zeit von Alexander bis Augustus.* Jena, 1930.

—— *Wirtschaftsgeschichte des Altertums.* Leyden, 1938.

Heitland, W. E. *Agricola.* Cambridge, 1921.

Herfst, P. *Le travail de la femme dans la Grèce Ancienne.* Utrecht, 1922.

Hicks, E. C. and Hill, G. F. *Manual of Greek Historical Inscriptions.* Oxford, 1901.

Hoffmeister, E. W. *Kritische Untersuchung zur Charakterentwicklung der Athener.* Hamburg, 1932.

Hörnschemeyer, A. *Die Pferdezucht im klassischen Altertum.* Giessen, 1929.

Jardé, A. *Les Céréales dans l'Antiquité Grecque.* Paris, 1925.

—— *La Formation du Peuple Grecque.* Paris, 1922.

Jones, W. H. S. *Malaria: A Neglected Factor in the History of Greece and Rome.* Manchester, 1911.

Kaeppel, C. H. *Off the Beaten Track in the Classics.* Melbourne, 1936.

Keil, B. *Die Solonische Verfassung in Aristoteles Verfassungsgeschichte Athens.* Berlin, 1892.

Kinkel, J. *Die Sozialökonomischen Grundlagen der Staats- und Wirtschaftslehre von Aristoteles.* Leipzig, 1911.

Knorringa, H. *Emporos.* Amsterdam, 1927.

Köster, A. *Das Antike Seewesen.* Berlin, 1923.

Laistner, M. L. W. *Greek Economics.* London, 1923.

Laum, B. *Das Eisengeld der Spartaner.* Braunsberg, 1925.

Leaf, W. *Homer and History.* London, 1915.

—— *Strabo on the Troad.* London, 1924.

Lenormant, F. *La Monnaie dans l'Antiquité.* Paris, 1878.

Lucas, A. *Ancient Egyptian Materials and Industries.* London, 1926.

Mallet, D. *Les Premiers Établissements des Grecs en Égypte.* Cairo, 1893.

Mauri, A. *I Cittadini Lavoratori dell' Attica nei Secoli 5 e 4 A.C.* Milan, 1895.

Meyer, E. *Geschichte des Altertums.* Stuttgart, 1897–1909.

—— *Kleine Schriften.* Halle, 1910.

Milne, J. G. *The First Stages in the Development of Greek Coinage.* Oxford, n.d.

Minns, E. H. *Scythians and Greeks*. Cambridge, 1913.

Motzki, A. *Eubulos von Probalinthos und seine Finanzpolitik*. Königsberg, 1903.

Murray, G. *Rise of the Greek Epic*. Oxford, 1924.

Myres, J. L. *Who were the Greeks?* Univ. of California, and Cambridge, 1930.

Neuberger, A. *The Technical Arts of the Ancients*. Eng. trans. London, 1930.

Neurath, O. *Antike Wirtschaftsgeschichte*. Leipzig, 1918.

Newbigin, M. I. *The Mediterranean Lands*. Edinburgh, 1924.

Oertel, F. "Die Soziale Frage im Altertum"; *Neue Jahrbücher f. d. klass. Altertum*. 1927.

O'Neill, J. G. *Ancient Corinth*. Baltimore, 1930.

Ormerod, H. A. *Piracy in the Ancient World*. Liverpool, 1924.

Poehlmann, R. *Griechische Geschichte und Quellenkunde*, 5th ed. Munich, 1914.

—— *Geschichte der Sozialen Frage und des Sozialismus in der Antiken Welt*. 3rd ed. Munich, 1925.

Radcliffe, W. *Fishing from the Earliest Times*. London, 1921.

Reinach, Th. *Histoire par les Monnaies*. Paris, 1902.

Richter, Gisela. *Craft of Athenian Pottery*. Yale Univ. Press, 1923.

Rider, Bertha C. *The Greek House*. Cambridge, 1916.

Ridgeway, W. *Origin of Metallic Currency and Weight Standards*. Cambridge, 1892.

—— *Early Age of Greece*. Cambridge, I, 1901; II, 1931.

Riezler, K. *Finanzen und Monopole im alten Griechenland*. Berlin, 1907.

Robertson, H. Grant. *Administration of Justice in the Athenian Empire*. Toronto, 1924.

Rose, J. H. *The Mediterranean in the Ancient World*. Cambridge, 1933.

Rostovtseff, M. *Iranians and Greeks in South Russia*. Oxford, 1922.

—— *History of the Ancient World*. 2 vols. Oxford, 1926–28.

—— *Caravan Cities*. Oxford, 1932.

Roth, H. Ling. *Ancient Egyptian and Greek Looms*. Halifax, Yorks., 1913.

Salvioli, G. *Le Capitalisme dans le Monde Antique*. French trans. by A. Bonnet. Paris, 1906.

—— *Il Capitalismo Antico*. Bari, 1929.

Sargent, R. L. *Size of the Slave Population at Athens in 5th and 4th Centuries B.C.* Univ. of Illinois Press, 1924.

Sauciuc-Saveanu, T. *Cultura Cerealelor in Grecia Antica*. Bucarest, 1925.

Schaal, H. *Vom Tauschhandel zum Welthandel*. Leipzig and Berlin, 1931.

Schaefer, H. *Staatsform und Politik. Untersuchungen zur griechischen Geschichte des 6. und 5. Jahrh.* Leipzig, 1932.

Schönbauer, E. *Beiträge zur Geschichte des Bergbaurechts.* Munich, 1929.

Segré, A. *Circolazione Monetaria e Prezzi nel Mondo Antico.* Rome, 1922.

Seltman, C. T. *Athens: its History and Coinage before the Persian Invasion.* Cambridge, 1924.

—— *Greek Coins.* London, 1933.

Semple, E. C. *Geography of the Mediterranean Region.* New York, 1931.

Seymour, T. D. *Life in the Homeric Age.* New York, 1908.

Sieveking, H. *Das Seedarlehen des Altertums.* Leipzig, 1893.

Spaventa-de Novellis, L. *I Prezzi in Grecia e a Roma nell' Antichità.* Rome, 1934.

Speck, E. *Handelsgeschichte des Altertums.* Leipzig, 1900–6.

Tarn, W. W. *Hellenistic Civilization.* London, 1927.

—— *Hellenistic Military and Naval Developments.* Cambridge, 1930.

Thiel, J. H. *Xenophontos Poroi.* Vienna, 1922.

Tod, M. N. *A Selection of Greek Historical Inscriptions.* Oxford, 1933.

Torr, C. *Ancient Ships.* Cambridge, 1895.

Toutain, J. F. *L'Économie Antique.* Paris, 1927.

—— Eng. trans. *Economic Life of Ancient World.* London, 1930.

Tozer, H. F. *History of Ancient Geography.* Cambridge, 1935.

Trever, A. A. *A History of Greek Economic Thought.* Chicago, 1916.

Ure, P. N. *The Origin of Tyranny.* Cambridge, 1922.

Vickery, K. F. *Food in Early Greece.* Univ. of Illinois, 1936.

Wallon, H. *Histoire de l'Esclavage dans l'Antiquité.* Paris, 1879.

Wilamowitz-Moellendorf, U. von. *Staat und Gesellschaft der Griechen.* Leipzig, 1923.

—— *Aristoteles und Athen.* Berlin, 1893.

Winkelstern, K. *Die Schweinezucht im klassischen Altertum.* Giessen, 1933.

Woodhouse, W. J. *Solon the Liberator.* Oxford, 1938.

Ziebarth, E. *Beiträge zur Geschichte des Seeraubs und Seehandels im alten Griechenland.* Hamburg, 1929.

—— *Eine Handelsrede aus der Zeit des Demosthenes.* Heidelberg, 1936.

Zimmern, A. E. *The Greek Commonwealth.* 5th ed. Oxford, 1931.

—— *Solon and Croesus.* Oxford, 1928.

INDEX

Printed in the United States
By Bookmasters